Primary Commodity Exports and Economic Development

Primary Commodity Exports and Economic Development

Theory, Evidence and a Study of Malaysia

John T. Thoburn
School of Social Studies
University of East Anglia, Norwich

JOHN WILEY & SONS

London · New York · Sydney · Toronto

Library of Congress Cataloging in Publication Data:
Thoburn, John T.
Primary commodity exports and economic development.

Bibliography: p.
1. Malaysia—Commerce. 2. Commercial products—Malaysia. 3. Malaysia—Economic conditions. I. Title.
HF3800.6.Z5T48   330.9'595'05   76-26337

ISBN 0 471 99441 3

Printed at Unwin Brothers Limited, The Gresham Press, Old Woking, Surrey.

To
June, Nicholas and Alan

Acknowledgements

In the time this book has been in preparation I have become indebted for help, comment and encouragement to many individuals. At East Anglia I have had useful discussions with Athole Mackintosh, Harold Lydall, Chris Scott, Cliff Attfield and Ashok Parikh; and I am especially grateful to Chris Edwards for commenting on the first draft of the Malaysia study, for much intellectual stimulus, and for very kindly allowing me access to his unpublished thesis on Malaysian industrialization. Contacts with the Institute of Development Studies at Sussex have left me particularly indebted to H. W. Singer, who has been generous with his comments on a draft of the book, and also to Frank Ellis, V. Selvaratnam and members of the International Problem Area Group seminar. With reference to my early work on the Malaysian case study I am grateful to P. T. Bauer, under whom I worked when I was a visiting student at the London School of Economics in 1966–7, for his continuing interest and his help in locating source material; and in Canada to my thesis supervisor, Tom Powrie, and also to Geoffrey Hainsworth for useful comments. I also have had helpful correspondence with Frances Stewart and Paul Streeten.

During three visits to Malaysia (in 1969, 1970 and 1974) I enjoyed the use of the facilities of the Faculty of Economics and Administration in the University of Malaya, to whose successive Deans, Yip Yat Hoong and Mokzani bin Abdul Rahim, I am grateful; and also to the numerous Malaysian officials and businessmen who provided me with information. There are in addition many Malaysian friends from whom I have learnt more about their country than they probably realized—among them Radzi bin Jaafar, Thian Thau Min, Ng Fong Cheng and Sow Ying, and Yuen Yin Hah.

The manuscript was typed by Sylvia Walker, Ann Hills and Kika Raba, whom I thank for their speed and efficiency.

I am particularly grateful to the Ministry of Overseas Development for a research grant for two years to write the study of Malaysia, and for a publication grant which has made possible that study's inclusion in the book. I have also received research finance from the University of East Anglia and (for the 1974 visit to Malaysia) from the Social Science Research Council. Of course, neither ODM, the SSRC, nor any of the people mentioned above necessarily agrees with any view expressed here, and I alone am responsible for any errors.

The Malaysian case study was submitted in an earlier draft as a report to the

Ministry of Overseas Development (then the Overseas Development Administration) in 1971, and was also accepted by the University of Alberta in Canada as a doctoral thesis. Parts of that report have subsequently been elaborated in articles appearing in the *Kajian Ekonomi Malaysia*, *Oxford Economic Papers* and the *Oxford Bulletin of Economics and Statistics*, to whose editors I am grateful for permission to reproduce some of this material here. I am also grateful to the editors of the *Journal of Development Studies* for permission to reproduce parts of a forthcoming paper on appropriate technology.

Finally, I should like to thank June, my wife, who has shared with me both the pleasures and the strains of this research.

Preface

At the present time developing countries depend for about three quarters of their foreign exchange earnings on exports of primary commodities. For many individual countries the dependence is greater still and is often on only one or two main products. Moreover, statistics on aggregate exports of manufactured goods by the Third World often obscure the fact that only a small number of countries, such as Hong Kong and Taiwan, have become significant exporters of manufactures. The focus of this book is on the role primary commodity exports can play as a source of economic growth and development, bearing in mind that *growth* (in the sense of sustained rises in income per head) and *development* do not necessarily occur together. In particular, it is widely accepted now that *development* includes at the very least the proviso that the poorest sections of the community should benefit from economic growth, and that growth should be of a form which will absorb into employment the large and generally growing number of unemployed workers in Third World countries. Development also has many non-economic goals, of which political liberty and social equality are probably among the most important.

At its most obvious level the debate is whether primary commodity exports should be encouraged, either with or at the expense of manufactured exports, or whether they should belong only to the colonial past and should be run down as as escape from the so-called 'artificial international division of labour' into which developing countries were then forced. Yet this is more of a long run question and much interest still centres—in the United Nations Conferences on Trade and Development for instance—on commodity price levels and whether a larger share of world income can be distributed to Third World commodity producers, either by OPEC—like 'commodity power' or by negotiated commodity agreements. Of course, these questions are of particular interest to countries heavily dependent on trade, about whom this book is mainly concerned, and in fact only a quarter of the *population* of the Third World lives in countries where exports generate more than 30% of national income. However, if the question is posed in terms of the number of countries, the average dependence on trade is much greater; and the first two chapters look at the position of developing countries in world trade, the major problems they face as commodity exporters, and their demands for better treatment under the 'New International Economic Order' resolution of the United Nations in 1974.

At a more fundamental level the 'primary commodity *versus* manufactured export' debate is concerned with whether different export products have different effects on development. It seems clear from historical experience that some countries have achieved high levels of income per head as a result of specialization on primary commodity exports—Canada, Australia and New Zealand are the best known, and also Denmark and the United States in its early years—and it is interesting that writers from such countries should have been among the first to suggest that even different primary commodities (or 'staples') could have different development effects. Thus Canadian 'staple theorists', such as Harold Innis, argued that the seventeenth century fur trade had retarded Canadian development, whereas wheat exports had encouraged it; and similar themes in relation to the Third World occupied much of the development discussions among academic writers in the 1950's and 1960's, surveyed in Chapter 3. An important result was a widespread acceptance among Third World governments of an overriding need to industrialize, and a belief that no primary commodities could be a source of development; though various economists argued against this naive approach—of whom P. T. Bauer, Gerald Meier and Hla Myint were probably the most influential.

In the event, industrialization has not proved an easy solution. Often it has had far worse effects on distribution and employment than even mineral exports (usually regarded as the worst offenders among primary commodities), and protected import-substituting industrialization has frequently come to a halt as the limits of domestic market size have been reached and high-cost producers have been unable to break into world markets. Even 'successful' labour-intensive manufacturing exports have not always generated more development than colonial agricultural exports.

The relative failure of industrialization as an easy solution to the development problem has led to a realization of the importance of issues which previously were either ignored or assumed to be essentially part of the distinction between primary commodity and manufacturing production. Most important of these issues, and closely interrelated, are the control and ownership of production and the control and appropriateness of technology. Thus gains from exporting can be lost just as easily by a developing country exporting electronic components, as by one exporting tea, if production is controlled by a foreign firm; and a multinational company can choose to buy equipment from an overseas subsidiary rather than local suppliers whatever its final product. Similarly, mineral exports, for example, do not have a monopoly of inappropriate, excessively capital-intensive technology.

The effects of primary commodity exporting in a wide range of countries are discussed in Part III, while Part II presents a detailed case study of Malaysia, the world's largest exporter of rubber, tin and palm oil. Malaysia is particularly interesting since its two traditional exports, rubber and tin, have been developed both by foreign and by local producers, and (especially in tin mining) the different effects of different ownership and technology are marked.

Norwich
March 1976

John Thoburn

Contents

Abbreviations and Notes

ABS	*Annual Bulletin of Statistics*, published by Statistics Dept., KL
AR	*Annual Report*
ASET	*Annual Statistics of External Trade*, published by Statistics Dept., KL
BSMI	*Bulletin of Statistics Relating to the Mining Industry*, published by Mines Dept., KL
CManI	*Census of Manufacturing Industries*, published by Statistics Dept., KL
CMinI	*Census of Mining Industries*, published by Statistics Dept., KL
DRC	Dry Rubber Content
ECAFE	Economic Commission for Asia and the Far East (United Nations), now known as Economic and Social Commission for Asia and the Pacific (ESCAP)
FELDA	Federal Land Development Authority, KL
FFB	Fresh Fruit Bunches (of oil palm)
FIDA	Federal Industrial Development Authority, KL
FM	Federation of Malaya
FMP	First Malaysia Plan (1966–70)
FMS	Federated Malay States
FSLC	*Report on the Financial Survey of Limited Companies Malaysia*, 1967, published by Statistics Dept., KL
GATT	General Agreement on Tariffs and Trade
HBS	*Household Budget Survey* (of FM), 1957, published by Statistics Dept., KL
HLS	*Handbook of Labour Statistics*, published by Ministry of Labour, KL
IBRD	International Bank for Reconstruction and Development (the World Bank)
IDS	Institute of Development Studies, University of Sussex
IIA	*Interindustry Accounts*, published by Statistics Dept., KL
IMF	International Monetary Fund
KL	Kuala Lumpur (capital of Malaysia)
MARA	Council of Trust for Indigenous People (Majlis Amanah Rakyat)
MBS (or MSB)	*Monthly Bulletin of Statistics*, published by Statistics Dept., KL
MIC	Malaysia Industrial Classification
MID	*Malaysia Industrial Digest*, published by FIDA
MTC	Malaysia Trade Classification
MTR	Mid-term Review (e.g. of SMP)
MU	Malayan Union
NA	*National Accounts*, published by Statistics Dept., KL
ODI	Overseas Development Institute, London
OPCTS	*Oil Palm, Coconut and Tea Statistics*, published by Statistics Dept., KL
OPEC	Organization of Petroleum Exporting Countries
PERNAS	The National Corporation, Malaysia (Perbadanan Nasional)
PR	*Preliminary Release* (of manufacturing, mining and construction statistics), published by Statistics Dept., KL

QBS	*Quarterly Bulletin of Statistics* (e.g. of Mines Dept., KL)
RRIM	Rubber Research Institute of Malaysia, KL
RSH	*Rubber Statistics Handbook*, published by Statistics Dept., KL
RSS	Ribbed Smoked Sheet (rubber).
SCI	*Survey of Construction Industries*, published by Statistics Dept., KL
SMP	Second Malaysia Plan (1971–5).
SMR	Standard Malaysian Rubber
SManI	*Survey of Manufacturing Industries*, published by Statistics Dept., KL
SS	Straits Settlements
TCCT	Trade Classification and Customs Tariff (of Malaysia)
UMS	Unfederated Malay States
UNCTAD	United Nations Conference on Trade and Development
UNESCO	United Nations Economic, Social and Cultural Organization
USS	Unsmoked Sheet (rubber)

Bibliographical References

References are made in the text only to author and year of publication, and full details are given in the bibliography. Where several authors of the same surname have written in the same year, the author's full name is cited. In Asian names, for instance those of Chinese, the surname is often written first. Most official publications are cited in full, however, using the abbreviations set out on pp. xv-xvi.

Abbreviations of journal titles in the bibliography are those of UNESCO (1972).

Symbols used in Tables

. . . not available
– zero or negligible
* estimated

Numbering of Tables, Sections, Subsections and Appendices

Table, section, subsection and appendix numbers are prefixed with a numeral which indicates the chapter number to which they refer (e.g. Table 4.2, Section 4.2, and Subsection 4.2.2 are in Chapter 4).

Malaysian Weights

Picul = 133.3 lb (16.8 piculs = 1 long ton)
Kati = 1.3 lb (100 katis = 1 picul)

Currency

Unless otherwise stated, the dollar sign ($) refers to the Malaysian dollar (or *Ringgit*, as it is now officially called).

£1 = $5 approximately (March 1976). The Ringgit has been allowed to 'float' since June 1973.

Part I
Primary Commodity Exporting in Theory and Practice

Chapter 1
Introduction—Developing Countries as Primary Commodity Exporters

1.1 PRIMARY COMMODITY EXPORTS FROM DEVELOPING COUNTRIES

Primary commodities are normally defined as products of the land, produced by forms of agriculture (including food, agricultural raw materials, livestock and timber) or extracted by mining, and subjected to a limited amount of processing.[1] The extent to which various primary commodities are processed before they enter international trade differs considerably, and not all producing countries process their product to the same extent as other producers. Natural rubber for instance has been exported from Indonesia in the past in the form of crudely coagulated, unsmoked sheet, for remilling in Singapore before final export. Copper is exported from the Philippines (and particularly to Japan) as concentrates, whereas much of Chilean production is exported as blister copper (i.e. smelted but unrefined). The major Asian producers of tin (Malaysia and Thailand) export smelted tin, while bauxite, though sometimes processed into alumina, is not exported from developing countries in smelted form (i.e. as aluminium). For most commodities generally accepted conventions exist to define the stage at which they cease to be primary products (so rubber processed into smoked sheet is a primary commodity and rubber footwear is a manufacture), though, at the margin, definitional problems may still arise (e.g. new-process, scientifically graded rubber exported under the Standard Malaysian Rubber scheme is often treated for tariff purposes by developed countries as a semi-manufacture, and non-ferrous metals such as smelted tin or copper are included in some official trade statistics as manufactured products).

In popular discussion, the fortunes of developing countries are often associated with the prospects for primary commodity exports. The contention that the terms of trade for primary commodities have deteriorated over some given period (which will be examined in Chapter 2), for example, has been used to suggest that developing countries have suffered thereby. Reference to Table 1.1 shows that this identification is correct in the sense that developing countries as a whole are dependent on primary commodities for three-quarters of their export earnings, compared to only a fifth in the case of developed Western economies. However, the *share* of developing countries in world primary commodity exports is quite low—only 40% in total, and under 30% if fuels (mainly petroleum) are excluded from the calculation. It is also the case that developing countries are relatively dependent on export sales to rich countries. In 1973, as Table 1.2 shows, nearly three-quarters of developing country exports went to

TABLE 1.1. INTERNATIONAL TRADE BY COMMODITY GROUPS, 1972

(percentages)

	COMPOSITION OF WORLD EXPORTS	COMPOSITION OF EXPORTS FROM INDUSTRIAL AREAS	COMPOSITION OF EXPORTS FROM DEVELOPING AREAS	SHARE OF DEVELOPING AREAS IN TOTAL WORLD EXPORTS
Primary Products				
Food	14.3	11.8	22.9	28.8
Raw Materials	5.6	4.1	8.6	27.7
Ores and Minerals	2.5	1.7	4.5	32.0
Fuel	10.4	3.4	38.6	66.9
Total Primary Products	32.8	21.0	74.5	40.9
Manufactures				
Non-ferrous Metals	2.8	2.4	3.5	22.7
Iron and Steel	4.8	5.7	0.9	3.4
Chemicals	7.1	8.8	1.9	4.9
Engineering Products	24.6	29.6	4.1	3.0
Road Motor Vehicles	7.7	10.3	0.1	0.3
Textiles and Clothing	6.4	6.4	7.2	20.2
Other Manufactures	11.9	13.9	6.2	9.3
Total Manufactures	65.3	77.2	23.9	6.6
TOTAL EXPORTS	100.0	100.0	100.0	18.0

Sources and Notes

(1) All figures from GATT (1974, Table G).

(2) Australasia and South Africa are included in world totals, but not elsewhere.

rich, capitalist countries (and another 5% to the Eastern bloc), while three-quarters of rich countries' trade was with other rich countries (there being no discrepancy between the two statements since rich industrial countries account for over two-thirds of *total* world trade).

The impression that developing countries have a low share in primary exports changes somewhat if particular commodities are considered which are of major importance in the export earnings of the Third World as a whole. Table 1.3 lists thirty-five commodities of major interest to developing countries. Of the twelve most important, the developing countries' world export share is only less than 50% in two cases (iron ore and rice) and even in those it is around 40%. In petroleum, coffee, sugar, rubber, cocoa, timber, tin and tea the share is about three-quarters, or more; and many of these very low world market shares are concentrated in temperate zone products such as wool, wheat, beef, maize, which are of much less importance to

TABLE 1.2 DISTRIBUTION OF WORLD EXPORTS BY AREA, 1960 AND 1973

(percentages)

	SHARE OF WORLD EXPORTS		DESTINATION OF EXPORTS (% POINTS FROM SHARE OF WORLD TOTAL)					
			INDUSTRIAL AREAS		DEVELOPING AREAS		EASTERN BLOC	
	1960	1973	1960	1973	1960	1973	1960	1973
INDUSTRIAL AREAS	63.8	69.0	42.5 (66.6)	51.7 (74.9)	16.3 (25.5)	12.3 (17.8)	2.3 (3.6)	3.2 (4.6)
DEVELOPING AREAS	21.4	18.1	15.0 (70.1)	13.3 (73.5)	4.9 (22.9)	3.5 (19.3)	1.0 (4.8)	1.0 (5.5)
EASTERN BLOC	11.7	10.1	2.2 (18.8)	2.8 (27.7)	1.0 (8.5)	1.5 (14.8)	8.5 (72.6)	5.8 (57.4)

Sources and Notes

(1) Figures from GATT (1974, p.3).

(2) World totals include Australasia and South Africa, which are not included in the major areas.

(3) Bracketed figures show the exports by destination as a percentage of the total exports of the exporting area (e.g. In 1973 exports by countries in industrial areas to other countries in industrial areas constituted 51.7% of total world exports and 74.9% of the total exports of industrial countries).

TABLE 1.3 PRIMARY COMMODITIES OF MAJOR INTEREST TO DEVELOPING COUNTRIES, 1967-69 AVERAGES

(percentages)

	COMMODITY SHARE OF DEVELOPING COUNTRY EXPORTS	DEVELOPING COUNTRY SHARE OF TOTAL WORLD EXPORTS		COMMODITY SHARE OF DEVELOPING COUNTRY EXPORTS	DEVELOPING COUNTRY SHARE OF TOTAL WORLD EXPORTS
Petroleum	33.09	76.04	Groundnuts	0.52	81.99
Coffee	5.62	94.37	Copra	0.50	99.07
Copper	5.59	56.44	Bauxite	0.45	79.61
Sugar	3.65	75.31	Wheat	0.41	4.22
Raw Cotton	3.17	57.07	Jute	0.38	93.81
Rubber	2.34	72.28	Zinc	0.33	23.38
Iron Ore	1.99	39.41	Silver	0.32	23.56
Cocoa Beans	1.59	100.00	Lead	0.28	27.02
Timber	1.57	87.92	Coconut Oil	0.28	79.56
Tin	1.37	80.71	Groundnut Oil	0.25	81.99
Tea	1.28	82.55	Manganese Ore	0.24	60.49
Rice	1.22	43.09	Palm Oil	0.23	82.76
Bananas	1.16	95.35	Sisal	0.18	96.24
Maize	0.98	26.39	Linseed Oil	0.07	65.84
Beef	0.86	26.09	Abaca	0.04	98.92
Tobacco	0.70	21.99			
Fishmeal	0.55	60.04	Total 35 Commodities	72.80	60.10
Wool	0.54	13.72			
Phosphate Rock	0.54	60.15			
Hides and Skins	0.53	30.65	Other LDC Exports	27.20	5.93
			Total	100.00	16.99

Sources and Notes

(1) All figures from IBRD (1973), which lists the original sources.

TABLE 1.4 DEVELOPING COUNTRY EXPORTERS OF TEN MAIN PRIMARY COMMODITIES, 1967-69 AVERAGES

(percentages)

	THREE LARGEST DEVELOPING COUNTRY EXPORTERS	SHARE OF LARGEST DEVELOPING COUNTRY EXPORTERS IN WORLD EXPORTS	SHARE OF COMMODITY IN EXPORTERS' TOTAL EXPORT EARNINGS		THREE LARGEST DEVELOPING COUNTRY EXPORTERS	SHARE OF LARGEST DEVELOPING COUNTRY EXPORTERS IN WORLD EXPORTS	SHARE OF COMMODITY IN EXPORTERS' TOTAL EXPORT EARNINGS
Petroleum	Venezuela	15.0	92.7	Rubber	Malaysia	38.4	35.0
	Iran	10.6	95.4		Indonesia	13.5	24.9
	Saudi Arabia	10.0	91.4		Thailand	7.4	14.3
	(Total Three Largest)	(35.6)			(Total Three Largest)	(59.3)	
Coffee	Brazil	31.4	39.2	Iron Ore	Venezuela	6.8	4.8
	Colombia	14.0	60.7		Liberia	6.0	71.3
	Ivory Coast	5.0	30.4		Brazil	5.8	6.1
	(Total Three Largest)	(50.4)			(Total Three Largest)	(18.6)	
Copper	Chile	18.3	76.2	Cocoa Beans	Ghana	26.1	57.3
	Zambia	19.3	93.9		Nigeria	22.9	20.5
	Zaire	8.5	65.1		Ivory Coast	12.0	19.4
	(Total Three Largest)	(46.1)			(Total Three Largest)	(61.0)	
Sugar	Cuba	26.9	78.3	Timber	Phillipines	25.4	20.0
	Phillipines	7.1	15.1		Malaysia	24.2	12.2
	Dominican Rep.	4.3	50.3		Ivory Coast	12.6	22.9
	(Total Three Largest)	(38.3)			(Total Three Largest)	(62.2)	
Raw Cotton	Egypt	12.6	44.3	Tin	Malaysia	39.8	19.0
	Brazil	6.1	7.1		Bolivia	13.8	51.8
	Sudan	5.7	57.3		Thailand	11.6	11.7
	(Total Three Largest)	(24.4)			(Total Three Largest)	(65.2)	

Sources and Notes

(1) All figures from IBRD (1973) , which lists the original sources.

(2) These ten commodities are the first ten in order of importance in LDC export earnings (see Table 1.3).

developing countries either as a whole or (in most of these cases) individually (with the important exception of the Argentine).[2] Of course, a high world market share does not necessarily mean an absence of competition from rich countries. Sugar exports (mainly cane) face competition from (usually highly protected) sugar beet industries for the Western European market. Much of the United States and Japanese demand for rubber is met by their domestic synthetic rubber production, which displaces natural rubber imports or slows their rate of growth. Raw cotton faces competition from rich countries' exports of synthetic fibres. Other high market shares may be misleading if the products have very close natural substitutes exported by rich countries in quantity. For example, the high shares in coconut oil, groundnut oil and palm oil disguise the fact that soya bean and other vegetable oils, produced on a large scale by the United States, are almost perfect substitutes in most of their industrial uses.

An indication of the dependence of individual countries on individual commodities for their export earnings is given in Table 1.4 for ten major exports. Petroleum and copper, for the three largest exporters of each, show very high degrees of dependence (though the share of the exports in national income would give a fuller picture).[3] Other countries, such as Cuba with sugar or Liberia with iron ore also have a high dependence which is not shared by other large producers. Some countries, too, depend heavily on a small range of goods—Malaysia for instance on tin, rubber and timber for 66% of its export earnings (and also on palm oil). Some countries, such as Brazil for coffee or Malaysia for rubber and tin, (and palm oil) occupy dominant positions of much greater importance than other producers.

1.2 TRENDS IN PRIMARY COMMODITY EXPORTING AND WORLD TRADE

In what is probably one of the most influential works ever written on trade relations between rich and poor countries, Ragnar Nurkse in the 1959 Wicksell lectures contrasted patterns of trade and development in the nineteenth century with those since the First World War (Nurkse, 1962). Extremely rapid expansion in world trade (by 270% 1850–1880, and by 170% 1880–1913) in the nineteenth century was closely associated with the growth of the British economy. Over the period 1815 to 1913 a threefold increase in population and a tenfold increase in national output put intense pressure on the British resource base. As a result, imports into Britain over the same period increased twenty-five times and imports as a proportion of British national output rose from 12% to nearly a third (Nurkse, 1962, p. 14). Trade in these circumstances acted as an 'engine of growth' in Sir Dennis Robertson's phrase (1938, p. 5), serving not only to offset diminishing returns in food and raw material production in Britain but also transmitting growth from the countries of the 'centre' of the world economy to those of the 'periphery'.

Whereas over roughly the last half of the nineteenth century (i.e. 1850–1913) trade had increased at double the rate of world output (Wells, 1965, p. 1), after 1913 world trade growth was slow, and Nurkse (1962, p. 19) records an increase in volume over the period 1928–58 of only 57%. Although the slow growth of trade in the inter-war period reflects world depression, Nurkse particularly associates slow trade growth both then and after the Second World War with the relative decline of Britain and the emergence of the United States as the dominant member of the countries of the

TABLE 1.5 COMPOSITION OF WORLD TRADE 1953-73

	% SHARE OF WORLD EXPORT VALUE			VOLUME INDICES 1973 (1960=100)		
	1953	1963	1973	WORLD OUTPUT	WORLD EXPORTS	RATIO OF EXPORT TO OUTPUT INDEX
Agricultural Products	40.8	31.2	21.1	139	164	1.18
Minerals (including fuels and non-ferrous metals)	19.7	16.7	16.2	192	231	1.20
Manufactures	38.1	50.2	60.8	232	350	1.51
Total	100.0	100.0	100.0	202	276	1.37

Sources and Notes

(1) 1953 figures from Briscoe (1975, p.211), and all others from GATT (1974, p.1).

centre. Not only does the United States have a much smaller import share of national output than the U.K., but in addition the U.S. economy became more 'closed' over Nurkse's period of interest—imports were 5.7% of Gross National Product in 1896–1914 and 3.0% in 1955—and there were increasing economies of raw material use in rich countries, the development of synthetic substitutes for primary products, a changing composition of output towards services and heavy industry (both less materials—intensive), and many agricultural commodities' demand was income—inelastic (Nurkse, 1962, pp. 22–5).

Reference to Table 1.5 shows that since Nurkse wrote (i.e. since the 1950's) world trade has increased rapidly, in volume terms over a third as fast again as world output, 1960–73. To some extent the expansion in trade has been the result of the lowering of trade barriers (about which more in Chapter 2) following the 1947 U.N. Havana conference, the Dillon round of 1952 and the Kennedy round of negotiations in 1964–7 (Briscoe, 1975, p. 212). Perhaps more important a factor has been the changing composition of the centre, with the share of 'centre' (i.e. rich industrial country) trade accounted for by the United States falling from 34% in 1948 to 20% in 1968, while the share of the countries of the European Economic Community and Japan, all highly open economies compared to the U.S. and much faster growing rose over the same period from 19% to 46% (see Pinto and Knakel, in di Marco, 1972).

However as Table 1.5 also shows, the most rapid increases have been in manufactured trade and although developing countries have certainly increased their manufactured exports (witness the 20% world market share of developing countries in textile exports, in Table 1.1), the main increases have been in manufactured trade *between* developed countries. The result of these trends has been an increase to 75% of the proportion of rich country trade with other rich countries (which in turn accounted in total for nearly 52% of world trade in 1973), and a rise in the share of manufactured products in world trade from 38% in 1953 to over 60% in 1973.

The reasons for rapid growth in 'intra-centre' manufactures trade are to be found mainly in the advantages of intra-industry specialization and product differentiation combined with economies of scale.[4] In the face of this manufactures expansion, agricultural and mineral trade has increased however. Indeed minerals (including petroleum) have almost maintained their world market share (see Table 1.5), and it is agricultural products which have fallen in relative importance, though they have increased in absolute value and volume. However, much of the increase in primary commodity exports has come from rich countries. Since the Second World War the United States has become the world's largest exporter of wheat, oils and fat and maize, and a major exporter of rice, having been a net *importer* of wheat in the 1930's, and a minor and intermittent exporter of the other commodities (Rowe, 1965, pp. 110–1). U.S. consumption of raw materials, however, though rising much more slowly than national output, has exceeded American domestic raw material production and turned the U.S. into a net importer (Nurkse, 1962, p. 25). Statistics published by the United Nations Conference on Trade and Development (UNCTAD, 1972, p. 193) show that over the periods 1950–60 and 1960–67 rich country exports of food and beverages and of raw materials (excluding fuels) grew substantially faster than those of poor countries, though a slight reversal of the trend occurred in the late 1960's. Only in the special case of fuels (a category dominated by petroleum) was poor country performance in aggregate better than that of rich countries.

Although, therefore, poor countries' primary commodity exports have been expanding over the post-war period in both value and volume (though volume indices are beset with weighting difficulties), nevertheless the really rapid expansions of trade generally have bypassed these countries except where they have exported certain light manufactures. Whether their terms of trade (in any or all of its definitions) have deteriorated (and, if so, over what period) is taken up in the next chapter, together with issues of commodity price stabilization and the significance of the commodity price boom in the early 1970's.

The post-1945 period with its rapidly expanding manufactured exports and apparent polarization of world trade seems to contrast sharply with the experience of the nineteenth century. Over much of the *late* nineteenth century (see next section) primary commodity and manufactured exports *as a whole* grew at similar rates. Indeed, even up to the early post-1945 years there was a remarkable stability in the manufactured export share, which Arthur Lewis (1952, p. 109) noted varied only a few percentage points from 37% for seventy years to 1950, though the *composition* of primary commodity exports changed considerably (Yates, 1959, p. 44). What is often omitted from discussion is that much (though by no means all) of the nineteenth century trade expansion bypassed the tropical countries of Asia, Africa and Latin America,[5] in that the very large rises in (especially) food exports were met by the so-called 'regions of recent settlement' (Canada, Australia, New Zealand, though also including the Argentine). This tendency is especially marked when one takes into account the importance of capital exports from the United Kingdom as a means of promoting commodity exports (though mainly by portfolio investment in infrastructure, rather than direct investment), and realizes that in 1913 two-thirds of the outstanding foreign investments of the U.K. were held in the relatively rich primary producing areas of North and South America (i.e. excluding most of the poorer Latin American countries except the Argentine and possibly Uruguay) and Australasia. Of the total British foreign portfolio investment (and over 85% of British foreign investment was portfolio) some 40% was in foreign railways and only 10% in mineral or raw material extraction (Dunning, 1964, pp. 18–19).

1.3 THE ESTABLISHMENT AND EARLY GROWTH OF PRIMARY COMMODITY EXPORTS FROM DEVELOPING COUNTRIES, AND PATTERNS OF OWNERSHIP

From 1857/9 to 1911/13 the share of 'new' countries (Canada, South Africa, Australasia and the Argentine) in British imports rose from 8% to 18%. The shares of the U.S.A. and of industrial Europe (both roughly 20%) stayed constant, and other areas' (including tropical countries') share fell from 52% to 40%; and Nurkse notes that '*in the years before 1914* exports of primary products were expanding more rapidly than exports of manufactures' (Nurkse, 1962, p. 20, my italics). These pieces of information together suggest that the great nineteenth-century expansions of primary products were associated with particularly fast export growth for 'new' regions rather than countries we would now consider 'underdeveloped'. In apparent contrast to this view, Charles Stover (in Lewis, 1970, p. 49, and based on Lewis's 1969 Wicksell Lectures) writes that from 1883 to 1913 'the picture which emerges is of a world economy in which industrial production,[6] trade in manufactures, the trade of tropical countries and the trade of temperate countries were all growing at about the same rate.' This picture is reinforced by League of Nations statistics (Hilgerdt, 1945, p. 159), which show almost identical rates of expansion (in both value and volume) of primary products and manufactures from 1876/80 to 1913. In other words, though primary commodities exports from 'new' countries were the fastest growing component of trade earlier in the century, by the last quarter of the nineteenth century tropical countries were sharing equally in the general export expansion (though their share of foreign investment was relatively small).

Indeed, as Arthur Lewis suggests,[7] it is in the last quarter of the nineteenth century that a widespread and rapid development of the tropical world began. Although certain commodities (tea, silk, spices, sugar) had been exported since long before then, industrialization in Britain, Europe and the United States generated a rapid rise in demand for tropical products; and the widespread introduction of steamships, and the opening of the Suez Canal markedly reduced the cost of transportation. Within poorer countries, as in 'new countries', railways often were introduced to collect produce over a wide area. In 1883 only one tropical country (India) had exports of over U.S. $100 million, and only five others had exports of over U.S. $50 million (Egypt, Cuba, Brazil, Indonesia and Malaya). India's large exports are perhaps mainly a reflection of the large size of her economy. Of the others, Egypt's cotton, Cuba's sugar and (to a lesser extent) Brazil's coffee were quite long-established exports, whereas the export of tin in large quantity from Malaya and Indonesia was of very recent origin though its growth had been rapid. By 1913 seven tropical countries (Egypt, Cuba, Mexico, Brazil, India, Indonesia and Malaya) had exports over U.S. $100 million and a further three (Ceylon, Indochina and the Phillipines) had exports over U.S. $50 million. Many others whose exports in 1885 in most cases had been minimal, in 1913 were exporting output over U.S. $25 million in value (e.g. the Gold Coast, Nigeria, Bolivia, Colombia, Peru, Thailand). Nor are these increases in aggregate simply a reflection of increasing prices, since from 1881/5 to 1913 the League of Nations primary product price index rose only from 94 to 100 (Hilgerdt, 1945, p. 157), though this index includes exports from temperate countries and the price experience of tropical commodities varied considerably.

Of course not all tropical countries shared equally in the export expansion. Lewis (1970, p. 15) shows how indices of the total value of exports (with 1883 = 100) varied, for instance, from 118 for the West Indies, 146 for Venezuela, to 212 for the Philippines, 235 for India, to 523 for Ceylon, 539 for Thailand and 548 for West Africa (with an average of 271). Based on ten short case studies of tropical development from 1880 to 1913, Lewis offers an interesting range of explanations for the variation in experience. While he stresses, as one would expect, the existence of such factors as internal peace and security, suitable climate and rainfall, adequate transportation and development-orientated government (though there were few of these!), Lewis's most interesting point concerns the availability of land. Except in tea and sugar, which required immediate and large-scale processing, local peasants could produce in principle most agricultural exports (though some such as tobacco, and also tea, required quite skilled management). Yet the risk in *switching* land from food production to an export crop was considerable, and (in the frequent absence of loan finance) impossible in the case of a crop with a long gestation period, such as coffee or rubber. The availability of uncultivated land near the peasants' existing holdings completely alters the situation. Land can be cleared and planted during slack periods. Many tree crops require little attention during their immature period, so growing the existing food crop is not hampered. When the export crop reaches maturity, allocation of labour time between food and export crop production can be determined by relative prices, marketing opportunities and physical effort involved (rubber cultivation, for example, is much less physically demanding than is that of rice). Thus some of the largest agricultural expansions have occurred—in the Gold Coast, Indonesia, Malaya—where there has been abundant agricultural land available to peasants (in much of Latin America abundant land also existed, but was held by large landowners who did not always wish to cultivate it (Lewis, 1970, pp. 24–5)). Of course, where the cash crop was also the subsistence crop (e.g. rice in Thailand and Burma, exported in order to feed immigrant workers in neighbouring countries) the risk element was greatly reduced, but still, rapid expansion relied on new land.

In Lewis's view, except in sugar and tea where large-scale production held considerable advantages, the development of foreign estates was the result more of political than economic factors (Lewis, 1970, p. 24), and estates were not necessarily more efficient than smallholdings. Many colonial governments favoured estate development, leasing state land to estates at low rates for instance; and in Indonesia peasants were forced to lease (scarce) land to plantations, while in Kenya and Southern Rhodesia African agriculture was confined to reservations which were too small to support subsequent African population growth. A particular problem faced by estates where there was also an ample supply of land for local peasants was how to obtain labour; and therefore immigrant workers frequently were recruited in large numbers (witness the many Indians and Chinese in South East Asia today). Non-European immigrants also set up as traders acting as middlemen between foreign buyers and local producers, as in many African countries and in South East Asia. The development of local estates (as opposed to foreign-owned ones) varied greatly between countries. Lewis records that wealthier people in Ceylon who owned land set up estates of their own, whereas in the Philippines, India and Sumatra it was more usual to let to smallholders (Lewis, 1970, p. 25).

The coexistence of large- and small-scale producers of agricultural products persists to the present, both within the same countries and between different countries. One important development has been that some crops requiring large-scale and fairly immediate processing (such as tea, sugar, and, at least in South East Asia, oil palm products) are now more frequently grown by smallholders who sell their produce to separately owned processing factories. In such cases much depends on there being an efficient transport system, and some element of choice between processers to strengthen producers' bargaining power. Another development has been that in some cases smallholder production has proved more efficient than that of estates (in copra, for instance; and in rubber too prior to the development of high-yielding varieties, which involved replanting and which estates therefore found it easier to introduce–see Chapter 6). Sometimes such changes have involved the discovery of efficient, more labour-intensive techniques, as in sisal where a small hand machine for tearing out fibre became the basis of a smallholder industry in Brazil (Rowe, 1965, p. 21). Nationalization of foreign estates has also occurred in some cases (e.g. Indonesia), and state land development is important elsewhere (e.g. Malaysia).

In mineral exporting there has been less diversity of ownership patterns. With the important exception of tin among the major mineral exports of developing countries, export expansion occurred rather later than in the case of agricultural products. In oil and aluminium, technological innovation reduced costs and stimulated a search for new markets, while expansion of the motor industry after 1900 created rapid growth in demand for both these products and for copper (Girvan, 1970, p. 493).

Technological development in copper too reduced costs, by applying large-scale production techniques to low-grade (and hitherto unworkable) ores. Economies of scale in processing led, Norman Girvan suggests, to the development of an oligopolistic market structure in these three major industries, and a consequent search for new sources of supply outside as well as within their home economy (in this case predominantly the U.S.A.). In aluminium, and later in petroleum, large-scale extraction techniques and the difficulties of independent producers selling in an oligopolistic market, prevented entry by local producers, and in copper local producers dropped out of business in Chile (the largest producer in the developing world) as high-grade ore deposits grew scarcer and as they lacked the access to technology to work low-grade ores. In tin, developed somewhat earlier than many other minerals, there has been much less vertical integration, though perhaps rather more horizontal combination than the obvious facts about the mining companies would suggest (see Chapter 5 for more details). Recent nationalizations and state enterprise have also altered the situation greatly in some minerals, particularly in copper and to a lesser extent in petroleum (both of which are discussed further in Chapter 10).

In the light of the frequent coexistence of domestic and foreign agricultural sectors in developing countries, both past and present, and the frequent dominance of foreign firms in mineral extraction, Malaysia—the subject of the case study in Part II—is of particular interest. In Malaya (as it then was), rubber was first developed by European (mainly British) firms following experimentation by the government with a number of crops.[8] Local estates and a large local smallholding sector (the latter predominantly Malay but with substantial Malayan Chinese and Indian elements too) developed rapidly soon after, and by the time rubber output was restricted in face of falls in demand in the early 1920's, it seems quite likely that the smallholding sector was economically the more efficient producer, with higher planting densities and an absence of overheads compensating for slight economies of scale in processing by estates. Dealers (usually Chinese), greatly facilitated the spread of rubber among local peasants, while the estate workforce was mainly recruited from India. Thus Malayan rubber represents an almost archetypal pattern of primary commodity development. Tin in Malaya was developed some thirty years earlier, by immigrant Chinese, some self-financing their passage from China and others under indenture to Chinese already resident. As in Chilean copper, a flourishing local (in this case Malayan Chinese) sector existed prior to the entry of foreign firms. Unlike Chile, however, foreign firms were at first unable to compete with Chinese firms using highly labour-intensive methods (and they also had difficulty in recruiting labour due to the activities of Chinese secret societies in Malaya). Most unusually, compared to the experience in other minerals, when foreign firms did eventually develop a large-scale, capital-intensive technique, entry into which was effectively barred to local firms because of shortages of capital and lack of access to the technology, the local sector was not driven out of existence. Instead, Chinese mining firms, with access to extensive credit facilities from local Chinese suppliers, and to short-term capital from local Chinese merchants, were able to develop a technique which was more mechanized and able to treat lower grade ores than hitherto, but whose capital intensity (whether measured in terms of initial capital to output or to labour force, or to the flow of capital services over time) was substantially less than that of the European technique, and which could be set upon a much smaller scale. Thus in contrast to most other forms of Third World mining, local and foreign firms coexist (and use different production techniques). Whether this coexistence is the result of the characteristics of the mining production function or whether it is more a reflection of the relative strengths (in terms of social cohesion, access to capital, etc.) of the different groups in altering technology to suit their economic needs is discussed further in Chapter 11.

Malaysia is also interesting (and typical), in that its early growth was of the classic 'surplus venting' variety (Lewis, 1970, p. 22), with increases in agricultural output (mainly rubber, later palm oil and much later timber) resulting from extension of the cultivated area (and given of course a highly suitable climate and rainfall, and a good transport system inherited from tin mining and developed by the colonial administration). Analysis of the basis that this growth laid for future development, in terms of diversification of economic activity through linkages, raising agricultural productivity, use of export revenue by the government, etc., is an important part of the case study.

NOTES

1. For other discussions of the definition of primary production see Rowe (1965, pp. 1–2) and Brown (1975, pp. 2–3).
2. Argentina in fact has a rather higher income per head than most developing countries—U.S. $828 in 1969 compared to U.S. $475 for Latin America as a whole, U.S. $200 for developing countries as a whole and U.S. $351 for Malaysia (UNCTAD, 1972, pp. 239–43). This puts Argentina (given the difficulties in making national income comparisons at market exchange rates) at about the same income level as some of the poorer countries of Europe—higher than Yugoslavia for example but lower than Spain.
3. For commodities chosen for further study, in Chapter 10, information on their shares of the national income in the main producers is given, in addition of course to the tin and rubber industries of Malaysia which are discussed at length in Part II. In general, the share of exports in national income is lower the larger is the population of the country being considered, though the export share does tend to rise, in both time series and cross-sectional terms, with the level of *per capita* income (see Chenery and Syrquin, 1975, pp. 40–1 and pp. 130–1).
4. For explanations of intra-rich country trade in manufactures see Linder (1961) and Grubel (1967). It is worth noting too that a quarter of world trade is intra-*firm* (Briscoe, 1975, p. 222), though, as the next section will show, this is not all in manufactures. For a discussion of the role of 'product-cycles' in intra-firm trade, see Vernon (1966).
5. Though the (at least partial) bypassing of less developed countries in the nineteenth century trade expansion is carefully noted in Nurkse's own discussion of that period (1962, pp. 13–9) he (correctly) implies in his treatment of the 'current lag in exports of the poorer countries' that poorer countries fared very differently in the past compared to when he was writing. As will be shown in Section 1.3, by the 1880's at least, tropical countries were participating in the 'centre's' export demand expansion.
6. Trade, however, rose faster than *total* production (Nurkse, 1962, p. 20).
7. Much of the rest of this section draws on Lewis's extremely useful essay 'The Export Stimulus (1883–1913)' in Lewis (1970), although Lewis does not discuss mineral exports. Detailed accounts of the early growth of rubber and tin in Malaya are given in Chapter 4, and for some other major commodities in Chapter 10. Lewis's definition of 'tropics', incidentally, excludes the Argentine, Chile, Uruguay, North Africa (except Egypt) and the Near East.
8. Experimentation with rubber had its origins in British colonial interest in the crop's potential for development in India. Official interest declined when India proved an unsuitable habitat, but individual government officers kept experimentation going in Malaya, and laid the basis for the industry's future growth (see Drabble, 1973, p. 6).

Chapter 2
Commodity Exporting — Problems and Prospects

2.1 THE SEARCH FOR A NEW INTERNATIONAL ECONOMIC ORDER

Changes in the pattern of trade since the nineteenth century have been outlined in Chapter 1. The great expansion of demand for primary commodities tailed off after the First World War and into the inter-war depressions. The 1950's and 60's saw rapid expansions of trade in manufactures, especially between industrial countries, while the demand for primary commodities (especially agricultural products) lagged behind.

The institutional context of these post-war trade expansions derives its philosophy from the Havana Charter, adopted after the United Nations conference on trade and employment at Havana in 1948. The original intention of the UN was that a specialist International Trade Organization (ITO) should be established as the third of a trinity of organizations, whose other members were the International Monetary Fund and the International Bank for Reconstruction and Development.[1] In the event, the ITO failed to gain the approval of the U.S. Congress, and the General Agreement on Tariffs and Trade (GATT), which embodies the treaty provisions of an earlier post-war conference, became in effect a permanent organization under whose auspices trade would be regulated and negotiations about reductions in trade barriers conducted.

Almost certainly the main motivation of these post-war negotiations was to move away from the restrictionist policies of the inter-war years, and, implicitly, to return to a system resembling more that of the free trade of the nineteenth century.[2] By the early 1950's however, substantial criticisms were being made of the notion that the (relatively) free play of market forces in the international economy worked to the benefit of all participants. Chapter 3 will discuss arguments in the academic literature by writers such as H. W. Singer and Gunnar Myrdal that specialization according to an apparent comparative advantage in primary commodities had done little to generate growth and development in poor countries, and (especially where exporting was controlled by foreign investors) that it may actually have retarded it. Criticisms too were being made by United Nations organizations, particularly the Economic Commission for Latin America (ECLA) and most influentially by Raul Prebisch, its executive secretary.

Thus the second UN world trade conference in Geneva in 1964—the United Nations Conference on Trade and Development (UNCTAD)—had an almost totally different focus from that of Havana. Under the Secretary Generalship of Prebisch, its explicit aim was to move towards a new order, away from free trade and non-discrimination, to a system taking specific account of the special problems of developing countries (Prebisch, 1964, p. 3). Since then, UNCTAD has become a permanent organization with its own secretariat, and a multiplicity of specialist committees, with four-yearly conferences—in New Delhi in 1968 and Santiago in 1972—with UNCTAD IV due to meet in May 1976.

Three main issues have concerned the developing countries (or 'Group of 77')[3] in UNCTAD and other forums. First is the level of prices for primary commodities, which as Chapter 1 showed, still account for about three-quarters of their export earnings, and particularly this level in relation to the prices of manufactured products, their main import. Second, there is the problem of fluctuations in commodity prices, which, it is claimed, produce domestic instability, retard growth and investment, and generally make planning difficult. Third is the fact that attempts to diversify out of primary production, either by the further processing of primary commodities for export or by the export of manufactures, are frustrated by a structure of tariffs in industrial countries, and also freight rates,[4] which escalate according to the degree of processing, and by various non-tariff barriers and 'voluntary' agreements to restrict exports of goods such as textiles which compete with relatively stagnant sectors of industry in the West (see e.g. Meier, 1973, pp. 92–183). Barriers also have been imposed on commodities which compete with temperate agricultural production (sugar, for instance has been subject to much negotiation in this regard) and heavy excise duties have been levied on certain tropical products (such as coffee) in several European countries to raise revenue.

While these three issues have appeared again and again in international discussions (and are examined in more detail in the next three sections of this chapter), important recent changes have taken place in the international development climate. Following the unilateral action of the Organization of Petroleum Exporting Countries (OPEC) in 1973, and subsequently, in quintupling the price of oil, and following the commodity price boom of 1973–4, an element of power politics has replaced the earlier *pleas* for a better deal for developing countries. Talk in particular has been heard of 'commodity power', and the problems and needs of developing countries have been expressed in a call for a 'New International Economic Order' (NIEO), embodied in the UN resolution following the Sixth Special UN Session in May 1974. Though the NIEO declaration repeats most of the previous UNCTAD demands, several new proposals have been made—in particular that primary commodity prices should be index-linked to those of manufactures, that commodity problems should be approached in an 'integrated' fashion (and specifically that a composite buffer stock should be established for eighteen—now reduced to ten—commodities), and that better facilities should be provided to compensate individual countries for income shortfalls resulting from fluctuations in export earnings, thus extending the facilities initiated by an IMF scheme and the EEC's 'Stabex' scheme under the Lomé Convention (about which more later). Also important in these recent discussions is a concern for better prospects for the poorest developing countries (and especially those who have little commodity power to exercise), for measures (including market access for labour-intensive manufactures) which will generate employment,[5] and in general for measures which (like employment creation) will improve the position of the poorest people in individual countries. Both for the poorest people and the poorest countries, improved techniques in food and fertilizer production, easier access to fertilizer imports (made more expensive by increased oil prices), and of course more aid, are of great importance; although domestic policies to improve income distribution are also crucial.[6] Other issues under discussion are measures to transfer technology and make it more appropriate (see also Chapter 9) and to regulate the operation of multinational companies both in primary commodity and manufacturing production.[7] Further international discussions have taken place in the Seventh Special Session of the UN (in November 1975), where the approach to problems has been more consiliatory and less confrontationist (*Financial Times*, 10 and 17 September 1975) (though major issues such as indexation have been strongly opposed to the West); in the Kingston meeting of Commonwealth Heads of Government in May 1975 (see British Government, 1975), and in the conference at Lima in March 1975. Major advances, however, still await UNCTAD IV and the conclusion of the present 'Tokyo Round' negotiations under GATT (see Section 2.4).

2.2 COMMODITY PRICE LEVELS

2.2.1 The Terms of Trade

Although the notion that the terms of trade for developing countries have deteriotated is only one of several ways in which developing countries' potential gains from commodity exporting are claimed to have been lost (as Chapter 3 will show), the terms of trade doctrine is of particular importance since it forms the basis of many of the policy recommendations of UNCTAD.

In his report for UNCTAD I Prebisch (1964, pp. 3–19) was mainly concerned with a persistent tendency towards external imbalance associated with developing countries' growth. Taking the target of 5% annual growth as set out in the UN's first 'Development Decade' (1960–70), he anticipated an annual growth of 6% in import requirements (growing faster than national output because of the need to import capital equipment) against a projected export volume growth of 4% a year based on the experience of the 1950's. Moreover, during the 1950's, because of deterioration in the terms of trade, exports grew in total value by only 2% annually in terms of real purchasing power. Attempts by developing countries to diversify out of primary commodities were frustrated by trade barriers, and Prebisch called for compensation to be paid to make up for productivity gains in primary export production, the benefits of which had accrued to rich countries in the form of lower prices.

Prebisch estimated (1964, pp. 18–19) that from 1950 to 1961 the terms of trade of primary commodities fell by 26% compared to manufactures, and the terms of trade for developing countries *vis-à-vis* rich countries fell by 17% (the difference being due to the fact that, as Chapter 1 has shown, much primary export production takes place in rich countries, and some developing countries also export manufactures). The terms of trade referred to here are the *commodity* or *net barter* terms of trade—a price index of exports divided by a price index of imports. If the net barter terms of trade are weighted by an index of export volume, the *income* terms of trade are derived; and weighting by an export productivity index produces the (single) *factorial* terms of trade. Thus a deterioration in the commodity terms of trade may be accompanied by increase in total export purchasing power, and the relative price fall need not necessarily cancel out totally all productivity increases (Meier, 1968, pp. 41–6).

Commodity terms of trade may alter over time for a variety of reasons—changes in demand and differential rates of productivity growth being the most obvious. What is more important is that Prebisch has argued that those of developing countries *necessarily* deteriorate over time.[8] The basis of the argument is that, because of low incomes elsewhere in the economy, export sector workers in developing countries are unable to bargain successfully for a share in productivity increases, which are then passed on to foreign consumers in the form of lower prices.[9] In rich countries on the other hand workers successfully bargain for shares in increased productivity. Moreover, developing countries lack the flexibility to shift resources into other lines of activity and to prevent supply expansions and the bidding down of prices.

The UNCTAD terms of trade doctrine has generated enormous controversy, and has been dismissed by many writers as totally erroneous—a 'mistaken view ..... enshrined by constant repetition into a myth' (Little, 1975, p. 227). Certainly the available evidence is not conclusive. Prebisch's period of 1950–61 covers a commodity price peak to a trough. Lewis's (1969, pp. 22–6) figures for tropical crops against manufactures suggest that although the terms of trade fell during the 1950's, even by late in the 1950's they were still as high as from 1880—1900 (which was a period of generally rapidly expanding commodity demand). Of course, any long period comparison suffers from problems of weighting (since television sets and aeroplanes were not exported in 1880!), and from the fact that primary commodity terms of trade deterioration against manufactures would overstate commodity producers' losses since manufactures tend to change in quality far more over time than do primary commodities. A study of the net barter and income terms of trade of developed and developing countries 1950–65 (Wilson, Sinha, and Castree, 1969), taking a 1950–53 (equals 100) average as the base (i.e. including the Korean boom years) showed that developing countries' net barter terms of trade fell to 98.3 (1954–7), 92.3 (1958–61) and 90.7 (1962–5). Their income terms of trade consistently improved, though, reaching 156.8 in 1962–5. Moreover, for certain countries both the net barter and income terms of trade improved—including those of Peninsular Malaysia whose net barter terms were 117.0, and income terms 187.7, in 1962–5.[10]

While the 1973–4 commodity price boom casts doubt on the notion that relative commodity prices usually decline (though the prices of some commodities since then have fallen drastically), the more important point given the conflicting empirical evidence, is whether the commodity terms of trade need *necessarily* worsen. The moral of the Prebisch arguments is surely that appropriate policy measures need to be taken to transfer resources out of export activities whose productivity is increasing to prevent oversupply (although much depends here on demand elasticities, as the next subsection will show), and for increases in productivity to be sought over a wider range of activities.[11]

2.2.2 Cartels and 'Commodity Power'

In 1970, the estimated market price of oil was U.S. $1.30 a barrel, having fallen by about a third over the previous fifteen years. Prior to the 1973 October war between Israel and the Arabs, the price stood at about U.S. $2.70. Yet by January of the next year collective action by OPEC countries including a temporary export embargo, had tripled the price.[12]

Although cartels had been formed before among primary producers (witness the attempts to support the tin price between the wars, as Chapter 4 will show) OPEC appears in the short run at least, to have been spectacularly successful in raising the oil price, and the question naturally arises whether other commodity producers could act in a similar fashion. While most popular discussion centres on *price*, it is obviously net *revenue* from exports which is important, and more particularly the stream of net revenues over some time horizon. Even if demand is at present highly inelastic over the range of the projected price increase, it will almost certainly become less so over time (as new sources of supply are sought, substitutes found, and resource-saving technology developed), and some set of time weights (or social rate of discount) is necessary to determine the price behaviour which will maximize the desired value of the net revenue time stream.[13]

The elasticity of demand for a cartel's product will depend not only on substitutability and user technology development, but also on potential supply from outside the cartel. Thus the Stevenson scheme to control rubber during the inter-war years foundered on massive supply expansions by Indonesian smallholders. Chapter 1 has identified commodities of particular interest to the Third World and has shown how control over supply varies between commodities. Copper and bauxite, for instance, are mainly produced by developing countries, and the main rich country producers (except Canada for copper and Australia for bauxite) are net importers. Tin is almost entirely produced in the Third World (including China), except for minor amounts by Australia, whereas iron ore is produced very widely even though it is an important item in Third World exports as a whole.[14] In copper (or indeed oil) where deposits are found in several rich countries, Third World supply restrictions to raise price are likely to stimulate intensive exploration and to make viable the workings of marginal deposits.

Of the three major metals which have some potential as candidates for cartelization—copper, tin and bauxite[15]—a producers' organization interested in price support—CIPEC (Conseil Intergovernmental des Pays Exportateurs de Cuivre)—has existed in copper since 1967 (Prain, 1975, pp. 248–60). Its success to date in raising prices has been slight, however, despite production cutbacks,[16] and despite the fact that its members (Chile, Peru, Zambia, Saire and Indonesia, with Australia and Papua New Guinea as associates) control over 70% of present world trade.

In bauxite, a newly established Intergovernmental Bauxite Association (IBA) has seven members producing two-thirds of world bauxite (Barker and Page, 1974, p. 85). IBA has failed recently to agree on a fixed price for bauxite (*The Guardian*, 5 May 1975), reportedly because of Australian objections, but Jamaican bauxite prices at least bear a relation to those of the final aluminium (British Government, 1975, p. 4). Tin output is restricted periodically to support prices under the International Tin Agreement (about which more in the next section).

Most commentators (e.g. Prain, 1975) are less hopeful about successful cartelization in copper, bauxite and tin than in oil. In tin for instance although the short-run price elasticity is low,[17] very great economies have been achieved in tin use and higher prices might induce further economies (including recycling), especially by such new consumers as Japan.[18] Also, the poorest producers frequently lack 'commodity power' and, as with oil, may be disadvantaged by higher prices for their imports. Substitution of one metal for another, however, can be reduced by producer agreements, copper and bauxite being a good example.[19]

For agricultural commodities, probably the greatest difficulty for cartels is the potential supply from Western competitors, either by production of the same commodity (e.g. rice),[20] or natural substitutes (beet for cane sugar, soya bean oil for palm oil) or synthetics (rubber, artificial fibres). Some tropical products do not normally have substitutes—tea, coffee and cocoa are the best examples since they comprise the bulk of 'beverage' supply (though Germany produced (apparently highly inferior) *ersatz* coffee during the war)—and here *joint* action might be effective. Storage is often more of a problem with crops than minerals—if supply embargoes are to be used—and of course minerals can be stored in the ground.[21] Supply embargoes also require financial reserves, with which most OPEC countries are well endowed and most other Third World countries poorly endowed.

For some agricultural commodities long-run demand elasticity may be high. Malaysia's two main agricultural exports,[22] rubber and palm oil, are probably in this category. In the absence of extreme oversupply, the minimum price for natural rubber is likely to be determined by the cost of its very close (stereoregular) synthetic substitutes, and so natural rubber cost reductions could appreciably increase its market share. Palm oil exports are less than 10% of world vegetable oil supply and great substitutability exists between different oils. Hence cost and price reductions (based mainly on agricultural research) could well increase export revenues,[23] unless importing countries restrict their purchases to protect import-competing industries.

2.3 COMMODITY EXPORT INSTABILITY

Commodity 'instability' refers to fluctuations in prices and export earnings, and to related vaiables such as producer incomes and government revenue. There is little doubt that primary commodity markets exhibit considerably greater instability than those of manufactures. In a study of commodity stabilization by the IMF and the World Bank in 1969, fluctuation indices (average annual percentage deviations from trend) for prices, quantities and export earnings for 1953–65 were 2.1%, 4.5% and 4.2%, respectively for industrial countries (three-quarters of whose exports are of manufactures), and 6.8%, 8.0% and 9.6%, respectively, for developing countries (three-quarters of whose exports are primary commodities); and the instability indices increased if the years 1950–52 (i.e. the Korean boom years) were added. Moreover for export earnings the standard deviation was only 1.6% of the mean instability index for developed countries, but 6.1% for developing countries, indicating even more extreme fluctuations for *some* developing countries.[24] The reasons for instability lie partly in low short-run supply elasticities. Copper or bauxite mines, or tin dredges, may take several years to come into production; many tree crops too have even longer gestation periods. On the demand side, in the short run again inelasticity of demand means prices respond sharply to shifts in supply (bad harvests, new sources of supply, etc.) or to cyclical demand changes.[25] In primarily supply-shift markets (wheat may be an example) price fluctuations could *stabilize* export earnings, but the evidence quoted above suggests that prices and quantity changes in the aggregate magnify each other rather than cancelling out.

Price fluctuations may be undesirable in themselves if they reduce consumer demand. Copper is thought to have lost some advantages over its substitute, aluminium, in the electrical industry for instance since the copper price has been highly unstable[26] while the price of aluminium, (whose raw material enters international trade mainly in transactions between branches of multinational companies) has been much less volatile. Similar arguments would apply to natural *versus* synthetic rubber. Nevertheless most concern with instability refers to export earnings. Fluctuations in export earnings, even around a correctly anticipated trend would require the exporting country to hold larger foreign exchange reserves than would be necessary for more stable exports, unless it were willing to allow its imports to fluctuate too. More important, especially in a highly open economy, such fluctuations may transmit themselves by means of a multiplier–accelerator mechanism to the domestic economy where, it is sometimes claimed, they will generate inflation and retard growth and investment.

Empirical investigations of these effects of fluctuations have been many and inconclusive. First, because of sliding-scale export taxes (imposed originally in colonial times, and discussed below) and because incremental export earnings often accrue to domestic or foreign capitalists rather than workers, fluctuations are often damped by leakages into taxation, savings and profit remittances abroad. Malaysia for example, with its exceptionally open economy, and exceptionally high export instability, had an instability index (for 1955–66) of only 3.5 for its Net National Product at factor cost compared to 12.2 for its export earnings (Ariff, 1969b, p. 66).[27,28] Second, fluctuations may not discourage investment, but may work with a ratchet effect, raising investment more in booms than they depress it in slumps, though low-income producers who cannot withstand periods of very low proceeds may prefer a lower risk activity even if its average income is lower. Ariff's study of Malaysia found there was no statistically significant relation over the period 1955–65 between export earnings and domestic investment, for instance (1969b, p. 62). More generally, the evidence from cross-sections of large numbers of countries is conflicting, though there is some tendency for more recent studies, generally using more sophisticated econometric techniques, to find some inverse relationship between instability and growth.[29] Inflation and instability is even more contentious—certainly Malaysia until 1973 had one of the most stable price levels in the world, despite exceptionally high export instability, and despite a money supply closely tied to the external sector (Munro, 1973b).

In spite of this conflicting evidence, great interest has been shown in commodity stabilization (though often the interest is linked with a wish to raise commodity prices—see e.g. Prebisch, 1964, p. 16). Devices to deal with fluctuations may work at either a national or international level and the national devices may seek either to control fluctuations or to insulate the domestic economy from their effects. Insulation may be achieved by sliding-scale export taxes (such as that on rubber in Malaysia, though the tin export tax in Malaysia has only very recently been made progressive), or by national buffer funds[30] (which withhold revenue from producers in good years and return it—or some of it, since in West Africa it has often been a form of taxation—in bad years). In a demand-shift market, though, this stabilization of producer incomes (and the consequent reduction of multiplier effects) will be achieved at the expense of increasing the fluctuations in price, since producers are likely to produce less than otherwise in good years (because their earnings are held down) and more in bad years (when their earnings are held up).

Attempts to control the commodity markets directly may be carried out either by individual major producers—Malaysia for instance has operated a national rubber buffer stock since the 1960's (see Brown, 1975, pp. 266–77)—or by collective action.

Collective action is most familiar in the form of international buffer stocks, which buy at low prices and sell at high prices (with the 'floors' and 'ceilings' determined as part of the agreement). It may also take the form of multilateral contracts, whereby minimum sales and purchases at agreed prices are decided with the rest of output channelled through a residual market. Since the Second World War commodity agreements have existed at various times in coffee, cocoa, sugar, wheat and tin. The International Tin Agreement—a buffer stock strengthened by the right to impose export quotas in face of low prices—was the only agreement in operation at the start of 1976, and the fifth five-year agreement is due to start in May 1976, with a larger buffer stock. The tin agreement includes all major producers except China and Brazil, and some consuming countries (though not the U.S.A.).[31] The International Cocoa Agreement, also using a buffer stock and export quotas, was signed in 1973 but has yet to come into effect. The coffee agreement using export quotas, broke down in 1971, and, though renegotiated, has yet to be ratified, and in 1973 the sugar agreement broke down in face of rising prices (British Government, 1975, p. 44; *The Guardian*, 29 December 1975). Indeed, high prices have been a particular problem for commodity buffer stocks genuinely aiming at stabilization since speculative pressure often makes it difficult to hold ceiling prices.[32] The wheat agreements have used multilateral contracts (Brown, 1975, p. 166).

Although negotiations are proceeding currently on several agreements—including a joint Malaysian-Thai-Indonesian attempt to establish a rubber buffer stock (*Straits Times*, March 1975)—the most interesting development is the proposal for an 'integrated' approach to commodities put forward by UNCTAD's Secretary General. Under this scheme, a joint buffer stock would be established for ten commodities (cocoa, coffee, copper, cotton, hard fibres, jute, rubber, sugar, tea and tin) (*Grindlays Bank Review*, November 1975, p. 8).[33] These commodities are mainly those of particular interest to developing countries, and it is hoped that considerable cost reductions will be achieved by operating an integrated stock, with purchases of some commodities being offset by sales of others. Negotiation on this scheme is likely in UNCTAD IV.

Negotiations are also in prospect at UNCTAD for schemes to supplement commodity stabilization by direct measures to stabilize export earnings. Two such schemes exist. The scheme operated by the IMF at present concentrates on primary commodity exports (thus disadvantaging somewhat countries which have started to export manufactures) and allows for financing of export income shortfalls based on recent (five yearly) trends with allowance for projected growth (British Government, 1975, p. 23). The IMF's terms are quite stringent, with a repayment period of 3-5 years and interest at 4-6%, with the result that the facility has been little used (*Grindlays Bank Review*, November 1975, p.7).[34] The other scheme—operating under the EEC Lomé Convention (see next section), covers forty-six countries of Africa, the Pacific and the Caribbean (the 'ACP' countries). Apart from its smaller coverage of countries and the fact that it is limited to exports to the EEC, Stabex differs from the IMF facility in two other important respects. Compensation for export shortfalls, though not necessarily full, is in the form of an outright grant[35] to the 'least developed' countries[36] (over half of the total number) based on the shortfall over recent trends plus projected growth, and to the others countries it is on significantly easier terms than the IMF's. Second, it is limited to a specific range of exports, and to shortfalls in the product in question for the country concerned. Export earnings stabilization schemes like Stabex are valuable in that they can concentrate on the problems of particular countries (especially the poorest), whereas schemes to raise commodity prices also benefit rich country producers. Indexation of a sort may also be introduced if export earnings shortfalls are calculated in real rather than money terms, which avoids the reservations felt by many commentators (including the framers of the background documents to the Kingston declaration) that the linking of, for instance, commodity agreement floor prices to an index of manufactured prices would freeze price relations undesirably (British Government, 1975, p. 22).

2.4 MARKET ACCESS[37]

Faced with low and fluctuating commodity prices, many developing countries' governments wish to diversify, (though if fluctuations *per se* are the problem a better solution would be stabilization measures, if these can successfully be achieved). Further processing of primary commodities adds to the producer country's share of value-added in the final product,[38] and labour-intensive manufacturing also offers scope for export expansion.

With the exception of some developing country exports which compete directly with those of rich countries (vegetable oils for example) and of commodities such as coffee, cocoa and bananas on which certain countries (especially in the EEC) levy excise duties, primary commodities have relatively free access to rich country markets. Severe problems arise, however, when developing countries attempt to diversify their exports out of primary commodities. Prior to the conclusion of the 'Kennedy round' trade negotiations in 1967, for example, the EEC common external tariff escalated from 1.5% for raw materials and energy to 10.7% for semi-finished goods, and 11.7% for capital goods, and similar escalations characterized the U.K. and U.S. tariff structures (Cutajar and Franks, 1967, p. 109). Similarly, in 1973, log imports could enter the EEC duty free, sawn timber faced a duty of 7% and plywood 20% (Singer *et al.*, 1973, p. 114). Moreover, since the raw material enters duty free, the protection on domestic value-added (i.e. the effective rate of protection),[39] is understated by the nominal rates;[40] though this effect can sometimes be offset by the use of countervailing export duties on the primary commodity (Helleiner, 1973, p. 25). Problems of market access may also be improved by customs unions *between* developing countries, but in Asia the Association of South East Asian Nations (ASEAN), of which Malaysia is a member, is very much in its infancy and its intra-trade is very small.

Under the auspices of GATT six series (or 'rounds') of trade and tariff negotiations have been completed (of which the most recent was the 'Kennedy round' 1964–7). A seventh round started in February 1975—the Tokyo round[41] Multilateral Trade Negotiations—due for completion in 1977. Under the Kennedy round and earlier negotiations it is generally agreed that products of special interest to the Third World received smaller average tariff reductions than other products. In the Kennedy round in particular the greatest tariff cuts were on advanced-technology, capital-intensive products (IMF, November 1975, p. 67). Non-tariff barriers too (quotas, 'voluntary' agreements to restrict exports, strict health regulations on food imports, etc.) have apparently increased considerably in the last ten years and appear to bear more heavily on exports of developing countries.[42]

Improvements in market access, in addition to those under the GATT 'rounds', have occurred following UNCTAD I and various treaties negotiated by the EEC. The Generalized System of Preferences, dating from UNCTAD in 1964, allows preferential access (subject to various escape clauses) to developing country exports. The U.S.A. did not join the scheme,[43] though, and in fact only 9% of the Third World imports into the participating countries are covered by the GSP. A large proportion of their total imports (63%) are already admitted duty free, but many industrial products are excluded and the main beneficiaries are few in number (e.g. Hong Kong) (Singer *et al.*, pp. 89–95). The Lomé Convention, signed in February 1975, by the EEC and forty-six ACP countries also offers a range of non-reciprocal trade concessions (in addition to the Stabex export stabilization concessions scheme already discussed), and widens the scope of the earlier Yaoundé Conventions (1960–75). One of its most widely discussed provisions is to allow a substantial quantity of sugar imports (the same quantity as under the U.K.'s earlier Commonwealth Sugar Agreement) at basically the same price as that received by the EEC's own sugar (beet) growers, thus providing some degree of indexation in terms of the Community's own support-price adjustment.[44]

Nevertheless countries outside Lomé's provision suffer a decline in their relative position and in the opinion of influential commentators the gains from Lomé and other agreements designed to improve Third World trade prospects are greatly outweighed by the growth of non-tariff barriers over the last decade and the countinuing existence of escalating tariff structures. (Green and Singer, 1975, p. 434).

NOTES

1. Much of this discussion of the formation of GATT and, later, the background to UNCTAD is taken from Cutajar and Franks (1967, Chapters 7–9). Other useful sources on the early years after UNCTAD 1 are Johnson (1967 and 1971).
2. The desire to return to the nineteenth century system should not be exaggerated. The International Monetary Fund, following the Bretton Woods conference, was an attempt to replace the nineteenth century international payments system by what Keynes regarded as the 'opposite' of the gold standard—since currency exchange rates would be allowed to be altered in face of any 'fundamental disequilibrium'. The World Bank of course was explicitly concerned with development problems, again a new departure, and even in the field of international trade *per se*, the GATT rules permitted tariffs to be used for protective purposes (though it was hoped eventually to reduce tariff levels) and were more concerned with eliminating discriminatory practices and non-tariff barriers.
3. The term 'Group of 77' dates from UNCTAD I and refers to the number of developing country participants in UNCTAD in the early 1960's. The 'Group of 77', though retaining its name, now has over 100 members (Wood, 1975, p. 2).
4. Freight rates tend to discriminate against further processing since they are often levied according to the value of the product rather than its bulk or weight (Edwards, 1975, p. 276). Also, as Singer *et al.* (1973, pp. 114–6) point out, fabricated primary products are often bulkier and genuinely costlier to transport than the minimally processed article, e.g. tyres *versus* block rubber.
5. Estimates by H. W. Singer suggest that the fall in the share of developing countries in world trade since the Second World War could account for much of the unemployment and underemployment in developing countries (often estimated at 25–30% of the labour force) (Singer *et al.*, 1973, p. 17).
6. A vehement espousal of the importance of domestic policies and the (at least partial and relative) irrelevance of international measures in this regard (and indeed for development problems in general) is made by I.M.D. Little (1975). Little's main point is that for the Third

World as a whole international trade is relatively unimportant (equivalent to 11.6% of GNP in 1972 if petroleum exporters are excluded, and 15% including petroleum exporters). He points out that half of the population of the Third World lives in countries with populations over fifty million, for whom trade is of minor importance in GNP. However, he concedes that the dependence on foreign technology is greater. Of course, a large number of developing *countries* are small and heavily trade dependent—and Malaysia, the country to be the subject of this book's case study, is certainly one of these. One must however agree with Little in feeling cynicism about certain governments demanding a better international income distribution while doing almost nothing to improve distribution domestically. Other countries though, *are* making efforts to help their poorest sections (see Chapter 9).

7. See Green and Singer (1975), Wood (1975), *Grindlays Bank Review* (November 1975) and UNCTAD (1974). Some very useful popular discussions of NIEO are given in the *New Internationalist* (October 1975).
8. The arguments cited here are those of Prebisch (1964). Other arguments by Prebisch include the notion that worker bargaining power works in a ratchet fashion in industrial countries during booms, whereas prices and wages fall in developing countries during slumps. See Chapter 3 and also the review article by June Flanders (1964). Thoburn (1971, pp. 75–82) gives a fuller account of the Prebisch doctrine than space permits here. It is also worth noting that Bhagwati (1958) has shown that it is theoretically possible for a growing country to face such a deterioration in its terms of trade that it is made worse off by growth—'immizerising growth'. (See also Melvin, 1969 and Bhagwati, 1969 for further discussion of this problem.)
9. Presumably the gains accruing to domestic capitalists (or foreign investors) from the workers' poor bargaining power are not retained since new producers enter the industry or existing firms expand output—thus lowering price and transferring (at least some of) the productivity gains to foreign consumers.
10. However, between 1958–61 and 1962–5 Peninsular Malaysia's net barter terms of trade deteriorated slightly, though the income terms of trade improved; and according to the Malaysian Treasury, *AR*, 1974–5, Peninsular Malaysia's net barter terms of trade deteriorated somewhat over the period 1965–74, the commodity boom notwithstanding. (Thus, with 1970 = 100, *Px/Pm* was 114 in 1965, 79 and 1972 and 92 in the first half of 1974.)
11. An interesting aspect of this problem is discussed in Arthur Lewis's Wicksell lectures (1969) in which he argues that labour productivity gains in primary commodity exports will necessarily be passed on to foreign consumers unless productivity in domestic food production rises (pp. 17–27).
12. These details are from Ellis (1974, p. 29). The oil price referred to is Saudi Arabian light (34°) crude, and oil prices vary with quality, Libyan or Venezualan oil, for instance, fetching a higher price. Market prices, in general are somewhat lower than 'posted' prices, which are used for tax reference purposes—thus the market price per barrel was U.S. $8 on 1 January 1974, and the posted price U.S. $11.65.
13. The potential time horizon will be determined by the size of deposits in the case of a mineral (though changes in technology, and increased exploration in the face of shortages make this 'size' an illusive concept). For an agricultural commodity it will be infinite (subject to changes in demand, and the need to prevent soil exhaustion). Most discussions (e.g. Barker and Page, 1974) concentrate on minerals, but agricultural products may also be cartelized (though, as will be shown, probably less successfully). For a discussion of optimal rates of resource depletion see Pearce (1975).
14. Details additional to those from Chapter 1 are taken from British Government (1975) which is an extremely useful source of basic data on commodities.
15. Zinc, lead and silver are generally regarded as the other 'major' metals (copper, tin, lead, zinc and silver are the metals traded on the London Metal Exchange, for instance,—though bauxite has been mainly traded internationally *within* aluminium-producing companies). These however (excluding bauxite), are mainly produced by developed countries.
16. The main reason for this failure apparently has been a large volume of stocks overhanging the market (*The Guardian*, 29 December 1975).
17. Lim (1974, p. 81) cites an estimate for the world price elasticity of demand for tin of −0.2 (and with a standard error large enough to suggest that it may not be statistically significantly different from zero.) Of course, demand elasticity normally rises with price, and might be higher outside (and above) previously experienced price ranges.

18. Over the period 1925/9 to 1965/9 world tinplate output (the main end use of tin) rose nearly fourfold, while world tin output rose only 8% (Munro, 1973a, pp. 56–7).
19. This important point is made by Barker and Page (1974, pp. 89–90). In the electrical industry, a very important end-user of copper, aluminium is a close substitute. In other uses (in the construction industry for instance) plastics, mainly produced by Western countries, can be substituted for copper (Prain, 1975, pp. 154–8).
20. There are however some strong consumer preferences for rice of different types, especially in South East Asia, and in fact most Third World rice trade is *within* Asia.
21. This is also true to a limited extent for natural rubber, since resting the tree would slightly increase later output, and also make safer the subsequent use of yield stimulants such as 'Ethrel'.
22. In this context Malaysian timber is best regarded as a kind of mineral since the rate of export expansion in the recent past could hardly be maintained if the forests were to be replanted with hardwood and the industry developed on a permanent basis.
23. These points are made strongly in Gordon Munro's projections of the Malaysian balance of payments to 1980 (Munro, 1973a, p. 61).
24. Figures cited by Helleiner (1972, p. 79).
25. A very full discussion of the causes of instability is given in Brown (1975, Chapter 1), from which much of this discussion is drawn. Lim (1974) is also useful, and a simpler presentation is given in Helleiner (1972, Chapter 5).
26. 'The' copper price referred to is the price on the London Metal Exchange, which is used as a reference price for most international trade in copper even though only a small proportion of traded coper actually passes through the LME. Sales in the U.S.A. are conducted at the U.S. 'producer price' which has been much more stable (Prain, 1975, pp. 94–6). The LME in fact is not primarily a 'physical' market, and its main function is as a futures market for hedging by dealers and manufacturers, and as a source of reference for determining world prices. In fact probably only about 5% of the world trade in the metals it handles (copper, tin, lead, zinc and silver), actually passes through the LME, and in copper only 15–20% of transactions are physical (Cairncross and McRae, 1974, pp. 174–82). For tin, for instance, the main 'physical' market is Penang in Malaysia.
27. See Ariff (1969b, p. 58) for derivation of the index (Coppock's logarithmic variance method), which is basically proportional fluctuations in a time series corrected for trend. Lim (1974, pp. 77 and 85) notes, however, that Peninsular Malaysia (to which Ariff's calculations refer) was nevertheless more unstable than most other developing countries. This is a reflection of the fact that Malaysian export proceeds were almost twice as unstable (in terms of the Coppock index) than those of a sample of forty-five developing countries, 1946–58. A more general discussion of Malaysian export instability is given in Ariff (1969a).
28. See also Chapter 7 on final demand linkages.
29. In a wide-ranging study of export instability Coppock (1962) found almost no relation between export instability and growth of GNP; indeed it was the lowest correlation coefficient of his entire analysis, and growth of GNP per capita also had a very low correlation coefficient (pp. 106–7). Probably the best-known study is MacBean (1966) who found no significant relation of export instability with economic growth, using time series for eleven developing countries in the 1950's. MacBean's findings were attacked in a long and highly critical review by Maizels (1968b) who disputed MacBean's statistical techniques and the quality of his data, and suggested that when certain maverick observations (such as those for Morocco and Iraq) were excluded, there was a significant relation between instability of exports earnings and the rate of growth of investment (p. 579). More recently Kenen and Voivodas (1972) have attempted to refine and update MacBean's study. They find that though there is no 'pervasive connection' between export instability and economic growth, that some of MacBean's results (e.g. his perverse-signed coefficients for instability in the 1950's) were not true of the 1960's, and that there *is* a relation between export earnings instability and the *level* of investment. Discussions of the literature on export instability are also given in Lim (1974) and Brown (1975).
30. Brown (1975) gives an exhaustive discussion of control devices, national and international.
31. The U.S.A. late in 1975 announced a willingness in principle to join the new (fifth) tin agreement, subject to Senate Approval (*Tin International*, November 1975).
32. The tin agreement also has been affected by uncertainties about potential releases from the

U.S. General Services Administration's strategic stockpile. In March 1973 for example Malaysian government opinion was incensed by an unexpected decision by President Nixon to sell large quantities of tin and rubber from the stockpile (which then covered forty commodities of strategic importance to the U.S., valued at U.S. $6000m) (*Straits Times*, March 1973).

33. The list originally was eighteen, and included wheat, maize, lead, zinc, iron ore, bauxite, rice and wool. Thus the reduced list has excluded mainly commodities in which rich countries have a large or dominant producer interest (except bauxite, where production is in the hands of a few multinationals).
34. The IMF will also lend funds to establish buffer stocks.
35. Of course such resource transfers should really be seen as part of a more general aid policy. For a discussion of aid policy towards the Third World see for example Green and Singer (1975, pp. 435–6), who stress the need for a 'third window' facility (i.e. 'soft loans' between the very low rates available from some sources such as the International Development Association and the commercial terms of e.g. the World Bank's standard loans). OPEC countries too are seeking Third World investment outlets, which could be arranged through international agencies.
36. See Hodgkinson (1975, pp. 12–4). She points out that the 'poorest' countries are defined to include 'island' and 'landlocked' countries, so the group includes some countries with relatively high incomes.
37. An extremely useful survey of market access problems, on which my account draws heavily, is given in Singer *et al.* (1973). Accounts of the subsequent Multinational Trade Negotiations (discussed later) are given in IMF (10 March 1975) and Anjaria (1975).
38. Barker and Page (1974, p. 83) cite the case of aluminium which sells at U.S. $570 a ton, compared to its earlier stages of alumina (U.S. $20–30 for four tons). This does not necessarily mean that further processing is desirable. It might for instance, generate very little employment in a labour-surplus situation. Singer *et al.* (1973) suggest that agricultural expansion is likely to generate far more employment than the processing of many industrial raw materials (pp. 45 and 116–7). See also Chapter 3 for a discussion of 'good' and 'bad' linkages.
39. ERP is usually measured as $=\frac{Vd\text{-}Vw}{Vw}$, where *V*d is domestic value-added and *V*w is value-added at free-trade prices.
40. Exceptions to this are some imports into the U.S.A. from subsidiaries of U.S. firms located overseas, on whose products duty is only levied on the value-added generated abroad.
41. Named after the declaration of September 1973, following an intergovernmental meeting in Tokyo to launch the negotiations.
42. The evidence relates to the numbers rather than the incidence of non-tariff barriers (Singer *et al.*, 1973, pp. 86–7).
43. Under the 1975 Trade Expansion Act the U.S. government is now empowered to extend duty-free treatment to developing country imports, excluding textiles, shoes and some other products (IMF, 10 March 1975, p. 70).
44. The sugar arrangements under Lomé are discussed at length by Harris and Hagelberg (1975), who compare them to the earlier Commonwealth Sugar Agreement. They are sceptical about the likelihood of full indexation occuring in sugar since they expect Community support prices for sugar to lag behind other prices as a result of possible sugar overproduction. Expansion of ACP sugar and EEC beet production, or both, may mean that excess production is sold on the world free market, thus depressing prices and disadvantaging the producers outside Lomé. Indeed the EEC common agricultural policy in general is extremely complex in its effects on developing countries, and space does not permit full discussion here. The arrangements prior to Lomé especially with regard to their effects on tropical crops are well covered in Singer *et al.* (1973, pp. 54–71).

Chapter 3
Exports and Development — Theory and methods of Analysis

This chapter provides a theoretical framework and a methodology by which the development effects of export expansion can be assessed. The first section reviews existing theories of trade, growth and development; from classical writing, to neoclassical, to 'dependency' and 'imperialist' theory. The second section, drawing on these ideas, presents the author's own approach; which is then used in the third section to develop a methodology for the quantitative analysis used in the case study of Malaysia, which follows in Part II.

3.1 THEORIES OF TRADE, GROWTH AND DEVELOPMENT[1]

Analyses of the role of foreign trade in promoting economic growth can be traced back to Classical economics.

Classical economists, particularly Adam Smith (1776) and John Stuart Mill (1848), thought trade could be a major stimulus to growth. Three main elements can be distinguished in their thinking. First, there is the 'vent for surplus' principle.[2] Second, there is the idea that by removing the constraint of domestic market size, exporting gives scope for division of labour. Thus, Smith writes:

> 'The importation of gold and silver is not the principal, much less the sole benefit which a nation derives from its foreign trade. Between whatever places foreign trade is carried on, they all of them derive two distinct benefits from it. It carries out that surplus part of the produce of their land and labour for which there is no demand among them, and brings back in return for it something else for which there is demand. It gives a value to their superfluities, by exchanging them for something else, which may satisfy a part of their wants, and increase their enjoyments. By means of it, the narrowness of the home-market does not hinder the division of labour in any particular branch of art or manufacture from being carried to the highest perfection. By opening a more extensive market for whatever part of the produce of their labour may exceed the home consumption, it encourages them to improve its productive powers, and to augment its annual produce to the utmost, and thereby to increase the real revenue and wealth of the society. These great and important services foreign trade is continually occupied in performing, to all the different countries

between which it is carried on,' [Reproduced by permission of Methuen and Co. Ltd. from Smith (1776, p. 413.), *An Enquiry into the Nature and Causes of the Wealth of Nations* (Ed. E. Cannon), 1930 edn.] [3]

And again, speaking of the discovery of America:

'By opening a new and inexhaustable market to all the commodities of Europe, it gave occasion to new divisions of labour and improvements of art, which, in the narrow circle of the ancient commerce, could never have taken place for want of a market to take off the greater part of their produce. The productive powers of labour were improved, and its produce increased in all the different countries of Europe, and together with it the real revenue and wealth of the inhabitants.' [Reproduced by permission of Methuen and Co. Ltd. from Smith, 1776, p. 414.]

For Smith, division of labour is a means of directly improving labour productivity (Smith, 1776, pp. 7–10). In Mill it is more concerned with the use of machinery and improved technology, and later writers have elaborated the concept to include specialization both between firms and between industries (Young, 1928; Stigler, 1951). This amounts to what Hla Myint has called a 'dynamic productivity theory' of trade (Myint, 1958, p. 318), whereby the gains from trade come not only from securing imports at lower real cost within the framework of an existing cost structure, but from altering that cost structure itself.

The third element is the effect of trade on economic incentives, found mainly in Mill[4] and written in part with explicit reference to the countries of Asia. After considering the direct (i.e. comparative advantage) gains from trade, he writes of the indirect benefits, which are benefits of a higher order:

'One is the tendency of every extension of the market to improve the processes of production. A country which produces for a larger market than its own, can introduce a more extended division of labour, can make greater use of machinery, and is more likely to make inventions and improvements in the processes of production. Whatever causes a greater quantity of anything to be produced in the same place, tends to the general increase of the productive powers of the world. There is another consideration, principally applicable to an early stage of industrial advancement. A people may be in a quiescent, indolent, uncultivated state, with all their tastes either fully satisfied or entirely undeveloped, and they may fail to put forth the whole of their productive energies for want of any sufficient object of desire. The opening of foreign trade, by making them acquainted with new objects, or tempting them by the easier acquisition of things which they had not previously thought attainable, sometimes works a sort of industrial revolution in a country whose resources were previously undeveloped for want of energy and ambition in the people; inducing those who were satisfied with scanty comforts and little work, to work harder for the gratification of their new tastes, and even to save, and accumulate capital, for the still more complete satisfaction of those tastes at a future time.' [Reproduced by permission of Longmans Green Co. Ltd. from Mill, 1848, p. 351.]

In Asia, Mill thought, the principle of capital accumulation was itself weak:

> 'where people will neither save, nor work to obtain the means of saving, unless under the inducement of enormously high profits, nor even then if it is necessary to wait a considerable time for them; where either productions remain scanty, or drudgery great, because there is neither capital forthcoming nor forethought sufficient for the adoption of the contrivences by which natural agents are made to do the work of human labour.' [Reproduced by permission of Longmans Green Co. Ltd. from Mill, 1848, p. 117.]

In these circumstances exporting acts to raise the rate of profit to a level corresponding to the low desire to accumulate. Imports provide economic incentives to increase wealth. Trade occurs within a framework of international factor movements. Imported technology also raises rates of profit, capital imports free the country from the constraint of domestic saving, and the economic activities of foreign capitalists provide an example for local people to follow.[5] In addition trade allows goods of low growth potential (primary products) to be exchanged for goods of a high growth potential (capital goods) (Hicks, 1959, Chapter 8).

All this adds up to an extremely optimistic view of growth through trade, and one which came under attack in the early 1950's when economists again became interested in trade and growth as part of the general post-war concern with the problems of less developed countries. Long before this time Marxist writers also had been interested in the problem and had fitted foreign investment by advanced countries in primary product exports of poor countries into their theory of imperialism, and to some extent the 1950's writers revived Marxist theories[6] (which are discussed later in this section, together with 'dependency' theories). However, the major developments in the 1950's and early 1960's were the hypotheses proposed by H. W. Singer (1950), Gunnar Myrdal (1956a, 1956b, 1957)[7] and R. Prebisch[8].

Singer's position is that export sectors based on foreign investment in less developed countries, though *geographically* part of the country in which they are located, are *economically* part of the investing country. The cumulative additions to income, employment and technical knowledge which one might expect do occur, but they accrue to the lender. Indeed, foreign investment may actively harm the recipient by diverting investment and entrepreneural resources away from the domestic manufacturing industry which might otherwise have developed.[9,9a] Myrdal adds to this analysis the concepts of 'spread' and 'backwash' effects, in combination with a principle of 'circular and cumulative causation' (his term for a vicious or a virtuous circle). Developing various principles of regional inequality which he later relates to the international economy, he traces a process whereby a growing region 'spreads' its growth to other regions by demanding consumer goods and agricultural products, but also generates 'backwash' effects by inducing an immigration of capital and high quality labour. In a less developed country spread effects from the growing export sector will be weak because of poor transport and communication, low levels of education, and so on, and 'backwash' effects will occur through the destruction of local industries by imports and through a loss of the best of the economy's productive resources to the export sector.

The other theme running through the work of all three writers, but usually associated with Prebisch, is that in addition to the adverse effects of foreign investment in primary product exports, primary producers will receive little return from their investment because of a secular deterioration since the nineteenth century in the terms of trade of primary products *vis à vis* manufactures.[10]

The Singer–Myrdal–Prebisch position is an extreme one, coming close to saying that poor countries have been made poorer by trade. The export sector is seen as an enclave,[11] having little effect on the rest of the economy other than employing unskilled labour and draining off capital and entrepreneurial ability. (This is seen as a bad thing because primary product exports are assumed to yield fewer growth effects—in the form of improved skills and education, the creation of new technology and new demands, and the dynamism accompanying urban civilization—than would domestic manufacturing. In fact this notion is merely an untested assertion.) There are large leakages abroad in the form of remitted profits and imports. Skilled workers are likely to be imported from abroad, and these 'foreign factors'[12] will consume imported consumer goods not local produce. This position has been the subject of much attack. For example, P. T. Bauer has argued that enclaves are a focal point of development, and that the concept of an enclave is designed solely to give a spurious reconciliation between the 'vicious circle of poverty' and the existence of manifest evidence of widespread economic progress in underdeveloped countries (Bauer, 1959, p. 113, and 1971, pp. 31–68). Cairncross has argued (1961) that it is difficult to see how dynamic influences can be contained completely within an enclave, and asks by what magic a steel mill producing for the domestic market could revolutionize an economy when an export good could not. Boris C. Swerling (1961) has pointed out the importance of the foreign trade sector as an easily available source of tax revenue in economic systems where scarce administrative skills must be carefully husbanded. The terms of trade doctrine has also been widely attacked, and the arguments against it are now commonplace (see also Chapter 2). A decline in the ratio of export to import prices (*barter terms of trade*) does not necessarily mean a decline in the *factorial terms of trade*, i.e. the terms of trade allowing for productivity changes. So poor countries need not have lost all of their productivity gains. Nor need the *income terms of trade* have deteriorated (i.e. the fall in price does not necessarily mean a drop in total revenue from exports). Moreover, many of the arguments are based on price series of British imports and exports, yet poor countries export a wider range of products than those imported by Britain. The decline in primary product prices may reflect a decline in ocean freight rates at the end of the last century also. In any case, it is invalid to lump together the experience of all poor countries; some may have gained even if others lost.[13] Also, much attack has been levelled at the Singer–Myrdal–Prebisch policy recommendations, usually various forms of protection, both from the more orthodox neoclassical viewpoint (especially Little, Scitovsky and Scott, 1970), and by 'dependency' writers (see below).

Following this controversy a number of less extreme accounts appeared (mainly in the late 1950's and early 1960's) of why many present-day poor countries have gained much less from export growth than did Canada, Australia and other temperate-zone nations which also had large export expansions. G. M. Meier argued that foreign investment in export industries has not been competitive with domestic investment: there is no evidence to suggest that the latter would have been greater in the former's absence. What limited development was a lack of 'carry-over' from the export sector due to domestic market imperfections and values minimizing incentives to economic change. If these obstacles could be lessened, Meier feels optimistic about growth through exports (see Meier, 1953, 1968).

H. Myint (1954, 1954–5, 1965, 1967) sees the explanation for limited economic development in terms of the nature of the way in which countries were 'opened-up' to trade. Where exports were developed by foreign investment a cheap labour policy became fossilized. As employers found it difficult to recruit local labour at existing (low) wage rates, they imported labour from abroad, thus keeping wages down to a level appropriate to the overpopulated areas (in the case of Asia particularly India and China) from which most immigrants were drawn. Thus the incomes of local people were raised very little and a market was not created for local products except simple foodstuffs. Where exports were developed by local smallholders the key feature was that productive techniques were not improved, the expansion being simply a vent for surplus labour time and land. There was a once and for all rise in income but no further growth.[14] Gains to local people were also lessened as a result of monopsonistic exploitation by foreign firms and middlemen. However Myint is optimistic about the future of primary product exports, once improved techniques are adopted, and he feels that there is no reason to suppose that had the past export expansions been of manufactures rather than primary products that more growth would have resulted (1967, p. 162).

Probably the fullest, and the most convincing analysis of export growth has been given by R. E. Baldwin (1956, 1963), whose work is closely linked with the so-called 'staple' approach used by economic historians to explain growth in Canada and the early United States. It is Baldwin's work, and indirectly the staple theories, which are the main influence on the view of exports and growth set out in the next section. The term 'staple' refers to any resource-intensive export and the key feature of the approach is the belief that in a given initial, socio-economic environment, different exports will have different effects on growth. Harold Innis, the founder of the Canadian 'staple' school conducted a series of commodity studies—from cod fishing, to fur hunting and trading, lumber, and wheat, in the belief that the study of history provided a potential source of relevant economy theory for a 'new' country, and that this involved the working out of the economic history of each major industry in turn (Innis, 1956, pp. 3–16). These studies were also a reflection of his view that an understanding of the country's development had to be approached through its foreign trade, whereby growth took the form of increasing integration into the international economy.[15] Unfortunately Innis did not develop an explicit theoretical framework, though some of the more important of his generalizations about the role of price incentives, transport technology and excess capacity in influencing the establishment and subsequent effects of various staples are set out in essays.[16] However, Watkins (1963) has provided a useful restatement of Innis's approach in terms of a theory of capital accumulation, and Douglas North, the other leading staple writer and student of early American history, has also provided a theoretical contribution (1955) though his later work (1959, 1966) explicitly uses Baldwin's (1956) theory.

In Baldwin's work, as in the staple theories, the stress is on the character of the export product and explicit account is taken of causes and effects of factor inflows. In his 1956 paper Baldwin contrasts a family farm crop and a plantation crop to illustrate his approach. Each is grown in separate, sparsely populated regions, 'West' and 'South', equidistant from an old region from which both can draw capital and labour,[17] the regions being identical except that South has land and climate suitable for a plantation crop and West for a family farm crop. Both new regions have an abundant supply of mineral resources such as coal and iron ore, but these initially are at a prohibitive distance from the export ports. The family farm crop is not subject to large economies of scale in production based on extensive use of cheap unskilled labour. Moreover, the elasticity of substitution between capital and labour is relatively large. Also, less technological and managerial skill is necessary to manage the optimum size of farm. In contrast, the plantation crop involves labour-intensive production for a wide range of factor price ratios, has a low substitutability of capital for labour after a point, and is subject to increasing returns to scale in both cultivation and processing. Thus large amounts of capital and labour are necessary for the optimum size. It also needs much technical and managerial skill to operate a plantation efficiently. These characteristics have a crucial significance for the effects of the export goods. South imports large quantities of cheap labour. Little labour skill is needed, so little develops, and this inhibits the subsequent development of any manufacturing industry even if there is demand for the products of such an industry. Workers find it difficult to set up on their own because of the large optimum size of plantation. The few managers and capitalists consume imported luxuries, and the workers consume only simple goods. Thus there is little demand for local residentiary industry. Profits tend to be repatriated or reinvested in the export sector or in luxury construction only. West, on the other hand, imports immigrants who are more skilled and who also own capital. The result is that income distribution is more even, and demand for local consumer goods is stronger. Moreover workers in the family farm sector are more suitable as domestic entrepreneurs or skilled workers than are the workers in South.

In this analysis the technological characteristics of the export goods production function, both with respect to input coefficients and economies of scale, are crucial. Probably the most important single consequence is the type of factor inflow. West is able to import workers who are themselves already 'developed', as it were, and therefore starts the growth process with a big advantage over South. Successive development is determined by the type of market which grows up for local consumer goods; and, as D. C. North stresses, by the investment opportunities offered to industries producing intermediate products for the export sector or using the export good as an input (North, 1966, pp. 170–171)—backward and forward linkages in A. O. Hirschman's terminology (Hirschman, 1958, pp. 98–119).

Given the initial factor inflows, successive development from the export base can be seen in terms of a theory of capital formation working through a disaggregated multiplier–accelearator mechanism—export expansion raises income through a multiplier process, and linkages are an acceleration concept.[18] Baldwin's later work goes into this successive development in more detail. This time however he concentrates on exports as a means of spreading advanced technology through a less developed economy, though again the analysis is organized around the export production function.[19] Export growth both offers opportunities for new economic activities (i.e. embodying more advanced technology) to develop elsewhere in the economy and it conditions the responsiveness of the economy to those opportunities. The establishment of particular exports in less developed countries depended on comparative cost considerations, taking into account factor movements. Unskilled labour and many natural resources were, at existing exchange rates in the late nineteenth and early twentieth centuries, much cheaper in less developed than in advanced countries. Therefore the industries established were those using some or all of these factors intensively. Baldwin distinguishes two main types of export product—plantation exports and mining exports.

Plantation exports require large quantities of unskilled labour, large amounts of capital (because of economies of scale) and a small number of technical and managerial staff, whose considerable skills locals (says Baldwin) find difficult to attain. The large wage bill could provide a large domestic market for simple consumer goods, but because of lack of labour skills, local people are not able to set up as entrepreneurs on their own. On the other hand, such industries are unlikely to require complex capital and material inputs. Often capital goods (as opposed to circulating capital) may consist mainly of construction outlays. The production functions for such capital goods use inputs more nearly in the proportions available domestically. Thus, brick, cement and timber are not highly using of skilled labour. Moreover, they can be produced efficiently on a small scale, and are protected from imports by high transport costs. In contrast, mining exports often require higher degrees of labour skill, which locals can acquire over time. However, in spite of their higher *per capita* income the mining workers are not sufficient in number to provide a large domestic market. On the other hand, they may be able to set up as entrepreneurs to supply goods to the export industry, because of their acquired skills and possibly because their high wages have allowed them to accumulate savings. The capital good and input requirements of mining exports were often complex. They had to be imported since their production was more suited to factor supplies in advanced countries. Similarly, processing of the export good depends on how well domestic factor supplies match processing input coefficients.

Baldwin's argument could be paraphrased thus: domestic production of goods supplying the export sector or using the export good as an input, can be established if domestic factor supplies are not *too* divergent from input requirements.[20] However, neither must the match to too exact if growth is to occur. Room must be left for qualitative changes in factor supplies, e.g. the requirement must be for *moderately* skilled labour, which the domestic economy can hope eventually to provide. Thus neither plantations nor mineral exports, if they have the economic and technological characteristics assumed by Baldwin, offer much scope for growth. Neither provide a large market for domestic consumer goods nor are intermediate or capital goods likely to be produced locally. Whether particular crops or minerals fit Baldwin's assumptions is another matter, and is considered later in this study (in Chapter 11).

The 'staple' model, particularly as interpreted by Baldwin, with its stress on capital formation and new technology as sources of growth, presumably has seemed to some writers to be too narrowly an *economic* approach to trade and development. A wider and possibly alternative approach, which has gained considerable popularity since the late 1960's, is to view development problems in terms of 'dependency'.[21,22] Dependency theories have important similarities to Marxist theories of imperialism and can usefully be discussed in relation to those theories, though by no means all dependency theorists would regard themselves as Marxist.

The essence of imperialism, as exemplified in the British colonial empire, is that the economies of underdeveloped countries were forced into a position of complementarity with those of the metropolitan economies (Kidron, 1973, p. 11), or into what Barratt Brown has called an artificial international division of labour (Barratt Brown, 1974, p. 96). Moreover, the free-trade policies followed by Britain in the nineteenth and early twentieth century were designed to perpetuate this division by reinforcing the already established preeminence of the U.K. in world export markets (and thus other countries, such as Germany, which wished to industrialize, had to do so behind tariff barriers) (Barratt Brown, 1974, p. 148).

The driving force behind Western imperialist expansion was partly a search for new sources of raw materials and new markets for manufactures; and, apparently more important, for new sources of labour to exploit. Thus by investing overseas in countries where labour could be paid low wages, Western capitalists were able to find outlets for their accumulated surpluses and maintain their rate of accumulation.[23] Colonial control therefore became the agency for such profitable exploitation.[24] Most important, however, is that Marx himself and other early Marxist writers (particularly Lenin) expected that this incorporation of poor countries into the world capitalist system would bring about their economic growth and development, albeit with the contradictions inherent in capitalism. While some countries such as Australia, New Zealand and Canada, fit into this pattern, most former colonies clearly have not achieved the real income levels to be found in rich capitalist economies; and the modern Marxist view, dating according to Barratt Brown (1974, p. 71) from the 1928 Congress of the Comintern, is that colonial expansion generally acted as a positive force for *underdevelopment*. Thus as a result of their concentration on primary production for the world market, poor countries have had a large part of their economic surpluses extracted by foreign investors for use in rich countries, have been prevented from industrializing, and have developed a class structure in which a 'comprador' bourgeoisie directly serves the capitalists of the imperialist countries (Barratt Brown, 1974, p. 261) rather than promoting domestic capitalist development.

This view of colonial exploitation, and its neocolonial counterpart to be discussed later, provides a convenient approach to dependency theory, especially as outlined by its most famous exponent A. G. Frank.[25] Frank has been portrayed by Booth (in Oxaal, Barnett and Booth, 1975, p. 52) as a synthesizer of Marxism on the one hand, and on the other, of the structuralist tradition developed by the United Nations Economic Commission for Latin America in the 1950's, which saw the world economy split between a rich 'centre' and a poor 'periphery' and was especially concerned about the poor prospects for continuing primary product exporting (see the discussion earlier in this section on Prebisch on the terms of trade). Frank sees centre–periphery relations as a chain of exploitation, in which a series of economic and social relations transfer surplus value from satellite to metropolitan areas *within* poor countries and thence to rich countries (Frank, 1966).

Rather surprisingly at first sight, dependency theories, which have been developed primarily in Latin America, have been less a reaction to underdevelopment brought about by primary commodity exporting than to underdevelopment of a newer kind (though this is not true of Caribbean dependency theory, discussed below). This newer kind of underdevelopment has resulted from the failure of the import-substituting industrialization policies proposed by ECLA, and widely adopted in Latin America, to provide a satisfactory alternative to (and as a reaction to) the traditional outward-looking development strategy based on primary exports (O'Brien, in Oxaal, Barnett and Booth, 1975, p. 10). Instead, industrial investment has increasingly depended on foreign firms, income inequality has increased as industrial investment, by creating fewer highly paid jobs, reinforces the pattern of foreign firms producing luxury goods for a small, privileged section of the community. Industrialization too has made little impact on unemployment. In sum, a situation on 'neocolonialism' exists in which, in spite of political independence, underdeveloped countries find themselves increasingly under the influence of metropolitan economies, with control most frequently exercised through the operations of multinational companies, though primary production has usually been maintained in order to provide foreign exchange.

Frank's view has been chosen as one of the most popular, and extreme statements of dependency theory, in which poor countries are actually made worse off as a result of the activities of rich countries. Development and underdevelopment are seen as two sides of the same process, whereby dominant countries are made rich at the expense of the countries dependent on them. Frank's views are by no means shared by all dependency theorists or by all Marxists. In particular, Barratt Brown (1974, pp. 264–84) and several Latin American writers such as Cardoso and Dos Santos[26] have argued that development *does* occur in a neocolonialist setting, though it is of a dependent nature (mainly because it is usually brought about by the activities of multinational companies who have a monopoly of modern technology). More forcefully the Marxist writer Michael Kidron has argued that imperialism is a redundant concept, imperialist expansion being no longer necessary for the support of the Western capitalist system. In Kidron's view the export of capital on the nineteenth century pattern in order to find raw materials has been rendered unnecessary by increases in economy of raw material use, and the use of underdeveloped countries as an outlet for surplus value is no longer necessary because the Western capitalism is now supported by the world arms economy (Kidron, 1973, pp. 12–16). Although Western firms are active in underdeveloped countries, the export of capital has been greatly reduced from the Western world (e.g. in the U.K. capital exports were 10% of domestic savings in the 1960's compared to 50% in the late nineteenth century).[27] Moreover modern firms, argues Kidron, have entered into effective partnership with local capitalists, whereas in the nineteenth century local capitalists were forced out of existence (witness the demise of the handicrafts industry in India). Capitalism, rather than just capital, has therefore been exported to the Third World and Kidron foresees the development of many more centres of capital in the world economy (Kidron, 1973, p. 16).

Dependency theories are useful in that they offer a broad and interdisciplinary approach to the development process. While the notion that the growth of some countries (the 'satellites') is dependent on the growth of metropolitan areas (i.e. the industrialized West) is hardly surprising, the theories do show how external structures of expropriation can be paralleled by an analagous internal structure (including exploitation of the domestic export sector by the foreign one—see Section 11.3), so that the restructuring of the domestic economy and society becomes an even higher priority than altering external economic and political relations. They show how different forms of production (for the world market, for internal élites, etc.) conditions the formation of classes, and how social and economic factors interact in the reproduction of dependency.[28] They are rather less satisfactory in formulating testable hypotheses about the mechanisms whereby development (or underdevelopment) occurs as a result of dependency. Partly this is because they are essentially a framework of analysis rather than a specific set of theories (O'Brien, in Oxaal, Barnett and Booth, 1975, p. 19) and partly because certain assertions such as foreign investment misdirecting domestic resources are intrinsically difficult to test because one cannot know what would have happened had history been different! Nevertheless

Frank's vertical chain of exploitation[29] could in principle be tested by studies at each successive level, e.g. in the case of primary export production by comparing dealers' margins and income with those of peasant producers.

Two specific points of difficulty, both with important general implications, arise from dependency and imperialist theories. First there is the question posed earlier in the section of why some obviously 'dependent' countries, principally the British Dominions, achieved much higher income levels than others. Barratt Brown argues that the main reason is that Australia, Canada, etc., had no really significant indigenous population, so that capitalism could start, as it were, from scratch; and also that they developed as high-wage areas[30] because of favourable man/land ratios, and were able to impose protective tariffs to encourage industry (Barratt Brown, 1974, pp. 261, 243, 140). The second, and related issue is why, when it is conceded that dependent industrial development brought about by multinational corporations can bring about capitalist economic growth, that this possibility is denied for primary export production, either by foreign firms or by domestic producers. This is relevant for the expansion of Canada and Australia too, because though they now derive only a relatively low proportion of national output from primary production, it can hardly be denied that their early growth owes much to primary commodity exporting. Here the arguments tend to become vague and (especially unfortunate in an interdisciplinary approach) of a naive economic kind. Barratt Brown (1974, p. 100), argues that industry provides levels of *per capita* output seldom found in agriculture, though he fails to note in this context that (reciprocally!), this means small numbers of workers employed per unit of output[31]—which is hardly to be desired in situations of high unemployment (unless high output/labour ratios are accompanied by low ratios of investment cost per worker). Other dependency theorists (see O'Brien, in Oxaal, Barnett and Booth, 1975, p. 16) argue that industry has built-in technical progress whereas agriculture does not, again hardly an assumption which stands up to empirical evidence.[32] On these particular arguments dependency and imperialist theories appear to have little to add to more standard economic analysis.

The dependency theories developed by Caribbean writers, most influentially by George Beckford (1972) and Norman Girvan (e.g. 1970), do specifically concern plantation and mineral economies, and offer a number of hypotheses,[33] some potentially testable. Beckford, writing about plantations, lists four main ways in which they have inhibited development. First, they compete for land resources, reducing potential food production, which has a higher income-elasticity of demand and therefore offers better long-run prospects. Second, they have normally imported their labour forces, and the subsequent racial pluralism has reduced economic and social mobility. Third, there has been a concentration of research on plantation crops to the exclusion of others; and fourth, potential linkage investment has been lost, often to branches of the plantation company located overseas (Beckford cites the Tate and Lyle sugar company as a bad offender in this regard) or to foreign firms located in the underdeveloped country. Girvan, concerned with mining investment by multinationals, also stresses the loss of linkages. He feels the geographical location of linkage investment has more to do with ownership and control than with domestic resource endowment. Thus foreign firms may prefer to locate their processing facilities in the home country in order to mix their sources of supply, and may prefer to use metropolitan suppliers in order to standardize the equipment they use in several countries.

3.2 A VIEW OF DEVELOPMENT THROUGH EXPORTS

This section presents a conceptual framework for studying exports and development, and discusses at greater length the more important of the ideas set out in the previous section.

As a preliminary it will be useful to distinguish between the value-added component of an export industry's output and its purchases of intermediate goods. Following W. M. Corden, a product can be said to be produced by two factors: a *produced product* and a *value-added product*, the latter being simply a bundle of primary factors (Corden, 1971, pp. 28–9). While this distinction is commonplace in national income accounting and input–output analysis, economic theory, especially international trade theory, has tended until fairly recently to assume industries to be vertically integrated[34]—with constant returns to scale each industry can produce its own intermediate goods. In fact, since economies of scale are common, industries can in practice be vertically disintegrated, and the degree of vertical disintegration is a matter of economic decision.[35] To treat industries 'as if' they are vertically integrated can be seriously misleading both for an understanding of economic events and for the formulation of policy. A country may be able to compete efficiently at world market prices in one stage of a production process, but other stages may require quite different factor proportions, managerial techniques, labour skills, etc. and be unsuitable for local production.

Consider first only the value-added component, and take the case of an export industry set up entirely by foreign capital, in which all capital goods and all produced inputs are imported. Assume that all management and supervision is provided by foreign residents who come to the country on a temporary basis and import all their consumption needs. The labour force is supplied either by workers withdrawn from a domestic subsistence sector (comprising the whole of the rest of the economy) where the marginal product of labour is zero, or by immigrants who plan to settle permanently in the country;[36] so that domestic-sector output does not fall. This example is chosen as a polar case in which further development would be least likely. It approximates for instance to the early stages of the Malayan rubber industry. (In contrast, tin mining was started in Malaya by immigrant Chinese, using capital raised locally.)

The question here is not the profitability of the investment to the private foreign investor but the benefits it gives to the host country. These depend crucially on the disposition of export-income flows. The distribution of export income between foreign profit receivers and foreign residents temporarily in the country, on the one hand, and domestic residents (including immigrants) on the other, determines how much export income leaks immediately out of the country. The larger the leakages, the more aptly can the export sector be described as 'enclave'. There is a rise in *domestic* income to the extent that the host government taxes exports[37] and local workers are given employment. If the local workers are immigrants income per head does not rise (unless their earnings are higher than those in the subsistence sector) as a result of this employment however.[38]

What brings about further growth? At first incomes earned by workers in exports may be spent entirely on imports or saved.[39] A switching of these purchases to locally produced goods marks the start of a process of domestic market creation. In the short run this demand may be met by the use of underemployed resources, though it may generate rising prices if the economy is fully employed. Investment may be switched from other activities or, if the investment opportunity creates new savings, there will be a net increase in domestic capital formation. Obviously much depends too on the ability of local entrepreneurs to seize these opportunities, and, as shown by Baldwin's work in the previous section, on the income levels of the wage earners.

The range of investment opportunities generated by the export sector is greatly widened whe the analysis is extended from the value-added component of the export good to its intermediate products, and to its own use as an intermediate product by other industries. The way in which an export sector generates these investment opportunities, or 'linkages', has been described already in the first section. Linkages, however, are a much abused concept and have been subjected to considerable criticism.[40] It is necessary, therefore, since they are to be an important part both of the case study of Malaysia and of other empirical work (see Chapter 10), to look critically at linkages. It will be contended that, once certain limitations are recognized, they remain useful.[41]

In his original presentation Albert Hirschman distinguished between *backward linkage*, which refers to investment in the production of inputs for the industry in question, and *forward linkage*, which refers to investment in industries using the output of the industry as an input.[42] These linkages refer to the *direct* effect of one investment on another and are distinguished from the type of induced investment behaviour assumed in most macro growth and trade-cycle models, where investment in one period is made a function of the income generated by investment in previous periods. The essential difference between the two mechanisms lies in the strength of the inducement to invest. Investment in a given industry concentrates linkage inducements on the small range of industries which supply inputs to it or buy inputs from it, whereas the inducements to invest which it generates through the multiplier–accelerator mechanism are spread for the first round of the multiplier over all industries whose products are consumed by its primary factors of production and thereafter spread even more diffusely throughout the economy.[43] Later writers have tried to bring the multiplier–accelerator mechanism within the framework of the linkages analysis by calling such investment inducement *final demand linkage* (Watkins, 1963, p. 145). Final demand linkage is a useful notion in the sense that the size and distribution of factor income in an industry determines the size and type of domestic market which develops for local consumer goods, but it must be remembered that it is 'linkage' in a rather different sense from that of forward and backward linkage. It can in principle induce new capital formation in the same way as backward and forward linkages (as will be discussed later in the section) but the investment inducement it offers to particular industries is likely to be weaker since final demand purchases are spread over a wide range of goods. Linkages are best understood in terms of the theory of external economies, and in particular Scitovsky's distinction between *pecuniary* and *technological* externalities (Scitovsky, 1964, p. 74). A pecuniary externality is generated where the actions of one firm affect the profitability of another through the market mechanism. A technological (or *unpriced*) externality is generated where the actions of a firm affect another's profitability through non-market interdependence. In a fully employed economy in static general equilibrium, pecuniary external economies would be simply part of the signalling mechanism of the price system. As one industry expanded, prices of its inputs for example would rise and investment in input-producing industries (i.e. backward linkage) would become profitable. Investment would be diverted from other sectors into the input-producing industry. But the theory of static general equilibrium is hardly a suitable framework for the analysis of investment decisions. The allocation of investment funds is essentially a dynamic problem and the economic system may not be tending to equilibrium as investment occurs during an industrialization process (Scitovsky, 1964, p. 77). Thus, Scitovsky explains, investment in an industry A might raise profits and induce expansion in industry B, which uses A's output as an input or supplies inputs to A, and the expansion in B would then make A investment more profitable. If A does not foresee that the pecuniary external economies it generates for B would make A itself more profitable, insufficient investment may take place in A from a social point of view. In contrast to pecuniary externalities, unpriced externalities make for a divergence between private social profitability even in a purely static context. An example would be where industry A finances the training of skilled workers who subsequently take employment in B.

In some of the development economics literature the term 'linkages' is used in the sense of Scitovsky's pecuniary external economies operating in non-equilibrium conditions. In social cost-benefit analysis in particular linkages seem often to have this meaning.[44] Yet in Hirschman's account, linkages have another and most important dimension. In a poor country the savings function itself may shift upwards in response to investment opportunity, a rise in investment being matched by a rise in saving at a given income level. This occurs whenever the desire to save is 'frustrated' by lack of outlets for investment (Hirschman, 1958, p. 57). When such outlets appear, investments will often bring with them their own savings (Streeten, 1961, p. 64). In such circumstances the explanation of how linkages are generated becomes a theory of capital formation; and the explanation fits either the neoclassical view that growth may be impeded by a lack of savings or the Keynesian view that it is an absence of investment outlets which needs to be remedied (see for instance Barratt Brown 1974, p. 41).

If investment in industry A induces (say) backward linkage investment in industry B, it would appear that A's potential for spreading growth will be understated unless the linkage is taken into account.[45] Before reaching this conclusion, however, a policy maker would need to satisfy himself that certain conditions were satisfied, these conditions being in effect limitations on the applicability of the linkages concept. First, it would be necessary to determine whether the economy did indeed suffer from a shortage of investment outlets such that savings would be likely to respond to opportunities to invest or that existing savings were being 'wasted'.[46] Second, it would be necessary to ensure that the linkage investment itself was socially profitable.[47] There can be 'bad' as well as 'good' linkages, in the sense that the social cost of importing the intermediate product in question might be less than that of producing it locally—one would not wish to suggest for instance that Britain should have grown its own cotton during the Industrial Revolution merely because cotton growing was a linkage of textile manufacture. Similarly, if A generates a forward linkage to B, and B is socially unprofitable, it would be better to export A directly.

The third condition which must be fulfilled before linkages become relevant to the calculation of social profitability of the industry A, is that there must be some limitation on the ability of the country concerned to engage in international trade in product B. In principle an industry set up through backward linkage could equally well be established as an export industry supplying intermediate products to industries located overseas, and an industry set up through forward linkage could equally well buy its inputs from overseas, without waiting for them to be locally produced (Little and Mirrlees, 1968, Vol. II, pp. 209–19). Thus a critic might argue that if an industry B did not develop through trade it must be because it is a 'bad' linkage, in which the country does not have a comparative advantage. In fact a variety of reasons may prevent industries in practice being established through trade. As the critics themselves recognize, there is the important special case where the products concerned (outputs of backward linkages, and inputs for forward linkages) are subject to heavy transport costs, including the extreme case of non-traded goods. Second, potential backward linkage industries may be unable to export because of import restrictions imposed by other countries, a situation especially common with respect to poor countries' exports of manufactures to rich countries. Third, there is the reason stressed by Hirschman himself that exporting is a more difficult and risky activity than is production for the home market (Hirschman, 1958, pp. 98–116). Linkages are a means of economizing scarce entrepreneurial ability in a situation of limited information. Opportunities to supply inputs (i.e. backward linkage) would be seized more readily by local entrepreneurs than would the chance to export the same products. The market would have been marked out by imports of intermediate products which local production could then replace. The argument applies far less strongly to forward linkages since there is less difficulty in buying imports than in exporting to a new and unknown market. Indeed if industries could not be set up using imported inputs (i.e. rendering forward linkage unnecessary) backward linkage could not occur! Thus potential forward linkage industries are more likely to develop on their own using imported inputs and so forward linkage is likely to be a weaker inducement to new investment than is backward linkage (Hirschman, 1958, pp. 116–7). Finally, at least one influential international trade theorist, Staffan Linder, has argued that for a country to gain a comparative advantage in a product, especially a manufactured product, it must first gain experience of producing it for the home market before trying to export (Linder, 1961, p. 87). If Linder's contention is correct, one would not expect production of any intermediate (i.e. potential linkage) products to develop through exports, and backward linkage would be the normal mechanism through which such production would be established.

Linkages are particularly important in the analysis of the economic effects of export growth, since a given industry is more likely to generate linkages if it produces for export than if it produces for the domestic market alone. In many cases the demand for the products of potential backward linkage investment (or the supply of inputs for potential forward linkage) must be of a certain minimum size before linkage investment becomes profitable (Hirschman, 1958, p. 101). Since the growth of exports is by definition not constrained by domestic market size, exports are more likely to provide the minimum demand for backward linkage products (or supply of inputs for forward linkages).

Before it can be concluded, however, that an export industry which generates more linkages is (*ceteris paribus*) more likely to spread economic growth than one which generates less linkages a further qualification must be made. It has been assumed implicitly so far that the industry would be set up at the socially optimal scale. Yet for an export industry in particular the socially optimal scale may be very large indeed and might take many years to establish. If the economy suffers from a shortage of investment outlets an initial small investment in the industry (e.g. by the government or by foreign investors) could 'show the way' to local private investors[48] to further investment in the industry and this would generate new savings in exactly the same way as would a linkage.

Linkages have so far been discussed mainly in terms of whether they generate new capital formation. There is also the possibility that they can introduce new technology into the country, and the same is true of investment in the export industry itself. This idea was the basis of Baldwin's important paper 'Export Technology and Development from a Subsistence Level' (1963) outlined in Section 3.1. His analysis of the spreading of new technology by an export good is almost identical to one in which the spread effects from exports generate new capital formation, and one must ask whether it represents a real improvement in the understanding of the trade-and-growth mechanism.

Exporting generates a range of investment demands, both in exports themselves and in linked industries. If the export good or the linkage goods were not previously produced in the country, a 'new' technology is required by definition,[49] but the relevant feature of 'new' technology here is that it must raise factor productivities above those in the factor's existing uses in the domestic economy.[50] Analysing the spread of new technology in the same way as the generation of new capital formation is useful in that it shows how income can be increased even if net capital formation initially remains constant, e.g. if linkage investment is financed by resources drawn from elsewhere in the economy. Thus, more advanced technology in an industry may raise labour productivity and might also so increase the return on capital over alternative investment outlets that the income and savings potential of local capitalists would increase. This point having been established, the Baldwin analysis can then be used to show the conditions under which technology will be adopted. Since in most cases the new technology is embodied in new industries (either exports or linkages), the analysis turns on the conditions under which these new industries will be established, and on the conditions under which local people will enter the industries as capitalists if they were originally set up by foreigners. Two main features emerge. First, the establishment of new industries should in principle depend on the 'appropriateness' of their technology to the host country's pre-existing factor endowment. The second feature is that the adoption of new technology in an industry (the export industry itself in the first place, and then linked industries) may condition the responsiveness of the rest of the economy to adopting new technology and establishing new industries. Thus the export industry's demand for skilled workers may result in local workers being trained (either formally or by learning on the job) in skills useful for other activities. It may result in managers acquiring familiarity with buying inputs and selling outputs, in supervisors developing their organizational skills,[51] and in general people acquiring what Solo (1966, pp. 96–7) has called the 'cognition of mechanism', the familiarity with mechanized means of production which facilitates industrial growth. Similarly, linkage industries, once established, may also provide these unpriced externalities to other sectors of the economy.

What is required, therefore, is not exact conformity of factor use by new industries to the pre-existing factor endowment, but enough difference to give room for factor improvements which the domestic economy can hope to make. It is in this sense that technology should be 'appropriate', and many of the arguments that export expansion has failed to promote further economic growth, or actually has retarded it, spring from a belief that inappropriate technology is often in use.[52]

Foreign firms, particularly if they are branches of multinational companies, are likely to have access both to world-wide capital markets and to best-practice Western technology. In the past they have also enjoyed the support of colonial government in importing labour. If they are more familiar with capital-intensive production methods, or simply wish to avoid the problems of using a large local labour force, they may instal techniques with high capital/labour ratios and requiring large initial amounts of capital (which is basically how Baldwin describes mining ventures). If local capitalists do not have easy access to new funds, or if the technology is monopolized by foreign firms, entry may be difficult. It may indeed be impossible if, in addition, the capital-intensive technology 'dominates' any available labour-intensive techniques (i.e. the techniques with relatively high K/L ratios have not only high O/L ratios but *also* high O/K ratios—i.e. capital productivity *increases* as the capital: labour ratio increases). Such 'domination' is by no means unusual, and it results mainly from a concentration of technical progress in advanced countries, which have high-cost labour and therefore seek new techniques to lower labour use (Streeten, 1971; Stewart, 1972). The use of such capital-intensive techniques, even if they are the most profitable to the foreign investor, are likely to be inappropriate to the host economy.[53] Not only do they generate little new employment and create a more uneven income distribution (and employment creation and more equal distribution are important aims of development policy) but they also reduce the spread effects of exporting, as already described.[54] Similarly, highly labour-intensive methods based on mass-imported labour (e.g. rubber in colonial Malaya or Ceylon) may have been inappropriate in that they kept local wages down to the level of large, overpopulated underdeveloped countries.

Linkage technology also may be inappropriate, especially if foreign firms enter linked industries, though inappropriate technology may also be used by domestic firms, often as part of a protected import-substitution programme (in other words they may be 'bad' linkages in terms of the earlier discussion in this section). The problem is especially acute where foreign firms monopolize the export industry, and control linkages with their orders for imports and their sales for further processing (as has been stressed by the Caribbean dependency writers).

3.3 METHODS OF ANALYSIS OF EXPORTS AND DEVELOPMENT

The conceptual approach having been spelt out, it remains to develop methods by which export-growth effects can be quantified.

Since the disposition of export-income flows is crucial, the first stage of the analysis is to split the payments made out of current export income into their constituent parts, the term 'current' here being used to distinguish expenditure from export income from capital expenditure. (Some linkages, it will be shown, are generated by payments made for investment goods.) Current payments are wage and salary payments, payments for intermediate products and gross profits. Gross profits split into depreciation allowances, dividends, retained earnings and payments to the government (both company tax and export duty). For each type of payment a local and a foreign component is identified (e.g. dividends paid to local residents, and to overseas residents).

The analysis is carried out on a sectoral basis. In the Malaysia study different sectors are distinguished: in the tin industry there is dredging and gravel pump mining, and in rubber there is an estate sector and a smallholding sector, (and in palm oil there are estates and smallholders on land development schemes). Dredging can be identified (at the cost of some oversimplification) as being foreign owned and controlled[55] and approximates to the stylized industry set up with foreign capital described in the previous section. There is a presumption in such a case that part of export income may flow immediately out of the country as remitted profits. The proportion of export income retained initially in the country is the industry's net foreign-exchange contribution, or 'retained value',[56] and the proportion retained in the foreign sector (i.e. dredging) can be compared to that in gravel pumping, the local sector (though most 'locals' in this case are Malaysian Chinese). Rubber estate development also approximates to the stylized process of the previous section, though, unlike dredging, there has been substantial direct local entry. A breakdown is not possible for smallholdings, however, owing to lack of data, but since smallholdings use few purchased inputs, employ no expatriate managers, and are entirely locally owned, no initial payments outflow would be expected. Hence the only relevant question at this stage[57] is how much income accrues to the smallholder. Palm oil is dealt with briefly (in Section 6.5) in comparison to rubber, but timber has been excluded because of lack of research time.

For the present day a wide range of input statistics is available for each of the three sectors (tin dredging, gravel pumping and rubber estates) for which the main analysis is conducted.[58] The input structure is assembled piece by piece. Employment statistics are used together with calculations of average wages to estimate the wage bill. Wages paid to locally resident people are treated as a local payment, and wages to expatriates as a foreign one. Detailed data can be compiled on intermediate product sales to each export sector, and *a priori* information, trade and production statistics are used to establish which are imported. Once the value of intermediate purchases and of the wage bill is determined, the non-wage component of value-added (i.e. gross profits) can be estimated as a residual, given the value of gross output. From this residual can be deducted export duty payments, easily available from official sources. For both rubber estate and tin dredging data are available from published company reports which allow gross profits to be split into dividends, tax payments, retained profits and depreciation allowances. In gravel pumping, where most mines are locally owned, such a detailed breakdown is not necessary since it is not expected that profits will be remitted abroad. Dividends are divided into local and foreign components on the basis of estimates from existing academic and government studies and from direct enquiry to a large number of companies, of the proportion of the value of shares owned by local people. The profit data in the company reports also provide a check on the estimates of wages and intermediate purchases, since they should be the same as the profits calculated as a residual, after allowing for depreciation, head office expenses, and so on.

It is interesting to trace the payments structure back into time to see if there have been changes in the local retention of earnings, in factor proportions, or in linkages. For all three sectors (i.e. excluding rubber smallholdings and palm oil), time series of most of the main inputs can be assembled back to about the First World War. The assembly of these series has been a major part of the study.[59]

These breakdowns of current export income are given for the two tin sectors in Chapter 5 and for rubber in Chapter 6, each being preceded by a section on the technology, structure and ownership of the industries. In Section 4 of each of these two chapters, backward and forward linkages are discussed. In the research time available it was not possible to go into great detail on each linkage. However as far as possible each major linkage is examined briefly in terms of the conceptual limitations on the validity of linkages set out in the previous section, i.e. limitations on direct export or import of the linkage product, and whether it is a good or bad linkage—the latter being examined in terms of Domestic Resource Cost statistics[60] from a new study of Malaysian industrialization (Edwards, 1975). In addition, the loss of linkages to foreign producers located in the host economy, or to branches of the foreign firms located overseas (both stressed by 'dependency' writers) is also examined. The general issue of whether Malaysia suffers or has suffered from a shortage of investment opportunities is discussed in Chapter 8, which presents a detailed study of one particularly important linkage, light engineering. In that chapter (as in Chapter 9) the discussion is widened to include palm oil, Malaysia's third export, the production of which has also encouraged the growth of engineering, and an analysis of which was excluded from the main part of the study because of lack of research time and because much data on the private estate sector do not allow material on oil palm meaningfully to be split from that on rubber (see Section 6.5, which compares rubber to oil palm). This linkage is not one generated out of current export income but by the export industries' investment purchases. Therefore breakdowns of tin and rubber capital expenditure are given too, in the Section 3 of Chapters 5 and 6 (and on oil palm in Section 6.5).

The role of linkages and of exports themselves in diffusing new technology through the economy is discussed Chapter 9. The chapter is particularly concerned with the development of labour skills by local workers, and whether those skills are transferable to other occupations (so that unpriced externalities are generated). Hence a detailed analysis of the skill structure of the tin and rubber industries (and of oil palm) is made, based both on interviews and published labour statistics. Chapter 9 also looks at employment creation by the export industries and at their effects on income distribution.

Final demand linkages, discussed in Chapter 7, depend on the income and the consumption pattern of workers (and of individual profit receivers, but the consumption data available cannot be used for them because their incomes are unknown). For Malaysia, detailed data on personal consumption are available, broken down into hundreds of products and numerous consumer categories. By fitting export sector workers and smallholders into these categories, their consumption patterns can be established. It is then necessary to decide whether a particular product is bought locally. In those cases of backward and forward linkage investment covered in Chapters 5 and 6, this was relatively easy. Most of the linkages were manufactured products, of which the export sector is often the main consumer and for which there is production data, against which export sector purchases can be measured (e.g. if purchases greatly exceed local production, it can be concluded that the product is largely imported).[61] For many of the goods whose local production could have developed through final demand linkages there are no production data. Moreover, they are products which are often the same as those consumed by workers outside the export sector. To try to establish whether they are locally produced, consumption figures must be compared to imports. As a rough guide (given the differences between consumption and trade statistics product categories) if consumption is larger than imports it is assumed there is local production. If consumption is less than imports there can still be substantial local production since export-sector workers are only roughly a third of the working population. Moreover, since these are mostly commonly consumed goods it is difficult to compare consumption of a relatively small group of workers (say those employed on tin dredging) with total imports. Therefore the total consumption of tin and rubber workers and rubber smallholders is aggregated, and compared to imports. Thus it is hoped to obtain an estimate of the proportion of the wage bill spent locally, together with information on the types of goods locally produced to meet this demand.

This calculation shows, *ex post*, what have been the average propensities of workers and smallholders to consume locally and to import out of export income; and it is not possible, given the data, to estimate their marginal propensities. Much of the literature refers to the 'multiplier–accelerator' effects of export expansion, to estimate which it would be necessary to know marginal propensities.[62] To apply this description to backward and forward linkages is perhaps somewhat misleading,[63] since export expansion generates such investment *directly*, and not through indirect process of income expansion leading to accelerator effects. Final demand linkages however *are* true multiplier–accelerator effects.[64] Knowledge of the marginal propensity to import of local export-sector factors of production, together with their marginal propensity to consume, would determine the size of first round of multiplier expenditure following any rise in export income. These could not be calculated[65] but one important preliminary to any multiplier effects can be estimated at least crudely. This is the extent to which income accruing to the local export-sector factors varies with a change in export income. This is crucial in determining the size of likely multiplier effects. Where export income accrues to foreign factors (e.g. overseas shareholders) there will be no multiplier effects. To this end the major component of local factor incomes, the wage bill, is regressed on total export income. Data on locally received profits were calculated only for the present day, as the time series of local profits necessary to do a similar regression on export income were not available. Regression analysis is not necessary to establish the share of export income accruing to the government as export duty, since the rates of duty are published, and data are not available in time series form for tax receipts from foreign export profits.

NOTES

1. This section aims at highlighting certain major developments in the literature, and is by no means a complete survey. For a fuller survey, to 1971, see Thoburn (1971, pp. 16–140). It is also worth pointing out here that discussion of the development literature of the mid-1970's on income distribution, poverty and employment creation is left mainly until Chapter 9, which deals with these issues in the context of Malaysian development. This is because most of this work (e.g. Chenery, Ahluwalia, Bell, Duloy and Jolly, 1974) is more empirical than theoretical in character, and is mainly concerned with providing evidence (now increasingly convincing) that economic growth often does not 'trickle down' to the poorest sections of society and does not necessarily generate enough jobs to employ the available (and usually rapidly growing) workforces in the Third World, and in formulating policies to improve matters. Nevertheless much of the earlier work reviewed in the present chapter (e.g. that of the 'dependency' theorists) has recognized that growth can sometimes proceed with such highly adverse effects on income distribution and employment that it can hardly be termed 'development'.
2. The 'vent for surplus' concept is at first sight merely the extreme case of differences in comparative costs, but it has been used by Myint (1958) to explain trade expansion in certain less developed countries. This is discussed later in the section.

3. Cited also by Myint (1958).
4. Ricardo also thought trade would benefit a country by affording 'incentives to savings and to the accumulation of capital'. (See Ricardo, 1817, p. 80.)
5. In addition, foreign political control often accompanied the introduction of foreign capital. Such control, whatever its other merits and defects, usually increased security of person and property, a change which Mill felt would strengthen the desire to accumulate (Mill, 1848, p. 117). For instance the extension of British control to the Malay States increased freedom from arbitrary expropriations of property by the aristocracy and eventually abolished the institution of debt-slavery. (See Chai, 1964, pp. 7–8.)
6. See in particular Baran (1952). However, Marx and Lenin (see for example Lenin, 1917) expected that countries colonized by these imperialist powers would *develop* within the capitalist framework. Barratt Brown (1974, p. 71) argues that the Marxist hypotheses that countries could become 'underdeveloped' as a result of imperialism did not appear until the Sixth Congress of the Communist International in 1928.
7. These references contain much duplication and the present account relies mainly on Myrdal (1957), together with the review articles by Meier (1958) and Bauer (1959). There is also Myrdal's later treatise (1968). This restates his earlier positions (see especially Chapters 10, 13 and 14); but he does lay greater stress on plantation agriculture being a form of 'industrialization', which he considers more appropriate for Asian development than is often suggested (see Myrdal, 1968, pp. 445–6).
8. Raul Prebisch's writings are scattered over many sources. Three are particularly important—1962, 1963 and 1964. There is also an excellent review article by June Flanders (1964).
9. At the time when Singer wrote (1950), in most cases where advanced countries had invested in poor countries' export industries, those industries were primary products.

9a. Since the final draft of this chapter was written, a most interesting paper has been published by Singer (1975a), in which he revises his view that industrialization (as opposed to primary commodity exporting) will promote development. Singer II (i.e. Singer, 1975a) feels that because of rich countries' monopoly power, especially in technology, neither path may be successful. Singer II is discussed in Chapter 11.

10. This is relevant only where exports are produced by peasants or other locally owned forms of organization. Indeed, if the contention is true, it is hard to see why foreign investors should be interested in producing primary products, unless they themselves are consumers whose related companies purchase these products (e.g. tyre manufacturers developing rubber estates). This issue is taken up again in Section 11.3.
11. Superficially, the enclave notion seems closely connected with the 'dualistic' theories of structure and growth in poor countries put forward by Eckhaus (1955), Lewis (1954) and Fei and Ranis (1964), where an 'advanced' sector and a 'backward' sector coexist (usually in a closed economy). In fact these theories describe the sectors in simple terms (e.g. difference in factor proportions and substitutability between the products produced by each sector), and the analysis of why the advanced sector may or may not spread growth into the backward sector is much fuller in the export-growth models themselves, especially those of Meier, Myint and Baldwin (discussed later in the section). In any case, as Beckford (1972, pp. 49–50) has pointed out, export sectors requiring large numbers of workers could rarely obtain them (at least at prevailing wages) in sufficient quantity locally, and therefore the work forces (especially on plantations) were often imported. In the early 1970's, several models of 'dualistic' development in open economies have appeared, such as Findlay (1973), Fei and Ranis (1971) and Hicks and McNicholl (1971, Chapters 1 and 3). Hicks and McNicholl, for instance, base their theory on the assumption of the specificity of capital goods (i.e. the inability to transform domestic resources into capital goods through domestic manufacturing, either directly or by exporting manufactures), and on the role extractive exports (both mineral and agricultural) can play in a land-surplus economy (Hicks and McNicholl, 1971, p. 141). It is assumed that domestic manufacturing is of a high-cost, protected, import-substituting variety, and is heavily dependent on capital goods imports. To maintain essential imports, agricultural and mineral export are necessary, therefore, since manufactures cannot compete on world markets. If agriculture growth proceeds by extending land margins, and with minerals being non-renewable, growth must eventually halt as resource constraints are reached, and meanwhile little has been done to generate any other basis for sustained

growth. These conclusions are rather similar to those of some 'dependency' writers (see later in this section). They also bear some relation to earlier work (e.g. Chenery and Bruno, 1962; Chenery and Strout, 1966; Bruton, 1969) on the identifying and removal of specific constraints to growth such as domestic savings and foreign exchange (the 'two-gap' approach). However, it is the specificity of capital goods rather than foreign exchange as such which Hicks and McNicholl stress (e.g. p. 170). The specificity of capital goods has also been stressed by Linder (1967), and Maizels (1968a) has used a varient of the two-gap analysis to project growth in countries of the Overseas Sterling Area. One problem with using the two-gap analysis, as J. K. Lee (1971) has shown, is that savings themselves may be highly sensitive to export-income changes (as in Malaysia or Sri Lanka), so the 'trade gap' and 'savings gap' are interrelated in this way.

12. This description is used by Levin (1960, p. 7).
13. For a full statement of the terms of trade arguments see Meier (1968, Chapter 3).
14. For a useful synthesis of vent for surplus notions used in staple theories (see below) and by Myint, see R. E. Caves, ' "Vent for Surplus" Models of Trade and Growth' in Baldwin (1965).
15. Summarizing Innis's work is difficult because his interests were so wide and he used the staple approach as much as an economic interpretation of history as a theory of growth. Again, he was as much interested in *extensive* growth (i.e. increases in population, settlement, GDP *per se*) as in *intensive* growth (rises in *per capita* income). Indeed Dales, McManus and Watkins (1967) have argued that he was *only* interested in *extensive* growth, but, as Douglas North has pointed out, *extensive* growth often will lead to *intensive* growth (North 1966, p. 11), though in 'surplus venting' situations this may not be the case. For a fuller discussion of staple theories see Thoburn (1971, pp. 33–64). An attempt to test staple theories in the Canadian context has been made by Chambers and Gordon (1966 and 1967).
16. See in particular his essays on 'The Penetrative Power of the Price System' (written in 1938), and 'Unused Capacity as a Factor in Canadian Economic History' (written in 1936), reprinted in Innis (1956).
17. The assumption that the two new regions have virtually no population before the development of exports is more realistic for West (presumably meant to represent Canada, Australia, etc.) than for less developed countries like South. In the latter case the type of factor inflow is still of great interest, but so are the determinants of the degree of participation by the indigenous population in export production.
18. The point that export expansion works through a disaggregated multiplier–accelerator mechanism is made by Watkins (1963, p. 145). This idea, to which some objections can be made, is discussed further in the next section.
19. In fact much of his analysis of the spread of technology follows almost exactly the same lines as would a theory based on exports as a means of capital formation. This is discussed in the next section.
20. Hughes (1959) suggests that a major reason for Western countries' successful response to trade stimuli was the ability to respond to the new factor combinations required for exports or industries complementary to exports.
21. The staple model is interpreted by economists such as Baldwin (1963) or Watkins (1963) would be presumably more objectionable to dependency theorists than the original formulations of Innis and North, who used it in an historical context. A major criticism of the conventional economic approach to development made for example by Frank (1966, p. 5) is that it lacks a sense of the history of developing countries.
22. In fact very few criticisms of the sort made by dependency theorists are levelled *directly* at models such as Baldwin's. More usually what is criticized is neoclassical economics in general as an approach to development (particularly the stress on capital formation, shortages of savings, non-economic 'impediments' to development, etc.). It is also interesting that theoretical economic criticisms of the neoclassical model, based on the Cambridge neo-Ricardian school (see for example Robinson, 1971), are also being applied to development economies. As has been demonstrated by Sraffa (1960), neoclassical economics cannot determine distribution *and* product pricing simultaneously, hence there is considerable scope both domestically and internationally for bargaining to determine distribution, and then product prices (see for instance Evans, 1975).
23. This concerns the familiar Marxian notion that as accumulation proceeds, the organic composition of capital (the capital/labour ratio) increases, and the rate of surplus (i.e. the

ratio of profit to labour) and the rate of profit (profit/materials, capital goods, and labour) becomes more difficult to maintain. In order for capitalists to stay in the competitive struggle, new sources of labour must be found to exploit. For further details see Barratt Brown (1974, especially Chapter 3) on which much of the present discussion of imperialism is based.

24. However, even at what may have seemed the height of colonialist exploitation in the nineteenth century, only a third of British overseas capital was invested in the Empire (Barratt Brown, 1974, p. 133). It is strange, if overseas investment was designed to exploit cheap labour (and cheap sources of raw materials), that so much of it should have gone to other industrial countries. Part of the explanation of this low proportion of investment in poor countries may be that most foreign investment was portfolio rather than direct, and domestic savers were attracted to issues of securities from other capitalist countries.
25. Frank's work is well summarized by Booth (in Oxaal, Barnett and Booth, 1975), and the present account relies on Booth, O'Brian (also in Oxaal, Barnett and Booth, 1975), together with Frank's statement of his views in 'The Development of Underdevelopment' (Frank, 1966). Leys (1975b, Chapter 1) also provides a useful survey. Since Frank writes as a Marxist, it might be argued that he is not a 'pure' dependency theorist. Nevertheless his views have probably been more influential in popularizing dependency theory than anyone else's (Oxaal, Barnett and Booth, 1975, p. 2) and he provides one of the clearest statements. Other writers have criticized him, for example, for his stress on vertical patterns of expropriation (e.g. Long, in Oxaal, Barnett and Booth, 1975, p. 262) and a neglect of horizontal relations between groups of producers.
26. See O'Brien (in Oxaal, Barnett and Booth, 1975, especially p. 23) for references to this Latin American work.
27. Increasingly foreign firms have been financing their investment in developing countries through reinvested funds and local capital markets. In 1965 only 20% of U.S. foreign investment in developing countries came from the U.S.A., while 40% was generated by reinvested profits and 40% from locally raised capital (Barrett Brown, 1974, p. 269). The use of reinvested capital is not new, however; and there was no *net* capital export from the U.K., though funds were switched from colonies (especially India) to the Dominions.
28. For example, Barnett (in Oxaal, Barnett and Booth, 1975) has provided a most interesting case study of this process in the Gezira scheme in the Sudan, where the reproduction of dependency is achieved through low peasant incomes generating a need for indebtedness to traders, thus giving both classes an interest in the continuation of the existing set-up.
29. A study concentrating on horizontal as well as vertical relations is Long's chapter on Peru in Oxaal, Barnett and Booth (1975).
30. The importance of high wages is strongly advocated by Emmanuel (1972) who argues that high wages result in high productivity and therefore high product prices. The low wages established in former colonial territories result in domestic producers receiving low prices for their products, while high-wage Western countries receive high prices—a situation of 'unequal exchange'. As Evans (1975, p. 44) has pointed out, the theory has little explanatory power when applied to situations, common in practice, where productivity differentials exceed wage differentials.
31. However, Barratt Brown argues this with regard to the income levels of primary producers and industrial countries in the world division of labour. With regard to underdeveloped countries, he does note that dependent capitalist development leads to a form of dualism where high-wage/high-profit sectors (dependent usually on multinational companies) coexist with low wage and profit sectors (Barratt Brown, 1974, Chapter 10).
32. See for example the very large increases in output per acre and per worker, with little increases in capital input, in the rubber industry in Malaysia (Chapter 6).
33. It is interesting in this context that Beckford (1972, pp. 50–1) regards the work of writers such as North, Watkins and Baldwin, discussed earlier in this section, as being a valuable starting point, though they need widening in scope. This is very much my own position (see next section).
34. See for instance Caves (1960, p. 147). For a recent treatment of pure trade theory taking intermediate products into account see Schweinberger (1975).
35. Input proportions are also a matter of economic decision, though Corden (1971, p. 29) assumes they are fixed.
36. Immigrants planning to settle permanently in a country are teated as 'local' (as opposed to

'foreign') in the Malaysian case study which follows this chapter. Before the Second World War there was considerable turnover among Chinese and Indian immigrants to Malaya, but since then they have become permanent communities. It is the author's value-judgement that growth in their incomes should be considered part of the 'development' of Malaysia. Of great importance too is the extent to which the indigenous Malay people have shared in the country's growth. Malay participation is considered, as a separate issue, at many points in the case study.

37. Taxes on imports would not increase the share of export income accruing to the host country unless they were on items consumed by expatriates or imported inputs. Import and export duties might however alter the terms of trade.
38. And even if workers are drawn from the subsistence sector any rise in *per capita* income will be reduced to the extent that subsistence output falls. The fact that the marginal product of labour time may be zero does not mean that individual workers are unemployed and can be withdrawn with no loss of output. It has to be assumed that remaining workers will raise their labour input to make up for the departed workers. See Sen (1966).
39. To the extent that they are saved, there will be a balance of trade surplus.
40. The best known critics of linkages are Professors I. M. D. Little and J. A. Mirrlees (1968, 1972, 1974). Their arguments are less directed against the theoretical validity of linkages than at the belief that linkages are in practice widespread and important in project appraisal. In particular they think that linkages often have been used in the past spuriously to justify otherwise socially unprofitable projects. See especially Little and Mirrlees (1974, Chapter 16).
41. Much of the argument which follows is taken from my paper 'Exports and the Malaysian Engineering Industry. A Case Study of Backward Linkage' (Thoburn, 1973b).
42. Hirschman also described what later writers have called *horizontal* and *negative* linkages. (See Stewart and Streeten, 1972, p. 76.) A horizontal linkage occurs when investment in an industry encourages investment in industries producing complementary goods (e.g. office building inducing investment in car parking facilities), and negative linkages refer to existing industries being forced out of business by new industries (e.g. traditional handicrafts forced out by modern manufacturing) (Hirschman, 1958, pp. 68–72). One reason for the subsequent lack of attention to these two concepts may be that they do not fit into the neat input–output framework used by Hirschman for backward and forward linkage.
43. Some qualification of the term 'multiplier–accelerator' is necessary since there is unlikely in a poor country to be the unutilized plant capacity assumed in a Keynesian multiplier. To the extent that there are substantial lags in accelerator-induced investment creating new capacity, 'multiplier' demand in the meanwhile is likely to raise only money incomes and imports. To the extent that accelerator-induced investment is financed out of new savings, additional inflationary pressure is not generated. See Rao (1952).
44. See for example, Little and Mirrlees (1968, Vol. II, pp. 212–19).
45. In project appraisal terms, A's social profitability will be understated unless the linkage is taken into account because the social cost of inputs purchases from B will be less than their private cost, if the resources newly invested in B represent new savings. If the government of the country in question believes that the economy would benefit if there were more savings and investment (and if it is not in a position to raise savings and investment by means of government investment projects financed from taxation), then the social valuation placed on resources withdrawn from consumption will be less than that placed on resources drawn from existing investible funds, and therefore less than the private valuation placed on those consumption resources. The general issue of the valuation of savings relative to consumption has been discussed at length by Little and Mirrlees (1968, Vol. II, pp. 35–6). However they believe that savings and investment are constrained by the supply of savings, whereas Hirschman's 'unbalanced growth' approach suggests that the supply of investment opportunities, as perceived by local entrepreneurs, is the relevant constraint. Moreover, the social valuation of capital inputs in B will be further overstated by the private valuation if the resources used in B have been withdrawn from what Streeten (1961, p. 64) calls 'waste in the economy'. Such waste might include 'excessive' expenditure on ceremonial (lavish wedding celebrations, etc.) or purchases of gold for hoarding. If the government chooses to make the *value-judgement* that such expenditure is socially valueless, the social opportunity cost of the investment resources in B becomes zero. For a general discussion of such 'waste' as a source of potential saving, and of the likelihood of savings responding to investment opportunities, see Wolf and Sufrin (1955, pp. 11–13).

46. (See also note 45.) If the linkage investment is *not* expected to be financed out of new savings, but the subsequent two conditions are fulfilled, A's social profitability will still be underestimated if A fails to take account of any fall in the price of B's inputs which may result from the investment induced in B. This is of course the case described in the Scitovsky pecuniary externalities argument outlined above. An important qualification to these arguments is that even in an economy not short of investment outlets, but where 'extensive' growth is proceeding through inflows of capital and labour, rises in *per capita* income *could* occur as a result of improved economic organization such as inter-firm, intra-industry specialization. This possibility has been discussed by the 'staple' writer Douglas North (see above), and ultimately derives from Stigler's classic paper 'The Division of Labour is Limited by the Extent of the Market' (1951).
47. Obviously there are severe practical limits to examining all the linkage effects of a project (Little and Mirrlees, 1972, p. 164), but if a project is advocated on the grounds that it generates linkages, the social profitability of at least the major linkage effects would have to be considered.
48. An important exception to this case would be if local investors were unable to enter industry A. For example industry A might be subject to such large economies of scale that the minimum scale on which the industry could be entered would require capital sums beyond the scope of local investors. This is often true of mining ventures set up by foreign investment, and was true for instance of the dredging sector of Malaysian tin mining until the early 1960's.
49. This problem would not be merely definitional in cases where the export good was previously produced for purely local use, as is the case with rice in Thailand and Burma. Here export production might or might not involve a new technique.
50. The way in which factor productivities may be raised can vary considerably, and many such possibilities are familiar from macroeconomic growth theory. The output/capital ratio could rise for example with the output/labour constant (Solow–neutral technical progress), or vice versa (Harrod–neutral technical progress); or both the output/capital and output/labour ratios could alter, including the special case where they rise together in such a way as to leave the capital/labour ratio constant (Hicks–neutral technical progress). A convenient discussion of technical progress is given in Allen (1967, pp. 236–57).
51. The development of organizational skills and familiarity with making market transactions are stressed by P. Kilby in his very interesting paper 'Farm and Factory: a Comparison of the Skill Requirements for the Transfer of Technology' (1972).
52. Some aspects of this problem are implicit in Baldwin's technology analysis, but they have been developed further by writers on appropriate technology and by 'dependency' theorists (see Section 3.1). This is not the place for an extended discussion of appropriate technology. Useful introductions to the issues are given in Streeten (1971) and Stewart (1972), and a very full treatment is contained in Sen (1975). Thoburn (1976) presents a case study of appropriate technology in Malaysian tin mining, which is discussed in Chapters 5 and 9.
53. For an export project marginal to the economy 'inappropriateness' could be tested by social cost–benefit analysis. Where an industry is being considered which has had major repercussions on the rest of the economy (such as rubber in Malaysia) the problem of imputing shadow prices to inputs in the 'without-rubber' situation would be enormous. (This is also discussed in the next section, on methodology.)
54. A further possibility of loss to the host economy, if export production is in the hands of foreign firms, is that those firms may engage in 'transfer pricing' (e.g. overinvoicing machinery imports, underpricing sales to head office overseas) to transfer profits to other branches of the firm overseas, if local taxation is relatively high. See Lall (1973).
55. Ownership of both tin mines and rubber estates and smallholdings is discussed in Chapters 5 and 6, respectively.
56. These terms are used in Mikesell (1971). The term 'returned value' is also used sometimes, especially by writers on Latin America (e.g. Mamalakis and Reynolds, 1965), though they often mean it to include capital inflows. Retained value may be artificially reduced by transfer pricing (see note 54), but data were not available for this to be investigated. However, the standardized nature of rubber, tin and palm oil makes overpricing of sales unlikely, and very little machinery or other inputs is bought from subsidiaries overseas.
57. Later, the consumer patterns of smallholdings are used in the analysis of final demand linkages. Studies of smallholder income are discussed in Chapter 9.

58. In 1975 the latest statistics available in most cases are for 1972.
59. Unfortunately the economics of publishing today are such that some of these series, originally given in a longer set of Appendices have had to be deleted. Any reader interested in further details is invited to contact the author at the University of East Anglia. Detailed series to 1968 are given in Thoburn (1971, pp. 459–510).
60. *Domestic Resource Cost* is a measure of the economic efficiency of production (Bruno, 1972). The DRC coefficient relates output valued at border prices (i.e. c.i.f. import prices for importables or f.o.b. export for exportables), and measured net of indirect import content, to the cost of domestic inputs (including an imputed rate of return on capital employed). If output is sold, and imported inputs bought, at free-trade prices, then the DRC coefficient measures only the degree of economic rent accruing to the activity if inputs are measured at market prices. If inputs are measured at shadow prices DRC measures the gain (or loss) from reallocating resources from other activities where there real opportunity cost is lower (or higher) than their market value. Alternatively, if tradable outputs or inputs are subject to (positive or negative) protection, revaluation at border prices will indicate gains or losses from such protection. In fact DRC ratios given in Chapter 5 and 6 (and taken from Edwards, 1975) do not revalue inputs at shadow prices, and their main purpose (in the Edwards study) is to measure net gains or losses from protection. The DRC ratio should be used in comparison to a shadow foreign-exchange rate to determine whether there is net gain from an activity (i.e. net gain if DRC<SER). For Malaysia the SER should be assumed for purposes of Chapters 5 and 6 to be approximately 1.1 (Little and Tipping, 1972—this is the reciprocal of the Little–Tipping 'standard conversion factor'). Of course, since it takes into account only a single time period, DRC is a short-cut measure compared to a full social cost–benefit analysis.
It is also necessary to explain why the DRC measure is not used to assess the gain from the export industries themselves in the Malaysian study, particularly as a recent collection of studies of commodity exports and growth in Africa (Pearson and Cownie, 1974) has used a variant of DRC. There are two major objections. First if shadow prices for inputs are to be used, it is extremely difficult to assess what they should be in the hypothetical 'without-rubber' or 'without-tin' situations (i.e. in the absence of industries which have generated about half of national income and induced mass inflows of factors), but it would be necessary to do so if the impact of the whole rubber or tin industry is to be measured in terms of DRC. Whilst DRC could be used to evaluate marginal rubber or tin investment projects this is far less satisfactory than a full social cost–benefit analysis, and some cost–benefit results are set out in Chapter 9 for locally owned rubber and tin investment. Second, even if shadow prices are not calculated, differences in rent generation would be expected anyway between the non-exhaustable nature of resources used in rubber and the exhaustible resources used in tin. In contrast, in cost–benefit studies this difference could be taken into account by difference in resale value of the relevant land resource at the end of the life of the relevant project, which would raise the net present value of the project using non-exhaustible resources in a way in which the DRC measure would not.
61. The major difficulty here is that definitions of products may vary between different types of statistics. Input categories in say, the censuses of mining industries, may differ from the product classifications in the census of manufacturing, which may in turn differ from those in the trade statistics.
62. Estimating local purchases by export workers indicates how large multiplier effects were at a particular time in the past, and identifying local production of consumer goods bought by them indicates past accelerator effects. Estimating the actual multiplier and acceleration coefficients is a more complicated procedure. However, these coefficients are likely to change over time, e.g. the average propensity to import may fall over a long period as local supply increases to meet potential demand, even though the marginal propensity to import may be high in the short run. Hence the procedure used in this study may give a truer picture than estimates of multiplier–accelerator effects alone.
63. Watkins (1963, p. 145) tries to circumvent this difficulty by describing the multiplier–accelerator effects as 'disaggregated'. Certainly there will be multiplier effects working through intermediate products as primary factors employed in their production spend their income. Nevertheless, intermediate product investment is not created through response to rises in aggregate income and the linkage process cannot be described as an acceleration mechanism,

unless the accelerator is defined more widely than usual to include *any* induced investment. Thus, although the 'disaggregated' multiplier–accelerator notion is useful as a preliminary approach in the sense that it provides a symmetrical treatment of the different types of linkage (see my paper 'Exports and Economic Growth in West Malaysia', Thoburn, 1973a, p. 89) in the rest of this study the multiplier–accelerator idea is used only in conjunction with final demand linkages.

64. Though the lags in the investment response may be considerable, supply elasticities in less developed countries often being low.
65. Pierre R. Crosson has tried to estimate directly a simple export multiplier for Malaysia by regressing time series of non-export GNP on export income. He found that there was probably no relation between the two (Crosson, 1964, p. 10).

Part II
A Case Study of Commodity Exports and Development in Malaysia

Peninsular Malaysia

Chapter 4
An Overview of the Growth and Structure of the Malaysian Economy-The Export Industries in Context

4.1 SOME GEOGRAPHY AND HISTORY

Peninsular Malaysia is situated in South East Asia on the southernmost part of the peninsula below Thailand and Burma, bounded on the east by the South China Sea and on the west by the Straits of Malacca. The country is less than 500 miles north–south and 200 miles east–west at its widest point, the southern tip is only a degree of latitude north of the equator. Average daily temperature is 85° to 90°F with little seasonal variation, and rainfall is heavy (100" per year on average). The east coast is subject to monsoon rains from November to March, while rainfall on the west coast is relatively even. A central range of mountains separates the western and eastern parts of the country, except in the southern states. Over two-thirds of the land area is covered by forests or swamps. It is estimated that there are nearly ten million acres of unused land suitable for agricultural development, (compared to the present planted acreage of under eight million, of which half is under rubber), and another twenty million acres in East Malaysia (Prime Minister's Dept., 1971, p. 131).

Malaysia is an independent country within the British Commonwealth, with its own king, the Yang di-Pertuan Agong. The country is a federation of eleven states in Peninsular Malaysia, while Sabah and Sarawak on the island of Borneo are the two states of East Malaysia. The Peninsular Malaysian states are (from north to south) Perlis, Kedah, Penang, Perak, Selangor, Negri Sembilan and Malacca on the west coast; and Kelantan, Trengganu and Pahang on the east coast. The southernmost state is Johore. Individual states have their own rulers and certain rights, particularly the right to alienate new land. The present population of West Malaysia is 8.9 million of whom 50% are Malays, 36% Chinese and 11% Indian.[1] Malay is the country's national language ('Bahasa Malaysia'). English also is widely used, as well as Chinese[2] and the South Indian language, Tamil.

From its early development to its independence ('Merdeka') in 1957, the country was under the influence of the British. Already established in the 'Straits Settlements' of Penang, Malacca and Singapore,[3] British control was extended to the Malay Peninsula proper in 1874. In that year the Sultan of Perak accepted under the Pangkor treaty a British adviser, or 'Resident', whose advice he was bound to accept on all matters except Malay custom and religion. This form of indirect role was soon extended to other Malay states, and in 1895 the Federated Malay States were formed, comprising Perak, Selangor, Negri Sembilan and Pahang. Soon after, all states in the

Malay Peninsula were under British control, Perlis, Kedah, Kelantan and Trengganu having been ceded from Siam. The whole area was known as British Malaya, comprising the States Settlements, the Federated Malay States (FMS) and the Unfederated Malay States (UMS). Only the Straits Settlements were under direct rule.[4] British Malaya was invaded by the Japanese in December 1941 and occupied until September 1945. The country was reorganized after the war into a Malayan Union, replaced by a Federation of Malaya in 1948, comprising the whole of British Malaya except Singapore. From 1948 to 1960, a state of 'emergency' was in force, while government and Commonwealth forces put down a communist insurrection (Short, 1975). Malaysia was formed in 1963 out of the former Federation of Malaya together with Singapore, Sabah and Sarawak. Singapore left in 1965.

4.2 THE DEVELOPMENT OF THE ECONOMY TO 1922[5]

4.2.1 The Growth of the Tin Industry

At the time of British intervention in 1874 the country was almost entirely covered in jungle, with settlement confined to Malay communities along the coast and on the banks of rivers, the Chinese mining community of Larut in Perak, and a number of Chinese agriculturalists practicing shifting cultivation of such crops as pepper, gambier and tapioca. (Jackson, 1968, pp. 34–83).

The early development of the economy, in the second half of the nineteenth century, was closely connected with tin.[6] Tin had been produced in Malaya since the ninth century,[7] but its large-scale exploitation dates from the discovery of the Larut tin field in 1848 and an accompanying influx of Chinese miners. By 1870 40,000 Chinese were mining tin in the district, (compared to a peak mining force in the Federated Malay States as a whole of 225,000 in 1913). Disputes, culminating in open warfare between rival Chinese clans, led to an exodus of population, a large fall in tin output, and to the intervention of the British, but by the end of 1874 output had recovered and many of the Chinese who had left the district returned. Exports of tin from Larut rose rapidly, reaching a peak of approximately three-quarters of Perak's output in 1884 (Perak, *AR*, 1887). In Selangor also tin was being mined, with 7000 Chinese working in the mines around Kuala Lumpur in 1874. This rose to 23,000 by 1884. Three-quarters of Selangor's output came from the Kuala Lumpur area (Selangor, *AR*, 1884–5).

The Kinta Valley around Ipoh, the centre of the present-day tin industry, began to rival Larut as the main tin area in the mid-1800's. In 1885 the Resident of Perak noted an extensive migration of Chinese miners from Larut to other parts of the state (Perak, *AR*, 1885), which would have been mainly to Kinta. By 1889 Kinta's output surpassed that of Larut, and in 1910 its output was nearly seven times that of Larut (Perak, *AR*, 1910), and approximately 40% of the output of the FMS. Indeed, this was the start of a strong regional bias in tin mining which continues to the present day, with, as Table 4.1 shows, the bulk of output coming from Perak and Selangor.

Until the last years of the nineteenth century tin mining was almost exclusively a Chinese concern. Capital for the industry came initially from the Chinese merchant communities of the Straits Settlements, and apparently very little was from China (Wong, 1965, pp. 60–4). Wong Lin Ken shows how a system of advances allowed the

TABLE 4.1 EXPORTS OF TIN FROM MALAYA 1875-1915, SELECTED YEARS

(Tons)

	PERAK	SELANGOR	NEGRI SEMBILAN	PAHANG	TOTAL FMS	TOTAL UMS	TOTAL MALAYA
1875	1,762	...	...	...	...	...	...
1880	5,247	3,007	...	...	...	...	...
1885	9,680	4,935	1,264	...	...	...	...
1890	14,117	10,389	2,142	327	26,975	...	...
1895	23,960	21,515	2,332	403	48,210	...	...
1900	21,166	16,041	4,301	936	42,444	...	...
1905	26,594	17,254	5,067	2,077	50,992	...	...
1910	25,080	14,297	2,065	2,421	43,863	1,137	44,999
1915	27,771	13,938	1,244	3,808	46,761	3,135	49,896

Sources and Notes

(1) All 1915 figures from Fermor (1939, p. 58).

(2) All other figures from Wong (1965, p. 249), and from AR's of individual states.

cost of fixed and working capital to be shared between a mine owner and an advancer. Use too was made of trade credit, with a pyramiding of facilities from large to small suppliers to miners.[8] Fixed capital costs were low because little equipment was needed for opencast mining.[9] Working capital costs were kept down by the practice of not paying workers until the end of six months or even a year, and in fact many workers worked on 'tribute', a system whereby they in effect 'lent' their labour to the mine owner in return for a share in the eventual profits of the mine. Additional profits were made by advancing food and opium to mine workers and by the leasing of revenue 'farms' from the government, which gave the holder the right to levy taxes on a particular commodity or activity, such as opium or gambling, in return for a fixed cash payment. Until the coming of rubber, tin mining was the major investment opportunity in the country and it seems likely that the rapid expansion of the industry from 1874 to the depression years of 1896–9, was in large part financed through reinvested profits, including those of advancers.

The labour force of the Chinese mines was drawn directly from China. Immigrants first came mainly under an indenture system, whereby their passage was paid by prospective employers, with whom they had to work off their debt. Later, workers were drawn from a pool of people who had paid off their indentures or who came from China under their own finance. By 1914 when the indenture system was officially prohibited it had virtually died out (Li, 1955, p. 86). Participation by Malays as either owners or workers was practically non-existent. Malays apparently were unwilling to work in the exacting conditions of the mines, at least for the prevailing rates of pay. In any case differences in language and social custom, the activities of Chinese secret societies and the feeling of local Chinese public opinion made their employment difficult, except as clearers of the jungle prior to the establishment of a mine (Wong, 1965, pp. 64–5).

At the turn of the century, when Malaya was already supplying over half of world tin output (Wong, 1965, p. 53), European firms were beginning to make their first inroads into Chinese predominance in tin. Apart from the Pahang Corporation, an underground mine which was the sole survivor of a 'tin rush' in Pahang in the late

1880's (Wong, 1965, pp. 137–41), most Western firms had been unsuccessful in their attempts to establish themselves in Malaya. While easily accessible high-grade ground was being mined by labour-intensive Chinese methods, Western firms proved unable to compete, being encumbered by a top-heavy administrative structure and inappropriate equipment (Allen and Donnithorne, 1954, pp. 150–2). Moreover secret society pressures made it difficult for them to hire Chinese labour, and indeed the subsequent supression of secret societies by the government was an important factor in promoting the growth of European firms. In Wong's view, by the end of the 1890's, however, Chinese firms were experiencing difficulties. Drainage problems and the difficulties of raising ore-bearing earth to the surface from deep mines made the use of mechanical equipment more appropriate. (Wong, 1965, pp. 216–21). The mining of lower grades of ground following the exhaustion of the richest deposits gave an edge to methods with a higher throughput of tin-bearing ground, and from 1905 competition for labour by the rubber industry raised wages. It was European experimentation in Malaya first with hydraulic methods (which were subsequently taken up by the Chinese, and which are now those used by the largest sector, gravel pumping), and then with dredging, which formed the basis for the growth of Western firms. Dredges required large capital outlays which the Chinese system of credit could not finance. The European dredging firms were joint-stock companies with capital raised from abroad, and by the late 1930's they were producing half of Malaya's tin output.

Although government policy in the years immediately before the First World War was said to favour European firms (Wong, 1965, pp. 220–1), the British-controlled governments of the individual Malay states took various measures to encourage mining during the period of Chinese dominance, the export duty on tin being the main source of government revenue. Most of the major towns on the west coast grew up as mining centres—Ipoh in the Kinta valley, Taiping in Larut, Kuala Lumpur in the biggest Selangor tinfield and Seremban in Negri Sembilan—and the government used tin revenue to construct railways from these centres to seaports, whence the ore could be shipped to Penang or Singapore for smelting.[10] In 1885 eight miles of track from Port Weld to Taiping were built by the Ceylon government under contract to the British authorities. Kuala Lumpur was connected to the port of Klang in 1886, Seremban to Port Dickson in 1891 and Ipoh to Telok Anson in 1895. By 1910 a line had been built from Prai (on the mainland by Penang Island) to Johore Bahru, and extended over the causeway to Singapore in 1923. This connected all the main mining centres and constitutes the basic west coast railway system of the present day. Such railways not only facilitated the growth of tin mining, but opened up the country to further settlement and development. The importance of communications was clearly seen by the government. Thus, F. A. Swettenham, as Resident of Selangor, declared:

> 'The government of Selangor has been anxious to improve, or rather to make, communications between the various states, to bring the mines within reach of the bases of supply, and to induce immigrants to come into the country and plant, giving them good roads to a market.' (Selangor, *AR*, 1883)

Until the development of rubber from 1905, tin mining was the principal sources of growth in the Malayan economy. Although the Malay economy benefitted from a ready market among the Chinese miners for the Malays' fruit and livestock (Perak, *AR*, 1886), nevertheless the output of the main Malay crop, rice, did not expand to meet the potential demand, in spite of help by the government for irrigation schemes (Chai, 1964, p. 147). Chai attributes this failure to the lack of widespread irrigation and the primitiveness of the existing agricultural equipment. Malay participation in the export sector had to await the coming of rubber.

4.2.2 The Introduction of Rubber

The first commercial planting of rubber in Malaya as a separate crop is thought to date from 1896, when five acres of rubber were planted on a European coffee estate in Selangor (Allen and Donnithorne, 1954, p. 110). By 1922, when exports were restricted and the alienation of rubber land was banned, the estate sector had already achieved almost its present size, in terms of acreage.[11]

Experimental work, carried out mainly by the Straits and Malay States governments, pre-dated commercial planting by twenty years. In 1877 rubber seeds sent from Kew Gardens, England, on the instructions of the British India Office, were planted in the Singapore Botanical Gardens and at the experimental gardens at the Residency at Kuala Kangsar, Perak, started by Sir Hugh Low in that year.[12] By 1896 seeds of the trees at Kuala Kangsar were being distributed to Singapore, Java and Ceylon, and seeds were being planted experimentally at a number of sites in Malaya with different soils and growing conditions (Chai, 1964, p. 153). In 1884–5 the famous administrator Sir Frank Swettenham planted four hundred trees in Perak from Low's seeds, which in turn yielded a good crop of seeds for further cultivation (Swettenham, 1907, p. 263). That this experimental work should have been carried out appears to have depended much on personalities. Men like Low and Swettenham encouraged the early rubber experimentation as part of a desire to promote development in general and agricultural development in particular. More specifically connected with rubber was the work of H. N. Ridley, director of the Singapore Botanical Gardens from 1888. With the encouragement of the director of Kew Gardens Ridley experimented with rubber cultivation, and with methods of tapping which would not permanently damage the trees. By 1897 he had devised the so-called herring-bone tapping method, an important technological innovation which greatly facilitated the development of commercial growing. Ridley also was an enthusiastic propogandist of rubber growing, travelling the country to influence planters to grow rubber.

Rubber was one of a number of crops grown experimentally by government plantations. Others included coffee, tea and chinchona. Coffee had been grown commercially elsewhere, particularly in Ceylon, while tea and chinchona never achieved much commercial importance. Rubber was the real achievement of government experimentation. By the time commercial planting had started, not only had an efficient tapping system been devised (by Ridley and others in Malaya) but the most suitable variety of rubber, *Hevea brasiliensis* or *Para* rubber had been selected.[13]

Rubber was taken up commercially at a time when a number of conditons had been created which facilitated its development. First, there existed a nucleus of estate agriculture. Experienced planters from Ceylon had come to Malaya in the 1870's and early 1880's following the destruction of the coffee industry by disease in Ceylon. Liberian coffee, the variety mainly grown in Malaya, is a crop requiring an investment similar to rubber in that it takes a number of years (three to four) to mature, and yields a return for a period of over twenty years. Thus when coffee prices declined in the late

1890's and the demand for rubber rose, the initial switch by estates from coffee to rubber involved little change in economic organization. In contrast the crops favoured by Chinese planters—gambier, tapioca, pepper and to a lesser extent sugar cane (which was also grown extensively by Europeans)—yielded quick once-and-for-all returns.[14] It is also worth noting that while coffee was grown predominantly by European estates, coffee holdings were also opened by Javanese and Malays,[15] mainly immigrants, and also Chinese and Tamils (FMS, *AR* Resident-General, 1896).

Second, a policy was in existence which favoured agricultural development. In 1888 the Resident of Perak, Sir Hugh Low, declared the government's great desire to encourage settlement by European planters, a policy started by his predecessors (Perak, *AR*, 1888). In 1893, Mr. Treacher, Resident of Selangor, felt that few could doubt the desirability:

> 'of giving every possible encouragement to agriculture, the soundest basis of permanent prosperity and of continued population in all countries, both among the native and foreign sections of the community.' (Selangor, *AR*, 1893.)

Encouragement also was to be given to non-European settlers. The Resident of Perak had earlier looked to agricultural development by permanent non-European settlers ('Eurasians, Malays, Chinese and Javanese') for the main future prosperity of the state (Selangor, *AR*, 1889). Policy measures to encourage agriculture included favourable terms for the holding of land,[16] loans to planters (Perak, *AR*, 1888) and help in the importation of labour, mainly from India, from 1887.[17]

Third, a pattern of communications already existed, developed largely for the tin industry. Thus much of the early planting of rubber in Selangor was in the Klang valley following the railway built to connect the Kuala Lumpur tinfields with the port of Klang (Jackson, 1968, p. 228). In fact it was government policy to invest its large mining receipts (mainly in the form of export duty) in the construction of roads and railways, which together with the climate and labour supply, 'afforded facilities to planters which probably (were) . . . not to be found in most tropical colonies' (FMS, *AR* Resident-General, 1900).

From 1896 falling coffee prices were accompanied by rises in the price of rubber. By 1897 many small planters had abandoned their coffee holdings (FMS, *AR* Resident-General, 1897) and in 1898 a plague of caterpillars ravaged the industry in Selangor (FMS, *AR* Resident-General, 1900). By 1900 coffee prices were so low that only the best estates could cover working costs. By 1902, J. C. Jackson records, almost every coffee estate in Malaya had been interplanted with rubber, and in some cases even mature intercrops such as coconuts were being cut out to make room for the new crop (Jackson, 1968, pp. 224–5).

An indication of the rate of new plantings of rubber is given in Table 4.2. Although in absolute terms the figures are not reliable, the rapid increase in plantings after the first rubber boom in 1905 is apparent. By this date the growth of the industry can no longer be seen in terms of a switch from coffee.[18] Planting gathered momentum to the 1910 boom when the London rubber price reached a peak of 12/9, falling to a trough in 1914 following the outbreak of war and poor prices in 1913, with a second peak in 1917–18.[19]

The initial inputs of capital and labour needed to sustain such increases in acreage came mainly from inflows from abroad in the case of the European estate sector, which by 1921 owned a little over half of the planted rubber area (see Table 4.6).

TABLE 4.2 ANNUAL NEW PLANTINGS OF RUBBER IN MALAYA, 1898-1922

('000 ACRES)		('000 ACRES)		('000 ACRES)	
1898	2	1907	73	1915	122
1899	2	1908	85	1916	140
1900	2	1909	79	1917	228
1901	5	1910	207	1918	228
1902	4	1911	209	1919	175
1903	5	1912	192	1920	120
1904	8	1913	132	1921	59
1905	18	1914	94	1922	20
1906	51				
(Total planted acreage		1900 : 6,000 acres		1922 : 2,260,000 acres)	

Sources and Notes

(1) Figures are from Figart (1925, p. 277).

Drabble describes how the large British merchant houses in Singapore, such as Guthries and Harrisons and Crosfield, acted as intermediaries between the industry and the overseas investor. They provided respectability to a venture which might otherwise have seemed too speculative and risky. Additional capital came in early years from rupee companies floated in Ceylon and from a number of dollar companies floated in Singapore and Penang (Drabble, 1967, pp. 55–6).[20] It is worth briefly trying to see the size of this inflow in perspective. Table 4.3. gives some very crude estimates

TABLE 4.3 ANNUAL CAPITAL EXPENDITURE ON RUBBER PLANTING IN MALAYA BY THE EUROPEAN SECTOR, 1905-1922

	Low Estimate ($M.)	High Estimate ($M.)		Low Estimate ($M.)	High Estimate ($M.)
1905	1.1	3.3	1914	12.6	37.8
1906	2.4	7.2	1915	11.9	35.7
1907	4.0	12.0	1916	12.3	36.9
1908	5.6	16.8	1917	14.3	42.9
1909	6.8	20.4	1918	13.9	41.7
1910	8.9	26.7	1919	13.2	39.6
1911	11.6	34.8	1920	13.4	40.2
1912	13.6	40.8	1921	13.7	41.1
1913	13.7	41.1	1922	12.9	38.7

Sources and Notes

(1) Low estimate assumes capital cost per acre of $175 (£20), and high estimate of $525 (£60) per acre, spread evenly over seven years (this is of course a simplifying assumption since somewhat heavier capital expenditure would be incurred in the first year). Low capital costs figures from Drabble (1967, p. 54) and Allen and Donnithorne (1954, p. 111) who estimate minimum capital costs to maturity of £20. Similarly, J.C. Jackson (1968, p. 248) quotes a 'usual rate of investment' of £25-£30 per acre to maturity during the 1909-12 boom, Figart (1925, pp. 51-2) however uses a higher figure (for 1924) of £61 to maturity, and such a high figure is supported even for earlier years by newer research by Drabble (1973, p. 99), who thinks that towards the end of the period newer estates might even be spending £70-£100 per acre.

(2) Total cost figures refer to capital costs of new planted acreage by estates (from Table 4.7).

of annual capital expenditure from 1905 based on simplifying assumptions.[21] The 'low' estimates assume a cost of £20 per acre for bringing an estate to maturity, which is slightly below the 'standard cost' figure of £25–£30 widely quoted in histories of the period. The 'high' estimate assumes a cost of £60 per acre, following recent research by Drabble (1973, pp. 98–100) based on a wider reading of contemporary sources. Ideally such estimates would be compared to national income. Of course, no national income statistics are available for this period and it is beyond the scope of the present study to calculate them. With higher than average expenditure in the first year of planting it is possible that total expenditure in the boom years reached, say $15m (low) or $45m (high) as shown in the table. These may be compared to known economic quantities. First, $15 is equal to about a third of total government revenue in 1912 and a quarter of 1917 revenue (FMS, *AR* Federal Secretary, 1938). It is equal to 18% and 19% respectively of 1912 and 1917 tin exports (see Chapter 5). Tin exports were an important component of national income, mainly a Chinese concern. If to the tin export figure is added a rough estimate of the *minimum* value of output of the Malay population, say $30 in 1911[22], the proportion of national income, (excluding the value of rubber exports) represented by European rubber investment is about 13% in the boom year of 1911 if the low estimate is used and 40% if the high estimate is used. Since the value of additional Malay output, and non-mining Chinese and Indian output might raise further the actual domestic product, it seems probable that the *gross* (i.e. before subtracting remitted profits) capital inflow represented an investment between 10% and 30% of domestic product, (excluding the value of rubber exports) a large but not enormous amount. What is more surprising is that an investment of similar magnitude should have been made in the non-European sector from domestic resources. Moreover, from 1910 onwards (and for all years for which profits can be calculated in Chapter 6 for the period to 1922, i.e. 1910–13, 1915, 1920) profits were consistently higher than the 'low' estimate of total investment, and in 1910, 1915 and 1920 profits were almost equal to, or greater than, the 'high' investment estimate. Thus if one accepts Drabble's view that £60 per acre is a more realistic figure than £20 for capital costs, in the peak of the boom in prices (1910) there was possibly no *net* capital inflow, and in other years often a third to a half of capital expenditure could in principle have been financed from profits; which provides evidence for the theoretical possibility put forward by Drake (1972) that some past export expansions in less developed countries apparently financed by foreign borrowing were in fact based on the use of *domestic* resources.

The labour supply problem was met by large-scale immigration of Tamils from South India. Various measures had been taken by the government to help foreign recruitment of labourers by planters, but 1907 marks the start of large-scale immigration, with government aid. In 1907 the Indian Immigration Committee was

TABLE 4.4 ETHNIC COMPOSITION OF ESTATE WORKFORCE, FMS 1922

	MADRAS INDIANS	CHINESE	JAVANESE	OTHERS
Total 167,259	78%	17%	3%	3%

Sources and Notes

(1) From FMS, AR Chief Secretary 1922.

(2) 'Others' include Malays.

(3) Estates include a small number of estate growing crops other than rubber.

formed, to devise a comprehensive scheme to import labour on a large scale.[23] The Committee was to administer an Indian Immigration Fund, financed by a levy on producers, which would provide passages from South India. Table 4.4 shows that by the end of the period of unrestricted expansion the workforce was mainly Indian.

Management and advisory services were in many cases provided by the Singapore merchant houses, or 'agency houses' as they came to be called (Allen and Donnithorne, 1954, p. 113). Development was facilitated by a generous land policy and by loans to planters (Jackson, 1968, pp. 234–241, 252).

TABLE 4.5 ACREAGES OF RUBBER BY STATE, MALAYA 1922

	('000 ACRES)		('000 ACRES)
Singapore	44.6	Johore	705.3 (1929 figure)
Penang and Province Wellesley	58.3	Kedah	121.2 (estates only)
Malacca	161.5	Perlis	5.0 (1929 figure)
Perak	447.5	Pahang	93.1
Selangor	417.4	Kelantan	73.1 (1929 figure)
Negri Sembilan	280.0	Trengganu	48.0 (alienated)

Sources and Notes

(1) Malaya, RSH, 1930.

The regional distribution of rubber acreages is shown in Table 4.5. The concentration on the west coast states, especially Perak, Selangor and Johore is obvious. Perak and Selangor were areas which already had communications before the rubber boom, while Johore had developed a rail link to the north by 1910. The extensive development in Kelantan relative to Trengganu is due mainly to the efforts of a particular company, Duff Development, which introduced rubber to Kelantan and itself planted a substantial acreage (Jackson, 1968, pp. 222–3).

By the start of rubber restriction in 1922 a substantial non-European rubber sector had developed. Table 4.6 shows that in 1921, the year of the first rubber census (Figart, 1925, p. 273), this sector accounted for almost half of Malayan rubber acreage. Over 80% of the Asian acreage was in smallholdings.[24] Nearly 90% of the estate acreage was European although by 1932 figures indicate that 25% of estate acreage was in Asian hands (of which over 70% in turn was Chinese) (Statistics Dept, *RSH* 1933).

Even before the turn of the century some Chinese estates had planted rubber (Jackson, 1968, p. 221). As rubber prices rose in the early 1900's rubber was planted as a catchcrop by many Chinese tapioca and gambier growers, encouraged by a regulation of 1900 in the western Malay states that new land was not to be alienated to gambier and tapioca unless a permanent crop such as rubber or coconut was also

TABLE 4.6 RUBBER ACREAGES IN MALAYA 1921

('000 ACRES)

	ESTATES PLANTED ACREAGE	ACREAGE IN BEARING	SMALLHOLDINGS PLANTED ACREAGE	ACREAGE IN BEARING	TOTAL PLANTED ACREAGE
All Races	1304	822	923	473	2225
European	1148	64	64	40	1212
Asian	157	858	858	473	1015

Sources and Notes

(1) From Figart (1925 pp. 274-7).

(2) "Smallholdings" are taken here as any holding under 100 acres. Figart distinguishes between smallholdings (which are all Asian) and European "estates under 100 acres". (p. 276).

(3) Figart's figures are those of the 1921 rubber census of Malaya.

TABLE 4.7 ANNUAL NEW PLANTINGS OF RUBBER IN MALAYA, 1898-1922, BY ETHNIC GROUP

('000 ACRES)

	EUROPEAN	ASIAN		EUROPEAN	ASIAN
1898	2	-			
1899	2	-	1911	117	92
1900	2	-	1912	97	95
1901	5	-	1913	55	77
1902	4	-	1914	26	68
1903	5	-	1915	40	82
1904	8	-	1916	70	70
1905	18	-	1917	166	62
1906	51	-	1918	102	126
1907	71	2	1919	71	104
1908	69	16	1920	61	59
1909	52	27	1921	38	21
1910	88	119	1922	10	10

Sources and Notes

(1) From Figart (1925, p. 277).

(2) Figures include new plantings in the small island of Labuan, but not Brunei.

planted (Jackson, 1968, p. 224), and Chinese and (to a lesser extent) Indian capital also entered the industry, especially from tin mining and from trading.[25]

Table 4.7 gives an indication of the timing of development in the European and Asian sectors, although the figures are unlikely to be very reliable.[26] Unfortunately the data do not distinguish between estates and smallholdings. After the end of the first rubber boom of 1905–8 Asian acreage showed spectacular expansions, reaching peaks during and after the boom periods of 1910–2 and 1915–7, although in the second case lagging behind the European sectors.[27] (Some of the earlier plantings were speculative, intended for sale to Europeans however. See for example Perak, *AR*, 1909. This led to the Malay Reservations Enactment of 1913, which forbad the selling of Malay ancestral land to non-Malays.) The tapping and processing skills required for rubber cultivation were easily learnt (McHale, 1967, p. 66). Smallholdings were of two main types. Larger holdings, often classed as 'medium holdings of 25 acres or more', are those which would use some outside labour both for establishment and cultivation. No figures are available for the period before the Second World War on individual smallholding size or racial ownership, but it is likely that the larger holdings would be predominantly Chinese with some Indian participation.[28] These holdings would require outside capital (e.g. from tin mining or trading) of the sort described already in this subsection. The development of smaller holdings below 25 acres, and often below 5 acres, was the means by which Malays participated in the boom. M. G. Swift describes how a typical holding of 2–4 acres would be cleared and planted with family labour alone using simple tools readily available to the Malay peasants (Swift, in Firth and Yamey, 1964, pp. 142–4).

The rubber tree fitted well into the Malay economy. It involved little essential work during the immature period, so that the owner could devote himself to other activities. Tapping and processing equipment involved minimal capital outlays. Also rubber, unlike rice or fruit, provides regular yields and income, which reduces the indebtedness frequently incurred before a harvest (Bauer, 1948b, p. 62).

Even less is known about the growth of Chinese ownership of the smaller holdings. Voon notes that in the 1900–10 period most applications for land in the Ulu Langat district of Selangor[29] came from manual workers, and were usually in the 10–15 acre size. He suggests that these workers would have been able to maintain themselves by paid employment during the immature period. Presumably such holdings would have required some outside labour to help in clearing and planting, and implies the prior accumulation of some capital.

Some indication of the relative importance of rubber and tin in the overall structure of the Malayan economy can be had from the occupational statistics given in the 1911 census, shown in Table 4.8, while Table 4.9 shows the changes in employment in selected occupations between 1911 and 1921.[30]

By 1911, employment in rubber was of a similar size to that in tin, and by 1915 the value of rubber exports from the Federated Malay States exceeded those of tin ore (FMS, *AR* Chief Secretary, 1915). Both rubber and tin at this time were larger in terms of employment than was the largest domestic sector, rice planting. From 1913 to the start of tin restriction in 1921, and beyond, tin exports declined steadily in volume (FMS, *AR* Chief Secretary, 1938), though the sharp fall in labour force shown in Table 4.9 was to a larger extent due to the use of less labour-intensive mining methods. Rubber expanded rapidly both in terms of employment and of output during the same period. Rice planting employment appears to have increased between the 1911 and 1921 censuses, but by no more than the overall increase in population.

4.3 THE ECONOMY, 1922–41

Sharply falling prices from 1920 marked the end of the period of expansion of Malayan rubber.[31] In 1922 the London rubber price reached a low of 6¾d compared to its peak of 12/9d during the 1910 boom (Drabble, 1967, p. 76).

From November 1922 to September 1928 exports of rubber from Malaya (and Ceylon) were restricted under the so-called Stevenson scheme. From June 1934 exports from virtually all rubber-producing countries were restricted under the International Rubber Regulation Scheme. This scheme, having been renewed in 1938, was still in force when Malaya was occupied by the Japanese in 1941. Tin exports too were restricted, from 1921 to 1923, and in 1929 and from 1931 onwards. Much has

TABLE 4.8 OCCUPATIONAL STRUCTURE, FEDERATED MALAY STATES, 1911

	('000 people)	
Government	24	
Pasture and Agriculture	323	
- Kampong owners		- 18
- Coconut planters		- 5
- Vegetable growers and sellers		- 17
- Padiland cultivators		-109
- Estate workers		-149
Personal Services	26	
Preparation and Supply of Material Substances	81	
Commerce, Transport, and Storage	53	
Professions	7	
Mining	164	
- Tin mine workers		-154
Unskilled Labour and Indefinite	43	
Independent Means	2	
No Occupation or Unreturned	286	
Total Population	1010	

Sources and Notes

(1) From British Malaya, Population Census, (1911).

(2) Preparation and Supply of Material Substances includes a wide range of manufacturing, retailing and semi-service activities, with small numbers of people employed in each individual occupation.

TABLE 4.9 EMPLOYMENT IN SELECTED OCCUPATIONS, FEDERATED MALAY STATES, 1911 AND 1921

('000 people)

	1911	1921
Estate workers	149	289
Rice planters	109	129
Fruit and vegetable growers and sellers	18	18
Tin mine workers	154	70
Total Population	1010	1297

Sources and notes

(1) From British Malaya, Population Census, (1911 and 1921). To assess the relative importance of tin and rubber in relation to other possible sources of growth in the economy is difficult. Since there are no national incomes statistics for any year before 1947, growth rates of the value of output of non-export sectors could be calculated only with great difficulty, and in most cases employment figures (and acreages in the case of agricultural commodities) must serve as a proxy.

been written on these restriction schemes already and only certain main points are set out here.[32] The Stevenson scheme restricted output on the basis of a set formula in relation to a standard tonnage based on actual 1920 output, in order to achieve a pivotal price of 1/3d a lb (raised to 1/9d in 1926). For all but nine months of the restriction period production was restricted to 85% or less of standard tonnage, and for half the period to 60% (Lim, 1967, p. 77).

The IRRS, introduced after the Great Depression, restricted output to a percentage of a quota based on 1929–32 output (with provision of increase of quota as immature areas came into bearing), the releases being determined by an International Rubber Regulation Committee. For the first two years of operation quota releases averaged 60%, rising to a peak of 90% in the last quarter of 1937 to a low of 45% in the third and fourth quarters of 1938. The 1939 quotas averaged slightly under 60% (Agriculture Dept., *AR*, 1934–40). Thus the reduction of output under both schemes was substantial.

The alienation of land for rubber was forbidden under the Stevenson scheme and from August 1930 to December 1938 (Bauer, 1948b, p. 5). It was discouraged from 1928 to 1930 by high alienation premiums and by administrative discouragement of alienation to smallholders (Bauer, 1947). New planting, allowed during Stevenson, was banned from 1934 to 1938. Replanting under the IRRS was allowed up to 20% of planted acreage during the whole restriction period (1934–8), with a maximum of 10% in any one year (Agriculture Dept., *AR*, 1935).

Thus the size of the industry and the distribution of acreage between estates and smallholders were effectively 'frozen' from 1922 to the Second World War although some increases in planted acreage occurred as new plantings took place on land already alienated (Drabble and Drake, 1974, p. 116), and limited new planting on newly alienated land occurred from 1939. Smallholdings seem to have been particularly hard hit by restriction.[33] Both under Stevenson and the IRRS their quotas were determined on the assumptions of yields per acre far below their actual capabilities. The restriction on replanting to 20% of total acreage in the 1930's combined with the overall restriction of new replanting during the whole period meant that the smallholders sector was unable to expand to the acreage already reached by estates and was unable to replant.[34] In fact, the estate sector did little replanting either, so that the relative efficiency of the two sectors in the long run was not affected.

Tin exports were first restricted by the so-called Bandoeng Pool. Following a sharp fall in the world price, Malaya and the Netherlands East Indies withheld a total of 19,000 tons of tin from the market, which amount they held until 1923 and subsequently sold at a profit. Following falls in the tin plate price in the late 1920's a voluntary Tin Producers Association was formed in 1929, controlling 20% of world output, to restrict production on a voluntary basis. Yip (1969, p. 171) notes the failure of this scheme as stocks continued to accumulate and prices decline. A wider scheme of control was agreed from February 1932 between Malaya, the Netherlands East Indies, Bolivia and Nigeria. A standard tonnage was agreed for each country based on its share of 1929 world output. Export quotas were determined on the basis of these standard tonnages. A second agreement was set up in 1934 and extended in 1937 so that control continued throughout the pre-1940 period. In 1938 as part of the scheme a buffer stock was set up to control price fluctuations.

TABLE 4.10 EXPORTS OF TIN AND RUBBER FROM MALAYA, 1920-35, SELECTED YEARS

	Tin		Rubber	
	Tons ('000)	$ million	Tons ('000)	$ million
1920	37	128	174	269
1925	49	175	210	757
1930	64	124	452	241
1935	42	117	377	259

Sources and Notes

(1) Tin tonnages 1920-30 are exports, 1935 figures are sales from FMS and exports from UMS, all from Fermor (1939, p. 61).

(2) All other figures from Lim Chong Yah, (1967, pp. 325 and 328).

Table 4.10 shows the course of tin and rubber exports during the inter-war period. Apart from a rise in rubber export earnings, and in tin earnings to a lesser extent, in the mid-1920's, there was little expansion in the two industries, tin output being relatively stagnant and rises in rubber output being outweighed by lower prices. Bauer has attempted to trace the effects of the world depression on the Malayan economy. Using imports of various consumer goods as a proxy for domestic consumption expenditure, he concludes that the period saw a sharp drop in the levels of consumption and general standard of living of the country, especially in the depths of the depression from 1929–33 (Bauer, 1948b, pp. 15–21).

As was the case with the period to 1922, it is difficult to determine the strength of other sources of growth in the economy at this time when staple exports ceased to expand. Certainly expansionary forces were not generated by the government, which during the depression undertook a programme of retrenchment. Some official attempts were made to promote the growing of rice by Malays, and these policies were pursued in spite of the fact that it could be shown that rice was a less profitable crop than rubber even at the depth of the depression (see Bauer, 1948b, p. 61).

TABLE 4.11 ACREAGE AND PRODUCTION OF RICE AND OIL PALM, MALAYA, 1922-39, SELECTED YEARS

	Rice		Oil Palm	
	Acres ('000)	Production ('000 Tons)	Acres ('000)	Production ('000 Tons) of Oil
1922	644	211	2	-
1925	656	185	8	1
1930	657	157	46	3
1935	735	331	62	25
1939	753	341	76	60

Sources and Notes

(1) All statistics from Agriculture Department, Malayan Agricultural Statistics (1939).

Table 4.11 shows some increases in rice acreage, and more substantial increases in rice output over the period. A start was made also on the planting of oil palm, new planting reaching a peak during the 1930 depression.[35] But even by 1939 its acreage was tiny compared to the two million acres under rubber.

Some growth appears to have occurred too in manufacturing employment, from nearly 44,000 in the Federated Malay States in 1921 to over 53,000 in 1931.[36] This manufacturing consisted of such industry as the making of wooden furniture, clothing manufacturing, some mechanical engineering and electrical work and construction, to name the main categories, mostly work of a simple small-scale kind to meet the needs of the domestic market.

4.4 PRIMARY COMMODITY EXPORTS AND POST-WAR DEVELOPMENT POLICY IN MALAYSIA[37]

The war and the Japanese occupation caused considerable damage, especially in mining. By 1947–8 the economy had recovered to a large extent, with rubber and rice production higher than before the war, and with tin output nearly at the level of the 1930's (IBRD, 1955, p. 19); and the primary export industries benefitted considerably from the boom in prices following the outbreak of the Korean War. At Independence in 1957 rubber and tin still accounted for some 85% of export earnings and exports generated almost half of national output. Manufacturing, probably accounting for 8–9% of national output if primary product processing is included (Wheelwright, 1965, p. 17), employed about 10% of the labour force, and much of the rest of the population outside the export industries was engaged in growing rice for domestic consumption. Several major problems, however, suggested a need to diversify the economy away from dependence on rubber and tin. First, though perhaps least convincing, were the fluctuations in economic activity caused by the fluctuating export earnings of those two industries.[38] Second, was the setback to natural rubber's market prospects resulting from the expansion of synthetic rubber production during the war, especially in the U.S.A. The third reason, particularly stressed by the influential mission to Malaysia from the World Bank, which reported in 1955, was that projected expansions in tin and rubber employment would be unable to cope with the post-war acceleration in population growth (IBRD, 1955, p. 27). Before the war Malaysia's primary exports had employed partly migrant labour forces, whose members often returned to India or China after a period in Malaya, and who would leave if employment prospects worsened. After the war and particularly after the formation of the People's Republic of China in 1949, this population became more settled. The proportion of females rose, and population growth rose from 2.4% in 1947 to 3.2% in 1953.

The World Bank mission recommended diversification into other forms of export agriculture and into manufacturing. Nevertheless it regarded Malaya's main priority as the rehabilitation of the rubber industry, where three-quarters of the acreage was planted with old trees of low and declining yield. Primary export production (and especially rubber) it was felt would remain the basis of living standards and a background to industrial development for a very long time to come (IBRD, 1955, pp. 30 and 428).

Rubber replanting has indeed been an important priority in development policy in Malaysia. The replacement of old, low-yielding rubber gained ground as a policy objective after the falling prices following the Korean boom, and in 1952 a Rubber Replanting Scheme was established, with separate funds (A and B) for estates and smallholders, respectively. Finance for the funds was provided by a replanting cess, refunded to estates unconditionally on proof of replanting, though smallholders had to apply for replanting grants[39] (see also Chapter 6). Very little replanting occurred in the smallholder sector in the early 1950's, however, since grants were inadequate to replant and in the main only larger holdings applied, which resulted in income being transferred away from small to large producers (Rudner, 1970, p. 324), and the smaller producers were mainly Malay. Nor was new planting by smallholders encouraged at that time, even though the ban on the alienation of new land to rubber was lifted in 1947.

Rudner (1970, pp. 322–5) attributes the initial failure to make adequate provision for smallholder rubber development to the bias of the then colonial authorities towards estates (a bias well illustrated by the unfavourable treatment of smallholders under the pre-war restriction schemes) and of the Malay élite towards a view that padi, not rubber, was the appropriate crop for Malay peasants; and he regards the 1955 general election as a political watershed in this regard, especially since rubber rehabilitation allowed the economic prospects of rural Malays to be improved without encroaching on the position of the Chinese. Rubber replanting was subsequently the largest single item in the First Five Year Plan, 1955–60,[40] accounting for 15% of public development expenditure. Further Malay political pressure following the 1959 election brought about an increase in smallholder replanting grants with special help given to the smallest holdings (mostly Malay), which were the most difficult to replant and on which the least replanting had occurred.

While estates have had advantages in the replanting provisions, especially before 1959, new planting has been concentrated almost entirely on smallholdings. It has mainly been on schemes of the Federal Land Development Authority (FELDA), founded in 1956, on certain state schemes (especially in Trengganu and Kelantan) and 'fringe' schemes, (see Chapter 6). In Rudner's opinion (1971, p. 82) this was associated with a switch from the ruling Alliance party's earlier view that padi should be the basis of the rural economy to an interest in more profitable crops, as conditions in padi areas deteriorated towards the end of the 1950's and rural Malays increasingly drifted into towns.

Replanting on estates has been almost total, with 93% of their acreage being under high-yielding material in 1972 (Statistics Dept., *RSH*, 1972). The estate acreage under rubber, however, has declined substantially (from about two million in 1950 to 1.5 million in 1972). This decline has been associated with diversification into oil palm (see also Section 6.5). Diversification into oil palm gained momentum in the 1960's as rubber prices fell and as new, stereoregular synthetic rubbers (particularly polyisoprene) were developed which were almost perfect substitutes for natural rubber.[41] By 1972 almost 30% of estate acreage was planted with oil palm (Statistics Dept., *RSH* and *OPCTS*, 1972), but the aggregate size of the estate sector had increased only marginally—from roughly two million acres in 1950 to 2.1 million in 1972. FELDA, too, had diversified into oil palm, and by 1970 its oil palm acreage exceeded its rubber acreage (Wikkramatileke, 1972, p. 111).

Diversification out of primary production and into manufacturing also gained momentum in the 1960's (Johns, 1973). Although the manufacturing sector after the war and at Independence was small by present-day Western industrial standards, and was confined to industries producing for the primary sector (smelting, off-estate processing, engineering) and for local consumption (foodstuffs, and also heavy items such as bricks and cement), the World Bank mission of 1955 had been impressed by the degree of labour and entrepreneurial skills, industrial experience and servicing facilities available locally, and had felt that a good base existed for further industrial development. The Mission recommended industrial development on a small scale but over a wide front, feeling that the country lacked the sources of power and the large domestic market necessary for large-scale industry. It was also sceptical of resource-based industries founded on rubber and tin, since these primary commodities constituted only small proportions of the total costs of the final product (tyres, tin plate, etc.). Yet among the list of potential products it compiled (though the list was intended to be suggestive not exhaustive) were included some rubber products, wood products, pineapple canning and further light engineering. It also recommended the development of improved sources of finance and further industrial training, and the use (though somewhat hesitantly) of tariffs to attract new industry (IBRD, 1955, pp. 31–2, 119–127).

Following the report of an Industrial Development working party which reported to the new Federal Government in 1957, and which largely endorsed the IBRD's recommendations (Wheelwright, 1965, p. 16), many of these proposals were turned into policy. Large increases in allocations to electricity and other utilities were made under the First and Second Five Year Plans (1956–60 and 1961–5), industrial estates were set up and agencies were established to consider tariff protection for particular industries and to provide industrial finance. The major piece of legislation was the 1958 Pioneer Industries Ordnance, giving tax exemption on profits for up to five years, depending on the size of the investment, and incentives were widened by the 1968 Investment Incentives Act which offered tax relief to non-pioneer firms and gave incentives for exporting, for the use of local materials and for location in less developed parts of the country (Lim, 1973, pp. 265–8).

Probably the most powerful stimulus to diversification out of primary exports and into manufacturing took place in the late 1960's. While growth in the Malayan economy was accompanied by export expansion during the First Five Year Plan (1956–60), during the next Plan period (1961–5) the main source of growth was increased public-sector expenditure, and in the formulation of the First Malaysia Plan (1966–70) heavy stress was laid on the country's poor immediate export prospects, potential balance of payments deficit, and the need consequently to industrialize to maintain growth. Moreover, this industrial growth was to be of an import-substituting character (Prime Minister's Dept., 1966, pp. 6–7).

In fact, the First Malaysia Plan greatly underestimated export performance. While the projections were quite accurate with regard to both the price and sales volume in rubber, the supply elasticity of tin mines (and especially the local, gravel pumping sector) was higher than expected (Munro, 1973a, p. 48), and oil palm products and timber grew at nearly 20% each in value terms (Prime Minister's Dept., 1971, pp. 22–3). Thus a substantial diversification of primary exports was achieved. Over the longer period of 1961 to 1974 rubber and tin, though retaining their respective first and second positions of importance in exports, fell in share from 65% of total Malaysian exports (including those of East Malaysia)[42] to 45%, while palm oil rose from 2% to 11%, timber (mainly from East Malaysia) rose 6% to 13%, and petroleum (from Sarawak) from 7% to 10% (Treasury, *AR*, 1974–5, p. 22). It is worth noting too that this diversification appears to have reduced export earnings fluctuations substantially. Lim (1975, p. 5) states that the size of vaverage percentage deviations from the trend in aggregate export earnings fell from 19.6 in 1948–58 to 5.7 in 1957–67.

During the 1960's the overall annual real rate of growth of the economy was over 6% on average, and the Second Malaysia Plan (1971–5) forecast real annual growth in output at 6.8% for Malaysia (6.3% for Peninsular Malaysia), with real income growing at the slightly lower rate of 5.8% as a result of an expected deterioration in the terms of trade (Prime Minister's Dept., 1971, p. 52). The growth objectives of the Plan have been supplemented, however, by a pressing concern for the redistribution of income and wealth, particularly towards Malays, (the poorest section of the community),[43] and presumably as a direct result of the May 1969 race riots in Kuala Lumpur and elsewhere, which indicated the depth of Malay dissatisfaction with their position (see Selvaratnam, 1974, p. 5, Abdul Rahman, 1969, and National Operations Council, 1969). These growth-and-redistribution aims are expressed in the New Economic Policy, whose two 'prongs' are the eradication of poverty regardless of race and the 'restructuring' of Malaysian society to remove the identification of 'race' (i.e. ethnic group) with economic function. To eliminate poverty among Malays productivity must be raised in low-productivity occupations (padi growing, rubber holdings planted with unselected material), Malays are to be shifted into higher-productivity sectors (such as manufacturing), and resources need to flow into the less developed and predominently Malay states, especially on the East Coast. Preliminary indications suggest these objectives will also be followed in the new Third Malaysia Plan (1976–80), due to be published in March 1976 (*Straits Times*, February 1976).

Probably the most pressing problem facing Malaysian planners, however, is the creation of new jobs to mop up present unemployment[44]—probably at least 10% of the labour force in 1970, if unregistered unemployed are added to the official estimates (Lim, 1975, p. 5)—and to absorb into employment new entrants to a labour force growing annually at about 3%. Employment creation also, of course, has an important impact on redistribution (see Chapter 9).

Raising productivity in rice is being tackled mainly by major irrigation schemes such as the Muda project in Kedah (260,000 acres) and Kemubu in Kelantan (47,000 acres), and by improved marketing arrangements. In addition, in October 1975, the Ministry of Agriculture announced plans to achieve self-sufficiency in animal products by 1990, with increases in domestic production of eggs, poultry and meat (*Straits Times*, October 1975). Rice self-sufficiency again appears to be an aim too, this time for 1985.[45] Rubber replanting, still only 63% complete on smallholdings in 1970, has also been part of Plan strategy, though in 1971–3 only a further 6% was completed, against a 12% target. The two main areas of expansion, both to create employment and raise productivity *and* to improve the economic position of the Malays, are the further growth of primary commodity exports and of manufacturing.

Plan targets to 1990 under the Second Malaysia Plan are shown in Table 4.12, which also indicates sectoral shares of output and employment.[46] Under this Plan a target of a million acres of new land development was set, mainly to be carried out by FELDA and including stages of the Johore Tenggara and Pahang Tenggara schemes (of 300,000 and about a million acres, respectively). Rubber and oil palm will both be planted under this expansion, with some possible diversification into other crops such as sugar or cocoa. The Plan's allocation to land development is large—18% of government investment and about 9% of total investment in 1973—but by itself new land development will create only about a third of the new jobs required. Thus 200,000 acres a year at roughly 14 acres per family creates some 30,000 jobs (allowing slightly more than two workers per household), and 200,000 acres per year is an extremely high target, previously reached in Malaysia only at the height of the planting booms of 1910–11 and 1917–18 and then by the estate and smallholder sectors combined; and it compares to a total land development of only 300,000 acres by FELDA for the *whole* of the 1960's.

Over the 1971–5 period, therefore, other sources of job creation have been necessary, and manufacturing expansion has been targetted to generate as many jobs as agriculture and forestry combined, and was exceeding its target by 1973 (Prime Minister's Dept., 1973, p. 30). Over the longer period from 1970 to 1990, manufacturing output is scheduled to grow at almost double the rate of GDP growth, and manufacturing employment to grow at more than double the aggregate employment growth rate (see Table 4.12). Thus manufacturing must become a major exporter.

Growth prospects in Malaysia suffered a sharp but apparently temporary setback during the world recession in 1974–5, following the commodity price boom. Rubber

TABLE 4.12 GROSS DOMESTIC PRODUCT AND EMPLOYMENT BY SECTOR OF ORIGIN, MALAYSIA, 1970-90

	1970		1990		Growth rates 1971-73		Projected Growth Rates 1971-90	
	Share of GDP (%)	Share of Employment (%)	Share of GDP (%)	Share of Employment (%)	Output (%)	Employment (%)	Output (%)	Employment (%)
Agriculture, Forestry & Fisheries	31.4	52.6	22.9	36.2	10.2	1.8	5.4	1.3
Mining & Quarrying	5.8	2.6	6.6	1.7	7.1	0.8	7.8	0.9
Manufacturing	13.6	9.6	35.2	21.7	16.1	9.5	12.3	7.5
Construction	3.9	2.7	3.5	4.0	16.1	6.2	6.5	5.1
Electricity, water & Sanitary services	2.6	0.7	4.6	1.2	10.5	6.8	10.3	6.2
Transport, storage & Communications	4.4	3.9	2.9	3.7	7.2	3.3	4.9	2.9
Ownership of dwellings	4.6	-	3.2	-	5.2	-	5.1	-
Wholesale & Retail Trade	14.1	9.3	9.3	12.1	9.7	4.7	4.9	4.6
Banking, Insurance & Real Estate	2.1	0.5	2.3	1.1	11.9	10.6	7.6	7.3
Public Administration & Defence	6.6	8.5	3.4	8.0	15.3	3.0	3.6	2.8
Other Services	10.9	9.6	6.1	10.3	12.4	3.6	4.1	3.5
GDP at Factor Cost (1970 prices)	$9551m.		$39334m.		11.3	(At Current Prices)	7.1	
Total Employment	3.3m.		6.2m.			3.4		3.2

Sources and Notes

(1) All statistics from Prime Minister's Dept., 1973, pp. 30, 40, 68-70.

export volume fell in 1974 compared to 1973, with total value only slightly higher, and during the course of 1974 the rubber price fell substantially (from 265 cents a kilo in January to 143 in October). Timber exports fell both in volume and unit value, though tin and petroleum exports grew, as did oil palm (Treasury, *AR*, 1974–5). By November 1975, the worst of the recession seemed to be over, and the Malaysian Treasury was forecasting a return to the trend annual growth rate of 6% (*Straits Times*, November 1975). Inflation too seemed to be coming under control—having reached a peak of 24% *per annum* in March 1974, in May 1975 it was down to the annual equivalent of under 5% (*Far Eastern Economic Review*, 29 August 1975).[47]

In the longer term, growth prospects for Malaysia still depend on export performance, which will also provide the expansions in export agriculture and manufacturing to bring Malays and other low-income groups into higher paid occupations. Munro (1973a), in an extremely useful set of balance of payments forecasts for Malaysia to 1980, is optimistic about commodity export prospects.[48] No major cost reductions are anticipated in stereoregular rubber, whose price provides a floor (for foreseeable increases in Malaysian output) well above the production costs of efficient estates. Moreover the higher petroleum prices following the action of OPEC in 1973 (see Chapter 2) worsen the competitive postion of synthetic rubber, as does the devaluation of the U.S. dollar *vis-à-vis* the ringgit as a result of the ringgit's upward 'float' since 1973 (Munro, 1973a, p. 51). Tin demand and output is likely to grow only gradually, but no disasters are expected in its performance. Palm oil, on the other hand, of which Malaysia is one of the lowest cost producers in the world, and which constitutes only about 7% of world oil and fat supply, faces a highly price-elastic demand, and (at least in other developing countries) a highly income-elastic demand too.[49] Timber, Munro suggests, could become Malaysia's prime export earner by 1980 (Munro, 1973a, p. 60).

On the supply side, perhaps some reservations may be expressed. The oil palm and rubber acreage expansions are concentrated on the public sector. FELDA'S development costs per job created are probably at present roughly the same as those for labour-intensive manufacture[50] (about $6–7000), but many doubts have been felt about FELDA's capacity to expand, particularly with regard to management and field staff (e.g. Wikkramatileke, 1972, p. 121). When the full development cost of schemes in new areas is included[51] costs per job may be very great and I have heard unofficial estimates in excess of $30,000. Certainly FELDA establishment costs are higher than those of the private sector, partly because of longer immature periods; and, it has been authoritatively suggested by the head of Economics and Planning in the Rubber Research Institute of Malaysia that some new developments could be given over to private estates and then purchased back—at a profit to the estates and at a lower cost to FELDA (Lim and Chong, 1973, p. 20).

Timber supply prospects seem good in view of the twenty million acres of forested, unused land in Sabah and Sarawak, but to date very little processing has been carried out[52] and timber exporting on the present scale is essentially of a 'vent-for-surplus' nature[53] offering no basis for future development once the stock is exhausted, though a smaller export industry could be established on a permanent basis if some forest areas are replanted.

Manufacturing export growth implies a considerable shift in the present orientation towards the domestic market.[54] In spite of the common view that until recently (i.e. up to the late 1960's) industry had developed in Malaysia with very little tariff protection (e.g. Lim, 1973, p. 255), C. B. Edwards in a new study shows that even in 1966 the average effective rate of protection (i.e. the protection on domestic value-added) was as high as 45% for manufacturing (having been only 15% in 1962) and had risen to 55% by 1972 (Edwards, 1975, p. 293). Since Edwards found very little correlation between ERP and profitability in particular industries, over much of domestic manufacturing therefore costs must be considerably greater than world export costs. In fact the proportion of output exported is low on average (15% in 1970—see Statistics Dept., *SManI*, 1970 and FIDA, *MID*, 1972, 3rd Quarter) and only in textiles (39% in 1970) and in the new (post-1972) electronics is the share of exports very much higher than average. Electronics is essentially an asembly industry, using imported components and locall labour.[55,56] Generous concessions (including those of the revised Investment Incentives Act, 1971, which gives tax relief on the basis of employment size) reduce its benefits to the economy to basically wage payments (+ some profits in the case of joint ventures) and one may also express some doubt about the long-run effects on improving income distribution if poor people are simply taken into unskilled industrial employment (though their wages in the short run will be more than their present earnings). However, the redistribution of *wealth* to *bumiputras* (Malays) through (e.g.) public ownership of shares through such organizations as PERNAS (the National Corporation) may be easier in an expanding sector consisting of large foreign firms (through joint ventures and stipulated minimum proportions of new issues of shares to be held by Malays, etc.) than if the growth was concentrated on smaller (probably unincorporated) local firms who would be mainly Chinese.

Successful development also depends in the long term on reducing the rate of population growth, especially before supplies of new land become exhausted. In the First Malaysia Plan (Prime Minister's Dept., 1966, p. 15) the objective was stated of lowering the population growth rate by means of birth control campaigns from 3% to 2% by 1985.

NOTES

1. These are 1969 figures, from Statistics Dept., *MBS*, June 1970. In ordinary Malaysian usage these groups are known as 'races'. For an account of the overseas Chinese in Malaya see Purcell (1948). A history written more from the Malay viewpoint is Winstedt (1968).
2. The main Chinese dialects spoken in Malaysia are Hokkien, Hakka and Cantonese. Hokkien and Cantonese are dialects of southern China. The Hakka dialect does not properly belong to any one region of China, but most Hakka people in Malaysia do in fact come from southern China too.
3. Also included in the Straits Settlement for a time was a coastal area known as the Dindings, later incorporated into Perak. Penang included Province Wellesley on the mainland, and Singapore included Christmas Island, Labuan Island and Cocos Island.
4. For an early account of the development of British influence see Swettenham (1907). Sir Frank Swettenham was one of the most influential of the early British administrators, and was first Resident-General of the FMS.
5. The year 1922 marks the end of a period of expansion based first on tin and then on rubber exports. In 1922 rubber exports were restricted by the Malayan government and the alienation of new rubber land prohibited. Tin exports were restricted from 1921. The restriction schemes are discussed in the next section.
6. For an economic history of the tin industry to 1914 see Wong Lin Ken (1965). A more general economic history is Yip (1969). Much of the account which follows is drawn from Wong's study, as well as from the annual reports of the Residents of the Malay states.
7. This point, and other information about the early development of tin, is from Fermor (1939, especially pp. 21–3).

8. That this system of extensive credit facilities persists to the present can be seen from Tan (1966).
9. Mining methods are described in some detail in Chapter 5.
10. For more details of railway development see Chai (1964) and FMS Railways (1935), from which much of the above information is taken.
11. The 1922 estate acreage was 84% of 1968 acreage. It was 69% of the maximum post-war figure (1953) and 68% of the largest estate acreage recorded (that of 1940).
12. General descriptions of the introduction of rubber in Malaya have been given in many works, in particular Jackson (1968), Allen and Donnithorne (1954) and Chai (1964). This account borrows heavily from these together with the *AR's* of the individual Malay States to 1896, and the *AR's* of the Resident-General/Chief Secretary FMS to 1925. Drabble (1973), now the standard work on the early rubber industry, is also extremely useful.
13. *Para* not only grew better in the Malayan climate than *Castilloa* or *Caera* rubbers, but it produced more regular yields than its main competitor *Rambong*. See Chai (1964, p. 155).
14. Nevertheless, J. C. Jackson, an authority on agricultural development in Malaya before rubber, suggests that the importance of coffee can be overrated. It was never of predominant importance, in acreage or value of output, except in Selangor in the 1890's. See Jackson (1968, pp. 205–6).
15. See Selangor, *AR's*, 1885, 1889, 1893.
16. For example, in Selangor, in 1884, all quit rent on agricultural land was waived for three years, and export duties were to be waived for the five years from 1885. See Selangor, *AR's*, 1884 and 1885.
17. This included a subsidy to steamers bringing immigrants from Negapatam, India, from 1887, and the establishment of a depot at Negapatam in 1890 where intending immigrants under monetary advances could be examined prior to departure. See Jackson (1961, especially pp. 96–108). However, the government was also accused of poaching labour from estates for employment in its public works (pp. 104–5).
18. In the last full year of the coffee boom, 1895, a total of 539 acres of rubber had been planted by European coffee estates in Selangor, the main coffee state, and 38,000 acres alienated to them. The total acreage of new rubber planted from 1906 is quite beyond this magnitude. Acreage figures from Selangor, *AR*, 1895.
19. This was in spite of the fact that from 1915 to 1919 it was difficult for British companies to obtain the official permission needed during that period to raise capital. In addition foreign companies were banned from 1917 to 1919 from acquiring new rubber land over 50 acres. See Drabble (1967, pp. 64–6).
20. A dollar company is one whose issued capital is denominated in (Malayan) dollars. The currency indicates the country in which the company was floated.
21. An alternative to the cost estimation used here is to estimate capital expenditure from rubber company accounts and records. Stillson (1971, 1974) has attempted to estimate investment by British companies using the value of authorized capital. His estimate of a total expenditure of $417m for 1905–22 (though part of this would be spread into the years beyond 1922 when there was still some investment though no new land alienation) is within the range for *total* investment estimated in Table 4.3 ($186 million–$558 million), but his methods have been severely criticized by Drabble and Drake (1974), partly for using *authorized* rather than *issued* capital, but more because of the inherent difficulties of using even issued capital as a proxy for capital expenditure (since shares were not always issued for cash, were not always sold at par value, may represent bonus issues, etc, and thus not represent a true inflow of capital into the industry).
22. This is calculated as follows. According to the 1911 *Census* the 'Malaysian' (i.e. Malays + Javanese, etc.) population was 1.37m. An adult Malay male consumes 4 to 5 piculs of rice per year (see Chai, 1964, p. 145). The average 1911 import unit value of rice was $5 per picul, (see FMS, *AR* Resident-General, 1911). If a minimum consumption of rice is taken as 4 piculs per year, (to allow for the average being lowered by inclusion of females and children), total value of Malay rice consumption is $27.4m, say $30m. This subsistence consumption can be taken, *faute de mieux*, as an indication of the minimum value of Malay's output. The inclusion of *total* Malay population is justified by the fact that to the extent that women and children did not work, they would be supported by the male members. Of course, this estimate raises all the problems of valuing subsistence output, and ignores the value of Malay production above the subsistence level, e.g. the growing of coconuts as a cash crop. It does not, however, involve

double counting, as little of the Malay output would have been sold to the (mainly Chinese) mining sector. Thus the value of tin output would include few Malay factor services or goods produced by Malays.

23. Parmer (1960, p. 39). For a history of Indians in Malaya see Sandhu (1969).
24. It can be seen from Table 4.6 that almost all smallholding acreage was Asian. The small European smallholder acreage ('estate under 100 acres') might have consisted of small estates operated by proprietory planters.
25. Drabble, (1967, pp. 56–7) notes that of the 190 applications for rubber land in Selangor and Negri Sembilan in 1909–10 made by Chinese (165) and Indians (25), 123 were from people described as already having other business interests, particularly tin mining, shopkeeping and contracting.
26. In particular, no Asian acreage is recorded for before 1907, in spite of many known cases of Asian rubber planting before that date. This point is made by Drabble (1967, p. 56).
27. Voon Phin Keong suggests that two reasons for the failure of Asians to take up rubber growing during the first boom were the lack of availability of tapping instruments and uncertainty about the tapping system. After 1910 more economic means of tapping and an abundance of rubber seeds aided smallholder development (Voon, 1967, pp. 12–13).
28. The 1952 figures given in Table 6.10 show that Chinese and Indians own over 80% of holdings of 25–100 acres, while Malays and Chinese own 55% and 35% respectively of holdings under 25 acres. Malays owned 40% and Chinese 47% of total smallholder acreage. Little new land was planted between 1922 and 1953, so these figures will reflect the pre-war position except for transfers of land betwen racial groups. However, Fryer and Jackson (1966) suggest that much land may indeed have been transferred to Chinese once the Chinese community became more permanently settled in Malaya after the Second World War. In fact, in their survey of Rasa, only 10% of Chinese holdings had been in their owners' hands for more than 30 years.
29. Since the obtaining of this type of information involves detailed study into Land Office records, the case-study approach is inevitable. There is little chance of determining how typical was the experience of Ulu Langat. It is certainly in contrast with Drabble's findings discussed above. It was one of the later districts to be developed in one of the most important planting states of Malaya.
30. The data in the 1911 and 1921 censuses are not set out in a form which allows comparison of figures of the sort set out in Table 4.8.
31. It could also be argued, as does Jackson (1968, p. 258), that unfettered expansion came to an end in 1917 when Land Offices could no longer cope with the flood of applications for new land.
32. For a discussion of the rubber schemes one of the most useful sources is Bauer (1948b). See also Bauer's article 'The Working of Rubber Regulation', reprinted in Silcock (1961). A convenient summary of the schemes is given in Lim (1967, pp. 76–83). Tin schemes, both pre-war and post-war, are discussed in Yip (1964).
33. P. T. Bauer is the most persuasive advocate of this case. His arguments are well set out in 'The Working of Rubber Regulation', in Silcock (1961). Most later writers have agreed with Bauer's general arguments, though not necessarily his implication of ulterior motivation on the part of the Malayan government. See for example, F. C. Benham, 'The Rubber Industry', in Silcock (1961).
34. Bauer argues that it is impossible to replant only 20% of a holding of a few acres. The young tres growth would be stunted by the other trees. Also a smallholder might not be able to afford to keep even 20% of his trees out of tapping. In the long run the inability to replant might have meant the extinction of the smallholding sector. See 'Working of Rubber Regulation', in Silcock (1961, p. 254).
35. Agriculture Dept., *Malayan Agricultural Statistics*, 1939. In 1930 over 14,000 acres of oil palm were planted. Of course this is very small compared to early plantings of rubber. In the boom years of 1910–11 and 1917–18 over 200,000 acres of rubber were planted annually (see Table 4.2).
36. British Malaya, *Population Census*, 1921 and 1931. The year 1921 was the first in which population was classified by industry.
37. This section is designed to provide a background, discussion and assesment of policy prior to the more detailed treatments in Chapters 5, 6 and 9. Certain topics (e.g. the development of FELDA) which are covered briefly here are dealt with more fully later. For a bibliography of

Malaysian development, see Challis (1968 and 1969). Some useful discussions of Malaysian development policy are given in Sumitro Djojohadikusumo (1968).

38. As Chapter 2 showed, fluctuations in export earnings in Malaysia since the war have had a much less than proportionate effect on domestic activity, and empirical work on export fluctuations covering many countries has shown little adverse effect on growth. However if, as is likely, smallholders and gravel pump miners become proportionately more important in the rubber and tin, the multiplier effects of export fluctuations may well increase (see Chapter 7). Also, with Keynesian policies in operation in western countries depressions on a 1930's scale are far less likely, so demand-induced export fluctuations are less likely too (though the 1973 commodity price boom is an important exception).
39. The regressiveness of export taxes in general and the replanting cess in particular, as applied to rubber smallholders, has been strongly argued by A. H. H. Tan (1967). Tan argues (p. 90) that a typical rubber smallholder pays in tax the same as people with *thirty* to *forty* times his income; and also that only a small proportion of smallholders (as of 1967) had benefitted from the replanting scheme (p. 97).
40. In spite of its name, the First Five Year Plan was not the first development plan for the country. The *first* Plan was the Draft Development Plan 1950–5. This was essentially a set of budgetary estimates. Subsequent plans have consisted of macroeconomic projections and targets, combined with sets of public expenditure allocations and discussions of policy towards the private sector. For a discussion of early planning in Malaysia see Silcock and Fisk (1963, pp. 242–75).
41. Diversification was aided by the fact that rubber replanting grants could be used to replant with oil palm. Between 1955 and 1962 18% of the increase in oil palm acreage was financed in this way (Khoo, 1964, p. 11).
42. Owing to lack of data for East Malaysia, the analysis of exports and development in Malaysia which follows in Chapters 5 to 9 concentrates on Peninsular Malaysia alone; but many of the projections and statistics in the First and Second Malaysia Plans are given for the whole of Malaysia. In 1970, East Malaysia generated 15% of Malaysian real output and had 16% of the Malaysian labour force. Most timber and (for the present) all petroleum exports come from East Malaysia. Some preliminary finds of petroleum deposits have been made in Peninsular Malaysia, e.g. at Kuantan.
43. Problems of income distribution are covered at much greater length in Chapter 9.
44. For a useful discussion of Malaysian unemployment, see Blake (1973). Inflation has also been a major problem since 1973, but by 1975 it was showing signs of coming under control. This is discussed later in the section.
45. Rice self-sufficiency has been an unsuccessful aim of Malaysian policy makers very often in the past (see, for instance, Lim Chong Yah, 1967, p. 177). Rudner (1971, p. 82) noted that under the First Malaysia Plan the padi self-sufficiency goal was 'finally laid to rest', (though it has since been brought to life again). Chapter 9 also discusses this point, and shows how much higher Malaysian costs are in relation to those of some neighbouring countries.
46. The share of manufacturing in total output may, however, be exaggerated in the 1970 figures since it receives a high level of effective protection on domestic value-added, (See Edwards, 1975, p. 287.)
47. Inflation had been virtually unknown in peace-time in Malaysia before 1973.
48. Munro (1973b) also argues that strong forces operate in Malaysia to constrain import growth as national output expands, unless exports expand too. This 'new (monetarist) view' assumes that the balance of payments plays a crucial role in determining domestic money supply, and Munro suggests that strong links still persist between the external sector and the domestic money supply (p. 71). The link persists in spite of the floating of the Ringgit in 1973, since the Malaysian authorities did not allow a 'clean' float.
49. On price projections which Munro (1973a, p. 54) still regards as realistic (and perhaps slightly pessimistic), Bevan and Goering (1968) estimated rates of return on oil palm investment of 17%, compared to 11% in rubber.
50. These estimates are based on job creation in manufacturing during 1971–3 of 33,000 *per annum* on average, and new investment in manufacturing in 1971 of $240 million (i.e. $7,278 per job.) (Prime Minister's Dept., 1973, p. 30, and Statistics Dept., *SManI*, 1971). FELDA's cost per household based on Second Malaysia Plan figures was $11,500 (i.e. just under $6,000 per job.)

51. It might, however, be argued that if FELDA develops new areas into which other industries might eventually move, then any appraisal of FELDA's social profitability should not include the full new development costs.
52. Munro (1973a, p. 60), citing work by A. J. Hepburn, suggests a number of reasons why processing has not occurred. These include shortages of skilled workers and management, higher freight costs for processed products and the fact that logging profits are so high (at least before the 1974 slump) that investment in processing is unattractive, especially if there are doubts about future supplies. Similar factors seem to have prevented the development of processing in the Indonesian lumber industry (see Manning, 1971).
53. Similar arguments apply to tin and petroleum, but Chapters 5 and 8 will show that tin's legacy to further development has been considerble.
54. Hoffmann and Tan (1973) have shown that between 1959 and 1968 industrial growth in Malaysia depended most heavily on import substitution, substantially on domestic market expansion, and only to a minor part on export expansion (p. 147).
55. 'Offshore assembly' of this kind is increasingly common in developing countries. See Helleiner (1973).
56. Another increasingly common form of manufacturing export development is where small local firms act as subcontractors to overseas manufacturers and retailers. This has been important in Hong Kong, for instance, and Malaysian Chinese firms in future may well be able to grow under similar arrangements. See Sharpson (1975).

Chapter 5
Tin

This chapter contains the first of the two major commodity studies. The core of the chapter is Section 5.2, which follows the methodology developed in Chapter 3 and undertakes a comparative analysis of the structure of payments made out of current export income by the two main sectors, gravel pumping and dredging. Section 5.2 takes the relative size of the two sectors as given at any one time, and an explanation is needed elsewhere therefore of why several sectors can coexist and what determines their relative growth rates. This explanation is attempted in Section 5.1 which looks at the technology and organization of the industry. Section 5.3 considers the investment purchases made by mining, and Section 5.4 discusses linkage effects.

5.1 THE TECHNOLOGY AND ORGANIZATION OF THE MALAYSIAN TIN MINING INDUSTRY

Malaysia is the world's largest supplier of tin, producing some 40% of world output, and in common with the other large producers in South East Asia, her deposits are predominantly alluvial (i.e. they consist of material deposited by the action of water and occuring in sediments relatively near the surface). The major mining methods are also common to several other producers,[1] and are described in Subsection 5.1.1 below, which also contains some historical information about the development of techniques, which will be helpful in understanding the analysis of the past structure of input purchases included in Section 5.2. Subsection 5.1.2 describes the organization of the industry, and looks in particular at the importance of the 'foreign' sector and its degree of horizontal and vertical integration. Subsection 5.1.3 outlines tin price stabilization schemes as they affect the structure of payments.

5.1.1 Mining Technologies

Dredging is in general the larger scale of the main techniques and as a first approximation (to be modified somewhat in the next subsection) it can be regarded as a 'foreign' sector.

A dredge is a structure which floats on a pond (or 'paddock') largely of its own making,[2] and is moved by means of lines fixed to the shore and attached to winches on the dredge. A continuous line of steel buckets at the front of the dredge digs the tin-bearing ground from the bottom. The buckets are attached to a chain mounted in a metal ladder, which can be raised or lowered to vary digging depth. Ground from the buckets is delivered to a primary treatment plant on the dredge, where ore is treated to about 15% purity,[3] and the waste material ('tailings') is pumped over the back of the dredge. Ore is taken from the dredge to a dressing shed on shore where it undergoes further treatment to a purity of about 75%, before shipment to the smelter.

The capacity of dredging, and other types of alluvial tin mining, is expressed in terms of a 'yardage'. The largest present-day dredges can mine over 750,000 cubic yards of tin-bearing earth a month. An average 'large' dredge has a capacity of 500,000. A cubic yard weighs over a ton and ground yielding one pound of ore from a cubic yard would be considered exceptionally rich, hence the need for large throughputs. The capacity of dredges has increased gradually over time. The earliest dredges, built just before the First World War, had capacity of 80–100,000 cubic yards and could dig to 50 feet (Ooi, 1955, p. 366). By 1924 new dredges could treat 200,000 yards a month (Mines Dept., *AR*, 1924) and by 1938 450,000 yards, with a digging depth of 130 feet (Mines Dept., *AR*, 1938), which is almost as deep as that of present-day dredges.

Technical changes in dredging have been mainly of two forms, both affecting the sector's input purchases, which are to be analysed in Sections 5.2 and 5.3. The first dredges were steam driven, using coal (first imported and later local) or firewood as fuel. By 1926 most newer dredges were using coal (Mines Dept., *AR*, 1926). In 1935 a third of the dredges were powered by electricity and the rest still used steam.

Today most use electricity. Second, machinery for the primary treatment plant has become more complex. The earliest dredges 'concentrated' (i.e. separated ore from waste material) on long sluices, similar to those of many present-day gravel mines. By 1925 sluices were being replaced by jigs (pulsating boxes in which waste material is floated off the ore), and by 1928 the number of dredges using jigs was roughly equal to the number using sluices (Mines Dept., *AR*, 1928). Today all use jigs. A further development has been the use of hydrocyclones and pumps to improve the feed to the jigs by dewatering and desliming. These are dealt with more fully in the account of gravel pump mining which follows below. In the dressing sheds too, advances have been made, with for example the use of sluice-type wash boxes being supplemented by magnetic and electrostatic separators and shaking tables.

Gravel Pumping involves breaking down of the tin-bearing ground by means of strong jets of water played against the walls of an open pit. The water is directed by rigid metal hose nozzles, or 'monitors', each operated by one or two men. The liquid ore-bearing material washed down by the monitors flows through crudely cut channels to a hollow, or sump, whence it is elevated by means of a pump–the gravel pump–to the primary treatment plant, usually a sluice.

The principle of this type of mining was imported from Cornwall, the centre of British tin mining, where high-pressure jets of water were used to mine china clay[4] (Allen and Donnithorne, 1954, p. 149). The first hydraulic mine in Malaya was Gopeng in Perak, started in 1892 (Perak, *AR*, 1893). This worked over 10,000 cubic yards a month with a workforce of only 20, using water under a natural head, brought over six miles from the Kampar River.[5] Originally the cut ground was recovered from artificial ditches by manual labour but subsequently hydraulic elevators were used to raise the ore-bearing material to a treatment plant (Osborne, 1920), as in a present-day gravel pump mine. By 1905 there were nine hydraulic mines in the Federated Malay States (Perak, *AR*, 1905). The first use of artificial motive power to operate the jets and elevators was in 1906 at the Tanjong Rambutan mine in Perak, introduced from Tasmania (Wong, 1965, p. 209). This was the so-called suction dredge. Pumps mounted on a floating pontoon, operated a monitor to break down ground on the wall of the excavation, and a centrifugal gravel pump to elevate the slurry. Because of its high operating costs the method never became popular but its importance lies in the fact that it demonstrated the possibility of hydraulic mining operating with artificial power (i.e. gravel pumping), and it was rapidly adopted by Chinese miners who adapted it for use without the floating pontoon. By 1915 the Mines Department's details of principal workings in the Federated Malay States listed three mines, all in Perak, hydraulicing with power plant, and by the 1920's gravel pump mining was well established (Mines Dept., *AR*, 1920 and 1924).

Technical change in the method of mining has been minor. In 1938 a new type of gravel pump was introduced, with an electric motor coupled to the pump in one portable unit (Mines Dept., *AR*, 1938). Steam engines were replaced by diesel oil engines, which were themselves replaced to some extent by electricity. The first hydroelectric mining plant was set up in 1911 (Wong, 1965, p. 209), but electricity was not available for commercial purchase on a large scale until the end of the 1920's. The Perak River Hydroelectric Power Company, which now supplies much of the power for the Kinta valley, started operations in 1928, and the first Government Steam Electric Plant was opened in 1927. Previously only Pengkalen, a mining company turned power station, had supplied electricity commercially, and only on a relatively small scale.

Primary treatment in some gravel pump mines has altered little in fifty years. The slurry raised by the pump is passed through the bars of a metal screen, or grizzly, to remove large pieces of stone, etc. The screen is manned by a single operator armed with a pole with which the screen is kept clear of blockages. From the screen the remaining solids are run onto a long downward sloping sluice box, the 'palong' where wooden strips (riffles) catch the ore on the bottom while the lighter material flows away to be pumped to a tailings dump.

Innovations have been of two kinds. First, from the late 1930's, but more especially in the last twenty-five years earth-moving equipment has been used extensively to remove the overburden before gravel pumping (United Nations, 1968, p. 99). Second, there is the use of jigs as on dredges. Although figures are not available at the time of writing, it would seem that this was ruled out for many years both by capital costs and technological sophistication, and economies of scale in mechanical treatment plants. However in 1959 a new type of treatment plant was developed by the Federal Department of Mines. This method, the hydrocyclonic jig plant, allows the rejection of a much greater proportion of the solids pumped up for treatment, which in turn allows treatment by one-quarter of the previous jig capacity. The recovery rate of ore is up to 50% higher than that of sluices treating the same amount of slurry, and the capital cost, expressed as an annual charge, is little over half that of a palong (Harris, 1959). By 1962 one gravel pump mine in six was using hydrocyclonic jig treatment (United Nations, 1968, p. 61). Today many gravel pump mines uses jigs installed at the end of the palong for treating the ore a second time to raise recovery, but the complete use of jigs for primary treatment is rare.

A typical gravel pump mine with a monthly yardage of 15–20,000, would employ approximately thirty men. A small dredge with a yardage of 250,000 would employ over a hundred men. This gives a yardage per man in dredges of over three times that of gravel pump mines. For the larger dredges this ratio would be still higher.

Other Mining Methods include open cast mining, underground mining and dulang washing. First, open cast mining. This name is somewhat misleading. All gravel pump mining, and in a sense dredging too, is open cast. 'Open cast' mining in Malaysian usage has the additional connotation that it is mining without the use of water—'dry mining' in the terminology of the industry.

Open cast mining is one of the oldest forms of mining in Malaya. The early open cast mines in Malaya in the nineteenth century, when open cast was the most important form of mining, were worked mainly by hand labour using only Chinese hoes (changkols) to dig the ground, and twin baskets slung on each end of a pole to raise the ore from the pit. Treatment was in simple sluice boxes or 'lanchuts'. Machinery was first introduced in 1877 with the purchase of a steam pump by the British Resident of Perak (Perak, *AR*, 1887). Such pumps enabled mines to be kept drained at a much greater depth than the earlier form of pump, the Chinese chin-chia water wheel. Their use spread rapidly, and by 1904 there were nearly a thousand boilers and engines in Perak alone (FMS, *AR*, Resident-General, 1904). By 1904 although most mines still used nothing except a steam pump, various other types of machinery were in operation in some European mines. Warnford-Lock (1907, p. 23) noted the use of steam engines to work lines drawing trucks on rails to remove overburden and carrying tin-bearing ground. Nowadays open cast mining is by means of mechanical excavators, and this dates from before the Second World War (Mines Dept., *AR*, 1936). The famous Sungei Besi mine near Kuala Lumpur, for example, which produces about half of the total open cast output of Malaysia, when visited in 1969 was using bucket wheel excavators, large self-propelled tracked vehicles with digging buckets on a single revolving wheel, each excavator equipped with its own crushing plant. Ore from the excavators was sent by conveyor belt to a central treatment plant. Other parts of the mine used gravel pumps to work lower grade deposits, while bulldozers and small excavators were used elsewhere. One especially rich deposit was worked by female dulang washers on contract. Other open cast mines use mechanical excavators and at least one other bucket wheel excavator is in operation.

Second, there is underground mining. Over three-quarters of underground tin output is produced by a single European company, the Pahang Consolidated Corporation Limited, which has been in operation since 1887 (Pahang Consolidated, 1967). Little explanation is needed as the methods used are essentially similar to those used to mine coal underground in Western countries.

Finally, there is dulang washing (so named after the 'dulang' or pan with which the miners work). Dulang washers, mostly Chinese women, pan for tin in rivers and streams in a similar fashion to gold miners in early America. They are sometimes employed on contract by mines but often work independently.[6]

5.1.2 The Organization of the Industry

An overall view of the structure of the industry in terms of its techniques of production is given in Tables 5.1 and 5.2. The predominance of dredging and gravel pumping is clear, and dates from the 1920's. Output figures by sector unfortunately

TABLE 5.1 PRODUCTION OF TIN IN PENINSULAR MALAYSIA BY MINING METHODS, 1930-74, SELECTED YEARS

(Percentages of Total Output)

	Dredging	Gravel Pumping	Hydraulicing	Open Cast	Underground	Miscellaneous	Dulang Washing
1928	30	45	8	6	6	2	2
1930	38	43	7	4	5	1	1
1935	45	41	5	2	4	1	2
1939	48	36	6	4	4	-	2
1950	49	35	4	1	5	-	5
1955	51	39	2	2	4	-	2
1960	54	34	2	2	4	1	2
1965	39	48	-	3	3	2	3
1974	32	53	-	4	3	2	4

Sources and Notes

(1) 1928-39 are for FMS only.

(2) 1928 figures from Fermor (1939, p. 113), 1930-39 from Mines Dept., AR 1939, 1950-65 from Mines Dept., BSMI's 1955-66, 1974 from Mines Dept., QBS, 4, 1974.

TABLE 5.2 PENINSULAR MALAYSIAN MINING EMPLOYMENT, BY MINING METHOD, 1903-72, SELECTED YEARS

(Percentages of total mining employment)

	DREDGING	GRAVEL PUMPING	HYDRAULICING	OPEN CAST	UNDERGROUND
1903	-		12	77	...
1910	-		17	72	11
1915	1		20	72	7
1920	3		39	47	11
1925	7		46	27	7
1930	15	51	11	15	7
1935	17	49	8	18	8
1939	23	50	5	16	7
1950	33	51	5	...	...
1955	37	48	3	...	...
1960	39	44	4	4	10
1965	24	65	-	3	6
1972	22	69	-	2	6

Sources and Notes

(1) 1903-39 are percentages of all mining employment and are for FMS only. No separate figures for tin employment by method of mining are available until 1967 except for dredging, which is given in the CMin I from 1964. However, dredging operations are virtually only for tin so little is gained from such information.

(2) The underground percentage will be slightly overstated from 1915 to 1955 since it includes coal employment (coal mining ceased early in 1960). Open cast mining may also include coal, and certainly includes iron, at least after 1921. Iron mining employment figures are available for the postwar period and have been subtracted from open cast employment to arrive at the figures for 1960 and 1965. A similar operation was not possible for 1950 and 1955 because of the difficulty of allocating coal employment between open cast and underground. Employment in other mining such as gold or bauxite is not large enough to have a noticeable effect on the percentages.

(3) Sources of figures are as follows - 1903 from FMS, AR of Resident General 1903, 1910-39 from Mines Dept., AR 1939, 1950-72 from Mines Dept., BSMI's.

(4) Dulang washers are excluded from the total.

are not available for the years before 1928, but the employment statistics in Table 5.2 show the rapid decline of the traditional open cast method over the decade from 1915. Clear too is the rise of dredging relative to gravel pumping over the 1930's to the late 1950's, and its relative decline in the last fifteen years. An important task of this subsection is to explain the coexistence and relative sizes of the sectors, but first their ownership and control is considered.

Dredging is normally regarded as a 'foreign' or 'European' sector. From the early days of dredging just before the First World War, to the 1950's, the foreign identity of dredging companies was unambiguous. They were founded by Europeans, managed by Europeans, registered abroad, raised their capital abroad (often in London), and consequently their shareholders, and also their directors, were mainly foreign; and British-based firms were particularly important in the industry. In the last twenty-five years important changes have occurred in the ownership of mining companies. Research by Yip (1969, pp. 346–73) and by myself (Thoburn, 1970), of which more details are given in Section 5.2, has shown that an increasingly large proportion of shares have been purchased by Malaysian residents, and this has been accompanied by some companies moving their headquarters to Malaysia. Moreover, there is in operation one virtually wholly Chinese public dredging company (Selangor Dredging), and at least one private Chinese dredging company (Senky Dredging in Selangor, with a subsidiary in Perak). However, although in locally incorporated dredging companies local ownership is now over 60%, in dredging as a whole foreigners still own possibly as much as two-thirds of the total capital.

Against these changes in ownership patterns must be set the pattern of control. George Beckford's (1972) and Norman Girvan's (1970) work, discussed in Chapter 3, have popularized the spectre in developing countries of foreign companies highly integrated among themselves, and vertically integrated into related activities within the host country and abroad; which are thus able to bring to bear substantial and possibly harmful influence on domestic activity and policies. This issue has been raised in relation to Malaysian mining by Putucheary (1960, especially pp. 81–95), and it is necessary to ask whether it is a correct view and if it is, what are its consequences.

Ownership can differ from control in practice if ownership is dispersed. Thus even where local individual shareholders own over 50% of the shares, if they are disparate and unorganized, control can still be exercised by foreigners owning a minority of shares. This appears strongly to be the case in Malaysia where increasing local ownership has not been matched by significant increases in local control (Yip, 1969, p. 371). The structure of control in the European sector has been described in detail by Putucheary and that structure has changed little in twenty years (Fox, 1974, p. 8), at least as far as the control pattern *within* Malaysia is concerned (i.e. there have been some changes in ultimate control, and ownership, by outside interests). Basically one group, Anglo-Oriental (a subsidiary of the London Tin Corporation), predominates, and in 1963 this group controlled companies accounting for 23% of total Malaysian tin output or about half the output of foreign mines; and three groups—Anglo-Oriental, Neill and Bell, and Osborne and Chappel—controlled companies producing 75% of the output of foreign mines (Yip, 1969, p. 21).[7] As Putucheary notes (1960, p. 91), this control, which is exercised through management functions and interlocking directorships, is backed by ownership;[8] though the ownership is a good deal less overwhelming than in the past.

Of considerable interest in terms of the Beckford–Girvan thesis, is how the foreign sector is linked to interests outside the country. Thus, at one extreme, firms might simply have foreign directors, shareholders and foreign registration, but no other foreign connections, or they might be part of vast international combines like Tate and Lyle (Beckford, 1972, pp. 128–40), highly vertically integrated and controlling production of the final product, manufacture of machinery, etc. Links might also be horizontal, to other countries or other commodities.

The Anglo-Oriental/London Tin Corporation group has been linked to the Patino group since before the Second World War (Fox, 1974, p. 9). Patino originally controlled half of Bolivian tin production (though it was nationalized in Bolivia in 1952) and currently controls about a third of the world tin smelting capacity (Fox, 1974, p. 10). Ultimate control in London Tin has changed somewhat. In 1973 the Singapore-based firm of Haw Par Brothers International bought 29% of London Tin's shares (Fox, 1974, p. 10). Haw Par Brothers, a firm whose original capital derives from the famous Tiger Balm fortune in Singapore, operates primarily in Malaysia, Singapore and Hong Kong, with interests including shipping, insurance, merchant banking and pharmaceuticals. Haw Par in turn was half-owned by the U.K.-based firm of Slater–Walker Securities from 1971to 1974, when Slater Walker sold its interests, half of which went to Charter Consolidated (*Straits Times*, July 1974), a U.K.-based international mining finance group with an exceptionally wide range of manufacturing and mining activities in many countries.[9]

Thus the European sector is highly integrated within Malaysia and has important connections with world smelting interests. Yet the minority interest of Charter Consolidated in Haw Par, and thence in London Tin, appears to be the only significant connection with mining activity other than tin outside Malaysia, though Charter Consolidated also bought into Tronoh Mines in Malaysia in 1965 (Fox, 1974, p. 27), and London Tin has some tin mining interests elsewhere, particularly in Thailand and Nigeria. These rather loose connections with other mining industries are illustrative of a much less integrated structure within the world tin industry than in other non-ferrous metals, and in particular there appears to have been little connection between tin and other metal developments (Fox, 1974, p. 8). Nor does the degree of vertical integration within Malaysia seem great. European mining interests own one of the two tin smelters in Malaysia (about which, more in Section 5.4), but the other smelter is largely independent, and there seems to have been very little backward integration into sources of mining supplies.

What is the effect of the high degree of horizontal integration in the European sector on 'local' producers? Wong Lin Ken has argued that the British colonial government favoured the European sector (including smelting) by means of preferential land alienation policy and other measures (Wong, 1965, pp. 237–8), and presumably their highly integrated structure enabled more effective representations to be made to the government (e.g. about tin control schemes). Putucheary argues that the major effect on local producers operates through European control of smelting charges and the advances made by smelters to miners (Putucheary, 1960, p. 93), but in fact much of the Chinese miners' output is smelted by the Straits Trading Company which is not obviously under European control (see Section 5.4). While smelting charges and advances may have some influence on local miners, and dredging companies control of land in some areas may also be important, it is nevertheless the case that there is a large and apparently thriving 'local' sector whose share of output has grown from 1960 to the present form a third to just over a half.

The coexistence of 'foreign' and 'local' producers is largely a question of the coexistence of two techniques of dredging and gravel pumping. Local producers, still almost exclusively Chinese, were not able to enter dredging until very recently because they could not mobilize the large capital sums involved. European companies have been largely confined to dredging, though the major open cast company (Sungei Besi) is European, and certain very old gravel pump mines such as Gopeng, are in European hands. The main reason for European companies' preference for dredging seems to be partly non-economic, in that they have preferred what they see as more advanced technology and dislike handling the large labour forces necessary in gravel pumping; and partly that in the past dredging may have been the more profitable technique.

To some extent the coexistence of gravel pumping and dredging can be explained in technical terms. Even if dredging were the more profitable technique for the private investor, there are certain areas which dredges cannot mine—hillsides, pinnacled limestone deposits, and in general any deposit of less than about 400 acres (necessary for minimum throughput). Conversely, gravel pump mines cannot operate in swampy areas or offshore[10], though they can operate (with double pumping) at the same depths (150') as the deepest dredges. However much ground worked by dredges *could* technically be worked by gravel pumps. The fact that gravel pumps are not working such areas may be due to the historical accident of their being alienated to dredging companies as a result of preferential government treatment in the past, or it may be that dredging was the more profitable technique at the time. Whether dredging is now a more profitable technique for the private investor (or socially) is an important issue. Much of the answer is implicit in Section 5.2, and rates of return on investment are considered explicitly in Chapter 9. Available evidence, to be presented in Chapter 9, suggests that at present (i.e. 1974–5) gravel pumping is the more profitable technique, both for the private firm and for Malaysian society as a whole. Indeed this may be an explanation of the relative decline in dredging since 1960 though it may also reflect foreign investors wishing to pull out of Malaysia (Yip, 1969, p. 367).

The coexistence of other mining methods is easier to explain. Underground mining operates on lodes rather than alluvial deposits, and alluvial methods could not be used. Hydraulicing is simply a form of gravel pumping using natural rather than artificial power and is used when a suitable nearby head of water exists. Open cast mining has extremely high operating costs per unit of throughput and works therefore only very rich deposits, and the same is true of dulang washing.

Finally, there is the question of Malay participation in mining. This is an important objective of Malaysian government policy (see Chapter 4), yet the earlier part of this section shows that tin mining has been basically split between Europeans and Chinese. Yip's research on shareholdings in locally incorporated dredging companies in Malaysia showed that in 1964 Chinese accounted for nearly 92% of local shareholdings while Malays owned under 3% (and Indians 5%) (Yip, 1969, p. 361). Since, until very recently, there were virtually no known cases of Malays owning gravel pump mines, it is clear that the Malay stake in the ownership (and control) of mining is negligible.

Entry by Malays into tin mining is hampered both by lack of skills and lack of finance. Lack of finance in the past would have been an overwhelming problem in dredging, just as it was for the Chinese, but with the development of the stock exchange and the widespread purchases of mining shares in the 1960's, this problem is now less severe. Nevertheless, the major scope for individual Malay enterprise seems to be gravel pumping. Here previous experience is of great importance. Table 5.3 shows how few Malays have been employed in mining, though the proportion has risen somewhat since the 1950's, and Table 5.4 shows that existing Malay employment is in dredging (and it is also predominantly unskilled). Yip (1969, pp. 377–8) records that the Mines Department had bought several gravel pump mines for leasing to Malays, and at present it is through public-sector initiative that Malay participation is

TABLE 5.3 ETHNIC COMPOSITION OF PENINSULAR MALAYSIAN MINING LABOUR FORCE, 1911-72, SELECTED YEARS

(percentages)

	MALAY	CHINESE	INDIAN	EUROPEAN	OTHER
1911	1	96	2	-	-
1915	1	94	3	1	-
1920	3	93	4	-	-
1925	2	86	9	-	-
1930	3	88	8	1	-
1935	5	84	10	1	-
1938	7	79	13	1	-
1947	13	76	10	1	-
1957	16	72	10	2	
1968	18	71	10	1	
1972	21	69	9	1	

Sources and Notes

(1) 1911-38 from Mines Dept., AR's: percentages of all mining labour.

(2) 1947 and 1957 from A Report on the 1947 Census of Population Malaya, (Malaya, 1947) and 1957 Population Census, Report No. 14, Final Report, (Federation of Malaya, 1957), respectively. These have been used in preference to Mines Department sources as they refer to tin mining employment.

(3) 1968 from Ministry of Labour HLS, 1968 and refers to proportions of tin mining labour force, 1972 from Mines Dept., BSMI 1972.

(4) Dulang washers are excluded.

TABLE 5.4 ETHNIC COMPOSITION OF MINING LABOUR FORCE, PENINSULAR MALAYSIA, 1972

(percentages)

	Malay	Chinese	Indian	Other
Dredging	40	34	24	1
Gravel Pumping	12	82	5	-
Underground	30	68	1	-
Open Cast	35	51	13	1
All Mining	21	69	9	1

Sources and Notes

(1) From Mines Department BSMI 1972.

(2) Figures refer to all mining employment, of which tin mining employment in 1972 was over 95% (and higher in gravel pumping and dredging).

preceeding, albeit rather slowly.[11] There are two main avenues. The first is PERNAS Mining, set up in 1972 as a subsidiary of PERNAS, the Malaysian National Corporation which operates as a trust for holding shares eventually to be purchased by individual Malays. PERNAS is primarily responsible for off-shore mining operations, though it has also prospected inland (e.g. in Kelantan, Pahang Tenggara, Penang) and in November 1974 it was planning the construction of an offshore dredge to work off the coast of Perak, the first dredge of its kind in Malaysia (interview, November 1974). At the time of writing, PERNAS, who already own 20% of London Tin, has been negotiating for a substantial (39.7%) share in Haw Par Brothers International who, it was noted earlier, have a large (and in practice a controlling) interest in the London Tin Corporation (*Straits Times*, June 1975), though negotiations are running into substantial difficulty especially with the Singapore Stock Exchange (*Far Eastern Economic Review*, 11 July 1975). The second avenue for increased Malay participation is through the new mining activities of State Economic Development Corporations, notably Selangor and Perak. Selangor SEDC is constructing a new dredge in Selangor, the Perak SEDC is to start a gravel pump mine in 1975, and it was reported in the Malaysian press that a joint venture between Associated Mines and the Perak SEDC was being negotiated (*Straits Times*, June 1974), though nothing has

TABLE 5.5 TIN EXPORT CONTROL 1931-73

Year	% Release	Year	% Release
1931	66.3	1958	58.8
32	32.8	59	61.9
33	24.3	60	92.7
34	32.8	1968-9	96.0
35	42.3	1973	Exports restricted to 1972 level
36	67.0		
37	77.7		
38	41.2		
39	53.0		

Sources and Notes

(1) 1931-39 figures from Mines Department AR, 1939. The percentage release figures refer to the amount of the FMS's "standard tonnage" which it was allowed to export.

(2) 1958-60 figures from Meerhaeghe (1966, p. 217) and 1968-9, and 1973 from Fox (1974, pp. 371 and 383).

been heard of this since. Joint ventures have also been reported in prospecting in Kelantan, with agreements by foreign mining companies to train Malay workers and managers for eventual Malay control (*Straits Times*, 1974, June).

5.1.3 Tin Control and the International Tin Agreements

Some information was given in Section 4•3 on international attempts to control production and to stabilize prices in the inter-war period. These attempts were revised after the war, and since 1956 four International Tin Agreements have been in force, each lasting five years; and the fifth Agreement, to run from 1976, has just been negotiated. All have combined the basic features of a buffer stock strengthened by the right to impose export control on producing members. Details of the agreements are given in Fox (1974) and the purpose of the present subsection is very briefly to outline the export controls which have been in force since the war, since such controls may influence the structure of payments to be examined in Section 5.2.

Table 5.5 shows the years since 1931 when exports have been under control. It shows how the very severe pre-war control, averaging about at 50% release from the producer's standard tonnage (a figure based on pre-control output), contrasts with relatively mild control in the post-war years. Only in 1958-60 has substantial control been in force, and the 1968-9 and 1973 controls have been minimal.

All major producers except Brazil and China are party to the Agreements, as are most of the main consumers—except for the U.S.A. whose interests are rather different because of its strategic stockpile. Contributions to the buffer stock are made almost entirely by producers, aided since 1970 by the right to use drawing rights with the International Monetary Fund to finance contributions. Among the consumers, only France and the Netherlands have made contributions.

5.2 CURRENT PAYMENTS STRUCTURE OF TIN MINING

This section examines the structure of payments made out of the income from tin exports, following the methodology of Chapter 3 (Section 3•3). It aims at a comparison between tin dredging (the predominantly 'foreign' sector) and gravel pump tin mining (the predominantly 'local' sector). The data split into four periods. The period 1963–72 is covered by the *Censuses of Mining Industries in West Malaysia*, though sectoral statistics for tin mining are not given until 1964.[12] For 1946–63 series can be constructed by sector for wages and some other important inputs. A wider range of input series is available for 1910–39, although the statistics themselves are less reliable. No regular series exist for before 1910, and a picture has to be built up from qualitative information and statistical fragments.

5.2.1 1963–72

The *Census of Mining Industries* gives aggregate values of wages, labour benefits, and materials for all tin mining for 1963, and for dredging and 'all other tin mining' separately from 1964. Table 5.6 is a summary of this information and provides the basis for a first comparison between the payments structures of the two sectors.

The picture which emerges is one of a high ratio of value-added product to produced product for both sectors. Value-added is currently over 60% of gross output

TABLE 5.6 CURRENT PAYMENTS STRUCTURE OF TIN MINING IN PENINSULAR MALAYSIA 1963-72

(percentages of Annual Value of Output)

	(i) Annual Value of Output ($ mil)	(ii) Total Wages & Salaries	(iii) Payment in kind	(iv) Total Materials	(v) Repair and Maintenance	(vi) Gross Profits	(vii) Total Value Added	(viii) Export Duty
All Tin Mining								
1963	445.0	19.5	...	13.6	...	66.9	86.4	15.9
Dredging								
1964	266.1	11.7	0.2	8.3	...	79.8	91.7	15.4
65	293.1	11.1	0.2	9.7	...	79.0	90.3	15.7
66	255.2	13.1	0.2	12.3	...	74.4	87.7	15.7
67	240.3	14.8	0.2	13.7	...	71.3	86.3	15.7
68	219.6	14.9	0.2	11.8	9.3	61.3	76.4	15.5
69	250.4	12.1	0.5	9.9	10.6	56.2	68.9	16.0
1970	262.3	11.6	...	15.9	...	72.5	84.1	16.0
71	255.1	12.9	...	18.4	...	68.7	81.6	16.0
72	248.3	12.9	...	20.2	...	66.9	79.8	16.0
Other Tin Mining								
1964	324.8	18.8	2.4	18.2	...	60.6	81.8	15.4
65	420.5	18.2	2.7	18.4	...	60.7	81.6	15.7
66	452.4	20.2	3.1	21.0	...	55.7	79.0	15.7
67	451.4	20.5	3.2	23.1	...	53.2	76.9	15.7
68	450.4	20.3	3.1	22.0	7.9	46.6	70.0	15.5
69	463.0	19.4	3.3	20.6	8.4	39.9	62.6	16.0
1970	503.4	18.7	...	29.2	...	52.1	70.8	16.0
71	433.8	18.8	...	35.2	...	46.0	64.8	16.0
72	443.0	21.1	...	36.8	...	42.0	63.2	16.0

Sources and Notes

(1) 1963-71 figures from Statistics Department CMin I 1963-71, and 1972 figures from Statistics Department PR 1972.

(2) Output value figures from Statistics Department, MSB's and from Mines Department BSMI's, 1955-72. Output values given in the CMin I are quoted net of export duty and smelters charges.

value for 'other tin mining' (predominantly gravel pumping) and nearly 80% for dredging, with wage payments of 10–15% in dredging and about 20% in gravel pumping. Profits make up the bulk of value-added, with gross profits (i.e. before tax, export duty and depreciation) ranging from approximately 60–80% of gross output in dredging and 40–60% in gravel pumping over the 1964-72 period.

In both sectors the share of wages has remained fairly constant over the period, but the share of materials purchases has risen substantially, to current figures of 20% and 35% of output for dredging and gravel pumping, respectively. In gravel pumping this is partly a reflection of a rise in power use per unit of output (which rose 32% 1964–72) and increases in materials costs (e.g. diesel costs rose nearly 20% over the same period—see Mines Dept., *BSMI's* 1964–72), and power use in dredging rose too (by

27%) though materials' costs rose by far less. Also important however, is the possibility that the coverage of materials purchased has risen in the *Census of Mining Industries* over the period, and that some expenditure on repairs and maintenance which was not included before 1969 now appears in the input figures.[13] More details of trends of wage and material costs and profits are given in Table 5.7, which shows

TABLE 5.7 TIN MINING COSTS AND PROFITS 1964-72

($ per picul concentrates)

	(i) Total Costs per picul	(ii) Material Cost per picul	(iii) Wage and Salary Cost per picul	(iv) Gross Profit per picul	(v) Price per picul metallic tin
Dredging					
1964	93.7	38.4	54.5	370.5	619
65	110.3	51.0	58.4	416.2	702
66	123.8	59.7	63.2	360.0	645
67	129.4	61.8	66.6	320.6	600
68	113.8 (153.1)	49.9 (89.3)	62.9	309.9 (270.1)	565
69	108.4 (158.2)	46.4 (96.2)	59.6	361.1 (311.3)	626
1970	137.2	79.3	57.9	361.6	665
71	148.3	87.0	61.3	325.7	632
72	155.6	95.0	60.6	313.9	626
'Other Tin Mining'					
1964	183.4	84.5	87.4	280.8	619
65	206.9	96.8	96.0	319.6	702
66	214.6	101.8	97.5	269.4	645
67	210.6	103.9	92.4	269.2	600
68	192.8 (226.5)	93.8 (127.5)	86.2	230.9 (197.2)	565
69	218.1 (257.9)	96.5 (136.3)	106.3	251.4 (211.6)	626
1970	239.0	145.5	93.5	259.8	665
71	256.0	166.7	89.3	218.0	632
72	228.1	145.0	83.1	241.4	626

Sources and Notes

(1) All data except prices from Statistics Department CMin I 1964-71 and PR 1972. Prices from Mines Department BSMI's.

(2) Column iv = (Column v x 0.75) - Column i

(3) Column i includes value of labour benefits not included in iii.

(4) Bracketed items are figures where repair and maintenance expenditure is explicitly taken into account.

that profits per picul have fallen somewhat since the mid-1960's in spite of a revival of the tin price which dipped in 1967–8, perhaps due to a declining grade of ground worked (from 0.29 katis per cubic yard in 1964 to 0.22 in 1972 in the case of dredges–see Mines Dept., *BSMI's*, 1966–72), though also due possibly to the increased coverage of costs in the mining census. The imposition of a minor degree of export control in 1968-69 (see subsection 5.1.3) has had no perceptible effect on the payments structure.

This picture of the overall payments structure of the tin industry corresponds to that given in the *Interindustry Accounts* of West Malaysia, (Statistics Dept., 1965).

TABLE 5.8

MATERIALS PURCHASES OF TIN INDUSTRY, 1963-71, SELECTED YEARS: MINING CENSUS DATA

($ Mil)	(i) Diesel Oil	(ii) Petrol	(iii) Wood for Fuel	(iv) Other Fuels	(v) Elect-ricity from CEB	(vi) Elect-ricity from Prhep Co.	(vii) Other Elect-ricity	(viii) Lubri-cating oil and Grease	(ix) Explo-sives	(x) Timber (not for fuel)	(xi) Iron Cast-ings	(xii) Cement	(xiii) Chem-icals	(xiv) Other Mater-ials
All Tin														
1963	——	——	21.8	——	19.5	15.3	15.3	2.9	0.3	——	——	0.8	——	——
Dredging														
1964	1.0	0.3	0.7	0.9	8.7	7.3	-	0.7	-	0.3	1.7	-	-	-
1966	1.1	0.3	0.7	0.7	9.6	7.8	-	0.7	-	0.4	1.9	-	0.2	8.1
1971	0.5	0.5	-	-	11.4	11.0	-	——	——	——	19.6	——	——	——
Other Tin Mining														
1964	22.1	0.5	0.2	0.2	4.6	14.9	0.3	3.4	0.4	5.3	6.8	0.2	-	-
1966	38.0	0.9	0.4	0.1	7.8	19.3	0.6	5.0	0.6	7.1	10.8	0.4	-	4.1
1971	50.5	1.3	0.4	-	6.2	25.6	-	——	——	——	45.0	——	——	——

Sources and Notes

(1) All figures from Statistics Department CMin I 1963-71.

(2) 1964 figures for Other Materials include only water.

(3) CEB = Central Electricity Board; PRHEP CO. = Perak River Hydro-Electric Power Company.

(4) 1971 'Other Tin Mining' figures refer to gravel pumping only.

These show that in 1965 in mining, (where tin mining is about 80% of the value of output) payments to primary factors of production (i.e. value-added) were 84.4% of gross output.[14] Labour payments were 27.9%, entrepreneurial income 72.1% of primary factor payments net of indirect tax, which is appreciably more capital intensive than for the economy as a whole, where labour earnings were 41.9% and entrepreneurial earnings 58.1% of value-added (excluding indirect taxation) in 1965 (see Table 5.27)

Moving from the value-added component to the 'produced-product' component of tin industry purchases, Table 5.8 gives detailed breakdown of materials purchased by the two sectors, and it is immediately apparent that most materials are fuel of various kinds, with diesel most important in gravel pumping and electricity in dredging. 'Other

TABLE 5.9 DREDGING COMPANIES PROFITS, TAX AND DIVIDEND PAYMENTS, 1963-73

(Percentages of Annual Value of Output)

	(i) Gross Profit Before Tax	(ii) Taxes	(iii) Dividends
1963	66.7	21.0	26.9
64	57.6	17.6	24.5
65	69.1	24.0	25.9
66	68.8	24.6	26.2
67	61.8	21.8	24.4
68	54.7	18.5	19.1
69	57.0	19.4	19.5
1970	59.6	20.4	20.3
71	55.0	16.7	20.3
72	55.1	18.2	19.0
73	53.5	20.8	14.4

Sources and Notes

(1) Column i figures are quoted before deduction of export duty.

(2) All figures obtained from company reports summarized, company by company, in Zorn and Leigh-Hunt (1970b and 1974).

(3) The companies listed in Zorn and Leigh-Hunt (1970b) produced 78% of all Malaysian dredging output in 1968, and the 1973 listed companies produced 83% of 1973 Malaysian dredging output.

[Statistics compiled from Manual of Tin Mining Companies, 1970 and Manual of Rubber and Tin Producing Companies, 1974, reproduced by permission of Messrs. Zorn and Leigh-Hunt (stockbrokers).]

TABLE 5.10 PAYMENT STRUCTURE OF EIGHT LARGE DREDGING COMPANIES, 1972-74

(Percentages of Annual Value of Output)

	Composition of Costs						Profits		Payments from Profits		
	(i) Operating Costs	(ii) (Repairs & Renewals)	(iii) Realization Charges	(iv) Depreciation	(v) U.K. Expenses	(vi) Total Costs	(vii) Total Gross Profits from Sale of Tin	(viii) Other Proceeds	(ix) Malaysian Export Duty	(x) Tax	(xi) Dividends
1972-3	38.8	(2.6)	3.1	4.1	0.8	49.2	46.8	9.0	16.0	22.1	15.4
1973-4	29.5	(2.3)	2.7	4.5	0.5	33.1	58.6	9.9	17.9	27.4	14.2

Sources and Notes

(1) Figures compiled from the 1973-74 Annual Reports of the following companies, which in 1973 produced 74% of Malaysian tin dredging output:- Southern Kinta Consolidated Ltd., Malayan Tin Dredging Ltd., Southern Malayan Tin Dredging Ltd., Kamunting Tin Dredging Ltd., Berjuntai Tin Dredging Bhd., Selangor Dredging Bhd., Ayer Hitam Tin Dredging Ltd., Tronoh Mines Ltd.

(2) Column ii included in column i figure. Figures for column i, iii, v, x excludes Ayer Hitam and Tronoh, for which figures were not given, and column ii based on Southern Kinta and Kamunting only. Column vi includes export duty and excludes other proceeds. In view of these differences between columns, components (e.g. of costs) will not necessarily equal the totals.

tin' in 1972 accounted for over 75% of the total materials purchased by tin mining (Statistics Dept., *PR*, 1972).

For dredging, to supplement the information from the *Census of Mining Industries*, data have been compiled from individual company statistics to be found in the *Manual of Tin Mining Companies* (now incorporated in their *Manual of Rubber and Tin Producing Companies*), produced annually since 1967 by the London Stockbrokers, Messrs. Zorn and Leigh-Hunt. The *Manuals* give data going back to 1963 (and to 1962 for a few companies) for all companies whose shares are traded on the London Stock Exchange.[15] Table 5.9 summarizes the Zorn and Leigh-Hunt data; and the importance of gross profits is clear. These ranged from over 50% to nearly 70% of gross export income in the 1963–72 period. Gross profits are less than those calculated as a residual after wages and materials payments were deducted from gross export income in Table 5.6. This is to be expected since companies have costs in addition to labour and materials, but the same trend towards declining profitability can be seen. Taxes and export duties take nearly 40% points of export income, leaving some 15% to 25% for dividends.

To supplement in turn the Zorn and Leigh-Hunt statistics, which give only profit, tax and dividend payments, the annual reports of eight of the largest dredging companies were taken which give details of operating costs, repairs and renewals, depreciation, overseas expenses and proceeds other than from the sale of tin. The results are shown in Table 5.10. Operating costs are shown to be some 5–10% points less than total costs, depreciation allowances are about 5%. U.K. expenses (and almost all foreign-incorporated companies are based in the U.K.) are slight, while 'other proceeds' are nearly 10% of export income. However, other proceeds are exaggerated since the companies hold investments in one another, leading to double counting.

An alternative source of information on the payments structure of tin companies is the *Report on the Financial Survey of Limited Companies Malaysia 1967*, published by the Department of Statistics. This covers all tin companies, both private and public, but unfortunately has not been published since 1967 though it is described as 'annual'. Thirty-one percent of 1967 tin output was produced however by unincorporated businesses which were not covered in the *Survey*, (Statistics Dept., *CMinI*, 1967). Since virtually no unincorporated firms exist in the dredging sector this statistic implies that less than half of 'other tin mining' output originated in firms covered by the *Survey*. Table 5.11 summarizes the *Survey's* findings. Foreign-controlled and foreign-incorporated firms will be predominantly dredging. Their profits, direct tax payments and dividends are slightly lower than the companies in Table 5.9. Their labour purchases are greater than is suggested in Table 5.6 and their purchases of materials and services are also larger. Malaysian-incorporated dredging companies appear to be slightly more profitable than foreign-incorporated ones. Malaysian-incorporated, locally controlled companies will include both some of the larger gravel pump mines and a few dredging companies. Profits in this sector seem very low in comparison with the figures in earlier tables either for dredging or gravel pumping and are difficult to interpret.

The first part of this subsection has built up a detailed and quite complete breakdown of the structure of payments from export income from both tin sectors, and the next step in the analysis is to determine what proportion of these payments is lost immediately to the domestic economy in the form of outflows abroad.

Turning first to dredging, the most interesting feature of the results so far is the size of profits. It was shown that gross profits are about 50% to 60% of export income.

TABLE 5.11 CURRENT PAYMENTS STRUCTURE OF PRIVATE AND PUBLIC TIN MINING COMPANIES IN MALAYSIA, 1967: SURVEY OF LIMITED COMPANIES DATA

(Items as Percentages of Annual Revenue from Sales of Goods and Services)

	(i) Malaysian Incorporated Locally Controlled Companies	(ii) Malaysian Incorporated Foreign Controlled Companies	(iii) Foreign Incorporated Companies
Current Profits before Direct Tax, Duty and Indirect Tax	15.2	50.1	45.5
Duty and Indirect Tax	3.8	14.8	15.1
Direct Tax	6.1	17.5	14.7
Wages and Salaries (including Contract Labour)	29.3	15.0	21.8
Purchases of Goods and Services	52.8	28.4	26.3
Depreciation and Depletion	7.4	5.2	6.8
Dividends Paid	4.2	20.2	15.7
Payments to Overseas Shareholders	0.2	13.4	...
Retained Profits	1.0	-2.4	...
Revenue other than from Current Sales	10.1	4.9	3.1
Annual Revenue from Sales of Goods and Services	$106.4m	$91.6m	$199.3m

Sources and Notes

(1) All data from Statistics Department FSLC 1967.

(2) A locally-controlled company is defined as a company with Malaysian ownership of over 50% of its voting shares. A foreign controlled company has less than 50% local ownership.

(3) For foreign incorporated companies "dividends paid" are assumed in the absence of more detailed information to be equivalent to "investment income accruing to Head Office" in Appendix Table F of the Survey.

(4) 'Current Profits' include 'Other Revenue'.

Profits are the obvious item to flow abroad from an export industry 'enclave'. In fact nearly two-thirds of these profits are retained by the Malaysian government as export duty and income tax. Export duty has been constant at about 15% of gross output value for the whole of this century.[16] Income tax was first imposed on companies in Malaysia in 1948 at 20%. It was raised to 30% in 1951 and to the present level of 40% in 1959 (Lim Chong Yah, 1967, p. 265). In addition there is a Tin Profits Tax,[17] dating from 1965[18] and a 5% Development Tax dating from 1967 (Bank Negara Malaysia, *AR*, 1967). Thus only 15%–25% of export income is left to flow abroad. The extent to which dividend payments actually do flow abroad depends mainly on the proportion of the *current* value of issued capital of the dredging companies which is owned by Malaysian residents (excluding resident 'Europeans'). Research on local ownership has been carried out by Yip Yat Hoong of the University of Malaya for Malaysian-incorporated companies (Yip, 1968). Yip's findings are elaborated,[19] and extended to include U.K.-incorporated companies. The results are presented in Table 5.12. The results for U.K. companies are based on a postal survey conducted in March and April 1970.

TABLE 5.12 OWNERSHIP OF CAPITAL IN TIN DREDGING COMPANIES, 1970

	1970 Value of Issued Capital ($ Mil)	Estimated Percentage of Capital Held by Malaysian Residents
Malaysian-incorporated	208.6	56.3
U.K.-incorporated	265.1	20.0
Malaysian and U.K.-incorporated	473.8	35.1

Sources and Notes

(1) Details are given in Appendix 5.4. Almost all non-Malaysian incorporated companies are incorporated in the U.K.

From these tables it can be seen that approximately a third of the current value of dredging capital is owned in Malaysia. Thus only some 25–30% of gross profits representing about 10%–15% of the value of gross output, flows abroad as dividend payments. Foreign tax payments are negligible.[20] Thus nearly three-quarters of dredging profits are retained in Malaysia. Tin dredging which it will be remembered represents the 'foreign' sector of tin mining, is an enclave whose isolation from the domestic economy has been much reduced.[21,22]

TABLE 5.13 LOCAL AND FOREIGN PAYMENTS IN TIN DREDGING, PENINSULAR MALAYSIA, 1972

(Percentages of Annual Value of Output)

	Total	Local	Foreign	Unallocated
Costs				
Wages (including payments in kind)	13.2	12.2	1.0	-
Materials	20.2	10.0	-	10.2
Other Operating Costs	5.7	-	-	5.7
Depreciation	4.1	4.1	-	-
U.K. Expenses	0.8	-	0.8	-
Other Costs	5.2	3.1	-	2.1
Total Costs	49.2	29.4	1.8	18.0
Allocation of Gross Profits				
(100 - Total Costs + 5.0% Other Proceeds)				
Export Duty	16.0	16.0	-	-
Tax	22.1	21.1	1.0	-
Dividends	15.4	5.7	9.7	
Other Payments	2.3	-	-	2.3
Total Allocation of Export Income (including 'Other Proceeds')	105.0	72.2	12.5	20.3

Sources and Notes

(1) Wages - Foreign component consists of number of Europeans (71) employed in dredging (Mines Department BSMI 1972) at an assumed monthly salary of $3000.

(2) Materials - Electricity is taken as the main local purchase (8.4%) of 1971 output, and this is rounded up to 10% to include other local purchases such as timber and iron castings.

(3) Dividends split according to information in Table 5.12.

(4) Foreign component of tax is U.K. tax estimated on information (not elsewhere shown) from company reports.

(5) 'Other proceeds' are scaled down from nearly 10% in Table 5.10 to take account of the fact that they include substantial earnings from shares in other dredging companies in Malaysia.

Table 5.13 is a summary of local and foreign payments in dredging and provides further evidence of how little isolated is the dredging 'enclave'. It indicates that nearly three-quarters of dredging current payments are local in the first instance.

Table 5.14 performs a similar exercize for 'other tin' which, it will be remembered, is predominantly Chinese gravel pumping. Assuming mining profits accruing to local Chinese are not exported, at least 80% of current export income is retained locally.

Taking into account the indirect import content of materials purchases would alter the results little, especially in dredging. In dredging, the total (i.e. direct and indirect)

TABLE 5.14 LOCAL AND FOREIGN PAYMENTS IN "OTHER TIN MINING", PENINSULAR MALAYSIA, 1972

(Percentages of Annual Value of Output)

	Total	Local	Foreign	Unallocated
Wages (including payments in kind)	24.4	24.3	0.1	-
Materials	36.8	20.0	-	16.8
Realization Charges	3.0	3.0	-	-
Allocation of Gross Profits (36.1%)				
Export Duty	16.0	16.0	-	-
Foreign Dividends	1.2	-	1.2	-
Malaysian Tax	8.0	8.0	-	-
Other Payments	10.6	10.6	-	-
Total Allocation of Export Income	100.0	81.9	1.3	16.8

Sources and Notes

(1) Wages - Foreign component consists of number of Europeans (9) employed in 1972 (Mines Department BSMI 1972) at assumed monthly wage of $3000.

(2) Materials - Diesel is the main purchase (11.6% of gross output in 1971) and two-thirds is locally purchased in the first instance (see Section 5.4). Other local purchases include electricity (7.3%), timber, cement, iron castings.

(3) Foreign dividends - In 1971 (Statistics Department CMin I 1971) non-Malaysian firms produced 15% of the ground pump output. Assuming they had profits similar to Malaysian firms (36% of output) and paid nearly half of those profits after duty in tax, only 1.5% of gross output value would be left for remission overseas, i.e. 15% of (36.1-16.0) x 0.4.

(4) Malaysian tax-take reduced to 40% to take account of depreciation allowance.

(5) 'Other payments' will be predominantly local profit.

import content in the main materials input, electricity is only 6.4% (Lo, 1972, p. 57), less than ½% of dredging output. In petroleum products it was 70% (Lo, 1972, p. 57), which is equivalent to 8% of gravel pump output value, but increasing quantities of East Malaysian crude oil are being locally refined and the import content may now be much less (since Lo's figures refer to 1965). Unfortunately no more recent input–output table than 1965 is available from which more up-to-date indirect import requirements could be calculated.

5.2.2 1946–63[23]

In Subsection 5.2.1 the present-day structure of current payments made out of tin export income was set out in detail. The present subsection tries to trace back the structure of these payments to the Second World War. Data for the 1946–63 period are not sufficiently complete for a proper breakdown between local and foreign payments to be made. Nevertheless any major changes in payments to inputs or government would indicate changes in the proportion of export income retained in the country, and show possible changes in linkage effects, etc.

Export duty payments are available from official sources, while electricity purchases by the tin industry can be compiled from Electricity Department records. Also, enough information exists to compile a reliable series for wage payments, and slightly less reliable ones for transport charges to port and for smelting charges.[24] Table 5.15 summarizes dredging current payments, and Table 5.16 summarizes those of gravel pumping. Reference back to Table 5.6 provides comparison with the 1964–72 period.

In dredging, wage payments have been fairly constant throughout the whole of the post-war period at about 15% of export income. There are dips in years of very high tin prices such as 1951–2 (and 1965–6), and in the years of export control (1958–60) wage payments seem somewhat higher than in subsequent years as a proportion of output. Export duty payments have been constant, while electricity purchases seem to have increased somewhat. Transport and smelting charges have also altered little in importance. Thus the payments structure appears to have been constant throughout

TABLE 5.15 TIN DREDGING CURRENT PAYMENTS, 1946-63

(Percentages of Value of Output)

	(i) Value of Output ($Mil)	(ii) Wages and Labour Benefits	(iii) Electricity Purchases	(iv) Transport Costs to Port	(v) Smelting Charges	(vi) Export Duty	(vii) Tin Price ($ per Picul)
1946	7.3	153.8 (sic)	...	0.7	2.6	12.2	170
1947	44.8	37.9	...	0.5	2.6	14.7	218
1948	99.8	15.4	...	0.4	1.9	14.6	281
1949	131.8	14.0	...	0.3	1.9	14.7	294
1950	171.9	12.6	2.9	0.3	1.5	14.8	367
1951	256.3	9.6	2.6	0.2	1.1	15.7	527
1952	238.8	11.2	3.5	0.3	1.1	15.2	480
1953	174.8	15.4	5.0	0.3	1.5	15.1	363
1954	187.1	15.5	4.4	0.3	1.5	15.2	354
1955	190.8	15.8	4.8	0.3	1.5	14.9	363
1956	199.7	15.2	4.8	0.4	1.4	14.6	387
1957	176.2	19.9	6.2	0.4	1.5	14.7	373
1958	123.4	17.6	11.3	0.4	2.2	12.4	369
1959	125.9	15.2	9.5	0.4	2.0	14.2	397
1960	185.3	14.6	6.5	0.4	2.1	16.1	394
1961	222.5	12.8	6.7	0.3	1.8	15.4	447
1962	214.7	13.6	7.5	0.3	1.8	15.2	448
1963	210.5	15.2	7.5	0.3	1.8	15.5	445

Sources and Notes

(1) Output values calculated from outputs and prices from Mines Department BSMI's.

(2) For details of the construction of the time series used to calculate the percentages in columns ii to v, see Appendices 5.1 (wages and labour benefits), 5.3 (electricity), and 5.2 (transport and smelting charges).

(3) Export duty figures from Mines Department BSMI to 1955, BSMI 1956-60, and Annual BSMI's 1961-63. Duty payments are allocated to dredging (and to gravel pumping in Table 5.16) according to the sector's share in total output.

TABLE 5.16 GRAVEL PUMP MINING CURRENT PAYMENTS, 1946-63

(Percentages of Value of Output)

	(i) Value of Output ($Mil)	(ii) Wages and Labour Benefits	(iii) Electricity Purchases	(iv) Transport Costs	(v) Smelting Charges	(vi) Export Duty	(vii) Tin Price ($ per Picul)
1946	9.4	66.0	...	0.7	2.6	12.2	170
1947	30.8	50.6	...	0.5	2.6	14.7	218
1948	74.0	41.4	...	0.4	2.0	14.6	281
1949	91.6	33.8	...	0.4	1.9	14.7	294
1950	130.5	21.4	4.7	0.3	1.5	14.8	367
1951	167.2	25.5	4.6	0.2	1.1	15.7	527
1952	174.2	24.1	4.8	0.3	1.1	15.2	480
1953	132.9	23.7	7.1	0.3	1.5	15.1	363
1954	134.1	26.5	7.1	0.3	1.5	15.2	354
1955	147.5	22.2	7.7	0.3	1.5	14.9	363
1956	162.0	31.8	7.6	0.4	1.6	14.6	387
1957	152.8	26.0	8.5	0.4	1.5	14.7	373
1958	87.1	36.8	10.1	0.4	2.2	12.4	369
1959	92.6	19.6	9.9	0.4	2.0	14.2	397
1960	117.9	20.7	9.8	0.4	2.1	16.1	394
1961	145.1	21.2	9.3	0.3	1.8	15.5	447
1962	166.2	20.2	8.9	0.3	1.8	15.2	448
1963	182.1	20.5	8.4	0.3	1.8	15.5	445

Sources and Notes

(1) As for Table 5.15.

the period, in terms of factor payments and duty payments. What has changed, however, is the proportion of profits paid in taxes to the government. This was noted in the previous subsection, and is the main cause of rises in the proportion of tin dredging export income retained in Malaysia during the post-war period, together with increases in local holdings of dredging shares.

In contrast to dredging where the input series in Table 5.15 are complete in all essential respects, one major series is missing for gravel pumping—purchases of diesel oil. Of the remaining series, wage payments seem to have fallen slightly during the 1960's in relation to earlier years, though the labour and power coefficients shown in Table 5.17 indicate an increase of power per unit of output with constant labour use since the early 1950's. Electricity purchases have increased, reflecting an increased use of power. Other input series show little change, though it is likely that diesel use, had statistics been available, would have shown increases. Increasing use of diesel would have increased foreign payments at least until the early 1960's when diesel production started locally (see Section 5.4). Since few profits are remitted abroad from gravel pumping, increased government taxation of profit would have altered little the proportion of export income retained in the country.

Finally, the proportion of tin export income retained in Malaysia depends on the distribution of output between the two main sectors. Reference back to Table 5.1

TABLE 5.17 LABOUR AND POWER COEFFICIENTS IN GRAVEL PUMPING AND DREDGING, 1928-72

	(Workers per 10 tons metallic tin)		(HP per 10 tons metallic tin)	
	Dredging	Gravel Pumping	Dredging	Gravel Pumping
1928	7.6	21.3	...	...
1929	6.2	20.4	...	...
1930	5.0	14.6	...	...
1931	4.2	12.6	...	...
1932	5.9	15.8	...	...
1933	6.1	20.2	...	...
1934	5.3	21.0	25.9	49.5
1935	5.8	18.6	27.6	45.7
1936	5.1	17.0	...	...
1937	4.5	16.5	...	...
1938	7.0	17.4	32.3	59.2
1939	7.0	20.2	...	...
1940	39.5	29.1	...	...
1947	9.7	21.9	40.7	96.9
1948	6.9	14.5	31.4	78.2
1949	5.6	12.1	27.9	76.0
1950	5.5	11.2	30.6	79.7
1951	5.1	12.0	31.1	95.7
1952	5.0	10.5	30.4	93.7
1953	4.6	7.8	33.3	83.8
1954	4.4	8.4	32.1	94.2
1955	4.6	7.9	32.9	98.5
1956	4.0	7.5	34.1	101.2
1957	4.9	6.9	38.6	97.2
1958	4.8	6.6	48.6	129.2
1959	4.5	7.6	43.0	124.0
1960	4.0	7.1	41.0	118.9
1961	3.8	7.9	38.9	134.7
1962	3.8	7.4	40.4	123.7
1963	3.6	7.5	43.7	128.1
1968	4.6	7.5	59.2	166.4
1972	3.9	7.1	60.6	196.3

Sources and Notes

(1) Output figures from the following - 1928 from Fermor (1939 p. 113), 1929-39 from Mines Department, AR 1939, 1946-72 from Mines Department, BSMI's.

(2) Employment figures to 1939 from Mines Department, AR 1939, 1946-72 from Mines Department, BSMI's.

(3) Power figures from 1934, 1935 and 1939 from Mines Department, AR's for those years. 1946-72 from Mines Department, BSMI's.

(4) Coefficients for whole period 1928-72 grouped in single table for convenience.

shows that the share of dredging rose somewhat over the 1946-65 period, though it has subsequently declined sharply. This would lower the proportion of export income retained locally, other things being equal, since the outflow abroad from dredging is greater than that from gravel pumping.

TABLE 5.18 TIN MINING CURRENT PAYMENTS, FEDERATED MALAY STATES, 1910-39

(Percentages of Value of Exports)

	(i) Value of Exports ($ Mil)	(ii) Wage Bill	(iii) Diesel Oil	(iv) Local Coal	(v) Foreign Coal	(vi) Fire-Wood	(vii) Elect-ricity	(viii) Smelting Charges	(ix) Transport Costs To Port	(x) Transport Costs for Fuel	(xi) Export Duty	(xii) Total Costs (ii to x)	(xiii) Tin Price ($ per Picul)
1910	57.1	...	...	...	...	...	...	...	...	...	12.5	...	78
11	69.7	...	...	...	...	...	...	...	...	...	12.6	...	94
12	84.1	...	...	...	...	...	...	...	...	...	12.9	...	103
13	83.6	37.2	...	...	...	1.0	...	3.6	...	0.5	12.8	(42.3)	100
14	60.7	39.0	...	...	...	2.2	...	5.7	...	1.0	11.6	(47.9)	73
15	61.4	36.2	...	0.1	0.8	2.4	...	4.1	...	1.0	11.8	(44.6)	78
16	64.5	31.0	...	0.3	1.3	2.8	...	3.0	0.3	1.3	12.2	40.0	86
17	72.8	23.0	...	0.3	1.5	2.8	...	5.4	0.3	1.2	12.8	34.5	109
18	94.5	22.3	...	0.5	...	3.2	...	4.1	0.2	1.0	13.9	(31.3)	151
19	74.9	22.0	...	0.8	0.1	4.2	...	3.7	0.3	1.4	13.3	32.5	121
1920	88.4	12.0	...	1.1	...	4.6	...	3.4	0.2	1.3	13.8	(22.6)	151
21	49.3	21.1	...	1.7	0.7	7.8	...	5.5	0.5	2.9	12.5	40.2	85
22	47.8	23.6	...	1.2	1.5	7.0	...	5.9	0.5	2.9	12.1	42.6	81
23	64.3	23.2	...	1.2	1.3	5.4	...	5.7	0.4	2.3	12.8	39.5	102
24	91.9	17.9	...	1.1	0.3	4.6	...	3.0	0.3	2.3	12.7	29.5	124
25	101.7	16.3	1.2	1.2	0.4	6.1	...	2.5	0.4	3.0	13.8	31.1	132
26	111.6	25.0	1.4	1.4	...	3.6	...	1.6	0.3	2.0	14.0	(35.3)	145
27	217.6	16.7	2.0	1.3	0.4	2.6	...	1.7	0.3	1.9	14.0	26.9	145
28	118.8	11.9	2.7	1.5	0.2	1.8	0.8	1.8	0.4	1.7	13.5	22.8	114
29	117.5	15.6	3.1	1.5	0.1	1.6	1.0	1.4	0.4	1.8	13.6	26.5	104
1930	75.0	14.8	4.2	1.6	0.3	1.6	2.3	3.9	0.5	2.2	12.0	21.4	73
31	51.1	11.1	3.6	1.8	...	1.6	...	5.3	0.6	2.1	10.8	(26.1)	60
32	31.3	13.8	3.5	1.3	0.1	1.8	...	2.2	0.6	1.9	11.5	(25.2)	70
33	37.7	18.9	2.2	0.7	...	1.2	...	1.7	0.6	1.1	13.0	(26.4)	100
34	67.5	15.5	1.7	0.6	...	0.8	...	...	0.2	1.0	13.2	(19.8)	114
35	76.2	15.6	1.8	0.7	...	0.6	...	...	0.3	1.0	12.7	(20.0)	111
36	109.4	14.0	...	0.8	...	...	6.2	...	0.4	...	12.2	(21.4)	100
37	151.4	18.5	2.7	0.8	0.9	0.6	5.2	...	0.4	1.4	12.9	(30.5)	120
38	64.3	14.6	4.4	1.4	0.5	1.0	7.6	...	0.5	1.7	12.6	(31.7)	95
39	100.2	18.3	...	0.7	...	...	3.9	...	0.4	...	13.1	(23.3)	114

TABLE 5.18 continued

Sources and Notes

(1) Column i from Mines Department, BSMI to 31 December 1955. Export figures used for whole period because production figures are available for 1931-8 only.

(2) Sources and methods for other columns can be found in the following Appendices: ii in 5.1, iii, iv, v, vi and vii in 5.3, and viii, ix and x in 5.2.

(3) Export duty figures calculated from Fermor (1939, p. 88).

(4) Bracketed items in column xii indicate that certain input items are not available for those years. Purchases of diesel are unimportant to 1924, and electricity is unimportant to 1927.

(5) Tin prices from Fermor (1939, p. 76) to 1938, 1939 from Mines Department, AR 1939.

5.2.3 1910–1939

This subsection performs a similar exercise for 1910–39 to that of Subsection 5.2.2 for 1946–63. Suprisingly there is a much wider range of input data available for this period than for 1946–63. They are however of greatly varying quality, and are available before 1928 only in aggregate form for all tin mining, or even in some cases, for mining of all minerals.

Table 5.18 shows for all tin mining, proportions of current payments for all input items on which data are available. Wages are calculated for each main sector separately, and aggregated for this table. No other inputs, except electricity, are available on a sectoral basis. Wages data are in no sense comparable in reliability to the post-1946 series. Separate wage figures for mining appear only after 1930, and those only for unskilled workers. In contrast, the post-1946 wages were based on averages calculated from detailed statistics. Diesel oil consumption is from Mines Department sources and may be inaccurately reported, although it is likely that the unit value figures are accurate. Local coal consumption figures may be more accurate to the extent that the Mines Department had access to Malayan Collieries' sales records. Foreign coal consumption is calculated as a residual after local coal mining purchases are subtracted from mining coal consumption. The firewood tonnage figures, also from the Mines Department, are only rough estimates. The unit value figures (not given by the Mines Department) have been estimated on heroic but (it is hoped) plausible assumptions, and the tonnage figures are somewhat suspect.

The proportion of wages falls from 1913 to the 1920's, reflecting the decline of open cast mining.[25] Growth of diesel consumption to the 1929 boom, probably reflecting use by Chinese mines, can be seen. The lack of diesel figures before 1925 is unimportant since the tonnage in 1924 and earlier years was very small.[26]

It is interesting to see the growth in consumption of both local coal and firewood from 1915. Firewood reached a peak in the early 1920's as dredge production and therefore consumption of firewood rose, and then fell as dredges switched to coal in the late 1920's. Again, coal consumption declines in the 1930's as dredges switched to electricity.

Export duty remained constant at the 10–15% level. Separate figures are shown for fuel transport costs, as coal unit value figures are given ex-pithead and imported fuel values given c.i.f. at port of entry.

The large drop in output in the early 1930's reflects the Depression and tin restriction, but it is difficult to determine any perceivable change in the payments structure as a result of these low outputs.

Separate output figures by sector are available from 1928. Table 5.19 shows these for dredging and gravel pumping. Wages and electricity figures are on a sectoral basis. Fuel consumption cannot be allocated between sectors according to output (or at least, the result would be trivial) and transport and smelting charges, and export duty, would be the same percentage as in Table 5.18. The figures show contrasts in labour intensity between the sectors. The large difference in electricity consumption is in contrast to the post-war experience where the two sectors consumed similar amounts of electricity as proportions of output. Presumably this reflects the fact that many dredges were still using solid fuels, and many Chinese mines had not switched to diesel.

Compared to the 1946–63 period, dredging is much less labour intensive, with an unweighted mean labour proportion of 8% for 1928–39 compared to 14% for most of

TABLE 5.19 TIN MINING CURRENT PAYMENTS BY SECTOR, FMS, 1928-39

(Percentages of Value of Exports)

	Dredging			Gravel Pumping		
	(i) Value of Output ($000)	(ii) Wages	(iii) Elect-ricity	(i) Value of Output ($000)	(v) Wages and Free Food	(vi) Elect-ricity
1928	35,822	8.9	...	53,436	19.6	...
29	47,543	8.0	...	50,723	20.5	...
1930	30,326	7.3	...	34,607	16.7	...
31	22,245	5.6	...	20,557	12.3	...
32	13,958	6.8	...	12,321	13.3	...
33	18,075	8.1	...	14,638	20.7	...
34	32,740	7.3	...	26,236	21.3	...
35	34,129	8.1	...	31,125	19.4	...
36	51,164	8.0	...	41,719	19.7	...
37	72,893	9.6	3.3	57,883	26.7	9.4
38	29,588	10.1	...	25,172	15.7	...
39	45,088	12.6	...	34,573	27.3	...

Sources and Notes

(1) Calculated from Appendices 5.1 and 5.3.

the post-war period; but, the average labour coefficient for 1930–39 is 5.6, which is higher than for the post-war from 1952 (see Table 5.17). However, the coefficient may be higher because of the restriction of tin output during the 1930's, when labour inputs were reduced by reducing wages as well as employment. For gravel pumping the mean labour proportion is 19.4%, similar to that of 1960–67. The labour coefficient is 17.4, substantially higher than in the post-war. This suggests a relative improvement in the quality of the gravel pump labour force (or at least an increase in the real wage).

Table 5.18 specifies most main inputs. Total costs for 1916 are 40% of output. By 1926 this is 35.3%, and by 1938 32.9% (assuming smelting charges to have remained constant at 1.7%). This compares to 33.1% in 1963, and 38.8% in 1968, (see Table 5.6) when gravel pumping output was again becoming more important than dredging. Thus the basic cost structure seems to have changed little since the 1920's, and it is again clear that the main determinant of the flow of payments into or out of the domestic economy is the distribution of profits. Ten to fifteen percentage points were retained by means of export duty. At least half of the rest (i.e. the proportion accruing to 'European' mines) would have been remitted abroad as foreign tax or ddividends payments.

Dredge inputs may also be compared to costs given by Griffiths, who cites an average recovery rate of 0.6 katis per cubic yard for eight dredges (Griffiths, 1917, p. 3). At the price of $78 per picul of metallic tin in 1915 the gross revenue per cubic yard would be $0.35. Griffiths' mean cost figure of 15c per cubic yard means that over 55% of the value of gross output is profit. Apart from the 10–15% points export duty virtually all of this would have been remitted abroad, either as tax or dividends.

5.2.4 1870–1910

Input series of the sort used for later years are not available, and therefore qualitative material must be relied on. An excellent economic history of Malayan tin mining to 1914 has already been written by Wong Lin Ken (1965) and there is also a more general history of the industry by Yip Yat Hoong (1969). This section does not attempt to duplicate their efforts but tries briefly to extract information of a similar sort to that assembled already for later years.

As outlined in Chapter 4, the period saw the development of the tin industry on a large scale. Most mining was by open cast methods, with some hydraulic and underground workings. European companies operated but they were in a minority: in 1910 they produced only 22% of FMS output (Mines Dept., *AR*, 1939).

In a typical open cast mine operating with little or no machinery, payments to labour would comprise over 80% of costs (Yip, 1966, p. 29). However, the concept of a distribution of earnings between labour and profits is somewhat artificial. As late as 1912 over 50% of workers in the FMS tin industry were employed on tribute.[27] These workers 'advanced' their labour to the mine owner for a share in the profits. Non-labour payments would have been for timber, and firewood or charcoal for smelting and as fuel for steam engines.

It is thought that the capital for Chinese mining came mainly from within Malaya itself, especially from Chinese traders in the Straits Settlements,[28] and was mainly in the form of advances of working capital.[29] Hence there would have been little outflow of profit, and much of the profit is likely to have been reinvested. A larger outflow would have been personal remittances by labourers back to China. Most workers came without their families, and many returned to China after accumulating a certain cash sum (Yip, 1966, p. 31).

However, to see the effects of the tin industry on Malayan development to 1910 purely in terms of the structure of its current payments is to take too narrow a view. During that period immigration provided a large population increase, which, combined with urbanization made for a substantial rise in the potential domestic market. Railways and roads were built, initially to service the tin industry but soon to develop the country. Tin provided a major source of market-orientated economic activity in a subsistence economy, although direct participation by local Malays had to wait until the spread of 'European' mining.

5.3 TIN MINING CAPITAL PAYMENTS

This section looks at the purchases of investment goods by the dredging and gravel pump sectors. As in Section 5.2 the aim is to split inputs into those of foreign and of local origin. The effects of the local payments on the domestic economy are examined separately in Chapter 8, which is a case study of the Malaysian engineering industry, and which also contains a description of the engineering aspects of dredge and gravel pump mine construction, which can be read usefully alongside the present section.

5.3.1 Tin Dredging

Information was gathered through personal interviews with dredge construction contractors and mining companies in Malaysia in 1970 on the capital cost structure of three dredges built during the last ten years.[30] Like most dredges now built in Malaysia, they are of roughly a half million cubic yards monthly capacity, or more. For reasons of confidentiality neither the names, dates of construction nor exact capacities are given. These dredges represent over a third of the new dredge building in Malaysia during the post-war period to 1970.

TABLE 5.20 SUMMARY OF LOCAL COMPONENTS OF CAPITAL EXPENDITURE FOR THREE DREDGES

($000)	DREDGE A	DREDGE B	DREDGE C
Fabrication	893	750)	1,066
Erection	516	500)	
Local Materials Purchases	815	188	341
Local Freight and Port Charges	...	130	256
Local Site Costs	242	400	639
Taxes and Import Duties	...	...	256
Total Local Expenditure	2,465	1,968	2,558
Total Dredge Cost	8,987	8,979	12,400
Local Expenditure as % of Total Dredge Cost	27.4	21.9	20.6

Sources and Notes

(1) For dredge A Local Materials Purchases includes $84,000 for local electrical work, and it also includes charges and taxes and import duties, but no further breakdown was available.

(2) For dredge B, Fabrication was included in Local Materials in the original data. Contract labour was $1.25 million and fabrication and Local Materials were calculated as residuals. At least half of Local Materials were steel castings. Site costs exclude estimated imported items.

(3) For dredge C, Local site costs may include imported items.

(4) Figures obtained from the mining companies concerned in 1970.

For Dredge A, of the estimated 27% points of local expenditure, nearly 16 are for fabrication and erection, (see Table 5.20). This figure, which in absolute terms is $1.41 million, is rather high. The usual payment to the labour contractor in 1970 was $1.25 million, but it is possible that a higher proportion of secondary steelwork than usual was bought locally or that the method used to estimate local content slightly overstates fabrication costs for secondary steel.[31] If fabrication and erection are reduced to $1.25 million, the total local content falls to 25%.

Summary figures for Dredges B and C are also shown in Table 5.20. Some further details, not shown, were provided for B, which helped interpretation of the figures. For C no supplementary information was given and the exact basis for certain estimates is not known. It is likely that some items included under Fabrication for A would be included under Materials for B and C.

It is impossible to discuss for each individual dredge exactly which items were locally purchased. However, none purchased everything which was available from Malaysian manufacturers. It is probable that with local electrical equipment and steel castings the local content could be raised to 35%. Problems of raising this proportion further are discussed in Chapter 8.

Total investment demand from dredging consists of new dredge construction and the rebuilding of old dredges. Table 5.21 shows dredge construction and reconstruction for the post-war period. However since the information collected

TABLE 5.21 DREDGE CONSTRUCTION IN PENINSULAR MALAYSIA, 1946-70

	NEW DREDGES (NAMES AND MONTHLY CAPACITY IN CUBIC YARDS)	DREDGE CONVERSIONS AND RECONSTRUCTIONS (NUMBERS)
1946	-	1
47	-	-
48	-	-
49	Petaling No. 6 (440,000)	4
1950	-	6
51	Malayan Tin No. 7 (396,000)	1
52	-	1
53	-	5
54	-	7
55	-	3
56	-	2
57	-	3
58	-	3
59	Malayan Tin No. 4 (432,000)	-
1960	-	2
61	-	3
62	-	2
63	-	5
64	Berjuntai No. 6 (500,000)	2
65	Malayan Tin No. 7 (600,000)	-
66	Selangor Dredging (450,000)	1
67	-	...
68	/Aokam No. 3 (390,000)/	...
69	-	...
1970	Berjuntai No. 7 (750,000); Petaling No. 7 (480,000) Conzinc Rio Tinto (815,000)	...

Sources and Notes

(1) 1946-66 figures from Mines Department, Dredge Data Chart 1965.

(2) 1966 figures from Dredge Data Chart may not include work started after 1965.

(3) 1966-70 figures from interviews.

(4) Berjuntai No. 7 and Conzinc Rio Tinto not yet completed at end of 1970.

(5) Aokam No. 3 was exported to Thailand.

refers mainly to the 1960–70 period, investment expenditure is calculated from 1961 only, and the 1946–61 construction figures are given simply for comparison.

The total value of new construction is relatively easy to calculate. A dredge of the 500,000–800,000 capacity cost, at 1970 prices, \$8 million–\$12 million, say \$9 million average, spread over two years.[32] The cost of dredge conversion is much more variable. To dismantle and reconstruct on a new site may cost \$5 million or more. Conversions such as lengthening the bucket ladder, converting from steam to electricity or from palongs to jigs, cost less. One recent conversion cost \$2 million, of which \$500,000 was for imported steel. Table 5.22 estimates investment expenditure at 1970 prices on the (heroic) assumption that the average cost of a reconstruction is \$2 million.

TABLE 5.22 DREDGING INVESTMENT IN PENINSULAR MALAYSIA, 1961-70

($MIL)

	NEW CONSTRUCTION	RECONSTRUCTION AND CONVERSION	TOTAL	ESTIMATED LOCAL PAYMENTS
1961	-	6	6	3.6
62	-	4	4	2.4
63	4.5	10	14.5	7.1
64	9.0	4	13.0	4.6
65	9.0	-	9.0	2.2
66	4.5	2	6.5	2.3
67	(4.5)	...	...	...
68	(4.5)	...	...	...
69	9	...	...	...
1970	14	5 minimum	19	6.5

Sources and Notes

(1) Table 5.21 figures (for numbers of constructions) are prorated with assumed costs of new constructions ($9m. per dredge) and reconstruction ($2m. per dredge).

(2) 1967-68 new construction figures are for Aokam dredge exported to Thailand.

(3) Local content taken as 25% for new construction, and 60% for conversions.

Official figures for tin mining investment are available from 1968 in the *Census of Mining Industries* (Statistics Dept., *CMinI*, 1968–71). The totals are set out in Table 5.23, together with maintenance expenditures and more detailed figures are given in

TABLE 5.23 PURCHASES OF FIXED ASSETS AND MAINTENANCE EXPENDITURE, TIN DREDGING AND 'OTHER TIN MINING' 1968-71

($MIL)

	TOTAL PURCHASES OF FIXED ASSETS	MAINTENANCE EXPENDITURE
Tin Dredging		
1968	30.9	20.5
1969	20.7	26.5
1970	23.7	...
1971	...	...
Other Tin Mining		
1968	48.1	35.8
1969	31.2	39.2
1970	36.8	...
1971	...	...
All Tin Mining		
1971	67.0	...

Sources and Notes

(1) Figures from Statistics Department, CMin I 1968-71.

Table 5.24 for dredging (and 5.26 for Other Tin Mining). These figures estimate annual capital expenditure in dredging at approximately $20-30 million over the period 1968 to 1971. These seem rather high figures compared to those in Table 5.22 for 1968 to 1970. Moreover, the 1970 estimate in Table 5.22 includes the Conzinc Rio Tinto dredge construction which started only towards the end of 1970. The official figure seems especially high since no new dredge construction occurred in 1968, except for export to Thailand, which should not be included in the official figures. $20 million of dredge conversion work would mean local purchases of up to $15 million, which is high in relation to the capacity of the dredging sector of the Malaysian engineering industry (see Chapter 8). It is possible that the 1968 figure includes planned expenditure in part or in total for either Petaling 7 or Berjuntai 7, or both. If this is the case, the local payments proportion would fall.

The local payments will vary according to the proportion of new dredge construction. As shown above, new dredge construction typically embodies 25% local content, while conversions may be up to 75% local. Total local purchases may rise to a maximum of some $8 million.[33] This sum is equivalent to 3% of the gross value of 1969 dredging exports (see Table 5.6). Thus in aggregate terms dredging investment purchases are small, although all concentrated on the engineering and construction

TABLE 5.24 PURCHASES OF FIXED ASSETS, AND MAINTENANCE EXPENDITURE, TIN DREDGING, 1969

($MIL)

	MACHINERY AND EQUIPMENT (EXCLUDING TRANSPORT BUT INCLUDING FURNITURE)	INTERNAL TRANSPORT EQUIPMENT	RESIDENTIAL BUILDINGS	NON-RESIDENTIAL BUILDINGS	OTHER CONSTRUCTION WORK	LAND	EXISTING BUILDINGS	TOTAL
New Fixed Assets	9.8	0.2	1.0	0.2	4.0	2.0	0.08	17.3
Used Fixed Assets	3.3	0.05	-	-	-	-	0.02	3.4
Total Fixed Assets	13.2	0.25	1.0	0.2	4.0	2.0	0.1	20.7
Maintenance Expenditure	23.0	0.5	2.0	0.2	--------	0.9	--------	26.6

Sources and Notes

(1) From Statistics Department, CMin I 1969. This is the last year for which such detailed breakdowns are given for maintenance and for capital expenditure by sector.

industries. Also concentrated on engineering are maintenance purchases amounting to 10% of 1970 export earnings, although the import content of dredge maintenance is much higher than for gravel pump tin mining. Dredge replacement items include digging buckets and other imported items.

5.3.2 Gravel Pump Tin Mining

Capital costs for a typical gravel pump mine, of 20,000 cubic yards capacity are given in Table 5.25.[34] It is clear from the figures that the only significant non-local expenditure is for the engines and pump items. In fact the pumps are made locally and the engines imported. The kongsi house, (accommodation for workers), palong and engine sheds are local construction items, normally built of wood. Bunds, drainage and roads are civil items, which are carried out by local contractors. The estimates indicate that about 40% of capital expenditure is local. Total capital and maintenance

TABLE 5.25 GRAVEL PUMP MINE CAPITAL COSTS: MINE IN KINTA, PERAK

	($000)	% LOCAL CONTENT
Water Piping	4	100
Steel Piping	4	-
Electric Wiring	10	...
Kongsi House	15	100
Palong-materials	17	100
-labour	3	100
Engine Sheds (3)	6	100
Roads	3	100
Drainage	3	100
Bunds	4	100
Engines and Pumps (3)	80	4
Total Cost	149	
% Local Content		39% (Min.)

Sources and Notes

(1) Figures from interview in Malaysia, December 1969.

(2) Items whose local content is not known are treated as non-local for purposes of calculating minimum local content.

TABLE 5.26 PURCHASES OF FIXED ASSETS AND MAINTENANCE EXPENDITURE, 'OTHER TIN MINING', 1969

($MIL)

	MACHINERY AND EQUIPMENT (EXCLUDING TRANSPORT, INCLUDING FURNITURE)	INTERNAL TRANSPORT EQUIPMENT	RESIDENTIAL BUILDINGS	NON-RESIDENTIAL BUILDINGS	OTHER CONSTRUCTION WORK	LAND	EXISTING BUILDINGS	TOTAL
New Fixed Assets	14.1	1.8	0.8	0.3	5.8	4.9	0.07	27.9
Used Fixed Assets	2.7	0.4	-	-	-	-	0.1	3.3
Total Fixed Assets	16.8	2.2	0.8	0.3	5.8	4.9	0.17	31.2
Maintenance Expenditure	24.9	2.8	1.5	1.1	---------	9.0	--------	39.2

Sources and Notes

(1) From Statistics Department, CMin I 1969. 1969 is the last year for which such detailed breakdowns are given for maintenance and for capital expenditure by sector.

expenditure for the gravel pump sector for 1969–70 are shown in Table 5.23, and a more detailed breakdown (for 1969) is given in Table 5.26. Total local capital expenditure, say 40% of fixed asset purchases[35] would be about $12.5 million, equal to 2.5% of 'Other Tin Mining' 1970 output (see Table 5.6). Maintenance expenditure, equivalent to about 8% of output is predominantly local and is larger than local investment purchases. Comparison with Section 5.2, especially Table 5.8, shows this maintenance expenditure is almost as large as the largest materials input, diesel fuel.

5.4 LINKAGE EFFECTS OF TIN

This section looks at the linkages generated by tin mining through its interindustry purchases and sales. In the research time available it was not possible to examine in detail all these linkages, and instead, one of them, engineering, has been chosen as the subject of a separate case study to be presented in Chapter 8. This section therefore confines itself to indentifying the main linkages, determining the extent to which they owe their existence to tin mining, and describing briefly their economic structure. It also confines itself to linkages generated out of current tin export income, since the engineering case study covers linkages generated by the investment purchases of the tin industry. Backward and forward linkages are dealt with in separate subsections, while a final subsection considers the linkages in terms of some of the objections to the linkage concept discussed in Chapter 3 and also asks how far the linkages simply represent increased vertical integration by the foreign sector and how far genuine local participation.

5.4.1 Backward Linkages

Reference back to Table 5.8 shows the materials purchased by the two sectors of tin industry and Table 5.27 shows interindustry purchases for tin as a whole. Electricity and diesel oil are the most important, at $54 million and $51 million, respectively, in 1971. Only two other inputs are of importance: timber (other than timber for fuel), and iron castings, the demand for both of which comes mainly from the non-dredging sector. Both are semi-capital items. Timber is mainly for repair and construction of palongs and other wooden equipment. Castings consist of liners for gravel pumps, spare monitors and other parts. Coal, an important input before the Second World War, and railway services, are also discussed. Both sectors purchase more or less the same range of material inputs, though in different proportions. Therefore no attempt is necessary here to separate linkages generated by each sector since the relative strength of each sector's purchases is quite clear from Table 5.8, which shows that both sectors buy large amounts of electricity but that 'other tin' has an overwhelming predominance in diesel purchases. Overall, however, gravel pumping now dominates in linkage generation, accounting for about 75% of the tin industry's purchases of materials.

Petroleum products were entirely imported until 1963. In 1963 and 1964 two refineries were established by Esso and Shell at Port Dickson in Negri Sembilan, both with 'Pioneer' status,[37] and Shell started construction of a further refinery in 1972 (FIDA, *MID*, 1971, 4th Quarter). Considerable import substitution has occured in petroleum since then, and by 1968 purchases of diesel by the tin mining industry

TABLE 5.27 INTERINDUSTRY PURCHASES OF THE MINING INDUSTRY, PENINSULAR MALAYSIA, 1965

	($ Mil)	PERCENTAGE OF ANNUAL VALUE OF OUTPUT	CUMULATIVE PRIMARY FACTORS
Forestry	0.8	0.1	
Products of Petroleum and Coal	14.1	1.6	
Electricity and Water	41.7	4.7	
Wholesale and Retail Trade	29.8	3.3	
Imports			
Chemical Products	1.2	0.1	
Manufacture of Petroleum Products	9.0	1.0	3.5
Basic Metal Industries	8.3	0.9	
Unspecified	34.4	3.8	4.7
Primary Factors			
Salaries and Wages	166.8	18.6	20.8
Entrepreneurial Income	431.0	48.2	52.2
Indirect Taxes less subsidies	157.4	17.6	18.8
TOTAL	894.5	100.0	100.0

Sources and Notes

(1) From Statistics Department, Interindustry Accounts, 1965.

(2) 1965 tin output (from Statistics Department, CMin I, 1965) was 79.8% of the value of all 1965 mining output.

(3) Cumulative primary factors (calculated using inverse input-output matrix for 1965) from Lo (1972, p. 57).

alone were substantially (60%) more than net imports (Thoburn, 1971, p. 227). Mining purchase of petroleum products are currently equivalent to about 25% of the output of the Malaysian petroleum products industry (see Table 5.8 and Statistics Dept., *SManI*, 1971).

Value-added (Primary Factors of Production) in Petroleum Products was only 3% of gross output in 1971, of which salaries and wages constituted only 0.3%. Non-wage value-added per head was exceptionally high at over $70,000, while average monthly wages were over $800 indicating use of high-quality labour, though total employment was only 551 (Statistics Dept., *SManI*, 1971).[38] However, though these figures seem to point to petroleum products as an industry 'inappropriate' to Malaysia, in fact there is evidence that it is both socially desirable and privately profitable (see Subsection 5.4.3.).

It is difficult to conceive of the local manufacture of petroleum products purely as a linkage of tin, in view of tin's relatively low (25%) share in the purchases of the industry's output. However, the existence of such a large consumer may well have played a part is establishing the minimum size of market required for at least the first refinery, though more recently the availability of local crude oil from the East Malaysian oilfields will probably have been a more important factor.

Electricity for tin mining is almost entirely locally produced.[39] As noted in Section 5.1, large-scale electricity generation dates from 1928.[40] The Perak River Hydroelectric Power Company supplies under licence to the National Electricity Board most Perak mines, while the NEB (and before the war the Selangor Government) supplies most mines in Selangor and other states. There can be little doubt that the large-scale generation of power in Malaysia is the result of tin mining. In 1936 and 1937 respectively, the earliest years for which such figures are available, mines (mainly tin) took 80.9% of the units generated by Perak River Company's and 83.8% of the Selangor Government's output.[41] In 1950 75% of the units generated by public utilities (including companies operating under licence) was sold to mines (Central Electricity Board, *AR*, 1950). By 1967 other large consumers were becoming important and mines consumed only 40% (Central Electricity Board, *AR*, 1967). The 1965 input-output table shows that value-added in 1965 was 66% of gross output, of which salaries and wages were 27 percentage points and entrepreneurial income 39.[42] Mining purchases as given in the input-output table were 21% of the value of electricity output.

Timber purchases by tin mining represent only a small part of the timber industry's output. In 1971 they were an amount equal to only 3% of the total exports of timber from West Malaysia, (Statistics Dept., *MSB*, April 1975).

The demand for iron castings is part of a more general demand by the industry for capital equipment and replacement items, which will be discussed in Chapter 8.

Coal was mined in Malaya from 1915 to 1960 by Malayan Collieries Limited, at Batu Arang in Selangor and briefly (1925-8) at Enggor in Perak. No figures for coal consumption by mines are available after the Second World War, but during the 1915-39 period mines consumed between a third and a half of the local output, the railways being the other main consumer. At its peak output in 1929 Malayan Collieries Limited, employed nearly 4000 workers, this total not being reached again until 1936.[43] Again, one cannot be certain that coal mining owes its existence to tin; only that the existence of a large-scale consumer would have been an important factor in the original investment decision. No wage or value-added figures are available for coal. Output declined progressively after a post-war peak during the Korean boom. It suffered both from exhaustion of deposits and the competition of imported fuel oil.

The beginnings of railway development were connected with the tin industry, (see Chapter 4) but the connection is not one of direct economic 'linkage'. In 1916, the earliest year for which such figures are available for the FMS, transport of tin ore accounted for only 2% (sic) of total railway revenue, and 5% of goods revenue (Railways Dept., *AR*, 1916). This low percentage was not due to any predominance of receipts from rubber, which were themselves only 5% of total receipts and 10% of goods receipts. The transport of coal, coke and firewood, much of which would have been for the tin industry, constitutes only another 4% of total receipts. Similarly, in the first year of operation of the Taiping-Port Weld line (a line built to connect the mining centre with a seaport) receipts from the transport of ore were only 7% of the total, firewood for mines was about 15%, passengers about 30% and the rest was from goods, parcels and sundries. Clearly the early railways derived their revenue from the general development resulting from tin mining (and later from rubber) rather than the transport of the ore (or rubber) itself.

Finance for railway construction in the FMS came mainly from current government revenue.[44] Much of this revenue in turn came from export duties. From 1884 to 1910 the peak period of railway construction, tin export duty contributed 36% of total FMS revenue. Railway receipts themselves (starting 1885) made up another 16%. By 1910 rubber export duty had not yet reached the $1 million level while tin revenue was over $7 million.[45] A further source of revenue connected with tin was receipts from the renting of opium 'farms', Chinese miners being the main smokers of opium. According to Lim Chong Yah's (1967, p. 254) figures such revenue comprised approximately 13% of total revenue over the period 1898 to 1906,[46] and it was probably a higher proportion in earlier years.

Railway construction was not merely a passive response by the FMS government to the needs of export industries. The FMS government, or more particularly the Resident-General, Sir Frank Swettenham, saw railways as a method of developing the new country:

> 'Seeing the value of railways as an investment in this country and recognising the enormous indirect benefits to be gained from them, I propose to join up the four isolated sections by the construction of about two hundred miles of line, that would probably at first reduce the percentage of earning, but would make the business of management easier and cheaper, would open up valuable mining and agricultural land, would substitute rapid and cheap means of intercommunication for the existing defective arrangements and would put all three Western States in direct Railway communication with Penang and ocean-going steamers.'[47]

Roads, also constructed out of current revenue, were used as feeders to railways, although after motor transport was introduced in 1902 they became increasingly competitive with rail transport.[48]

5.4.2. Forward Linkages

The only significant forward linkage is tin smelting; and virtually all Malaysian tin is smelted by two companies, in roughly equal proportions—The Straits Trading Company, founded in 1887, and Sharikat Eastern Smelting, founded in 1897 (see Tregonning, undated). No official information is available on the industry since the Statistics Ordinance forbids the publication of data for any grouping containing less than three firms. The discussion here is based on interviews with the two smelters in November 1970, supplemented by their published accounts (Stock Exchange of Malaysia and Singapore, 1973), together with historical information from Tregonning's history of the Straits Trading Company (Tregonning, undated) and the *AR's* of the Mines Department.

In 1970 each smelter had an annual throughput of about a million piculs of ore, for which a charge of approximately $5.25 was levied. This throughput, equivalent to about 88,000 tons of metal, exceeded Malaysian domestic output (72,000 tons in

1970) and the difference is the result of ores being imported for smelting from Indonesia and Laos, and more recently from Australia (Stock Exchange of Malaysia and Singapore, 1973).

Employment in each smelter was about 600, giving an output per head of about $8000 per year. Assuming an annual wage of about $2000 per year, NWVA must be substantially below $6000, which in turn is below the average for Pioneer manufacturing industries ($7976 in 1971) and similar to that in manufacturing as a whole ($5472). The size of the smelters is also indicated by the market value of their issued capital, which in 1971 was approximately $200 million for the two combined, compared to about $160 million for the largest dredging company (Berjuntai) (Stock Exchange of Malaysia and Singapore, 1973).

In addition the smelting industry is served by a network of ore-buying agencies of the two smelters, together with a number of licenced ore dealers in the mining districts, though most dredges deal directly with the smelters.[49]

The only other industry in Malaysia using tin as an input is the manufacture of pewterware, carried on by the Selangor Pewter Company in Kuala Lumpur. Pewter is over 95% pure tin. Pewter manufacturing is grouped in the *Censuses and Surveys of Manufacturing* under the Industry Code 4563, 'Brass, Copper, Pewter and Aluminium Products'. The grouped figures are sufficient to show that the industry is insignificant in comparison to the tin mining industry itself. Purchases of tin by the industry in 1971 amounted to much less than 1% of the 1971 value of tin output.

Tin cans are made in Malaysia, but the tin sheet is imported. Tin metal is a small proportion of the value of tin plate output, and its production is subject to economies of scale sufficiently large to ensure its location near the main consuming countries. It is not produced in Malaysia, though, as Edwards (1975, p. 275) has pointed out, now that Malaysia is producing steel products the Malaysian Federal Industrial Development Authority has begun to investigate the possibility of producing tin plate locally.

5.4.3 Tin Linkages—Summary and Discussion

In Chapter 3 it was argued that certain conditions had to be met before linkages could be accepted as evidence of an export industry spreading growth to the rest of the economy. Reasons have to be given to show why an industry producing intermediate products could not have exported them without waiting for backward linkage inducement, or why a forward linkage industry should not simply have imported its inputs. If there are no good reasons, and if a linkage is promoted by government policy,[50] the possibility exists that the linkage is a 'bad' one, in the sense of using a technology inappropriate for local factor supplies, which would in turn be reflected in a low or negative social rate of return. Also, the case for an export industry having spread growth through linkages is strongest if in addition it can be shown that the linkage investment represents new capital formation and not a mere reallocation of existing investible resources.

Of the backward linkages all but petroleum (and engineering products discussed in Chapter 8) are subject to some degree of natural restriction on direct export. Railway services are a non-traded good. Electricity can be transported only a few hundred miles (though alternative forms of power such as diesel oil can be and have been imported) and coal is subject to high transport costs in relation to value. Petroleum refining conceivably could have been established as an export industry before the emergence of large-scale diesel consumption by tin mining (and other domestic consumers), but in the absence until recently of local supplies of crude oil, crude would have had to be imported, and it is difficult to see why international oil companies would have preferred to locate refineries in Malaysia rather than in nearby oil producers (such as Indonesia) or in consuming countries. In the case of the forward linkages—smelting and the manufacture of pewterware—the antilinkage argument is that they could in principle have used imported tin, in which case their existence could not be said to be due to local tin mining. In the case of smelting, metals are normally smelted either in the producing or consuming country, and like the antilinkage used for petroleum, the reasoning seems to have a somewhat unreal flavour. This is especially so since tin mining was one of the earliest forms of modern economic activities to develop in Malaysia, and thus there might be no way of testing the hypothesis that forward linkage investments could have developed by importing their inputs. However, if a forward linkage industry imported the input on a large scale, it could be argued that the existence of local supplies was irrelevant. In fact tin smelting imports ore from nearby countries, but these amounts, though substantial are under 20% of total smelting output. In the case of pewterware all the tin used is local. It could in principle be imported but in fact the industry relies for much of its tourist appeal (and it is heavily dependent on sales to tourists) on the fact that the pewterware uses *local* tin.

If a linkage is developed as the result of government policy, it is necessary to ask whether or not it is a 'good' linkage. To answer this conclusively a full social cost–benefit analysis would be necessary in each case, which is not possible here in view of the available data and research time. Three pointers can be used as a substitute. First, there are the industry's factor proportions, described here in terms of annual non-wage value-added per worker. By comparing NWVA per worker to the average NWVA in manufacturing, some notion can be obtained of the industry's capital intensity, and there is a presumption that industries of low capital intensity are 'appropriate' to a labour-abundant economy like Malaysia. NWVA per head however can be an unreliable guide to the extent that rates of profit differ between industries (which they will do except in the unreal circumstances of static long-run equilibrium), but is particularly likely to be unreliable if profits are distorted by atypical levels of protection. Hence the second measure (though it is not available for all of the linkages) is that of the effective rate of protection (ERP), using Edward's (1975) data. This is also probably the most effective indicator of the governmental support required to establish the industry.[51] Third, and again from Edward's (1975) study, there is the domestic resource cost/foreign exchange ratio for the industry in question. The DRC/FE ratio is closely related to the ERP criterion,[52] but its major value for present purposes is that it provides a convenient short cut to a measure of social profitability.[53]

Two of the major tin linkages received government help. The early development of smelting was aided by a 35% export duty on ore (when the duty on metal was only about 12%) imposed from 1903, though exports of ore to the U.K. were later exempted from it (Wong, 1965 pp. 229–30). The aim apparently was to protect smelting against American competition (i.e. to prevent U.S. tin dealers from buying ore for overseas smelting), and illustrate the fact that tin smelting, unlike rubber processing (see Subsection 6.4.2), is by no means a satellite industry (i.e. a processing industry or supplying industry which must for technical reasons be located with the main product—see Hirschman, 1958, pp. 102–4). Since tin can be treated by mines to over 70% purity prior to smelting and (unlike rubber) does not deteriorate in transit, overseas smelting is possible, and until 1965 Malaysia smelted quite substantial quantities of ore from Thailand and also from Indonesia and Laos. However, the NWVA per head calculated in Subsection 5.4.2 as substantially below $6000, does not suggest an industry which is inappropriately capital intensive, and it will be argued below that it is extremely profitable privately.

Petroleum refining also received help in terms of tax concessions under 'pioneer' legislation, but though there are import duties on petroleum products they are mostly matched by excise duties, so cancelling out the tariff protection. Its NWVA, at $70,000, is extremely high and suggests 'unappropriateness', but in fact its DRC/FE ratio (i.e. the domestic factor cost of saving a unit of foreign exchange) is very low (0.4), (Edward's, 1975, p. 170) and this high social profitability presumably is the result of economies of scale and advanced technology associated with its high capital intensity (see Stewart, 1972, pp. 106–7).

The characteristics of the other main linkages—railways and electricity—were not further examined since they are non-traded goods. Of course, government-aided linkage investment in non-traded goods may also be 'bad', and the government played an important part in both railway and electricity investment, but there is no evidence that these have been historically inappropriate investments.

Whether these linkages discussed above represent new net capital formation is a question best deferred until the linkage case study in Chapter 8. Chapter 8 will argue that linkages in the period before the Second World War probably did result in rises in savings. In the post-war period this is much less likely in view of the large number of industrial investment outlets opened up by the growth of the domestic market and by government import substitution policy in the 1960's and 1970's.

Finally, how far do the linkages of tin mining represent genuine participation by Malaysians, and how far merely vertical integration by the foreign sector? Certain clear cases of foreign vertical integration can be found. Investment in coal mining, mentioned in Subsection 5.4.1, was undertaken by the mining firm of Osborne and Chappell who floated Malayan Collieries Ltd. in 1913 (Mines Dept., *AR*, 1913). Mining interests are linked to one of the two smelters, the Eastern Smelting Company (known since 1970 as the Sharikat Eastern Smelting Bhd.) through the London Tin Corporation–Consolidated Tin Smelters connection mentioned in Section 5.1. On the part of the mining companies very little backward integration appears to have taken place. An examination for instance of the accounts of the five major Anglo-Oriental Companies (Kamunting, Southern Malayan, Malayan Tin, Southern Kinta and Berjuntai) and of the two main Charter Consolidated Companies, Ayer Hitam and Tronoh which in 1974 produced nearly 70% of Malaysian dredging output, showed total investment holdings of only £10 million. This is overstated since several companies owned investments in other companies in the group, and it compares to a market valuation of the companies themselves of nearly £90 million (1972 figure, from Stock Exchange of Malaysia and Singapore, 1973). In fact, the companies' total holdings of cash and bank deposits (£20 million) were considerably in excess of their investments, though this *may* reflect a temporarily liquid position at a time of stock market uncertainty. In contrast far larger investment holdings were owned by the smelters. Straits Trading in 1974 derived almost half of its total profit from investment income, of which half in turn was derived from investments in mining companies (Straits Trading Company, *AR*, 1974). In 1969 Eastern Smelting owned investments of a par value of $31 million compared to its own market value of about $75 million (Stock Exchange of Malaysia and Singapore, 1970). These large investments may well be a reflection of the smelters' high profitability. The Straits Trading Company in 1974 for instance earned a trading profit of $12 million on a probable net turnover of $18 million ($740 million gross turnover, i.e. the value of tin smelted, less payment of $722 million for supplies of unsmelted tin).

Included in the smelters' investments are substantial holdings in mining companies (e.g. Straits Trading holds 14% in Tronoh, which in turn holds 17% in Ayer Hitam; and Eastern Smelting holds 10% in Southern Malayan and Southern Kinta), and there has also been diversification into real estate, plantations, and shipping. Control of one smelter (Eastern Smelting) is clearly in the hands of the mining industry, while the Straits Trading Company appears to be owned by Singapore interests, especially the Overseas Chinese Banking Corporation (Stock Exchange of Malaysia and Singapore, 1973). In spite of the high profitability of the two smelters, however, there appears to have been some underutilization of capacity (Interviews, 1970) and an attempt in 1965 by a new company, Oriental Tin Smelters, owned jointly by Malaysian and Japanese interests (United Nations, 1968), to enter the market was unsuccessful and the new firm closed in 1969.

NOTES

1. These other major producers include Thailand (with 11% of 1972 world production) Indonesia (11%) and Nigeria (3%). Bolivia produced 16% of world output in 1972 but her deposits are underground so different methods are used. See Mines Dept., *BSMI*, 1972.
2. Useful accounts of dredging technology, past and present, can be found in Griffiths (1917), Jones (1925), Deller (1963) and Fox (1974). Deller, Jones and Fox also describe other types of tin mining.
3. A higher percentage could be obtained but would increase the risk of theft on the way to the dressing sheds, several handfuls of ore at current prices being worth as much as a labourer's daily wage.
4. This method was not used to mine tin in Cornwall, since Cornish tin occurs in lodes.
5. As a point of comparison with respect to throughput and labour requirements G. C. Warnford-Lock (1907, p. 121) estimates that a single worker in an opencast mine could move two cubic yards in a working day, equal to about fifty cubic yards a month. Therefore an unmechanized opencast mine would have to employ 200 workers to treat the monthly Gopeng yardage, i.e. about ten times the number of workers actually employed by Gopeng.
6. For an interesting account of dulang miners see Siew Nim Chee 'Labour and Tin Mining in Malaya' in Silcock (1961).
7. Some further and newer evidence of integration is that of the fourteen tin dredging companies operating in Malaysia listed in Zorn and Leigh-Hunt (1974), which produced 82.6% of 1973 dredging output, all but two (Kinta Kellas and Renong, which together produce only 4% of total dredging output) had as Secretaries and/or Managers either Anglo-Oriental, Osborne and Chappel or Charter Consolidated/Associated Mines.
8. For example, Zorn and Leigh-Hunt (1974) listed ten tin dredging companies in Malaysia (and one in Thailand) in which the London Tin Corporation owns over 10% of the issued capital, and in all but three cases the ownership share was over 25%.
9. The 1974 *Who Owns Whom* U.K. edition lists over a hundred subsidiary and related companies under the Charter Consolidated heading.
10. Offshore dredging operations in Malaysia are still in the planning stage—principally by PERNAS Mining—but offshore dredges currently operate off Indonesia and Thailand.

11. Malay participation is also increasing in the dulang tin mining labour force. This was over 95% Chinese until the late 1950's, rising to 32% Malay in 1965 and 46% in 1972. In 1972 there were nearly 48,000 dulang licences issued, compared to a total tin mining labour force (excluding dulang miners) of nearly 46,000. See Mines Dept., *BSMI*'s, 1955–72.
12. At the time of writing the latest *Census of Mining Industries* is 1971, but preview figures are available for 1972 (Statistics Dept., *PR*, 1972).
13. In 1968 repair and maintenance figures were given for the first time, and in 1969 they were included in 'total inputs', but shown separately from materials purchases. In 1970 they were excluded from input, and were not shown after that year. However, the mining census questionnaire now asks firms to list only repairs and maintenance done by other firms, and it is probable that materials used by mines to do their own repairs and maintenance are now included as 'materials' in the *Census*.
14. This compares to 54.2% for the economy as a whole. This measure is adapted from Chenery and Watanabe (1958 p. 492). Chenery and Watanabe take intermediate purchases as a proportion of total value of output, which for West Malaysia is 45.8% (i.e. 100–54.2). This is within the range 40% to 50% which they found to be an average for a number of countries, both developed and less developed.
15. The companies quoted in the 1969 *Manual* accounted for 78% of all dredging output; and the companies in the 1967 *Manual* for 98%. Fewer dredging companies are now quoted on the London Stock Exchange than in 1967 and earlier years because, with increasing Malaysian ownership of shares, quotations tend to be shifted to the Malaysian Stock Exchange. (I am indebted for this point to the compiler of the *Manual*, Mr. R. T. Jacobson–interview, March 1970.) In the 1974 edition a few smaller companies have been omitted, but those included still account for 78% (sic) of dredging output.
16. See Tables 5.15, 5.16 and 5.18. Since April 1974 there has been imposed in addition a surcharge operating at prices in excess of $700 a picul, equivalent to about 1% of output value at $700–800 a picul and nearly 15% at $2000 a picul (private communication, Mines Dept., January 1975).
17. Levied on profits which exceed a standard profit of $100 a pikul of concentrates sold. *Malay Mail* (1969, p. 229).
18. This is the year when it was first mentioned in company reports.
19. In particular it was necessary to change the basis of enquiry from the proportion of *shares* owned (which was Yip's measure) to proportion of current value of issued capital. Yip's measure in effect weighs the percentage of shares owned in each company by the *number* of shares issued by that company. Thus the extent of local ownership of a company with, say, 10,000 shares currently valued at $10 million is given the same weight as a company with 10,000 shares currently valued at $1 million. Naturally since current share prices reflect current and expected earnings, the flow of dividends will be much greater for the former than for the latter company.
20. Before Malaysian income tax was instituted the outflow of profits took the form of payments of U.K. company tax (now remitted under double taxation relief) rather than higher dividends.
21. An interesting account of the breaking open of other such enclaves is in R. Vernon, 'Foreign Owned Enterprise in the Developing Countries', in Theberge (1968).
22. Yip's research indicates a considerable rise in local ownership over the ten year period to 1964 (Yip 1968).
23. 1963 is included because the *Census of Mining Industries*, used in Subsection 5.2.1, does not give information on a sectoral basis for 1963.
24. The assembly of the main time series used here is described in appendices, references to which are given in the notes to Table 5.15.
25. Of course proportions of input receipts in gross payments can change for cyclical as well as secular reasons. However, correlating the tin price as a rough indicator of the cyclical factors, and the proportions of wages in output, shows only a weak association. The correlation coefficient for 1910–39 is -0.21. Lagging wages one year behind prices lowers the correlation to -0.07. Fluctuations in the wages proportion were larger than those of the tin price. The standard deviation of tin prices was 23.6% of mean tin price, compared to 37.1% for the wage proportion.
26. The 1913–24 tonnage figures are given in Appendix 5.3. Unit value figures were not available for those years.

27. A further 16% only were employed directly for wages, and another 29% were employed through labour contracts. By 1920 only a quarter of workers were on tribute (Mines Dept., *AR*, 1912 and 1920).
28. See Wong (1965, p. 64). Only in Negri Sembilan did a large part of the capital come directly from China.
29. Capital was principally working capital. Wong (1965, p. 67) estimates that to set up a very large mine with 600 workers in 1880 a fixed capital investment of $4272 was needed, of which 30% was for buildings, 15% for drainage and mining equipment, 12% for ore-dressing and smelting apparatus, and 43% for collecting and importing labour. By itself this figure is of little significance (and in any case its accuracy must be spurious)—Wong simply observes that it is very small. A meaningful comparison can be made between this expenditure and operating costs. Doyle (1879, p. 10), states that mining wages at about this time were $6 to $8 a month. Six hundred men at $8 a month would earn $57,600 a year, giving an extraordinarily small capital/value-added ratio of 0.07 (assuming that profits were distributed as 'tribute' wages). Even halving this wage rate would make little difference. Wong also notes (p. 67) that $4272 was approximately the cost of a steam pump, the main piece of mining machinery at that time. Hence even with a steam pump, the fixed capital/output ratio would be very small, (even if a number of pumps were needed for such a large mine). A large amount of working capital was required because ore was often sold only once or twice a year. However, wages were often only paid at the same intervals. Profits were increased by advancing wages and charging higher than market prices for goods purchased with advances.
30. On this and all other dredges quoted, prior development of the site and construction of staff and worker housing may cost up to $2 million, almost entirely a local expenditure. (Interview with dredging company in Malaysia, October 1970.)
31. The method used was to subtract estimated cost of imported steel from fabrication costs, using steel tonnage and price obtained from interviews with dredge contractors. See Thoburn (1971, p. 238).
32. Since 1970 average dredge capital costs have risen to over $16 million for a half-million cubic yard per month capacity dredge (interviews Malaysia, 1974). This has been due in particular to the increased cost of imported steel, and this will have lowered the overall local content somewhat.
33. Calculated on 25% local content for new dredge construction ($9 million, from Table 5.22 for 1969) and 75% for conversion (assumed to be $8 million—see Table 5.24 where new fixed asset purchases are $17 million for 1969).
34. These figures can be compared with those in Tan Theong Hean (1966), which estimate total capital costs for a 20,000 cubic yard mine at $100,000, with a local content of 41%. Since 1969, and more especially since 1971, capital costs have risen substantially and a similar mine would cost over $200,000 (interviews, Malaysia, 1974).
35. However, the mine discussed here is of a quite traditional sort. Many more modern mines would treat their material by means of jigs as well as palongs, and also use electromagnetic separation, etc., for ore-dressing. Since these items are made locally, the local content of machinery could be somewhat higher. See Thoburn (1976).
36. Since the first draft of this section was written, some extremely useful results have become available from a study of Malaysian industrialization by a colleague at the University of East Anglia, Dr. C. B. Edwards. Edwards (1975, especially pp. 156–79) calculates domestic resource cost/foreign exchange (DRC/FE) ratios for a number of the linked industries studied here. However, he does not attempt to shadow-price any of the inputs, or foreign exchange. He takes 10% return on capital as his capital cost. The rationale of the DRC/FE ratio and other criteria used here is discussed in Section 3.3.
37. Under the Pioneer Industries (Relief from Income Tax) Ordinance of 1958 new industries can have freedom from company taxation for up to five years, together with certain other privileges. Tariff protection is often granted also. The Ordinance was revised and extended by the 1968 Investment Incentives Act, which includes export incentives and accelerated depreciation allowances. Pioneer status for the two refineries' main products ended in 1968 and 1969, though Pioneer status for some new refinery products has been granted since then. See Stock Exchange of Malaysia and Singapore (1970, pp. 44 and 139). Since 1968 the Act has been further amended to provide incentives for greater labour intensity of production (in 1971), and for location away from industrial areas and to promote exports (FIDA, *MID*, 1974, 3rd Quarter).

38. Pioneer industries can be taken as representing a standard of 'modern' industry, against which the capital intensity (measured here by non-wage value-added per worker) can be judged. In 1971, non-wage value-added per head was $7976 per year, and monthly wages were $206. The figures for all industries covered in the *Survey of Manufacturing Industries* for 1971 were $5472 and $183, respectively.
39. In South Johore until the early 1960's electricity was 'imported' from Singapore (ECAFE, 1962, p. 20).
40. Earlier generation of electricity on a small scale had occurred not only on mines but for public consumption. Thus the *AR* of the Resident-General, FMS, for 1905 notes the construction of a small power station to supply light for Kuala Lumpur.
41. See Perak, *AR* (1936) and Electricity Dept., *AR* 1937. However, since large power consumers are charged lower rates than domestic consumers, the percentages of *revenue* generated by mines would have been lower. This applies also to the post-war period.
42. For the economy as a whole value-added was 54.2% of gross output. Wages and salaries were 41.9% of total value-added (Excluding indirect taxation) and entrepreneurial income 58.1%. The latter figures change to 45.6% and 54.4% respectively if agriculture and rubber growing (where peasant and smallholder income is counted as entrepreneurial) are omitted.
43. See Mines Dept., *BSMI* to 31 December 1955 for output figures for 1915 and employment figures from 1929 to 1955 and *BSMI* 1956–60 for figures to 1960.
44. Lim Chong Yah (1967, p. 275), calculates that from 1884 to 1937 (the period during which most of the present system was built) over 75% of the total expenditure on railway building had come from current FMS revenues. The FMS government also undertook the construction of railways in the UMS, as well as being responsible for almost all railway building in the FMS itself.
45. Figures for 1889–1910 are calculated from FMS, *AR* Chief Secretary, 1938. The 1884–8 railway revenue and total revenue figures are from *AR*'s of Perak, Selangor, Negri Sembilan/Sungei Ujong/Jelebu. The 1884–8 export duty figures are from Wong Lin Ken (1965, p. 251). No export duty figure for Selangor is available for 1884, and no figures are available for Pahang to 1888.
46. Lim gives aggregate figures of opium revenue and total revenue for Perak and Selangor 1898–1906 and Negri Sembilan 1901–06, based on the SS and FMS, *Opium Commission Report* (1909).
47. From Colonial Office (1900). (Letter by Sir F. A. Swettenham to the Governor of the SS, 7 January 1897, p. 11.)
48. See Lim Chong Yah (1967, pp. 276–82) for a discussion of road development in Malaya.
49. For a description of ore marketing, see Yip's (1959) case study of Kampar, one of the most important mining districts in Perak.
50. If *locally-owned* firms develop through market forces in response to linkage inducement it is highly unlikely to be a 'bad' linkage. However, it is conceivable that it might produce undesirable externalities, or use intensively a particularly scarce resource whose shadow price is above its market price, to such an extent that it was socially unprofitable. These possibilities have not been investigated but they seem improbable in Malaysia, where there are no obvious resources (e.g. foreign exchange) whose market price is below their shadow price.
51. See David Lim (1973, pp. 262–3) for a summary of the argument that tariff and quota protection is a more effective means of inducing investment in an activity than are tax concessions (such as those given under 'Pioneer' Status).
52. See Bruno (1972) for a very full discussion of the relationship between DRC and ERP. See also Section 3.3.
53. A more familiar method of appraising social profitability would be to estimate the internal rate of return or net present value of an investment, using shadow prices derived according to e.g. the Little–Mirrlees method (Little and Mirrlees, 1974). The DRC measures only the social profitability in a single year, whereas the IRR or NPV takes into account the whole time profile of costs and benefits (though under certain circumstances single-period optimization may give the same result as optimization over time—see Bruno, 1972, p. 19). A useful discussion of the relation between DRC and the Little–Mirrlees method is given in Little and Mirrlees (1974, pp. 363–5), and the question is also discussed in Section 3.3. It should be remembered that Edwards (1975) DRC figures used here do not involve shadow-pricing and the divergences between private and 'social' profitability reflect only the rates of duty and other trade restrictions on inputs and outputs. Hence there is a particularly close relation between the DRC and ERP figures.

Chapter 6
Rubber and Palm Oil

Compared to tin, a much larger body of economic research has been built up on the rubber industry.[1] Studies have been made of agricultural developments immediately preceding and during the early years of rubber (Jackson, 1968), of the early growth of the estate sector (Drabble, 1967 and 1973), and of the industry between the two world wars (Bauer 1948b; Parmer, 1960). There is a major study of the Federal Land Development Authority (Ness, 1967), and there are investment appraisals both from a private and a social viewpoint.[2] In addition, since 1964 the Rubber Research Institute of Malaysia has produced many useful studies of the economics of estate and smallholder rubber production.[3]

Nevertheless, no breakdown of the payments structure of rubber over time is immediately available from existing work, and this chapter proceeds in the same way as Chapter 5, splitting payments made out of rubber export income into their component parts and estimating what proportion of payments are made locally. Data are not readily available (either for the present or for the past) for this exercise to be conducted for smallholdings,[4] so the chapter concentrates on estates. In fact, it could safely be assumed that apart from small quantities of imported inputs, almost all payments from smallholding income are made locally and the more interesting question would be to determine income levels of smallholders and the distribution of income between smallholders, sharetappers, dealers and landlords, and existing work on these questions is discussed in Section 6.1 (and also in Chapter 9).

As in Chapter 5 the first section introduces the structure and technology of the industry and discusses relations between the sectors,[5] Section 6.2 presents a breakdown of payments from export income, Section 6.3 discusses investment purchases and Section 6.4 linkages. In addition, Section 6.5 considers briefly the palm oil industry in relation to rubber.

6.1 THE STRUCTURE AND TECHNOLOGY OF THE MALAYSIAN RUBBER INDUSTRY

6.1.1 The Present Structure of the Industry

Natural rubber in Malaysia is obtained from the *Hevea brasiliensis* or *Para* rubber tree, so-called after the port of Para in Brazil from which the original rubber seeds from the Amazon were shipped. Rubber in liquid form, *latex*, is found in the bark of the tree and contains about 70% water and 30% rubber, the dry rubber content (DRC) of one gallon of latex being about three pounds of rubber. Latex is obtained by tapping, the making of an incision in the bark with a knife. The latex is collected in cups of earthenware or glass suspended on the tree below the tapping cut. Also, about 15% of the crop is collected as scrap rubber, mainly in the form of coagulated material collected on the previous days cut or in the cups—tree lace and cup lump respectively. The tree has a productive life of at least thirty years.

TABLE 6.1 RUBBER EXPORTS FROM PENINSULAR MALAYSIA 1968 AND 1972, BY TYPE OF RUBBER

		Percentage of Total Tonnage of Gross Exports	
		1968	1972
1.	Ribbed Smoked Sheet	60.5	51.5
2.	Crepe	17.1	9.6
3.	Latex Concentrate	14.3	15.5
4.	Heveacrumb and Comminuted, Exported under Standard Malaysian Rubber Scheme	6.9	22.0
5.	Other Forms	1.2	1.3

Sources and Notes

(1) From Statistics Dept. RSH, 1968 and 1972.

(2) Unit values will differ slightly and understate the relative importance of items 3 and 4 in total export value.

The raw material collected from the field can be processed into several forms, the relative importance of which are shown in Table 6.1. Sheet and concentrate are made only from latex. Crepe, heveacrumb and comminuted rubber can be made from latex or scrap. Sheet rubber (which is dried by smoking) is still the most important product, having superseded crepe by the 1930's.[6] Latex concentrate is a more specialized product and is used in the making of goods such as foam rubber which require the raw material in liquid form. New-process rubber such as heaveacrumb and comminuted rubber are produced under the Standard Malaysian Rubber (SMR) scheme, about which more in Subsection 6.1.2, and the growth in their importance since the late 1960's is clear from Table 6.1. They can be produced in converted estate factories originally designed for sheet, but are increasingly produced in purpose-built SMR factories.

The rubber industry, traditionally is divided into two sectors, estates and smallholdings. A rubber estate is defined officially in the *Rubber Statistics Handbook* as 'lands, contiguous or non-contiguous aggregating not less than 100 acres in area planted with rubber or on which the planting of rubber is permitted, and under a single legal ownership'. The definition of a rubber smallholding is the same, but refers to an area of under 100 acres. The relative importance of these two sectors is shown in Table 6.2. One important economic distinction between them lies in their degree of use of

TABLE 6.2 ACREAGES, PRODUCTION, AND WORKING POPULATION OF ESTATES AND SMALLHOLDINGS IN PENINSULAR MALAYSIA, 1972

	'000 Acres	Production ('000 Tons)	Working Population ('000)
Estates	1508	649	196
Smallholdings	2698	589	468

Sources and Notes

(1) Acreages, production and estate workforce from RSH 1972.

(2) Smallholding working population figures derived from Barlow and Chan's (1968, p6) estimate of 446,000 for 1966, prorated by the proportional increase in acreage to 1972.

wage labour (though they are also distinguished by somewhat different production methods and ethnic ownership). A smallholding would be characterized by its use of family labour. Table 6.3 shows the use of different types of labour by smallholdings, based on the 1960 *Census of Agriculture*. It should be studied in conjunction with Table 6.4 which shows the relative importance of the various size groups within the smallholding sector. The predominance of family labour on holdings below ten acres is

TABLE 6.3 TYPES OF LABOUR USED ON RUBBER SMALLHOLDINGS MALAYA, 1960

(Percentage of total workforce of each size group)

Size Group (Acres)	Family Labour Only	Family Labour & Share Cropping	Share Cropping Only	Contract Labour Only	Wage Labour Only
0 - 10	70	4	25	-	1
10 - 15	46	11	37	1	4
15 - 25	29	17	42	1	9
25 - 50	17	19	47	1	12
50 - 100	5	15	47	1	24
Over 100	2	6	24	2	62
All	65	6	27	-	2

Sources and Notes

(1) From Ministry of Agriculture and Cooperatives (1960, Volume 6).

(2) The 'over 100 acre' group comprises only 0.1% of the farms covered. It presumably includes those holdings over 100 acres which have not been listed under the estate category. It provides a comparison with what is in effect the smallest type of estate.

TABLE 6.4 SIZE DISTRIBUTION OF RUBBER SMALLHOLDINGS IN MALAYA, 1960

SIZE GROUP (ACRES)	% OF NUMBER OF HOLDINGS IN CENSUS	% OF CENSUS SMALLHOLDING ACREAGE
0 - 3	41	12
0 - 5	64	28
0 - 10	87	57
10 - 25	11	28
25 - 50	2	9
50 - 100	-	4
Over 100	-	2

Sources and Notes

(1) From Ministry of Agriculture and Cooperatives (1960, volumes 6 and 6A).

clear. Family labour merges into sharecropping (known in Malaysia as the *bagi dua* system—*bagi dua* being a Malay expression meaning to split into two parts), under which the sharetapper usually receives 40–60% of the value of the crop in exchange for his labour. In none of the size groups shown below a hundred acres, is wage or contract labour predominant. Since the larger proportion of Peninsular Malaysian smallholder acreage is in farms of under ten acres, the dependence of the sector on family labour is clear.[7] In contrast, virtually all estate labour receives money wages,

TABLE 6.5 SIZE AND ETHNIC DISTRIBUTION OF RUBBER ESTATE ACREAGE IN PENINSULAR MALAYSIA, 1966

SIZE GROUP (ACRES)	% OF ESTATE ACREAGE	% EUROPEAN	% ASIAN
100 - 500	16	3	97
500 - 1000	10	22	78
1000 - 2000	20	50	50
2000 - 3000	15	72	28
3000 - 5000	19	81	19
Over 5000	21	78	22
All	100	56	44

Sources and Notes

(1) From Statistics Dept RSH 1966 .

(2) 1966 is the last year for which statistics are broken down by ethnic group. Thereafter the breakdown is one of citizenship. This is not the same as the ethnic breakdown since resident Europeans may hold Malaysia citizenship and, more important, resident Asians may not always be citizens. Use of citizenship would overstate the size of the foreign sector.

(3) An estate is classified as European (or Asian) if 50% or more of its shares are owned by Europeans (or Asians). This may be misleading if there are substantial minority share holdings, e.g. by Asians in European estates.

nearly 85% are directly employed, and the rest are on contract. (Statistics Dept., *RSH*, 1972)

The estate sector has 75% of its acreage in estates of over a thousand acres (see Table 6.5) European ownership predominates in the larger size groups. Over three-quarters of the European estate acreage is controlled by fourteen leading agency houses, of whom Guthries and Harrison and Crosfields are the largest.[8] Tyre manufacturing companies also own rubber interests.

Of the Asian estates in 1952 61% were owned by Chinese, 15% by Indians and the remaining 24% by 'Others' (which would include Malays) (Lim Chong Yah, 1967, p. 331)—but more recent figures are unfortunately not available.

TABLE 6.6 RUBBER ESTATE LABOUR FORCE IN PENINSULAR MALAYSIA, BY ETHNIC GROUP, 1938-72 SELECTED YEARS

(Percentages of Total Labour Force)

	1938	1947	1957	1968	1972
Malays	2	20	19	23	33
Indians	80	52	51	46	40
Chinese	17	27	29	31	26

Sources and Notes

(1) 1938 figure from Statistics Dept. RSH 1938. 1947 and 1957 from Lim Chong Yah (1967, p 334). 1968 from Ministry of Labour HLS 1968 and 1972 from Statistics Dept. RSH 1972.

(2) Pre-war 'Malays' include Javanese.

Table 6.6 shows how Malay (and Chinese) participation in the rubber estate labour force has been increasing, a change largely occurring during the war. M. G. Swift (1965, p. 60) puts forward the idea that Malay participation also increased during the Emergency when Chinese were removed to new villages.

Estate acreage has declined after reaching a peak in 1953 after the Korean boom. The 1972 acreage is substantially less than that of 1929, as shown in Table 6.7.

TABLE 6.7 RUBBER ACREAGE IN PENINSULAR MALAYSIA, 1929-72, SELECTED YEARS

('000 ACRES)

	ESTATES	SMALLHOLDINGS
1929	1827	1144
1939	2068	1305
1947	1934	1580
1953	2030	1606
1968	1676	2582
1972	1508	2698

Sources and Notes

(1) 1968 and 1972 from Statistics Dept. RSH 1968 and 1972. 1929-66 from Thomas and Fong (1968).

Reasons for the decline include a partial flight of capital from Malaysia as a result of the communist Emergency (1948–60), Independence (1957) and switches in estate cultivation from rubber to oil palm. There is also the political factor that little new land has been alienated to estates since the war, which somewhat reverses the political preferences given to estates before the Second World War.[9] It was estimated that from 1951 to 1960 over 200,000 acres were sold by estates and subdivided into smallholdings.[10] Between 1947 and 1968 palm oil estate acreage rose by over 300,000 acreas and by another 200,000 acres to 1972.[11] During the First Malaysia Plan the government declared its hope of involving the private sector in large-scale land development, but little appears to have come of this so far.[12] In contrast to the estate sector, smallholding acreage has increased substantially since the war, with a peak increase, as Table 6.8 shows, in the early 1960's comparable in magnitude with the

TABLE 6.8 ANNUAL RATES OF NEW PLANTING OF RUBBER ON ESTATES AND SMALLHOLDINGS, PENINSULAR MALAYSIA, 1946–72

('000 ACRES)

	ESTATES	SMALLHOLDINGS		ESTATES	SMALLHOLDINGS
1946	-	-	1960	22	25
47	1	-	61	18	67
48	7	2	62	10	82
49	7	2	63	9	100
1950	6	3	64	6	57
51	15	5	65	5	40
52	7	7	66	3	27
53	5	6	67	2	22
54	7	3	68	1	10
55	10	8	69	2	15
56	15	13	1970	3	27
57	16	11	71	6	31
58	14	11	72	5	23
59	14	21			

Sources and Notes

(1) 1946-66 from Thomas and Fong, (1968). 1967-72 from Statistics Dept. RSH 1967-72.

peak years of the early growth of the smallholder sector 1910–19. Table 6.9 shows the forms in which new planting has occurred. It also shows the relative importance of smallholding sector can be divided into two: unassisted smallholders and smallholders on schemes, especially those of the Federal Land Development Authority (FELDA).

In the case of unassisted smallholders,[13] the predominantly small size and use of family labour has already been established (see Tables 6.3 and 6.4). A number of case studies have been made of smallholder areas, which are most useful supplements to the quantitative information available from the *Census of Agriculture* and elsewhere.[14]

TABLE 6.9

NEW PLANTINGS OF RUBBER ON SMALLHOLDINGSIN PENINSULAR MALAYSIA, 1952-67, AND DISTRIBUTION OF 1968 AND 1972 SMALLHOLDING ACREAGE ('000 ACRES)

	FELDA Schemes	State Schemes	Fringe Schemes	Other Subsid-ized Schemes	RI(R)B Schemes	Unsubsid-ized Individual Schemes	Unsubsid-ized Block Planting	Controlled Alienation				Total
New Planting	126	38	130	12	72	67	134	26				605
					OTHER SMALLHOLDER RUBBER				From Estate Subdivision 1954-68	Acreage Replanted Since 1952	Old Rubber	
1968 Acreage	128			578					257	914	705	2582
1972 Acreage	188					2510						2698

Sources and Notes

(1) New planting adapted from Noor and Arun (1968, p4). 1968 from Statistics Dept. RSH 1968 .

(2) Although some new planting occurred there was virtually a ban on land alienation until the late 1950's. Over 90% of the planting shown occurred after 1958.

(3) Other post-war new plantings are larger than those given in Noor and Arun, (1968), even including the acreage (40,000) planted in 1968.

(4) The dates from which figures for subdivision and replanting are given are those from which those items became important.

(5) For 1972 such detailed figures as those for 1968 were not given in the RSH.

TABLE 6.10 OWNERSHIP OF MALAYAN SMALLHOLDING ACREAGE, 1952, BY ETHNIC GROUP

(percentages)

	HOLDINGS BELOW 25 ACRES	HOLDINGS 25-100 ACRES	ALL SMALLHOLDINGS
Malay	55	5	47
Chinese	36	66	41
Indian	6	15	8
Other	2	13	4

Sources and Notes

(1) From J.C. Jackson, "Smallholding Cultivation of Cash Crops", in Wang (1964, p249).

(2) Ownership of acreage by ethnic group is available only for 1951-53 (in Statistics Dept. RSH).

Table 6.10 shows the ownership of smallholdings by ethnic group for 1952, one of the latest years for which such figures are available.[15]

The split between Chinese and Malay ownership corresponds to differences in the economic organization of the Malay and Chinese holdings. Chinese own most of the larger holdings, which use sharetappers and paid labour. Moreover even in the size group below 25 acres, there is what corresponds to an urban/rural split between the two races. Most Chinese smallholdings are near urban areas, where there has been a tradition of Chinese settlement. Tin mining areas are the prime example (Fryer and Jackson, 1966, p. 199). The urban nature of Chinese smallholding ownership was strengthened by the resettlement of Chinese into new villages during the Emergency.[16] Most Malay holdings are in areas removed from urban centres (Fryer and Jackson, 1966, p. 199). This difference is of great importance in terms of the outside earnings of smallholders.

It was shown in Table 6.4 that most rubber smallholdings are less than five acres (though such holdings accounted for only about a quarter of smallholding acreage). A rubber tapper can work three to four acres a day.[17] Assuming daily tapping, a typical holding of under five acres, offers full-time work for only one person.[18] Using data from the 1960 *Census of Agriculture*, Barlow and Chan (1968, pp. 6–8) estimated that 21% of the family members on smallholdings covered by the *Census*, and half of the economically active members, worked at least part-time outside the rubber holding. Fryer and Jackson in their study of the Rasa area of Ulu Selangor depicted Chinese smallholdings as providers of work often only for the females and children of urban families. Over two-thirds of the holdings with mature rubber in their survey had outside income. Typically, older daughters and daughters-in-law might be occupied as paid tappers on nearby estates (and indeed nearly half of the total estate labour force consists of women—see Statistics Dept., *RSH*, 1972). Twenty percent of families in the Rasa survey had men employed by tin mines, where average earnings are higher than on estates. Others had a variety of urban occupations. In the groups below five acres, 5–10 acres and 10–25 acres, 69%, 62% and 48% of family income, respectively, came from outside earnings (Fryer and Jackson, 1966, pp. 226–7). Similarly, Voon's study of Chinese smallholders in the Semenyih area of Ulu Langat (in Selangor) found that most had outside sources of income (Voon, 1967, p. 78).

Fryer and Jackson (1966, p. 199) contend that Malay smallholding families do not have outside earnings from modern capitalistic activity. Certainly there are areas of mixed Malay farming where the main alternative occupation is padi growing. M. G. Swift describes such an economy where rubber provides a steady stream of income, rice provides food and fruit sales provide seasonal income for lump-sum expenditures (Swift, 1965, pp. 26–77). The fact that a third of the estates labour force and a fifth of the mining labour force is Malay does not suggest a complete isolation from capitalist activities. Of course, these workers are not necessarily members of rubber smallholding families but it is at least intuitively plausible that many may be. Nevertheless, many Malay communities, at least in the west coast states, are isolated, in the sense that almost all dealer activity is carried out by non-Malays (Swift, 1965, p. 28). Also, even in Malay reservations, much of the income from rubber may accrue to non-Malays.[19]

Under Federal Land Development Authority schemes,[20] large blocks of land, usually about 4500 acres, are cleared and planted in phases by contractors. Settlers (mostly rural Malays) are moved in soon after, and after a period to accustom themselves to working on the scheme they are allocated land in plots of 8–10 acres.[21] Settlers are provided with fertilizers and a subsistence allowance while their rubber is immature, the subsistence allowance being granted at a daily rate against work done on the settler's holding or on approved economic activities. These, together with the establishment costs, are charged against the settler's loan amount to be repaid over a period of ten–fifteen years after the rubber becomes mature. FELDA has been the spearhead of land development in Malaysia.[22,23] Other schemes are set out in Table 6.9 Fringe alienation schemes are administered by State governments, usually providing land in plots of 3–5 acres on land near existing settlements (Ness, 1967, p. 176). Such schemes are intended to supplement income from existing smallholdings, and are subsidized (on loan) to the extent of clearing, planting, and some fertilizers (Noor and Arun, 1968, p. 3). Unsubsidized block plantings are sometimes considered under the general heading of controlled alienation. State schemes are similar in organization to FELDA schemes, and in most cases they have been taken over subsequently by FELDA.[24] In general the success rate on non-FELDA schemes, especially those not supported by State governments has been low, and rehabilitation of neglected rubber is often necessary.[25]
than have other types. In future FELDA land developments are likely to be in large concentrated areas (FELDA, 1966, p. 45), such as the Jengka Triangle project already underway in Pahang (PELDA, 1967) and the Pahang Tenggara and South Johore projects for which master plans have recently been prepared. Such developments are hoped to achieve economies of scale both in planning execution and administration (FELDA, 1966, p. 45).

As well as developing new land the government has had a major replanting programme underway since the early 1950's.[26] Replanting has been undertaken both to replace trees which werynear the end of their economic life,[27] and to take advantage of new high-yielding varieties. Replanting has been encouraged by government grants, financed in part by compulsory cesses on rubber exports since 1952.[28] Over the period 1953–68,884,000 acres were replanted on estates and 889,000 on smallholdings, representing about half of the acreage (excluding new planted areas) of each sector, respectively (Thomas and Fong, 1968, p. 20; Statistics Dept., *RSH*, 1968), and by 1970 89% of estate acreage and 69% of smallholder acreage had been replanted with high-yielding material (Pushparaja, Johar, Subramaniam, Ti and Yoon, 1973). There is evidence however that the burden of export taxation used to finance replanting has born more heavily on smallholders, at least to the early 1960's.[29]

In addition to the estate and smallholding sectors of the rubber industry there is a substantial marketing network of dealers and exporters and an off-estate processing sector. In Peninsular Malaysia there are over 2500 licenced dealers (Statistics Dept. *RSH*, 1972), together with an unknown number of unlicenced (illegal) ones. In the case of the smallholder rubber, marketing and processing are closely linked. About 75% of smallholder latex is sold as unsmoked sheet, to so-called first-level buyers who smoke it before passing it on to middle dealers or exporters (Barlow, 1967).[30] Scrap is sold by first and middle dealers to remillers who manufacture it into crepe. A minority of smallholders, particularly in Selangor, use commercial group processing centres, where, for a fee, their rubber is smoked prior to sale to the dealer.[31] There are also Malay Group Processing centres whose construction has been financed mainly by MARA,[32] and whose operations constitute about 15% of the total output of all group processing centres (Barlow and Lim, 1965, p.1).

A later development has been the setting up of a number of large central factories buying smallholder latex and scrap for processing into SMR.[33] These factories are the successors to a series of thirteen factories set up by MARA between 1962 and 1965 to produce sheet from smallholder latex. All made severe losses and were closed. Two were re-opened in 1966-77 by the RRIM, converted into SMR factories (Lim Sow Ching, 1968b, p. 16), and handed over to Malayan Rubber Development Corporation.

Most estates process their own latex although a number sell their crops to off-estate latex concentrating factories.[34] FELDA tends to sell its latex to outside buyers. They had in 1970 only one rubber factory (Bilut Valley in Pahang) which processed only scrap, although more factories were planned (interview, FELDA, October 1970).

6.1.2 Technological Progress in the Rubber Industry, and the SMR Scheme

Since the early development of the industry technical changes have taken place in a number of areas. In estate cultivation before the Second World War great reductions in both the number of workers and in labour expenditure per acre, with given output, were achieved, particularly in response to the need for cost reductions as rubber prices fell during the Depression of 1929–33. Labour expenditure was reduced not only by cutting wages and salaries, but by increasing the areas supervised by (highly paid) expatriates. Thus Bauer (1948b, p. 254) notes that between 1914 and 1932 the average number of acres per European rose from 500 to about 1500. Expatriate staff below the manager rank were replaced by Asians, and expenditure on field workers was reduced by abandoning the practice of clean weeding between the trees, a practice never used on smallholdings and highly conducive to soil erosion. The drastic reduction in workforce per acre during the Depression is clearly shown in Table 6.11. During the 1929–33 Depression important changes in factory practice also took place. Latex was coagulated in large partitioned tanks instead of small individual tanks, and fed through light sheeting batteries instead of heavy creping rollers.

Table 6.11 shows that the most important reductions in workforce per acre occurred before the Second World War. Since the war there has been further replacement of European managers by Asians. A development of possible future importance in reducing labour input per acre is the collection of latex in polybags

TABLE 6.11 OUTPUT PER WORKER AND PER ACRE, AND WORKERS PER ACRE ON RUBBER ESTATES, FEDERATED MALAY STATES AND PENINSULAR MALAYSIA, 1915-72 SELECTED YEARS

	OUTPUT PER WORKER (TONS)	OUTPUT PER PLANTED ACRE (TONS)	WORKERS PER PLANTED ACRE
1915	0.20	0.07	0.36
1929	0.56	0.15	0.27
1933	0.89	0.14	0.16
1968	2.71	0.34	0.12
1972	3.31	0.43	0.13

Sources and Notes

(1) Employment, acreage and output figures for 1915 from Agriculture Dept. AR 1915; 1929 and 1933 output from Malaya RSH 1930, employment from FMS, AR Chief Secretary 1930 and Malaya RSH 1933, and acreages from Agriculture Dept. AR 1929 and 1933; all 1968 and 1972 figures from Statistics Dept. RSH 1968 and 1972.

(2) 1915, 1929 and 1933 coefficients refer to Federated Malay States only, and 1915 and 1929 figures include a small number of workers employed on estates not producing rubber.

instead of cups (though whether the reduction of labour input per acre is desirable from a national point of view is another matter, in view of the government's intention to promote labour-intensive industries to combat unemployment). Bags can be collected at intervals of four to five days, thus reducing collection labour although increasing the risk of theft (Chang, Pillai and Chin, 1969).

Perhaps the most important single technological improvement, increasing both output per man and per acre, has been the development of high-yielding varieties of rubber.[35] Trees planted in the first two decades of the century yielded on average about 325 lb per acre (Figart, 1925, p. 185). By the 1930's clones were available yielding over 1000 lb per acre (Bauer, 1948b, p. 273). By 1972 average production per mature acre was nearly 1200 lb (Statistics Dept, *RSH*, 1972). Some clones in commercial practice by 1969 were achieving over 2000 lb per acre and a commercial experimental station was reported in 1969 to have produced a clone yielding over 4000 lb per acre in its early years and expected to yield eventually over 5000 lb (*Straits Times*, 31 October 1969). High-yielding material has achieved practical importance with the new planting and replanting programme started in the 1950's and 1960's. It has normally been a condition of government grants and loans that replanting and new planting should be carried out with approved high-yielding material. By 1968 87% estate acreage and over 60% of smallholding acreage was planted with high-yielding material (defined as all clonal seedlings and budgrafts approved by the RRIM) and by 1972 the estate proportion was up to 93% (Statistics Dept., *RSH* 1972). The dramatic increase in output per worker and per acre shown in Table 6.11 from 1933 to 1972 is mainly due to the use of high-yielding material. Yields have also been increased by the use of yield stimulants such as 'Ethrel' (normally used on trees only after some ten years of tapping), and much effort has

TABLE 6.12

CURRENT PAYMENTS STRUCTURE OF RUBBER ESTATE SECTOR, PENINSULAR MALAYSIA, 1964-72

	(i) Value of Estate Output ($Mil)	(ii) Output Unit Value (Cents per lb)	CURRENT PAYMENTS AS PERCENTAGE OF ANNUAL VALUE OF OUTPUT (iii) Total Payments to Labour	(iv) Estimated Value of Labour Benefits	(v) Expenditure on Fertilizer for Mature Acreage	(vi) Expenditure on Fertilizer for Immature Acreage	(vii) Maintenance Expenditure on Immature Rubber	(viii) Export Duty	(ix) Research Cess	(x) Replanting Cess	(xi) Transport Charges to Port	(xii) Profits before Tax: (100)-(iii + iv + v + viii + ix + x + xi)
1964	748.7	70.1	47.0	6.1	1.4	1.7	7.1	5.2	1.0	6.1	0.8	32.4
1965	774.2	70.4	42.7	5.8	1.6	1.8	6.7	5.6	1.2	6.0	0.8	36.3
1966	781.5	67.9	42.3	5.3	2.0	1.6	6.1	4.7	1.2	6.3	0.8	37.4
1967	677.0	57.5	46.0	5.7	2.2	1.4	5.7	3.5	1.6	7.4	0.9	32.7
1968	683.6	54.2	41.4	5.0	1.1	1.0	3.6	3.7	1.8	8.0	0.9	38.1
1969	1026.6	70.9	29.2	5.6	1.4	0.6	2.3	6.3	1.4	6.3	0.7	49.1
1970	891.8	59.8	33.0	6.7	1.9	0.7	2.6	4.9	1.7	7.5	0.8	43.5
1971	780.1	49.1	36.4	8.1	2.0	0.7	2.9	4.0	2.0	9.2	1.0	37.3
1972	704.6	44.5	39.8	9.0	2.1	0.6	3.0	4.0	2.2	10.1	1.1	31.7

Sources and Notes

(1) Column i is output figures from Statistics Dept. RSH 1964-72 multiplied by Unit Value(ii) For calculation of ii see Appendix 6.1. The output unit value is in effect the unit value of exports.

(2) Columns iii and v to vii are calculated from Statistics Dept. RSH 1964-1972. Column iv is calculated from data in Rubber Research Institute of Malaya (1968, p30).

(3) Export duty and cesses are calculated from Rubber Producers' Council of Malaya, MSB, (November 1969) to 1968 and from Treasury, AR 1974-75., for export duty; and research cess (1 cent per lb.) calculated as percentage of output unit value. Replanting cess is 4.5 cents/lb.

(4) Column xi calculated from Railway Dept. AR's., assuming all costs of transport per ton are the same as rail costs per ton,

TABLE 6.12 Continued

to 1967. Thereafter assumed to be 0.5 cents per lb. (Ng, 1972, p.15).

(5) Some proportion of labour payments will be for maintenance on immature acreage. Column vii, which would also include maintenance materials, indicates the maximum amount of such expenditure. Columns vi and vii represent capital expenditure and are not deducted in the calculation of column xii. Column x can be thought of as a sort of compulsory depreciation allowance.

been put into research to shorten the rubber tree's period of immaturity, which raises the rate of return and shortens the pay-back period of investment.[36]

The Standard Malaysian Rubber scheme announced in 1965 combines new presentation and new processing methods.[37] Before the scheme, rubber was graded visually into four grades of ribbed smoked sheet (RSS1 to RSS4) and various kinds of crepes. Under SMR, rubber is graded technically, primarily according to its dirt content.[38] Such grading methods are in keeping with those already used in the synthetic rubber industry (Bateman, 1965, p. 1). Processing methods used under the scheme involve new means of coagulation, coagulum size reduction and drying.[39] Scrap can also be handled by SMR processes. SMR factories can handle very large throughout at comparable costs to sheet production, and SMR grades fetch a premium over RSS.[40] More specialized types of SMR such as Tyre Rubber have also been developed (Nair and Lee, 1972).

The implementation of the results of research into new techniques in order to improve the performance of the smallholder sector is in the hands of the Rubber Industry Smallholder Development Authority (RISDA). The Rubber Research Institute of Malaysia now undertakes smallholder project research under the auspices of RISDA and research in smallholder central processing for use by the Malayan Rubber Development Corporation,[41]

6.2 CURRENT PAYMENTS STRUCTURE OF THE RUBBER ESTATE SECTOR

This section is set out in similar fashion to that of Section 5.2, where the current payments structure of the tin industry was presented. The presentation is organized around the tables, which give the main data, methods and references. Detailed calculations and methodology are set out in appendices and the text provides a commentary. As was the case with tin, more information is available for the later 1960's and early 1970's than for earlier years. The period 1964–72 is set out in Subsection 6.2.1 while Subsections 6.2.2 and 6.2.3 trace back some of the main series for the periods 1946–63 and 1906–39 respectively.

6.2.1 1964–72

Statistics on wage and salary payments, and expenditure on fertilizer, maintenance and new planting by estates are given for 1964–72 in the *Rubber Statistics Handbook*, published by the Malaysian Department of Statistics.[42] Table 6.12 is a summary of the *RSH* data supplemented by some other series. The importance of labour payments is clear. When labour benefits are included, these payments rise to over 50% for some years. After payment for labour and materials, and after deduction of duty and the research cess, a residual of 30% to 50% is left before any expenditure on the immature area.[43,44]

Public companies produce over half of Peninsular Malaysian estate output. (53.5% in 1972—see Statistics Dept., *RSH*, 1972). As a check on the *Rubber Statistics Handbook* results, the summarized annual reports of between 40 and 80 public companies were examined for the years 1964–5, 1967–8 and 1972–3; and average profits, dividends, taxes and net replanting and new planting expenditures were calculated, the results of which are given in Table 6.13. The profits figures are after

TABLE 6.13 PROFITS, TAXES, DIVIDENDS, AND PLANTING EXPENDITURES OF PUBLIC RUBBER COMPANIES IN PENINSULAR MALAYSIA, 1964, 1968 AND 1973

	(i) Number of Companies	(ii) Annual Value of Agricultural Output ($ Mil)	(iii) Annual Value of Rubber Output ($ Mil)	(iv) Pre-Tax Profits as % of ii	(v) Tax as % of ii	(vi) Dividend as % of ii	(vii) Net New and Replanting Expenditures as % of ii
1973 (RSS 1 Price = 74.9 cents/lb.)							
1. UK- & Malaysia Incorporated Companies							
Rubber Companies	20	37.0	37.0	38.6	18.0	10.3	4.5
Multicrop Companies	18	510.0	261.3	31.3	13.6	7.1	6.8
Rubber + Multicrop Companies	38	547.0	298.3	31.8	13.9	7.3	6.6
1968 (RSS 1 Price = 53.1 cents/lb.)							
1. UK-Incorporated Companies							
Rubber Companies	48	101.4	101.4	22.7	6.3	10.9	7.8
Multicrop Companies	10	269.7	185.9	32.4	12.4	15.0	4.0
Rubber + Multicrop Companies	58	371.9	287.4	29.7	10.7	13.8	5.1
2. Malaysian-Incorporated Companies							
Rubber Companies	18	31.6	31.6	26.1	6.9	10.5	2.2
Multicrop Companies	4	50.7	32.3	25.6	5.6	11.9	0.5
Rubber + Multicrop Companies	22	83.0	63.9	25.8	6.1	11.4	1.1
3. Malaysia + UK-Incorporated Companies	80	454.2	351.3	29.0	9.9	13.4	4.4
1964 (RSS 1 Price = 68.1 cents/lb.)							
UK-Incorporated Companies							
Rubber Companies	57	163.0	163.0	25.4	7.0	11.0	8.5
Multicrop Companies	7	136.4	101.2	37.3	12.4	15.4	4.4
Rubber + Multicrop Companies	64	299.4	264.3	30.8	9.5	13.0	6.7

TABLE 6.13

Sources and Notes

(1) Data on all UK companies from Zorn and Leigh-Hunt (1967a, 1969a, and 1974). Data on Malaysian companies for 1968 compiled from Stock Exchange of Malaysia and Singapore (1970), and major Malaysian companies 1973 from Zorn and Leigh-Hunt (1974). The 1973 figures omit a number of minor companies from this calculation.

(2) RSS 1 prices from Statistics Dept. RSH 1964 and 1968 and Treasury AR 1974-5.

(3) Pre-tax profits are profits after payment of export duty and cesses (excluding replanting cess, which was refunded automatically until recently to estates). Rubber export duties from Table 6.12, but 1973 duty assumed 8% (average of 1972 and 1973 duty payments) and duty on oil palm products for 1973 is taken as 15%, (based on figures from company reports).

(4) Net new planting and replanting expenditure is expenditure in addition to that financed by refunds of the replanting cess. Certain ambiguities for the 1968 dollar company figures for replanting make them unreliable. Although the replanting cess ceased to be automatically refundable to estates from January 1972, this change was retroactive and has not appeared in the 1972-73 company accounts.

(5) Output figures from the sources in note 1 are multiplied by unit values of net exports from Statistics Dept. MSB sources, except for 1973 where large price fluctuations made it necessary to calculate a weighted average value based on unit proceeds from company accounts.

(6) All years in the table refer to the companies' financial year ending in the year in question, e.g. 1973 is 1972-73.

payment of duty and research cess, and (except for 1972–3) after expenditures on new planting or immature areas.[45] The replanting cess is not deducted because in the period covered by Table 6.13 it was automatically refunded to estates. Adding net new planting and replanting expenditure to profits gives a residual of over 33% in 1967–8 for all companies covered. Taxes are predominantly Malaysian since almost all U.K. tax is refunded under a double tax agreement (and almost all foreign-incorporated estates are British). In 1963–4, when the rubber price was considerably higher than in 1967–8, the residual is larger, rising to over 37% with new planting and replanting expenditure added. In the boom price year of 1972–3 the residual would be slightly higher still (nearly 43% before export duties) but for the fact that export duties were higher, taking over 11% of gross output value for rubber and oil palm combined (through profits in Table 6.13 are shown for 1972–3 *before* deduction of replanting expenditure, so these should not be added for comparison with earlier years—see footnote 45).

TABLE 6.14 CURRENT PAYMENTS STRUCTURE OF PRIVATE AND PUBLIC RUBBER COMPANIES IN MALAYSIA, 1967 - SURVEY OF LIMITED COMPANIES

	ITEMS AS PERCENTAGES OF ANNUAL REVENUE FROM SALES OF GOODS AND SERVICES				
	(i) Malaysian Incorporated Locally Controlled Companies	(ii) Malaysian Incorporated Foreign Controlled Companies	(iii) Foreign Incorporated Companies	(iv) Total i to iii	(v) Total + Estimated Values for Non-Limited Liability Estates
Current Profits before Direct Tax, and after Duty and Indirect Tax	11.4	11.4	26.9	20.7	18.9
Duty and Indirect Tax	4.2	6.5	7.3	6.5	6.0
Direct Tax	5.5	3.0	8.2	6.6	6.4
Salaries and Wages (including Contract Labour)	38.4	41.2	37.5	38.4	38.4
Purchase of Goods and Services	49.6	35.6	27.0	31.8	35.3
Depreciation and Depletion	4.1	4.3	5.4	5.0	4.8
Dividends Paid	6.8	6.3	21.1	14.9	12.0
Payments to Overseas Shareholders	1.6	8.2	...	...	...
Retained Profits	-0.9	2.0	...	...	...
Revenue other than from Current Sales	13.9	1.6	5.5	5.9	4.7
Annual Revenue from Sales of Goods and Services	\$86.1m.	\$109.1m.	\$345.5m.	\$540.7m.	\$677.0m.

Sources and Notes

(1) All items in columns i to iv are from Statistics Dept. FSLC 1967.

(2) In 1967 79.2% of rubber estate acreage and 85.2% of rubber estate production was accounted for by public and private limited companies, (Statistics Dept. RSH 1967). Estimates for the remaining (non-limited liability) estates, in column v, assume that they have the same payments structure as those of column i (Malaysian incorporated, locally controlled companies), except that they are assumed to have no foreign dividend payments and no income other than that from current sales. The value of output in column v is from Table 6.12.

(3) A locally controlled company has Malaysian ownership of over 50% of its voting shares, and a foreign controlled company less than 50%.

(4) For foreign-incorporated companies "dividends paid" are assumed in the absence of more detailed information to be equivalent to "investment income accruing to Head Office" in Appendix Table F of the FLSC.

(5) 'Current profits' include 'other revenue'.

(6) It must be assumed that "Duty and Indirect Tax" does not include the replanting cess, since the latter (at 4.5 cents per lb.) would at the 1967 price of approximately 57 cents per lb.be7.9% of gross output value (i.e. more than the total of "duty and indirect tax" shown in the table).

Thus the company report statistics appear broadly to confirm the information from official sources in Table 6.12, though the Table 6.12 surpluses are somewhat larger because the range of costs included is not complete, and the relation between price and the residual is less clear in Table 6.12. Two points of caution about the company statistics are necessary, however. First for convenience small values of minor crop output (tea, copra, etc.) are excluded so the other crop included in total output figures is mainly oil palm. Second, and more important, some companies have diversified into other activities, profits from which are included in the profit figures, while output figures refer to plantation crop outputs only (and non-plantation crop turnover figures were not given in the Zorn and Leigh-Hunt manuals). Both factors overstate therefore the size of profits generated from rubber (and oil palm) as a proportion of output. However, examination of the annual reports of individual large, diversified, companies shows that plantation crop profits are a very large proportion of total profits, even though the proportion of turnover may be much lower.[46]

Other information on companies is available from the 1967 *Survey of Limited Companies* published by the Statistics Department of Malaysia, data from which are given in Table 6.14. This survey covers both private and public companies. In addition, Table 6.14 gives an estimate of payments by unincorporated estates. Profits for foreign-incorporated companies, mainly British, are slightly lower than in Table 6.13, and those for Malaysian-incorporated companies are strikingly lower than those of dollar public companies in Table 6.13. The low profit figure of foreign-controlled Malaysian companies is surprising since they might be expected to have similar performance to those of public dollar (i.e. Malaysian-incorporated) companies. Table 6.13 shows that profits of the latter are as high as for U.K. companies. Dividends in foreign companies in Table 6.14 are much higher than in Table 6.13 and conversely tax payments are lower. The main difference in the two sets of figures lies in the very large item Purchase of Goods and Services in Table 6.14. This is particularly confusing since if the lower profitability were the result of the sectors having lower-yielding trees, all cost items would be affected approximately uniformly; and no satisfactory explanation of this item can be offered.

Before estate payments can be split into their local and foreign components, it is necessary to know the relative shareholdings of Malaysians and foreigners in the sector in order to determine the foreign/local split of dividend payments. The 1967 *Survey of Limited Companies* gives the proportion of issued capital owned by Malaysian residents in Malaysian-incorporated companies (public and private), as set out in Table 6.15.[47]

To determine the proportion of capital held by Malaysians in foreign-incorporated companies, a postal survey of U.K.-incorporated rubber companies[48] was conducted in March–April 1971, whose results are set out in Table 6.15 and described at greater length in Appendix 6.2.

U.K. rubber companies were found to have a rather low average Malaysian shareholding (6%) although a minority of companies had Malaysian holdings of 40–60%. This is in contrast both to Malaysian rubber companies, and to the tin dredging companies discussed in Chapter 5 (see Table 5.12). The sample is sufficiently large relative to the population for a high degree of accuracy to be expected from the results.[49]

Table 6.15 summarizes the ownership of capital in the estate sector, showing that Malaysian ownership at the end of the 1960's was about 20%. This is lower than other official sources suggest. The *Rubber Statistics Handbook* for 1968 and 1972 (Statistics Dept., *RSH*, 1968 and 1972) show that estates in which Malaysians own over 50% of the capital owned 38% of the total acreage of rubber estates in 1968 and 43% in 1972. The discrepancy may be due in part to the different definitions of ownership used and the fact that there may be substantial holdings by foreigners in

TABLE 6.15 COMPARISONS OF SHAREHOLDINGS IN MALAYSIAN-INCORPORATED, AND UK-INCORPORATED RUBBER COMPANIES, AND UNINCORPORATED ESTATES

	(i) % VALUE OF SHAREHOLDING OWNED BY PRIVATE RESIDENTS OF MALAYSIA	(ii) 1967 DIVIDEND ($M.)	(iii) VALUE OF 1967 OUTPUT ($M.)
Malaysia-incorporated Companies (Public and Private)	45.1 (1967)	12.8	195.2
Non-incorporated Malaysian Estates	100.0 (ownership of assets)	8.0 (profits after all taxes and duties)	136.3
UK-incorporated Companies (Public only)	6.7 (1971)	70.5 (all foreign-incorporated companies)	345.5
All Malaysian Estates	20.3	91.3	677.0

Sources and Notes

(1) Shareholdings in Malaysian-incorporated companies from Statistics Dept. FSLC, 1967. All figures in columns ii and iii from Table 6.14. Virtually all UK-incorporated rubber companies are public.

(2) Shareholdings in Malaysian-incorporated companies are expressed in terms of the par value of issued capital. Shareholdings in UK companies are expressed in terms of the current (1971) value of issued capital. See Appendix 6.2.

(3) To estimate the overall Malaysian shareholding, the individual sectors' shareholdings are weighted by dividends (column ii). This weighting procedure is used instead of weighting by value of issued capital, since no information on the capital value of unincorporated estates is available. (Issued capital values tend to reflect past and expected dividends).

Malaysian-controlled companies, whereas it has been shown above that Malaysian share ownerhip in U.K.-controlled companies is generally minimal. In 1972 Malaysian-controlled companies still owned only 16% of the public rubber company acreage though as Section 6.1 showed there is evidence that local ownership in certain large companies (Highlands and Lowlands, Kuala Lumpur—Kepong) has increased very recently.

Table 6.16 brings together the information so far presented in an attempt to show the proportion of export income retained locally. This proportion for 1972 is approximately three-quarters of total export income, and is roughly similar to the

TABLE 6.16 LOCAL AND FOREIGN PAYMENTS OF THE RUBBER ESTATE SECTOR, PENINSULAR MALAYSIA, 1972

(Items as Percentages of Gross Value of Output)

	(i) Total	(ii) Local	(iii) Foreign	(iv) Unallocated
Costs				
Wages and Salaries	39.8	35.8	4.0	-
Labour Benefits	9.0	9.0	-	-
Materials	11.2	5.6	5.6	-
Total Costs	60.0	50.4	9.6	
Allocation of Gross Profits (40.0%)				
Export Duty	4.0	4.0	-	-
Research Cess	2.2	2.2	-	-
Tax	13.9	13.4	0.5	-
Dividends	7.3	1.5	5.8	-
Net Replanting and New Planting Expenditure	3.9	3.0	0.9	-
Other Expenditure	8.7	-	-	8.7
Total Allocation of Export Income	100.0	74.5	16.8	8.7

Sources and Notes

(1) Total wages and salaries and labour benefit figures from Table 6.12. Foreign component of wages and salaries based on 1964 RRIM estimate (Chan, Ng and Barlow, 1969) that management costs were 16% of wage bill, and assuming 10% points of this was for European managers.

(2) Materials total based on RRIM 1964 (Chan, Ng, and Barlow, 1969) estimate of approximately 5 cents a lb. for materials, on assumption that effects of inflation (raising the figure) and higher yield per acre (lowering it) approximately cancel out. A 50% local content for materials is a conservative estimate based on the high proportion of fertilizers, weedicides etc. manufactured locally.

(3) Export duty and research cess from Table 6.12. Replanting cess not deducted because it would have been refunded during the period covered (though subsequent legislation, with effect from 1973, makes it refundable only against approved replanting expenditure).

(4) Tax, Dividends, from Table 6.13 and Net Replanting and New Planting Expenditure from Statistics Dept. RSH 1972. Dividends split according to ownership figures in Table 6.15, and tax split on basis of data from company reports.

proportion retained in 1968 (not shown).[50] The main cause of this high retention figure is the large share (nearly half) of wages and salaries in total output, combined with payments to the Malaysian government of nearly 20% of export income. The tax and dividend figures are, however, those of U.K.-incorporated companies and

TABLE 6.17

RUBBER ESTATE SECTOR, PENINSULAR MALAYSIA, CURRENT PAYMENTS STRUCTURE, 1946-63

(Current Payments as Percentages of Annual Value of Output)

	(i) Value of Estate Output ($Mil)	(ii) Output Unit Value (Cents/lb.)	(iii) Total Wage Bill	(iv) Export Cess	(v) Research Cess	(vi) Replanting Cess	(vii) Schedule II Replanting Cess	(viii) Anti Inflationary Cess	(ix) Transport Costs to Port	(x) (100) - (iii to ix)
1946	...	...	...	...	...	-	-	-	...	...
47	310.3	38.3	82.0	5.2	-	-	-	-	1.3	11.5
48	390.9	43.3	55.6	4.7	0.5	-	-	-	1.3	37.9
49	345.0	38.5	50.9	4.6	0.7	-	-	-	1.3	93.4
1950	918.5	109.1	22.3	4.7	0.4	-	-	-	0.5	72.1
51	1,240.8	168.9	28.2	8.2	0.2	-	1.9	1.0	0.4	61.1
52	736.5	96.4	40.6	8.4	0.4	3.3	1.6	-	0.6	45.1
53	524.9	68.7	48.5	6.0	0.7	6.2	0.5	-	0.9	37.2
54	522.9	67.7	47.5	5.7	0.7	6.2	0.5	-	...	39.4
55	1,264.5	109.7	32.7	10.8	0.4	3.8	-	3.0	0.8	48.5
56	766.2	97.5	40.0	10.2	0.5	3.4	-	0.7	0.5	44.7
57	751.6	91.2	41.8	9.0	0.5	2.1	-	0.1	0.6	45.9
58	698.7	80.1	45.3	7.3	0.8	2.3	-	-	0.7	43.6
59	915.7	100.4	35.0	10.5	0.7	1.8	-	1.0	0.8	50.2
1960	1,012.6	109.4	37.4	10.4	0.6	3.7	-	2.1	0.6	45.2
61	804.6	83.9	41.1	8.0	0.8	4.8	-	-	0.5	44.8
62	780.4	79.5	44.0	6.6	0.9	5.1	-	-	0.7	42.7
63	765.8	74.6	42.5	5.9	0.9	5.6	-	-	0.7	44.4

Sources and Notes

(1) Column i is derived from output and price figures from Thomas and Fong (1968 p.1), with prices converted to output unit values according to the methodology of Appendix 6.1.

(2) Column iii is calculated from Appendix 6.3. It does not include labour benefits.

(3) Export duties and cesses are calculated from Rubber Producers' Council of Malaya, MSB, various issues from 1947 to 1964.

(4) Column ix is calculated from Railway Dept. AR's, 1947-63, and assumes average cost of transport by road is the same per ton as by rail.

Malaysian-incorporated companies quoted on the London Stock Exchange and it is possible that smaller, locally based companies' tax and dividend payments may differ somewhat from them, but no reliable information is available on this (given the reservations expressed above about the *FSLC* data).

6.2.2 1946–63

Table 6.17 sets out the available time series with which the analysis in Subsection 6.2.1 can be carried back to the Second World War. The main series is that of wages, the compilation of which is shown in Appendix 6.3.

Wages and employment statistics are available from Ministry of Labour sources, and are very close to the wages and salaries bills for the 1964–72 period from the *Rubber Statistics Handbook*. The residual gross profit (column x) in Table 6.17 is of

TABLE 6.18 PROFITS AND DIVIDENDS OF UK-INCORPORATED PUBLIC RUBBER COMPANIES IN MALAYA, 1951 AND 1957

	(i) Number of Companies	(ii) Annual Value of Output ($Mil)	(iii) Annual Value of Rubber Output ($Mil)	(iv) Pre-Tax Profits as % of ii	(v) Dividend as % of ii	(vi) Net New Planting and Re-planting Expenditure as % of ii
1951 (RSS 1 Price = 169.6 cents/lb.)						
Rubber Companies	260	687.7	687.7	38.8	12.9	...
Multicrop Companies	11	46.5	26.6	39.8	13.5	...
Rubber and Multicrop Companies	271	734.2	714.3	38.9	12.9	...
1957 (RSS 1 Price = 88.7 cents/lb.)						
Rubber Companies	196	325.7	325.7	30.9	22.7	7.0
Multicrop Companies	8	34.1	23.1	31.9	17.6	5.1
Rubber and Multicrop Companies	204	359.9	348.8	31.0	22.2	6.8

Sources and Notes

(1) Data compiled, company by company, from Zorn and Leigh-Hunt (1953 and 1959).

(2) RSS 1 prices from Thomas and Fong (1968, p.25), and converted to output unit values (see Appendix 6.1) to arrive at column iii. Unit values for oil palm and copra included in column ii are from Statistics Dept. MBS, June 1954.

[Statistics compiled from Manuals of Rubber Planting Companies, 1953 and 1959, reproduced by permission of Messrs. Zorn and Leigh-Hunt (stockbrokers).]

course larger than in the Subsection 6.2.1 tables because the input series are less comprehensive. Again, the importance of wage and salary payments is clear. If labour benefits were added, say 5% points, usually 40–50% of export income is spent on labour. In years of very high rubber prices, such as 1951 and 1955, the labour share drops, but a ratchet effect suggests itself in the years which follow, as wages, pushed up by union pressure, maintain at least part of their higher value as prices fall.[51,52] Export duties, on a sliding scale, have taken as much as 10% of export earnings in years of high prices.

Table 6.18 shows profits and dividends in U.K.-incorporated rubber companies for the boom year of 1951 and for 1957. Even in 1951 profits were below 40% of annual output and up to 30% of profits would have been channelled back into Malaysia in tax.

Thus, from the early 1950's the payments structure shown by Tables 6.17 and 6.18 appears similar to that in 1964–72. In 1951 and 1957 profits are slightly higher than either 1964 or 1968, as shown in Table 6.13, but in both cases the rubber price is substantially higher, and in the boom year of 1951 profits are greater than in 1973 (which is the year with the highest rubber price in Table 6.13). From 1952 the wage bill also is similar to that of later years, falling below 40% only in years of very high prices. In 1955, 1959 and 1960, when wages were from 32% to 37% of output, prices in each case were over 100 cents per lb. Detailed data on non-labour inputs are not available to allow a calculation of the local/foreign payments split. Unless there were major changes in non-labour inputs, which from the available qualitative information seems unlikely (see Subsection 6.1.2), the local retention of export earnings would be similar to 1972, except in years of very high prices when the dividends outflow would be higher. The outflow would also be greater because of lower local shareholdings in the earlier years, and a lower proportion of fertilizers, insecticides, etc. locally produced. Since overall local shareholdings in foreign-incorporated companies are still low at present, and since the growth of local ownership in local public companies is not of great quantitative importance,[53] the proportion of dividends flowing out of the country, in the early 1950's is likely to have been at most 10% more than in the late 1960's or early 1970's. This difference represents only 2% points of export income (assuming dividends to be as much as 20% of gross output value.)[54]

6.2.3 1906–39[55]

Table 6.19 shows the payments series available for the rubber estate industry to the Second World War. In view of the enormous fluctuations in the rubber price, from a high of 315 cents/lb in 1910 to a low of 8 cents in 1932, wide fluctuations in the proportion of export income retained might also be expected.[56] Moreover, the extreme price variations make comparisons with later years difficult. Also, the output, wages and employment data on which the series are based are less reliable than for later years.

With low outputs and large immature areas often intensively maintained (e.g. by clean weeding) wage bills in the years of the first rubber boom were high, at least while the price was in the $1 to $2 per pound range. Increases in output per acre by 1920 reduced the bill as a proportion of output. For 1923–9 the proportionate wage bill fluctuates inversely with the rubber price. In 1927 with a price of 65 cents (a price in the 1955–72 range) wages are 36% of output, though there are more than six times as many workers per ton of output as in 1972, when the price was 68 cents and wages were 42% of the value of output. Thus the low wages paid during this early period appear largely to have counterbalanced the much more intensive labour use, and wages were not so much more important in total payments relative to more recent times as might have been expected. It can also be seen how the large wages cuts from 1929 to 1932 prevented the wage bill from becoming proportionately large as prices fell. The low proportions of wages after prices rose from 1934 suggest wage rises lagged behind prices.

TABLE 6.19 RUBBER ESTATE SECTOR, FEDERATED MALAY STATES, CURRENT PAYMENTS STRUCTURE, 1906-39

(Current Payments as Percentages of Annual Value of Output)

	(i) Value of Estate Output ($Mil)	(ii) Output Unit Value (Cents/lb)	(iii) Total Wage Bill	(iv) Labour Benefits	(v) Export Duty	(vi) Transport Costs	(vii) 100 - (iii to vi)
1906	1.6	180.3	...	...	2.3	...	...
07	3.8	191.5	...	...	2.5	...	...
08	4.6	145.1	...	...	2.5	...	...
09	14.6	239.2	...	...	2.5	...	...
1910	39.8	315.6	27.1	...	2.5	...	70.3
11	44.2	202.8	54.8	9.0	2.5	...	34.2
12	57.3	180.2	53.8	8.4	2.5	...	35.3
13	48.3	106.7	57.7	9.0	2.5	...	30.8
14	46.4	79.3	...	...	2.4	...	...
15	60.8	73.6	36.7	5.8	2.6	...	54.9
16	...	105.0	...	...	...	...	...
17	...	105.7	...	...	...	...	...
18	...	66.3	...	...	...	...	...
19	...	79.3	...	...	...	...	...
1920	189.7	78.7	19.9	3.0	2.5	0.5	74.1
21	...	31.9	...	...	...	...	...
22	...	25.9	...	...	...	...	...
23	75.0	50.2	32.2	5.1	4.1	0.8	57.8
24	56.6	46.7	40.7	6.8	4.3	1.0	47.2
25	151.1	103.5	23.4	3.2	3.1	0.4	69.9
26	209.5	83.1	26.7	3.0	3.7	0.4	66.2
27	133.5	64.6	36.5	4.7	4.6	0.4	53.8
28	75.3	33.5	64.9	7.9	2.8	0.9	23.5
29	110.7	34.2	56.6	6.9	2.1	0.8	33.6
1930	60.8	19.3	37.4	6.7	1.0	1.4	53.5
31	35.6	11.3	49.4	8.2	0.9	2.0	39.5
32	24.7	7.9	42.9	6.9	0.9	2.3	47.0
33	31.2	10.1	51.3	7.2	1.0	1.8	38.6
34	84.8	25.7	26.3	3.8	1.5	0.5	67.9
35	61.2	20.5	33.5	5.5	2.5	0.9	57.6
36	74.0	26.5	30.8	5.0	2.6	0.7	60.9
37	121.2	32.5	29.5	4.8	2.6	0.5	62.6
38	69.5	23.9	38.6	6.6	1.7	0.7	52.4
39	...	31.0	...	...	...	0.6	...

Sources and Notes

(1) Output volume figures from the following: 1906-15, Agriculture Dept. AR's 1911-15; 1923-25 and 1931-38 from FMS, AR's 1923-25 and 1931-38; 1926 from Rubber Restriction Dept. AR, 1926; 1927-29 from Malaya RSH 1930.

(2) Output unit values derived from prices from Agriculture Dept. AR's 1918-25; 1926-39 from Thomas and Fong (1968, p.25). For 1906-17 export unit values are used from FMS AR's 1905-15 and Trade and Customs Dept. AR's 1916-17.

(3) Columns iii and iv from Appendix 6.3. Column v from export duty figures in FMS, AR 1938.

(4) Column vi from Railway Dept. AR's, 1920-39, and assumes road transport costs per ton are the same as those by rail.

Table 6.20 shows profits and dividends for U.K. rubber companies for 1921 and 1937.[57] It can be seen that even with the low prices of 1920 to 1921 a dividend could be paid as large as those paid today. The large reduction in costs following the great depression is suggested by a comparison of profits and dividends for 1938 with those of 1921, with the same price of rubber. From the wage data available it seems certain that the main cause of lower profits after the Second World War, and, therefore of greater local retention of export earnings, has been rises in wages.[58]

TABLE 6.20 PROFITS AND DIVIDENDS OF UK-INCORPORATED PUBLIC RUBBER PLANTING COMPANIES IN MALAYA, 1921 AND 1937

	(i) NUMBER OF COMPANIES	(ii) ANNUAL VALUE OF OUTPUT ($MIL)	(iii) ANNUAL VALUE OF RUBBER OUTPUT ($MIL)	(iv) PRE-TAX PROFITS AS % OF ii	(v) DIVIDEND AS % OF ii
1921 (RSS 1 Price = 31.9 cents/lb.)					
Rubber Companies	217	31.5	31.5	9.6	11.9
Multicrop Companies	16	4.2	2.7	28.2	21.7
Rubber and Multicrop Companies	233	35.7	34.8	11.8	13.0
1937 (RSS 1 Price = 32.1 cents/lb.)					
Rubber Companies	276	102.8	102.8	43.8	30.6
Multicrop Companies	14	8.5	6.4	49.5	34.6
Rubber and Multicrop Companies	290	11.3	109.2	44.2	30.9

Sources and Notes

(1) 1921 figures compiled, company by company, from Mincing Lane Tea and Rubber Share Brokers Association (1925). 1937 figures from Zorn and Leigh-Hunt (1938).

(2) 1921 profits figures are unreliable. Profits are given on different bases for different companies and insufficient means is given to reduce these figures to a common basis.

(3) RSS 1 prices from Thomas and Fong (1968, p. 25) for 1937 and Agriculture Dept., AR 1921.

[Statistics compiled from Manual of Rubber Planting Companies, 1938, reproduced by permission of Messrs. Zorn and Leigh-Hunt (stockbrokers).]

As was the case for 1946–63, the data are not comprehensive enough to allow a proper calculation of the proportion of export earnings retained. It is unfortunate that value of output data for estates are not available for the 1916–19 period of high prices and large expansion of output. The 1920 figure shows a large surplus of profit, but Figart's figures for 1919–22, which fully specify the inputs, show gross profits of only about 30% (Figart, 1925, p. 65), which is no more than the present-day companies of Table 6.13 earn. What seems likely is that labour use was so intensive that really large profits were not earned except in the early boom years. The period where profits appear strikingly high in relation to the present day is in the post-depression years of the 1930's, after the reduction in costs during the depression (see Subsection 6.1.2). As Table 6.20 shows, profits in 1937 with a price of 32 cents were larger than during the Korea boom in 1950–51 (Table 6.18) with a price of well over 100 cents. Moreover, no local tax was levied on these company profits in the period before the Second World War.

TABLE 6.21 FACTORY AND FIELD ESTABLISHMENT COSTS FOR RUBBER, 1970

	FACTORY CAPACITY (DRC PER DAY)		
	10 TONS	20 TONS	40 TONS
Mean Factory Capital Costs	$685,000	$685,000	$1.56m.
Acreage Served by Factory	2,700	5,400	10,800
Total Field Establishment Cost of Acreage Served by Factory (at $1385 per acre)	$3.74m.	$7.45m.	$14.96m.
Total Capital Cost	$4.24m.	$8.31m.	$16.52m.
Factory Cost as % of Total Cost	15.5%	10.4%	9.5%

Sources and Notes

(1) Mean factory capital costs calculated by averaging costs of nine factories of various capacities, with data obtained from interviews in Malaysia (1970), FELDA, (1967 Vol. II, p.192) and Bevan and Goering (1968, p.164). More details of factory costs are given in Thoburn (1971, pp 328-331).

(2) Field establishment costs are from Ng (1969), and include indirect costs (general charges, labour benefits, depreciation on buildings and equipment, etc.) of $545 an acre (Barlow and Ng, 1966). Direct costs in 1973 were estimated at $890-$1,214 per acre (Lim and Chong, 1973, p.19), but these more recent figures were not used since factory figures refer to 1970.

(3) Costs are undiscounted, though costs are incurred over 5-6 years on most estates.

(4) The acreages served by factory is calculated on the Jengka Triangle (FELDA 1967, p.192) assumptions of peak year crop of 1645 lb. per acre. Assuming 300 tapping days per year and that one eighth of crop occurs in peak month, the peak month capacity required in the peak year will be approximately 3.7 tons per day for 1000 acres. This is also similar to the figure implied in the Bevan-Goering calculation (1968 p. 164) which assumes that a 50,000 lb./day factory is needed for an estate of 6000 acres with maximum yield of 1800 lb. in peak year. 300 tapping days per year may however be a somewhat high figure, and it could be as low as 240.

6.3 RUBBER ESTATE CAPITAL PAYMENTS

Following the procedure used in Chapter 5, and following the methodology of Chapter 3, this section sets out rubber capital payments, concentrating on the relative sizes of local and foreign payments.

Table 6.21 summarizes 1970 costs of establishing rubber estates of varying sizes, and shows the relative importance of field establishment and factory costs. Since very little new planting has occured in estates in the post-war period (see Table 6.8) the field establishment statistics are taken from replanting data, but new planting and replanting costs do not differ markedly, provided the new planting is in an area where basic infrastructure already exists. Field establishment costs on FELDA and other official land development schemes appear to be at least 40% higher than on private-sector estates (Lim and Chong, 1973, p. 19).

Of the field establishment costs on private estates, *at least* 50% are for labour, while fertilizers and weeding chemicals are about 20% (see Ng, 1969, pp. 54–83). If a further 10% points of materials expenditure is assumed, at least two-thirds of direct field costs would be for labour. This accords with FELDA estimates of a 60–80% labour component in total field establishment costs (Interview with FELDA, November 1970). Since much of the fertilizer and other agricultural chemicals used on rubber are made locally the total local content of field expenditure could well be over 75%.

TABLE 6.22 ITEMIZED CAPITAL COSTS : SMR RUBBER FACTORY

(Capacity 8 tons/day DRC)

COST ITEMS	COST ($000)	% LOCAL COMPONENT
1. Site preparation	11.1	100.0
2. Main drains	8.6	100.0
3. Factory compound and approach roads	16.4	100.0
4. Factory buildings, including office, store and workshops	199.1	100.0
5. Machinery and equipment	268.7	28.9
6. Water supply	54.2	...
7. Electrical installation	34.8	...
8. Weighbridge and house	26.0	10.0
9. Fire fighting appliances	1.2	-
10. Equipment for office, store, and workshop.	2.6	100.0
TOTAL	622.7	51.4% (Minimum) to 65.4% (Maximum)

Sources and Notes

(1) Information from interview in Malaysia, October 1970.

(2) Factory not designed for further expansion.

(3) Local content of item 8 is estimated. The weighbridge is imported, and the house is local.

(4) Imported structural steel in item 4 will account for 50% - 75% of cost of buildings (based on oil palm and dredge building data). This reduces local content by between 21.6% and 32.4% points.

Further details of factory costs are shown in Table 6.22, where over half of expenditure is local, though the proportion would possibly fall to 30–40% if the indirect import content is taken into account. The factory described in Table 6.22 has a lower local content than several others for which figures were obtained (Thoburn, 1971, pp. 329–30).

If it is assumed that some 75% of field establishment costs and up to 60% of factory costs represent local expenditure, and that factory costs are 10% of total capital costs, then overall local content can be up to about 70%.

6.4 LINKAGE EFFECTS OF RUBBER

This section examines the linkage effects of the rubber estate sector through its intermediate purchases of inputs.[59] The approach is the same as in Section 5.4 on tin linkages.

6.4.1 Backward Linkages

The rubber industry makes few intermediate purchases of inputs. Table 6.23 shows the position for estates and smallholdings combined. Primary factors accounted for over 90% of current purchases. Allocated intermediate purchases account for 3.2% and unallocated items for a further 1.2%. The total (i.e. direct and indirect) import content is under 2%.

TABLE 6.23 INTERINDUSTRY PURCHASES OF THE RUBBER INDUSTRY, PENINSULAR MALAYSIA, 1965

	($MIL)	PERCENTAGE OF ANNUAL VALUE OF OUTPUT	TOTAL (DIRECT + INDIRECT) USE OF PRIMARY FACTORS
Chemical Products	6.5	0.6	
Products of Petroleum and Coal	0.4	0.04	
Wholesale and Retail Trade	8.3	0.8	
Imports			
Chemical Products	18.7	1.7)	
Products of Petroleum and Coal	0.3	0.03)	1.9
Metal Products and Machinery	0.7	0.06)	
Unspecified	13.5	1.2	1.4
Primary Factors			
Salaries and Wages	482.0	42.2	44.4
Entrepreneurial Income	520.1	47.7	48.4
Indirect Taxes	39.4	3.6	3.9
Subsidies	–	–	
Total	1089.9	100.0	100.0

Sources and Notes

(i) From Statistics Dept., IIA (1965), except the cumulative figures, which are from Lo (1972, p. 57).

Chemical Products are the largest input, the bulk of which was imported in 1965. Products of Petroleum and Coal (i.e. petroleum, since there was no coal production in 1965 or subsequently), purchased for use by vehicles and factory machinery, total less than $1 million. This is an insignificant proportion of local production representing

½% of 1965 output. Wholesale and Retail Trade purchases will include the value of dealers' contributions to the value of rubber output. Dealers were discussed in Subsection 6.1.1. The value of their services may be as much as $130 million, which is equal to some 10% of 1972 rubber exports, though this includes an imputed value for estates' own marketing networks, and for the value-added by Group Processing Centres and Central MRDC factories.[60] Purchases of metal products and machinery are discussed in Chapter 8 and their importance in current purchases is in any case very small. There are also local purchases of tapping equipment, not shown in the input–output table.

Chemical Products consist of acid for coagulation (usually formic acid), chemical fertilizer, weedkillers and other items such as anticoagulants. According to Table 6.23, $25.2 million were spent by the rubber industry on chemical products in 1965. According to *Rubber Statistics Handbook* figures, from Table 6.12 the rubber estate sector alone spent over $26 million on fertilizers in 1965, suggesting that the input–output table information on fertilizer purchases is incomplete (i.e. the unspecified item includes additional chemicals purchases). The 1971 rubber estate purchase of fertilizers of $20 million (Statistics Dept. *RSH*, 1971) was equal to 35% of the 1971 output of Industry 4113, Chemical Fertilizer Manufacturing (Statistics Dept., *SManI*, 1971). The reason for the fall in rubber industry purchases is partly a decline in the proportion of acreage immature and partly the switch of estates to oil palm.[61] In 1971 twelve establishments in Peninsular Malaysia produced chemical fertilizers with a workforce of 684 and a non-wage value added per full-time worker of $13,537 (very high by Malaysian standards) indicating high capital intensity. Wages per full-time worker, $366 per month, are also high by Malaysian standards. Further information on local production of fertilizers and other chemicals was obtained through interviews in Malaysia (in November and December 1970) and from the *Malaysia Industrial Digest* produced quarterly by the Federal Industrial Development Authority.

The largest producer of the chemical fertilizers in Malaysia and the only producer of *compounds*[62] is the Chemical Company of Malaysia Sdn Bhd, a subsidiary of the British firm Imperial Chemical Industries Limited. CCM's capacity is equivalent to about two-thirds of Malaysian market demand for fertilizers. The company was formed in 1963, and chlorine and fertilizer plants started production at Batu Tiga in 1965 and 1967, respectively, with Pioneer status. Fifty-one percent of the capital is held by ICI and 49% by the Malaysian public.[63] The establishment of CCM represents a pattern repeated in the establishment of production of most other agricultural chemicals in Malaysia. A foreign multinational corporation sets up a subsidiary in Malaysia with the tax concession of Pioneer status. Import duties are imposed,[64] and in CCM's case it seems unlikely that the company would be profitable without tariff protection, in view of the small market size. All CCM's straights are imported, except for ammonium nitrate (for conversion into nitrogen) hence the import duty on nitrogenous straights referred to already. Ammonia, for ultimate conversion into ammonium nitrate is bought from the Esso petroleum refinery at Port Dickson, where it is a by-product. The company employs over 400 people, although most of them work in the *godown* (warehouse).

Weedkillers are made by a number of recently established firms, mostly subsidiaries of multinational corporations. Ansul Malaysia Sdn Bhd opened its $3 million plant at Batu Tiga near Klang in April 1970, planning to produce arsenite weedkillers to meet total Malaysian demand. Ansul's staff is 40, and it is a subsidiary of the American Ansul company (FIDA, *MID*, 1969, 2nd Quarter, p. 1). Similarly, Pacific Chemicals Bhd, a subsidiary of the Dow Chemical Company of the U.S.A., was set up in 1969 to start production in 1970 with a $7 million plant making multiple herbicides, also at the Batu Tiga industrial estate (FIDA, *MID*, 1969, 2nd Quarter, p. 8). Again, the Canadian firm of Chemetics started production of weedkillers in 1971 with a $4.3 million factory in a joint venture with the local firm of Mega Chemicals Bhd (FIDA, *MID*, 1970, 3rd Quarter, p. 11). Monsanto Chemical Sdn Bhd, another American subsidiary has also started weedkiller production, and a joint Japanese/Malaysian insecticide plant, Agriculture Chemicals Malaysian, was completed in 1971 (FIDA, *MID*, 1971, 1st Quarter, p. 10). Some exporting to nearby countries also occurs.

Formic acid had been made locally by the private company, Malaysian Acid Works, for several years, and supplies most Malaysian demand. Formic acid imports are subject to a 25% duty (Malaysia, *TCCT*, 1969) presumably to encourage local production.

Thus the production of chemicals for the rubber industry (and for other crops) is essentially an exercise in import substitution, using highly capital-intensive methods, and with a high indirect import content.

6.4.2 Forward Linkages

Forward Linkages from rubber are of three sorts: the off-estate processing sector, the manufacture of rubber goods and the processing of rubber wood.

The off-estate processing sector is essentially a 'satellite' industry, in Hirschman's (1958, pp. 102–4) terminology.[65] It is an industry of average to low capital intensity.[66] Total full-time employment in 1971 was over 11,000 (compared to nearly 200,000 employed on rubber estates), most of which was in rubber remilling and latex processing. Less than 1000 workers were employed full time in commercial smokehouses.

The local manufacture of rubber goods dates from before the Second World War.[67] A wide range of products is made, including long-established items such as rubber shoes and items newly produced locally such as tyres. The main industries in the rubber products Group are 4010, Manufacture of Rubber Footwear; 4021, Manufacture of Tyres and Tubes; 4030, Foam Rubber Products; and 4090, Manufacture of Rubber Products. Combined statistics only are given for these industries in the *Census of Manufacturing.*

In 1971 there were 50 establishments with nearly 9000 full-time workers, and total value added was $46.6 million. Non-wage value added per head was $4935, a fairly low figure by Malaysian standards. The industry included five public companies, of which the tyre manufacturer Dunlop Malaysia would have been one, with very much higher capital industry of over $10,500 (NWVA per worker). This shows a new type of production being introduced into the industry often with Pioneer status and tariff protection. Over a third of the industry's employment was in these large firms. To keep the industry in perspective, however, it must be noted that total local consumption of natural rubber by Malaysian manufacturers in 1971 represented only 1.3% of West Malaysia's rubber output (Statistics Dept. *SManl* and *RSH*, 1971).

The third forward linkage is the manufacture of products made from rubber wood. With a replanting rate of about 3% per annum, about 6 million tonnes of rubber wood become available annually. Over half is used for smokehouse and brickkiln fuel and for making charcoal, but chipboard, blockboard, and other wood products are made by the local wood processing industry (RRIM, *Planters' Bulletin* November 1974, pp. 181–94). It is difficult to see this use as a 'linkage' since the existence of wood processing industries almost certainly results from the availability of local timber from ordinary logging operations, but 6 million tonnes of rubber wood is substantial compared to a current export of sawlogs and sawn timber of nearly 9 million tonnes (Treasury, *AR*, 1974–5).

6.4.3 Rubber Linkages—Summary and Discussion

The only important backward linkage is the production of agricultural chemicals, particularly fertilizer. Although in principle it would have been set up as an export industry, it has been established as a backward linkage to serve domestic agriculture. The unpublished study by C. B. Edwards (1975, p. 60, Vol. II) suggests that at least from 1969 chemical fertilizer production enjoyed an effective rate of protection (ERP) of 250 to 300%. This, combined with the industry's high NWVA per worker (nearly $14,000) raise the suspicion of a 'bad' linkage, which is further strengthened by its extremely high domestic resource content/foreign exchange ratio of 2.5 (Edwards, 1975, p. 173). Off-estate processing (and on-estate processing too though no separate figures are available for it) seems well suited to Malaysian factor endowment, with its low capital industry and a low DRC/FE ratio of 0.3 (Edwards, 1975, p. 173). The other forward linkage, rubber products, is an amalgam of relatively traditional and very modern capital-intensive production, witness the wide range of NWVA per worker (from $4,000 to $11,000). Edwards calculates that rubber products enjoy the high ERP of 170% and a high DRC/FE ratio of 1.6 (Edwards, 1975, p. 173), which suggests that *as a whole* the existing rubber products industry may not be socially profitable for Malaysia, though with such a wide variation in factor proportions between firms in the industry this certainly does not constitute an argument against the further *selective* development of rubber products.

Finally, there is the question similar to that posed in Chapter 5, of whether linkages generated by rubber constitute genuine local participation or an extension of foreign ownership by means of vertical integration. Of the backward linkages, chemical fertilizers are predominantly foreign controlled, with the ICI subsidiary CCM producing the bulk of output, though other, smaller firms may well be locally controlled. It does not however represent vertical integration by the rubber industry, though Putucheary (1960, p. 56) notes that the first important fertilizer factory in Malaysia was owned by the plantation agency Sime Derby. Of the forward linkages, Dunlop are an important local producer of rubber products and also own substantial estates whose rubber output was equal in 1971 to almost half that of the largest estate group, Guthries (Stock Exchange of Malaysia and Singapore, 1973). In off-estate processing rubber interests predominate though not mainly European ones—almost half of value-added is produced by a Singapore company Lee Rubber, but much of the rest is in the hands of U.K.-controlled rubber companies (Edwards, 1975, Vol II, p. 7).

The investments owned by rubber companies do not seem extensive,[68] but this in many cases is a reflection of the fact that firms in other activities have been taken over and included in 'group' figures. Thus the Guthrie Corporation in 1974 derived only 34% of its turnover from plantation activities (mainly rubber and oil palm), though these constituted 83% of total profits. For another large company, Plantation Holdings, the figures were 22% and 73% respectively. Most larger companies have diversified into oil palm.

In general the spread of activities of rubber companies is difficult to determine without far more research time than is available for the present study. This is because much of the foreign estate acreage is controlled by agency houses, a study of whose activities would be a major undertaking in itself. Putucheary's (1960) pioneering work has shown extensive agency house control[69] and activities which extend to shipping and insurance, import–export business and some manufacturing.

6.5 PALM OIL IN COMPARISON TO RUBBER

6.5.1 History, Organization and Technology

Unlike rubber, where Malaya occupied a predominant place in world export markets from the very early years of the industry's development, it was only in the late 1960's that Malaysia became the world's largest exporter of palm oil.

Experimental plantations of oil palm were planted by the FMS government in 1913—continuing the active agricultural experimentation which had led to the establishment of rubber—and the first commercial planting took place in 1917 (Grist, 1930). Further and more rapid development occurred in 1923 and 1924, when three rubber companies of the Guthrie group founded Oil Palms of Malaya Ltd. (Khoo, 1964, p. 3). In 1924 new planting was at the rate of over 2000 acres *per annum*, rising to over 7000 in 1927 and 1929 (Grist, 1930), and to over 14,000 in the peak new-planting year of 1930 (Agriculture Dept., *AR*, 1930). By 1930 there were nearly 60,000 acres, of which over half were in Selangor and Perak and a third in Johore. While oil palm had been an attractive crop in the late 1920's, with the alienation of new land for rubber virtually banned, prices fell from over £40 per ton (of oil) in 1927 to an average of £12 for 1934, in which year the Vegetable Oils Committee recommended a temporary reduction in rent and taxes to ease the industry's difficulties (Agriculture Dept., *AR*, 1934). From 1932 to 1938, according to the *AR*'s of the Agriculture Department, annual new plantings hardly exceeded 4000 acres, though in Johore alone in 1932 a reserve acreage (i.e. alienated to oil palm but not planted) of 32,000 acres was held. By 1938 72,000 acres had been planted, though this was minute in comparison to the two million acres planted on rubber estates, and another 1.3 million acres on rubber smallholdings (Agriculture Dept., *AR*, 1938). Nevertheless, in 1940, before the outbreak of war in the Far East, Malaya was producing 12% of world palm oil exports, following Indonesia (38.6%), Nigeria (29.3%) and the Congo (14.1%) as the main world suppliers (Lim Chong Yah, 1967, p. 133). Unlike rubber, where Malaya had pioneered estate production, oil palm estates had been planted in Indonesia at least ten years prior to the crop's commercial introduction to Malaya.

Before the Second World War (and indeed until the development of FELDA oil palm schemes in the 1960's) oil palm was entirely an estate crop. In the absence of government measures to develop an oil palm smallholder sector, the failure of smallholders to enter the industry seems mainly a function of the export technology available. Although oil palm is grown as a smallholder crop in West Africa, the type of fruit and the products produced differ considerably from those in South East Asia. The fruit of the oil palm consists of a thin skin (the *exocarp*) and a pulpy outer layer or *mesocarp*, which together are known as the *pericarp*. Beneath the pericarp is found a shell (*endocarp*) and this contains the kernel (Ministry of Agriculture, 1966). In West Africa the palm kernel (from which cattle feed, and also palm kernel oil can be made) is the main product, though there is some domestic consumption of oil for cooking and lighting (Lim Chong Yah, 1967, p. 129); and this difference in products between West Africa and South East Asia (which mainly exports oil) is the result of the pericarp layer (which contains the oil) being much thinner on the African varieties. Indeed, technical progress in oil palm in Malaysia has led to increasing proportions of pericarp (as for instance in the Tenera variety, developed in the post-war period from crossing a high-pericarp but low-yielding variety with the higher-yielding but lower-pericarp type previously grown). In an industry producing oil for the world market, the technical specification of the product is important, particularly in terms of its dirt and free fatty acid (FFA) content. For most of its industrial uses, for instance, the FFA content should be below about 7%. This is true of oil used for edible products such as margarine, or as a flux in tin plating. FFA content is less important in soap manufacture but the use of palm oil in the soap industry has declined with technical progress favouring other oils (Lim Chong Yah, 1967, p. 130).

Fresh fruit bunches (FFB) are harvested, when ripe, by cutting from the tree. Once harvested, FFA content builds up rapidly, and processing preferably should take place within twenty-four hours. This in itself would pose difficulties for smallholders, and they would require adequate transport, and dealers to take the fruit off their hands immediately. Processing, if FFA content is to be kept low, is a highly complex and capital-intensive operation (see Subsection 6.5.3), with the fruit needing to be sterlized with steam to stabilize the FFA content, then stripped from the bunch, digested and have the oil extracted (usually by means of hydraulic presses). This processing is entirely outside the means of smallholders, and the high initial capital costs and technical expertise required would put it out of the range of most dealers. Estates would be concerned about the quality of fruit from smallholders, which would make enlargement of factories to process smallholder fruit un unattractive proposition. Also working against smallholder entry is the need for greater expertise in harvesting than is needed in rubber tapping, the fact that oil palm grows well on a smaller range of soils than rubber, and, as the next subsection will show, oil palm requires more purchased inputs (especially fertilizer) per acre than does rubber.

The great expansion in acreage and production in the post-war period—from 121,000 acres in 1963 to some half-million acres in 1972 (Statistics Dept., *OPCTS*, 1972)—has been the result of rubber estates diversifying into oil palm, and (since 1960) of the development of FELDA and other official land development schemes. Estate diversification accelerated in the 1960's following falls in the price of rubber and large increases in output of rubber per acre with high-yielding varieties. In 1972 of a total rubber and oil palm estate acreage of over two million, estates on which some oil palm had been planted accounted for an acreage of 1.2 million, of which 600,000 acres were actually planted with oil palm. Of this 600,000 acres, only 221,000 was planted with oil palm as sole crop. The impression that oil palm has been used by rubber companies to diversify, while maintaining a large interest in rubber is strengthened by figures of the acreages of individual large companies and groups. Among the largest of these, for example, the Guthrie Corporation in 1973 had 36% of its 176,000 acres under oil palm (and almost all the rest under rubber), nearly 40% of Consolidated Plantations' acreage of 128,000 acres was under oil palm (and almost all the rest under rubber), and figures for other groups were—33% for Kuala Lumpur-Kepong (total 98,000 acres), 42% for Highlands and Lowlands (total 77,000 acres) and 37% for Golden Hope Plantation (total 68,000 acres) (Zorn and Leigh-Hunt, 1974). Thus almost all the main rubber estate groups have diversified into oil palm.

High initial capital costs (espeically for processing) seem to have deterred local (i.e. Malaysian-owned) estates, as well as (unassisted) smallholders from entering the industry. In 1972 66% of the oil palm acreage was controlled by non-Malaysians (of which only 6% were Singaporeans) and British-controlled estates (i.e. with more than 50% British ownership of capital) made up 48% of the total oil palm estate acreage (Statistics Dept., *OPCTS*, 1972). In contrast Malaysian-controlled estates made up 46% of the 1972 rubber acreage (Statistics Dept., *RSH*, 1972), Singaporeans 9% and British 38%.

FELDA's entry into oil palm dates from the establishment of the Kulai oil palm estate in Johore in 1960 (Khoo, 1964, p. 8). The growth of FELDA has already been described in Section 6.1. Its interest in oil palm has been as a means of diversifying out of rubber, and in 1970 its oil palm schemes exceeded its rubber schemes in acreage (164,000 compared to 148,000) (Wikkramatileke, 1972, p. 115). By 1972 FELDA's acreage had risen to 239,000 (Statistics Dept., *OPCTS*, 1972). There is also a substantial acreage (116,000 in 1971) on state-government oil palm schemes, mostly in Pahang and Trengganu (ECAFE, 1972, p. 115). It is through FELDA and other schemes that smallholders have been able to enter oil palm growing, though it is unlikely that settlers will operate individual plots as they do on rubber schemes, and the processing facilities will remain under FELDA control.

6.5.2 Current Payments Structure

Information from official sources on the payments made out of oil palm estates export income is far less comprehensive than for rubber and tin. The *Oil Palm, Coconut and Tea Statistics*, for instance, have only very recently given details of wage and salary payments, and the 1965 input–output table does not list oil palm as a sector separate from agriculture (as it does for rubber). Nor is data on individual companies very useful, since, as was shown in the previous subsection, in most cases it is grown with rubber as the main crop. Thus aggregate information on the whole estate sector cannot be given so easily as for rubber, and more reliance would have to be placed on individual studies of oil palm growing, where there is, of course, a problem of small-sample size.

In general oil palm is a less labour-intensive crop per acre than rubber, with only 0.08 workers per acre in 1972 compared to 0.13 in rubber (see Chapter 9). In 1972, calculations based on statistics from the *OPCTS* suggest that wages and salaries were equal to about 25% of the value of estate output,[70] compared to 40% for rubber. However, 31% of the 1972 estate acreage was immature in oil palm compared to only 14% on rubber estates, which would lower labour requirements on oil palm relative to rubber. Fertilizer use on oil palm was equivalent to 8½% of export value on the mature acreage (and another 2½% on the immature acreage) (Statistics Dept., *OPCTS*, 1972), very much higher than for rubber (which is about 2–3%).

In general, oil palm operating costs on a per acre basis are lower than those of rubber. For example, in a recent investment appraisal by Pushparaja, Chan and Ti

(1974), rubber costs in the peak yield year (15 years from planting) were estimated at $1872 per hectare, compared to peak year oil palm costs (10 years from planting) of $1093 per hectare. Conversely, capital costs (taken as the negative cash flow during the immature period), were $2080 per hectare for rubber, compared to $2859 for oil palm.

Thus the proportion of profits in gross output is likely to be higher for oil palm than for rubber at recent prices, and this impression is strengthened by the fact that the share of profits in the turnover of multicrop companies (which are mainly ones which grow oil palm as well as rubber) is in most years slightly higher than those of single-crop rubber companies. Profit outflows, however, are likely to be larger than rubber because of the higher proportion of foreign ownership noted in the previous subsection, and it is worth noting too that the share of local ownership in foreign-controlled companies is smaller for estates than it was, for example, in tin dredging. Export duty is at present 7½% of the f.o.b. price of palm oil, plus (from 1972) a surcharge levied at the rate of 2½% for every $50 increase in price over $350 per ton, to a maximum total duty of 30% at $700 a ton (Edwards, 1975, p. 254). In 1972 the export duty on kernels was raised from 10% to 20% to encourage local processing (Treasury, *AR*, 1974–5). Very crudely, we may estimate the gross profits in 1972 may have been over 60% of output value (before deducting tax, export duty, capital charges and other overheads). Export duty at a price just over $600 per ton would have been 22½%,[71] and tax would have taken about 40% of the remaining 40%

TABLE 6.24 FACTORY AND FIELD ESTABLISHMENT COSTS FOR OIL PALM

	FACTORY CAPACITY (TONS FFB PER HOUR)		
	10 TONS	30 TONS	50 TONS
Mean Factory Capital Costs	$2.09m.	$4.90m.	$7.16m.
Acreage Served by Factory	3220	9670	16120
Total Field Establishment Costs of Acreage Served by Factory (at $1190 per acre)	$3.83m.	$11.51m.	$19.18m.
Total Capital Cost	$5.92m.	$16.4m.	$26.34m.
Factory Cost as % of Capital Cost	35.3%	29.9%	27.2%

Sources and Notes

(1) Average factory costs derived from interviews for three mills and six other mills from secondary sources (see Thoburn, 1971, p. 332 for details).

(2) Field establishment costs are from Bevan and Goering (1968, p. 161), including housing and other general charges.

(3) All costs are undiscounted.

points of profit (after deducting various allowances). Thus perhaps 20–25% of gross output value may have been available to flow abroad as remitted profits, and some 60% of this would be in the hands of foreign-owned companies.

Income levels on FELDA smallholdings at FELDA's typical yields and 'low' price of 50 cents/lb for rubber and $370 a ton for oil are roughly similar on similar sized plots (Edwards, 1975, p. 260), but a settler family could work a larger oil palm holding (say 15 acres) than they could in the case of rubber (say about 10 acres) (Spooner, 1969).

6.5.3 Oil Palm Capital Payments

Although oil palm has a shorter gestation period than rubber (three to four years compared to five to seven), its capital costs per acre are higher, since oil palm's need for more expensive processing facilities outweighs the lower cost of field establishment. Table 6.24 shows the importance of factory costs in total costs for several sizes of estate or scheme, and can be compared to Table 6.21 for rubber. For a large estate of about 10,000 acres capital costs would be approximately $1530 for rubber and $1700 for oil palm, and the factory would be about 10% of total capital costs for rubber and 30% for oil palm. Given (as noted earlier) that fewer workers are employed per acre on oil palm, the difference in capital–labour ratios would be greater still.

Field establishment costs, like those of rubber, consist mainly of labour, local services and fertilizer, all purchased locally in the first instance. The local content of oil palm factories was determined through detailed breakdowns of capital costs obtained through interviews in Malaysia in 1970. All the mill data relates to relatively large-capacity mills (40–60 tons FFB/h) which are typical of mills built in the early 1970's (though prior to 1970 there were to my knowledge only two mills in operation with a capacity as large as 40 tons). In all cases, local content was over 40%, even after allowing for indirectly imported steel. Table 6.25 shows such a mill, where costs are broken down by stages (*stations*) of processing. Imported items are concentrated on a small number of stations—the pressing station and the boiler and power houses. Probably the absolute maximum local content, given existing engineering capacity in Malaysia, is that achieved recently (1970) by a local design consultant. In this case a 40 ton/h mill was built for $4.5m of which only $1.5m (33%) was imported. Unfortunately a detailed set of costs for this mill could not be obtained.

6.5.4 Oil Palm Linkages

Backward linkages made out of current export income from palm oil and kernels are similar, qualitatively, to those of rubber (see Section 6.4), though transportation requirements are more elaborate (primarily tanker lorries and rail trucks) and bulking installations, in wide use since the 1930's, are also necessary. The main current intermediate input is fertilizer and the 1972 purchases of fertilizer by oil palm estates alone was equivalent to 55% of the output of chemical fertilizers in Peninsular Malaysia (Statistics Dept., *OPCTS* and *PR*, 1972), reflecting the much heavier fertilizer usage of oil palm compared to rubber. Backward linkages generated by factory capital requirements are discussed in Chapter 8 (on engineering), but it is worth noting that some demand is generated for local transport equipment (rails, diesel locomotives, etc.) for field transport.

Forward linkages consist mainly of the manufacture of soap, but soap manufacturing in 1971 purchased an amount of palm oil equivalent only to less than

½% of 1971 palm oil output (Statistics Dept., *SManl* 1971 and *OPCTS*, 1972). There are also possibilities of further refining of palm oil and of further processing of kernels.

TABLE 6.25 ITEMIZED CAPITAL COSTS OF PALM OIL MILL

(Percentage Local Content by Stations)

Station	(i) % LOCAL CONTENT	(ii) TOTAL COST ($000)
1. Reception	90.0	400
2. Sterilization	50.0	400
3. Threshing	55.6	450
4. Pressing	14.3	700
5. Clarification	28.6	350
6. Depericarping	62.5	200
7. Kernel Recovery	46.0	500
8. Oil Storage	99.6	700
9. Steam Plant	31.3	1200
10. Power Plant	2.4	250
11. Piping, Valves, etc.	16.7	300
12. Water Supply	50.0	200
13. Electrical Installation	40.0	300
14. Buildings	85.7	350
15. Civil Works	100.0	400
16. Fees	50.0	250
TOTAL	45.3	6950

Sources and Notes

(1) Mill capacity is 54 tons FFB per hour.

(2) Only for item 14 is cost of imported structural steel known to have been deducted (estimated by manufacturer at 100 tons, at say $500 a ton). If structural steel for complete mill is estimated at, say, 600 tons (less 100 already included = 500 tons) at $500 a ton, total local is reduced to 41.8%.

(3) Information from interview with a manufacturer in Malaysia, October 1970.

NOTES

1. Not all of this work has been done by economists. Geographers, historians, sociologists and anthropologists have produced much material of economic interest, and an interdisciplinary approach is certainly necessary for an understanding of the smallholding sector at least.
2. A private investment appraisal, made as a comparison to oil palm, is Bevan and Goering (1968) and social appraisals are made in Helm (1969) and Syed Hussain Wafa (1972 and 1973). Some other work, conducted by the RRIM, is cited in footnote 3.
3. Two studies worth particular attention are Barlow and Chan (1968) and Lim Sow Ching (1972). Investment appraisals are given in Ng (1972) for estates, Pushparaja, Chan and Ti (1974) for rubber *vs* oil palm and Lim Sow Ching (1972) for smallholders.
4. In fact, the major gap in research which qualifies for study is the early development of smallholdings. This would be a difficult study—a book in itself involving fieldwork with Land Office records in Malaysia and extensive interviewing of existing smallholders. See, however,

P. T. Bauer's *Report on a Visit to the Rubber Growing Smallholdings of Malaya, July–September 1946* (Bauer, 1948a).

5. A discussion of rubber output restriction in the inter-war years is given in Section 4.3 and of current (1975) proposals for a rubber buffer stock in Chapter 2.
6. Today crepe is made mostly from scrap, though an exception is sole crepe which is made from latex into a form ready for attachment to shoe uppers in the consumer's factory. See Morris (1964).
7. An important qualification must be made here. The 1960 *Census of Agriculture* covered only about 0.9 million acres of a total smallholder acreage of 1.8 million. This was due mainly to the exclusion of holdings owned by certain city dwellers. It is likely that some of these were in the larger size groups, since the average holding of the city dwellers who were included was larger than the rural holdings. See Greenwood (1964, pp. 81–6). Nevertheless, it should not be assumed that most city-held smallholdings are in the larger (say, twenty-five acre +) size group. In a case study of mainly urban-held Chinese smallholdings in the Rasa mukim of Ulu Selangor, D. W. Fryer and J. C. Jackson found that 95% of Chinese smallholdings were below 25 acres, with average size of 5¼ acres. See Fryer and Jackson (1966).
8. The control is exercised through a complex of holding companies, cross company investments and interlocking directorships. See Fryer (in Wang 1964). Agency houses in Malaysia are discussed at length in Putucheary (1960, Chapter II), and their origins and organization are described by Stahl (1951, Chapter 4). However, the control is based rather less on ownership than in tin (Putucheary, 1960, p. 91) and more on management. According to statistics to be presented in Section 6.2, about 20% of the 1970 value of issued capital on rubber estates was in Malaysian hands, though Statistics Dept. *RSH* 1972 sources suggest that over 40% of the acreage is owned by Malaysian-owned companies (i.e. companies with more than 50% of their capital in Malaysian hands). The discrepancy is probably due to the fact that there may be substantial foreign minority interests in many Malaysian-owned companies.
9. The principal ways in which smallholdings were disadvantaged before the Second World War were in underassessment of their production quotas during the restriction schemes (Bauer, 1948b, pp. 203–15), and in a land alienation policy (prior to 1922 when *all* new land alienation for rubber was banned) which favoured estates (Drabble, 1973, p. 74).
10. Federation of Malaya (1963b, Vol. 1, p. 3) This subdivision partly reflects a flight of capital. In other cases land was sold to finance replanting or estates were subdivided under the same ownership in order to qualify for the larger replanting grants given to smallholders. See pp. 123–36 of Vol. 1.
11. The 1947 figures are from Agriculture Dept. *Malayan Agricultural Statistics* (1949); the 1968 and 1972 figures from Statistics Dept. *RSH*, 1968 and 1972.
12. However, an interesting idea has been put forward by Lim and Chong (1973) that estates might participate in public-sector land development by new planting of virgin areas part of which would then to sold to, e.g. FELDA schemes, since estate establishment costs are lower than those of schemes.
13. Unassisted here refers to smallholders who are not on subsidized new planting schemes. The definition includes smallholders who may have received help under replanting schemes, which are discussed below.
14. See in particular Fryer and Jackson (1966), Voon (1967), Swift (1965, and in Firth and Yamey, 1964). There is also Bauer (1948a) and McHale (1965).
15. Since 1952, Chinese have acquired an increased acreage from the subdivision of estates. Over 75% of such acreage was bought by Chinese (see Federation of Malaya, 1963b, p. 138), say 200,000 acres, which is about a third of the increase in planted area since the war. For the smallholder sector as a whole the increase in Chinese acreage may well have been outweighed by the predominance of Malays in official schemes.
16. The grouping of rural Chinese into some 400 resettlement areas, or new villages, was carried out to prevent communist insurgents (who were mostly Chinese) from obtaining food and supplies from Chinese squatters in rural areas. Although the Emergency was not formally ended until 1960, the worst was over by 1955. See A. Short, 'Communism and the Emergency', in Wang (1964); and also Short (1975).
17. An average tapping 'task' would be 550 to 600 trees, which is equivalent to 3 to 3.3 acres with a smallholding planting density of 180 trees per acre. Estates normally plant at a lower density, say 120 trees per acre. See Barlow and Lim (1967).

18. Most smallholders tap daily (or two days out of three) and most estates alternate daily. See Ng Eng Kok, Ng Choong Sooi and Lee Chew Kang (1968). Little maintenance work is done on many smallholdings and a tapper could process the latex he collected at the end of his morning's work.
19. Fisk's study of a Malay reservation, in an area of the (much researched) district of Ulu Selangor, showed that only 15% of potential income and less than a half of actual income from rubber accrued to Malays. Non-Malays owned 38% of the acreage, and over half of the Malay-owned farms were rented out (by the relatively small number of Malay landlords) to Chinese (Fisk, 1961, pp. 16–22).
20. The classic study of FELDA (then FLDA) is Ness (1967). Two other useful sources are FELDA (1966 and 1970). See also FELDA (undated) and Taib (1968). I am grateful to FELDA for arranging visits for me to two of its rubber schemes–Bilut Valley in Pahang and Sungei Tiang in Kedah, in November 1970.
21. This applies only to rubber schemes. Under oil palm schemes, settlers work blocks of about 200 acres, although receiving their share of profits on the basis of a hypothetical holding of 8–10 acres. Settlers on rubber schemes work on similar blocks before they are allocated individual plots (which are within the blocks in which they worked). In 1973 holdings were raised to twelve acres for rubber and fourteen for palm oil (Prime Minister's Dept., *MTR*, 1973, p. 8).
22. Federation of Malaya (1961, p. 37). Although FELDA was formed in 1956 the main expansion of its work dates from the start of the second plan period.
23. Its overall importance in Malaysian land development is understated in Table 6.9 since by 1968 it had developed an acreage of oil palm equal to that of rubber, whereas most acreage under other schemes was planted with rubber.
24. The state of Kelantan is the exception to this statement. Kelantan had (as of 1970) refused to hand over the administration of its schemes to FELDA.
25. See Lim and Ghazali (1974). To combat this problem the Federal Land Consolidation and Rehabilitation Authority (FELCRA) was set up in 1966. However, Lim and Ghazili question the *economic* desirability of further expenditure on many such schemes, preferring either minimal improvement or new land development elsewhere, because the increases in yield from rehabilitation generally do not produce a sufficiently high return on investment compared to opportunities elsewhere in Malaysia.
26. See Federation of Malaya (1954) (the Mudie report); and Federation of Malaya (1955), which is the government statement of policy following the Mudie recommendations on replanting.
27. Federation of Malaya (1954, p. 68) noted that half of the 1954 smallholding rubber acreage and a third of estate acreage had been planted more than 33 years previously.
28. A convenient description of the replanting cesses can be found in Lim Chong Yah (1967, pp. 122–7).
29. See Edwards (1970, pp. 238–47), and also Tan (1967). This resulted mainly from the fact that (from 1955 to 1972) all contributions paid by estates were refunded unconditionally on replanting, whereas smallholders' payments had to be applied for and were refunded only against approved replanting expenditure. From January 1973 under the Rubber Industry (Replanting) Scheme for Estates administered by the new Rubber Industry Smallholders Development Authority (sic), estates will also get refunds only against approved replanting expenditure. See Lim and Chong (1974).
30. See also Lim Sow Ching (1968a). Lim describes a hierarchy of dealers. Middle dealers are usually found in larger towns, and often finance first-level dealers, who work on a smaller scale.
31. These centres are operated and used mainly by Chinese. In Selangor 27% of smallholder rubber is processed in GPC's (1963–5) in contrast to less than 6% in all other states. See Voon (1967, pp. 115–6).
32. Majlis Amanah Rakyat–Council of Trust for Indigenous People. This organization was formerly known as the Rural Industrial Development Authority (RIDA).
33. There were by 1970 five such factories with capacities of 10–20 tons/day DRC. They were operated by Malayan Rubber Development Co-operation, an organ of the Malayan Rubber Research and Development Board (interview with MRDC, November 1970).
34. In 1971 nearly 130,000 tons of processed latex was produced by the off-estate processing sector (see Statistics Dept., *SManl*, 1971). This is equivalent to 19% of the 1971 estate output.

Very few smallholders sell their crops as latex (e.g. 2% of smallholding crop in Selangor is sold as latex). See Lim Sow Ching (1968b, p. 15).

35. Research by the RRIM has shown that the proportion of high-yielding material is the dominant factor both in the profitability of estates and in the family return to smallholders. For both estates and smallholdings area of holding within a given yield group was not significant in determining costs. See Barlow and Chan (1968, p. 21) and Ng, Barlow and Chan (1968, p. 2). The influence of planting density has also been investigated by the RRIM (see Barlow and Lim, 1967).
36. An extremely useful summary of the rationale behind this research is given in Lim, Ho and Yoon (1973). The main methods used to shorten the immaturity period include the use of 'precocious' clones which mature earlier (even at the expense of lower yields later), nursery techniques such as the establishment of rubber in polybags and subsequent transfer to the field, use of legume cover during the immature period and even the use of yield stimulants on virgin bark. Lim, Ho and Yoon, in fact recommended the reduction of the period of exploitation from thirty to twenty years, advocating obtaining high yields as soon as possible even at the expense of subsequent output.
37. Strictly speaking rubber produced by the old processes could be graded and packed as SMR. Only 6% of SMR exports in 1968 were of conventional rubber however, and by 1972 this had fallen to 1% (Statistics Dept., *RSH*, 1968 and 1972).
38. Thus the grades SMR 5, SMR 20 and SMR 50 have 0.05%, 0.20% and 0.50% dirt content respectively. SMR 5L is a rubber of especially light colour, if such is required by the consumer.
39. Latex is coagulated either in steel drums (the Promoci process) or in large concrete tanks (the GEC–AEI process), though in the case of a factory converted from sheet production the existing coagulating facilities could be used. The coagulum is then reduced in size by granulators (which slice the rubber into small pieces) or hammermills (which pound it into small pieces), and dried by air. There is much dispute in Malaysia about processing methods, and much of my own information is based on interviews with manufacturers in Malaysia in 1970. The heveacrumb process pioneered by the RRIM, in which castor oil, rather than any mechanical means, is used to crumble the rubber is now rarely installed in new factories. Some discussions of processing methods can be found in Graham and Morris (1968) and Sethu, Soh and Hoo (1972).
40. Bateman (1965, pp. 1–2) suggests that it was the larger throughputs expected from high-yielding new plantings and replantings which were the main impetus to research into new processing methods. SMR processing economizes particularly on drying time and capacity.
41. This information is from Pushparaja, Johar, Subramaniam, Ti and Yoon (1973), who give a summary of the technical advances which are currently available to modernize smallholder rubber production.
42. For earlier years it gives only payments to labour, and these only for 1962 and 1963.
43. It would not be correct to aggregate immature area expenditure and the replanting cess (a sort of forced depreciation allowance) since the former is partly financed from refunds of the latter. For a further discussion of this point see Edwards (1970, Chapter 9).
44. A more detailed breakdown of the estate current payments for 1964 is available from a survey of estates in Peninsular Malaysia carried out by the Rubber Research Institute (Chan, Ng and Barlow, 1969). The expenditure on labour by estates in the survey is slightly lower (40.9%) than in Table 6.12 for 1964. It would be slightly lower still if the RRIM costs were calculated as percentages of export unit values (70.1 cents per lb) instead of the gross amount received by estates (64.8 cents per lb). This is to be expected in view of the bias of the RRIM sample towards more efficient estates (Chan, Ng and Barlow, 1969, pp. 1–2). Materials in the survey amount to a little over 10% of gross output, leaving a residual of over 30%. The survey represents the RRIM's first attempt to acquire widespread economic data on estates. Before 1962 the RRIM was expressly forbidden to conduct economic research (Interview with head of Economics and Planning Division of RRIM, October 1969).
45. In the Zorn and Leigh-Hunt (1967a and 1969a) data for 1964 and 1967 there appears to be some inconsistency as to whether profits are stated before or after replanting expenditure. Of the major companies for instance, Highlands and Lowlands clearly (from its annual report) shows profits before replanting expenditure, whereas Seafield Amalgamated appears to deduct replanting expenditure from profits. For 1973 however, the *Manual* (Zorn and Leigh-Hunt, 1974, p. 2) states that because of differences in companies accounting practices,

it has standardized *all* profits so that they are shown *before* deduction of replanting expenditure.

46. For the largest company, Guthries, plantation crops in 1973 were 36% of turnover, but produced nearly 60% of total profits (and 83% in 1974). For Plantation Holdings the figures were 25% and 66% respectively. For the other major companies the share of rubber and oil palm in total turnover is much higher, e.g. 89% for Golden Hope and 99% for Highlands and Lowlands. Since not all company reports give turnover figures and most do not split profits according to their source, no overall figures can be given.
47. More detailed information on shareholdings in Malaysian public rubber companies is given in Mamajiwala (1963). Mamajiwala found from 1948 to 1963 the proportion of issued capital held by residents of Malaya (and Singapore) rose from 45.5% to 58.3%, and to 69.7% in 1958. Over the same period the proportion of issued capital held by Europeans (including European residents of Malaya and Singapore) fell from 75.6% to 57.8%, to 40.3% (see pp. 324). Mamajiwala suggest that as share prices rose during the Korean boom, Europeans took their chance to sell out, their commitment to Malaya having been weakened by war and the Emergency (pp. 402–10).
48. U.K.-incorporated companies form the bulk of foreign rubber companies operating in Malaysia. Thus the U.K. companies in Table 6.13 had an output of rubber in 1967–8 equal to 83% of the total output of foreign-incorporated companies in Table 6.14.
49. The 1967 output of the 31 companies covered in the sample was 61% of all foreign-incorporated companies given in Table 6.14; and the 1971 value of their issued capital was 78% of all U.K. rubber companies quoted on the London stock Exchange, as listed in Zorn and Leigh-Hunt (1969a). If the other companies had zero Malaysian share ownership, the overall figure would be 5% Malaysian ownership, and if the other companies had 100% Malaysian ownership the overall figure would be 25%.
50. For the 1967–8 the proportion was 75.1%. See Thoburn (1971, p. 304 and 1973a, p. 97).
51. For a history of trade unionism in the rubber industry see Gamba (1962) and Gul (1968).
52. Since 1958 estate wages have consisted of two elements: a cost of living, or basic, element, together with a price element which increases as the rubber price rises. See Gul (1968, p. 27). However, see Section 7.2 for an estimate of rubber industry export multipliers, which suggests that there is little immediate connection between changes in rubber export earnings and changes in wage payments.
53. Such companies accounted for only 29% of 1967 output and 14% of 1967 dividends. See Statistics Dept., *FSLC*, 1967.
54. The 10% increase is arrived at as follows: In 1967 45% of Malaysian-incorporated companies' capital was locally owned and these companies accounted for 14% of dividends. If local ownership were zero (an extreme assumption since many of the companies were private) dividend outflow would increase by 6% points. 10% is assumed in order to take account of the fact that in early post-war years replanting had yet to give foreign companies their present dominant advantages.
55. This subsection concentrates on the rubber industry in the Federated Malay States only, since figures for the FMS are in many cases the only ones available. The estate sector's economic structure would differ little between the FMS and the Unfederated Malay States.
56. In contrast, from 1906–39 the lowest tin price ($60 per pikul in 1931) was equal to as much as 40% of the highest tin price ($151 in 1918 and 1920).
57. No earlier years than 1921 are now available, although the manuals from which the figures are taken were published from the first years of the century. Even the British Museum does not have copies covering the 1910–20 period. Manuals published before 1910 did not have statistics in a usable form.
58. But see Section 9.4 which suggests that post-war real wages increases as rubber estates have been small.
59. In principle this section should deal only with estate-sector intermediate purchases and sales following the current payments analysis of Section 6.2. In fact much of the available information is for the industry as a whole. Input purchases and sales do not differ qualitatively between the estates and smallholding sectors, although inputs per unit of output may differ considerably.
60. The value of dealers' services is calculated as follows—according to Barlow (1967, p. 3) acreage dealer margins are 2.1 cents/lb on smallholder smoked sheet and 8.4 cents/lb on smallholder

unsmoked sheet. Three-quarters of smallholder output is sold as unsmoked sheet (p. 2). Taking 3 cents and 10 cents as the 1972 margin figures, and with a total 1972 smallholder output of 589 million tons (Statistics Dept., *RSH,* 1972), total margins are a maximum of $109 million. Assuming a smaller margin of 1.5 cents/lb for estates (649 million tons in 1972) gives a total maximum margin for both sectors of $130 million million.

61. The oil palm estate sector bought $31 million of fertilizers in 1972. See Statistics Dept., *OPCTS*, 1972.
62. Fertilizers can be divided into three. First, single nutrient fertilizers, or *straights.* Straights can be combined into *mixtures* and *compounds.* A mixture consists of straights mixed together physically, usually as a powder. Mixtures are liable to separate during transit. In a compound the various straights are bonded together by a chemical process, often into a concentrated liquid, and separation cannot occur. Rubber requires mainly compounds and oil palm mainly straights. Oil palm use of fertilizer per mature acre is four times that of rubber.
63. Of the 1966 issued capital of $30 million over 90% is for the fertilizer plant (FIDA, *MID,* 1970, 3rd Quarter, p. 4).
64. There is a duty of $60 a ton on all mixtures and compounds, and $50 a ton on straight nitrogenous fertilizers except urea (which is used by padi planters). Most fertilizer prices are in the range of $200 to $300 a ton, thus the duty is equivalent to about 25% *ad valorem.*
65. In other words, an industry which *must* be located at the source of its major input. Thus it would be difficult to imagine rubber latex exported unprocessed, since it coagulates naturally and would become scrap. Concentrating latex for export is as complicated a process as any other form of processing, and the only alternative to the present degree of processing would be to export unsmoked sheet or scrap.
66. Non-wage value added per full-time worker was $8402 in Rubber Remilling and Latex Processing Off-estates in 1971, and $3628 in Rubber Smokehouses Off-estates. See Statistics Dept., *SManI,* 1971. In fact the capital intensity of Remilling and Latex Processing has risen sharply since 1968 when it was just over $5400 per worker, probably as a result of the greater capital intensity of SMR production.
67. According to the British Malaya *Census* of 1931, 100 people were employed in the Federated Malay States in the manufacture of rubber goods.
68. An examination of the 1974 annual reports of eight of the largest companies which produced 50% of the output of all public rubber companies in Malaysia showed that these companies, with a total 1971 market value of capital of £330 million, owned outside investments with a market value (or director's estimate in the case of unquoted investments) of only £20 million. The companies were Consolidated Plantations, Golden Hope, Guthries, Highlands and Lowlands, Kuala Lumpur-Kepong, London Asiatic, Petaling and Plantation Holdings.
69. Control by agency houses over estate output does not seem to have lessened noticeably, with a few exceptions, since Putucheary wrote. Thus of the companies listed in the previous footnote, all had as secretaries major agency houses, except for Kuala Lumpur-Kepong whose control has recently been taken over by local interests (*Far Eastern Economic Review,* 18 July 1975). Also according to its 1974 annual report, another major company (Highlands and Lowlands) had 9% of its shares owned by PERNAS and a further 13% by Kuala Lumpur-Kepong.
70. This calculation assumes that the proportion of estate to total output is the same as the estate share of mature acreage. Estate production figures cannot be used because some FELDA output, for instance, is channeled through estate factories. Also, the wages and salaries bill in *OPCTS* is for December only, which is a relatively low-yield month, so the wage payments may be understated somewhat.
71. In April 1974 there was a further rise in the oil palm surcharge (and those of rubber and tin) (Treasury, *AR*, 1974, p. 105).

Chapter 7
Final Demand Linkages and the Development of the Local Market for Consumer Goods[1]

In Chapter 3 it was argued that one way in which the export sector could spread growth was through final demand linkage. If primary factors of production employed in the sector buy goods produced locally, domestic investment in these goods might be induced and a local market created. The type of local market would depend on the size and distribution of export-sector factor incomes. Not only might final demand linkage stimulate new capital formation[2] but, as in the case of other linkages, it could introduce new technology.[3] Section 7.1 therefore examines the size and local components of export-sector final demand expenditure.

In Chapter 3 also, final demand linkage was equated with the multiplier–accelerator mechanism. While Section 7.1 shows *ex post* how export income accruing to primary factors has been spent, Section 7.2 looks at the relation between export income and the income of primary factors, in an attempt to quantify the multiplier effects of changes in export income.

7.1 EXPORT-SECTOR CONSUMPTION EXPENDITURES

The principal source of information on consumption expenditure in Malaysia is the *Household Budget Survey of the Federation of Malaya,* 1957–8, published by the Department of Statistics. The Survey gives detailed breakdowns of expenditure, commodity by commodity, for Malay, Chinese and Indian households. For each group, information is given separately for households in rural areas and households in urban areas. For each of the six groups (rural Malay, urban Indian, etc.) consumption expenditure is split further according to six income categories.[4]

The aim of the present exercise is to determine what are the consumption expenditures made by export-sector workers and smallholders,[5] then to split these expenditures into their local and foreign (i.e. import) components, and finally to examine the effects of the local expenditures. Given the form of the expenditure data, the first step is to determine what proportion of the wage bill (or of total export income in the case of smallholders) accrues to each ethnic group (or 'race', in Malaysian usage). Second, it must be decided into which income category the various households fall, and, third, whether the households are rural or urban.

Table 7.1 shows the wage bills paid to each race on rubber estates, gravel pump tin mines and tin dredges. The total wage bills have been split first according to the

TABLE 7.1 DISTRIBUTION OF WAGE BILLS BY ETHNIC GROUP, 1968

		(i) PROPORTION OF EACH GROUP IN 1968 WORK-FORCE	(ii) WAGE BILLS ($000)	(iii) ROUNDED WAGE BILLS ($M.)
Rubber Estates	Indians	0.46	111,440	111
(Wage Bill:	Chinese	0.31	75,101	75
$242.262m.)	Malays	0.23	55,720	56
Gravel Pump Tin Mines	Indians	0.06	3,338	3
(Wage Bill:	Chinese	0.83	46,171	47
($55.628m.)	Malays	0.10	5,563	5
Tin Dredges	Indians	0.24	6,113	6
(Wage Bill:	Chinese	0.37	9,424	10
$25.469m.)	Malays	0.37	9,424	9

Sources and Notes

(1) Column i from Statistics Department, HLS 1968.

(2) Total Wage Bills from Appendix 6.3 for rubber, and Appendix 5.1 for tin. Wage bills exclude managerial and professional salaries, which frequently accrue to expatriates in estates and dredges.

(3) Column ii derived by multiplying Total Wage Bills by column i.

(4) Chinese Wage Bills in tin mining in column iii are rounded upwards to take account of the fact that Chinese tend to occupy more skilled positions.

proportions of each race in the workforce. In rubber, earnings differ little between the races. In mining, Chinese tend to occupy the more skilled positions, hence Chinese wage bills have been adjusted upwards, and Malay and Indian wage bills downwards, in the rounded wage totals. Table 7.2 shows the distribution of income among smallholders by racial group. An arbitrary 20% of Malay income has been reallocated to Chinese in the rounded figures to take account of the fact that much Malay-owned land is actually operated by Chinese (Fisk, 1961).

The estimation of household income raises a particular problem in the case of rubber estate workers. Normally a household may consist of a wage earner and his dependents. In rubber estates however nearly half the labour force is female[6] and other available information[7] suggests that in many Indian households living on estates[8] there are both male and female wage earners. This seems also to be true, but to a lesser extent, of Chinese. Unfortunately no cross-classification is available of the estate labour force by ethnic group and sex. The nearest cross-classification is in the 1957 *Population Census,* which refers to all employees in rubber planting, including a

TABLE 7.2 DISTRIBUTION OF SMALLHOLDER RUBBER INCOME BY ETHNIC GROUP, 1968

	(i) SHARES OF 1952 SMALLHOLDER ACREAGE	(ii) FAMILY RETURN FROM RUBBER ($000)	(iii) ROUNDED FAMILY RETURN FROM RUBBER ($M.)
Indians	0.08	21,553	22
Chinese	0.41	110,460	137
Malays	0.47	126,625	100

(Total Smallholder Family Return = $269.415m. = 50% of value of Smallholder Rubber Exports, 1968).

Sources and Notes

(1) Column i from Table 6.10. No more recent figures are available. Malay acreage will have increased as a result of participation in FELDA schemes, while Chinese acreage has risen because of estate subdivision and other purchases of existing rubber land. See Subsection 6.1.1.

(2) Family Return is the difference between net smallholding revenue from rubber, and all costs except family labour. Barlow and Chan (1968, p. 17), calculated that the family return in 1968 was from 28.4 to 30.0 cents/lb., depending on the type of planting material. These figures are approximately 50% of the 1968 net export unit value.

(3) Column ii calculated by distributing Total Smallholder Family Return according to column i shares of acreage.

(4) Case studies of Malay and Chinese smallholder areas indicate that Malay-owned rubber land is often worked by Chinese on a share-cropping basis (See Subsection 6.1.1). Thus the rounded figures in column iii include an arbitrary transfer of 20% of Malay income to Chinese. This may still understate the Chinese share, but it is a correction in the right direction.

(5) In calculating family return the proportion of gross income retained on FELDA schemes, which is likely to differ from 50% (see note 2) is disregarded, since FELDA schemes in 1968 accounted for only 5% of smallholder acreage (Statistics Dept. RSH, 1968).

minority of workers employed on smallholdings. For employees in rubber planting the ratio of males to females was 1.31 for Indians, 1.24 for Chinese, 1.47 for all workers, and 1.97 for Malays (Federation of Malaya, *Population Census,* 1957, Report No. 1). On the strength of this information, and given an average estate wage in 1968 of $98 a month with little variation around the mean, it has been decided to put

Indians and Chinese in the $151–$300 a month category and Malays in the $1–$150 category.

In gravel pump mining, the 1968 average wage was $114 (see Appendix 5.1), and all groups are placed in the $1–$150 category. In dredging, the average wage was $140, and Chinese tended to occupy skilled jobs with higher wages than the average, while Indians and Malays did less skilled jobs. Hence Chinese are placed in the $151–$300 group, and Malays and Indians in $1–$150.

In the rubber smallholding sector the average size of holding is 6.6 acres (Barlow and Chan, 1968, p. 3). Malays tend to have holdings well below the average size and Chinese have holdings above it. Barlow and Chan (1968, p. 17) calculate that the family return per acre, at the 1968 rubber price is $308 per annum if high-yielding material is planted, and $154 for low-yielding material. A holding of 6.6 acres gives family returns of $169 and $85 a month for high- and low-yielding material, respectively. On this basis Malay and Indian households are put in the $1–$150 category, and Chinese households in the $151–$300 category. Of course, these classifications, like those for wage earners on estates and mines, are rather arbitrary. It should be remembered, however, that the purpose is not to estimate exact income, but to decide which consumption pattern to use in the analysis which follows. Another difficulty is that various household members may work in several industries, thereby perhaps raising household income above the limits chosen here. Little quantitative information is available on this point.

TABLE 7.3 CLASSIFICATION OF HOUSEHOLDS IN RUBBER PLANTING AND TIN MINING

		URBAN (U) OR RURAL (R)	INCOME GROUP ($ PER MONTH)	WAGE BILLS ($ M.)
Rubber Estates	Indians	R	151-300	111
	Chinese	R	151-300	75
	Malays	R	1-150	56
Rubber Smallholdings	Indians	R	1-150	Family (22
	Chinese	U	151-300	Return (137
	Malays	R	1-150	(100
Gravel Pump Mines	Indians	R	1-150	3
	Chinese	R	1-150	47
	Malays	R	1-150	5
Dredges	Indians	R	1-150	6
	Chinese	R	151-300	10
	Malays	R	1-150	9

Sources and Notes

(1) See text for discussion of methodology.

The final step in determining which consumption patterns to use is to decide whether households are rural or urban.[9] In the case of estate workers, and workers on gravel pump mines and dredges, most of whom live at their place of work,[10] households are assumed to be rural. However, during the Emergency many rural Chinese were reallocated to new villages, often with populations of over a thousand. For this reason Chinese smallholders are classed here as urban.[11] Table 7.3 summarizes the classifications chosen.

Having decided into which income group each race of worker (or smallholder) in the tin and rubber industries should fall, and whether they are urban or rural, the proportions of total income spent on particular goods by each of the six groups in Table 7.3 are multiplied by the total income of each group (from Tables 7.1 and 7.2) to determine the group's demand for the goods in question.[12] The *Household Budget Survey* lists monthly income spent on each of about 200 goods. To reduce the calculations involved, the goods on which none of the six groups spent at least 1% of

TABLE 7.4 CONSUMPTION EXPENDITURE OF WORKERS IN THE TIN AND RUBBER INDUSTRIES, AND OF RUBBER SMALLHOLDERS, PENINSULAR MALAYSIA, 1968

	(i) TOTAL EXPORT SECTOR DEMAND ($MIL)	(ii) (i) / NET IMPORTS
Food		
Rice (polished)	77.7	0.8
Rice (parboiled)	8.1	0.3
Wheat Flour	3.1	-0.6
Bread	4.3	44.8
Biscuits	5.3	2.2
Buns, Cakes, Pies	12.3	9.3
Potatoes	1.8	0.4
Sugar	17.8	0.3
Bean Curd	2.2	...
Dhall	1.5	0.3
Coconuts	3.3	-11.3
Beef	4.7	1.1
Mutton	4.2	1.4
Pork	20.3	50.3
Miscellaneous Carcass Meat	5.0	0.9
Fowl	9.5	10.9
Kembong (fish)	4.1	...
Other Fresh Fish	14.8	...
Prawns and Shrimps	4.8	...
Preserved Fish	13.7	...
Duck Eggs	4.0	2.9
Fresh Milk	1.6	-11.6
Condensed Milk	14.9	-1.0
Coconut Oil	6.5	9.1
Coffee	5.6	1.4
"Other Curry Stuff"	1.6	22.0
Meals Out	21.4	NT
Drink and Tobacco		
Beer	2.1	0.6
Stout	3.9	-0.6
Toddy (an alcoholic drink)	7.1	NT
Cigarettes	19.0	-5.8
Cigars	3.1	18.4
Tobacco	4.4	10.9
Sirah, Betel, and Other Nuts	1.4	NT

TABLE 7.4 Continued

	(i) TOTAL EXPORT SECTOR DEMAND ($MIL)	(ii) (i) / NET IMPORTS
Manufactures		
Sarong (article of clothing)	3.2	1.5
Cotton Material	7.3	0.2
Other Materials and Tailoring Charges	3.6	0.5
Durable Household Goods	4.4	0.1
Joss Sticks, etc. (religious objects)	2.3	3.8
Kerosene	5.4	-0.9
Books and Periodicals	3.2	0.3
Utilities and Services		
Firewood	8.6	NT
Electric Power	2.5	NT
Bus Fares	6.1	NT
Other Fares	5.8	NT
Cinema	3.6	NT
Haircuts and Shaves	3.4	NT
School Fees	8.5	NT
Medical Fees	2.7	NT
Internal Eastern Medicine	3.2	...
Charity and Gifts	8.2	NT
Loan Repayments	13.6	NT
Pocket Money	10.8	NT
Miscellaneous Expenditure	6.1	...
Rent and Rates	14.9	NT

Total Expenditure on Items Listed above: $442.5m.

Total Expenditure on Items with Column ii Value of < 1.0: $132.5 m. (29.9% of Total Expenditure on items listed above)

Sources and Notes

(1) Consumption data calculated from Statistics Dept., HBS (see text for discussion of methodology). Net Imports are Imports less Exports and Re-exports, from Statistics Department, ASET, 1968.

(2) NT = non-traded good. A negative entry indicates positive net exports.

(3) The items listed above account for 74% (in the case of rural Chinese with incomes of $151-300 a month) to 81% (for rural Indians with $1-150 a month) of total expenditure. A necessary and sufficient condition for an item to be included in the table is that one or more of the six income-ethnic groups should spend at least 1% of their income on that item.

income were omitted. This reduced the coverage to about 75% of total consumption expenditure.[13] The demands of each group for each good are summed in order to arrive at the total demand by the tin and rubber industries for the good in question.[14] These demands are shown in column i of Table 7.4, which summarizes the results of the analysis.[15]

For most of the fifty or so goods in Table 7.4, local production data do not exist, so a direct measure of local market share (Local Demand÷[Local Production+Net Imports]) cannot be used. Instead, consumption can be compared to net imports. In column ii of Table 7.4 total demand is divided by net imports. If the export-sector households concerned constituted the whole population of Peninsular Malaysia, a column ii figure of 1 would indicate demand equal to imports (i.e. demand satisfied by imports, with no local production). In fact, workers (and smallholders) in tin and rubber are just over 30% of the Peninsular Malaysian working population. If their ratio of workers to dependents is roughly the same as for the rest of the population,[16] and their consumption patterns broadly similar,[17] a figure of 0.3 in column ii would indicate that export-sector demand was met entirely by imports. A column ii figure of 1 would show that demand was three times larger than imports. In Table 7.4 a column ii figure of 1 is chosen as a cut-off, above which export-sector demand is assumed to be met from local production. Only 29.9% of the value of consumption in Table 7.4 (equal to 22% of total consumption) is of goods where imports meet more than a third of local demand. Items for which no suitable import statistics are available constitute only another 11%, and 5% points of that is fresh fish which is almost certainly locally caught. Allowing for the import component in items with a coefficient of more than 1, up to 70% of Table 7.4 expenditure could be local.

The composition of local consumption expenditure as well as its total size is important in determining its development effects. New technology may be introduced if consumers demand more sophisticated products (Baldwin, 1963). In fact about 65% (at least) of expenditure[18] is on food, though it includes the high figure of 5% points on meals out. Manufactured foodstuffs include sugar (4% of expenditure), which is refined locally, various bakery products (1%) and condensed milk (3%). Beer is also brewed locally. Non-food manufactured items include cigarettes (4%), and a few small items. 'Modern' expenditure on services includes cinema tickets and bus fares, each about 1% of expenditure.

Thus household workers in the two export industries still spend the bulk of their income on simple foodstuffs, while manufactured commodities and Western-type services are but a small proportion of expenditure.[19] However, these results exclude managers and executives for whom no adequate data are available,[20] and who would earn an amount equivalent to another 10–20% of the wages bill.[21]

7.2 EXPORT-SECTOR MULTIPLIERS

The previous section provided an estimate of the average propensity to consume local products out of export income on the part of wage earners in tin and of wage earners and smallholders in rubber. The average propensity to import of these consumers appears to be slightly lower than that of the economy as a whole (40% in 1974, though of course the latter includes imports of investment goods and imports by government—see Treasury, *AR*, 1974–5). By indicating the types of products purchased locally by these workers and smallholders the previous section also gives an indication of the composition of accelerator effects of export income increases in the past.

Multipliers for exports as a whole in West Malaysia have been calculated by Ariff (1969b), and by Harvie (1964) for particular sectors. Ariff's estimates are based on time-series regressions for 1955–65, where GNP at market prices is regressed on export income and on gross fixed capital formation, and he calculates an export multiplier of 1.0 (and an investment multiplier of 2.2). Harvie's multipliers refer to the 1955–60 period and the estimates are 1.06 for tin exports, 1.16 for rubber and 1.33 for all other exports combined. Harvie's estimates are also based on time-series regressions. However, many of the relationships he calculates in order to estimate the export multipliers refer only to the economy as a whole;[22] and it would be desirable for our purposes to have estimates for a longer period and for individual sectors. However, the use of time series by sector would bias the results in favour of a higher multiplier for the rubber sectors than for either tin sector since the individual tin sectors are small in absolute size compared to rubber and regressions of national income on, say, tin dredging export income, might well not pick up that sector's multiplier effects (which could be swamped by other influences on income, even if those other influences were specified in the equation). Accordingly this section attempts to estimate the probable size of first-round multiplier effects indirectly. The assumptions may seem slightly heroic, but are in fact broadly justifiable.

The method used is to assume that the first-round multiplier effects from an initial export income increment depend on its distribution between the factors of production. If export-sectors workers (and smallholders) do not save, and if export-sector profit-earners do not consume their income from profits (or if they remit it abroad), then the marginal propensity to consume (MPC) out of export income (net of export duty) will depend on the relationship between export earnings and total wage payments. The subsequent multiplier effects will depend on the marginal rates of tax on workers' and smallholders' earnings, on their marginal propensity to import, and also on the marginal propensity of the government to spend locally out of export tax revenue. It will be assumed here that profit receivers' propensity to consume domestically is negligible,[23] that the responsiveness of government expenditure to marginal export revenue is also negligible[24] and that personal direct taxation on workers' and smallholders' income can be disregarded.[25] No estimates are available for export workers' and smallholders' *marginal* propensity to import, but Ariff (1969b, p. 67) has estimated that this is 0.44 (in real terms) for the economy as a whole. It has already been suggested that total tin and rubber workers' and smallholders' average propensities to import are lower than for West Malaysia as a whole, but whether this is also true for marginal propensities is not certain.

In order to estimate the MPC[26] out of rubber estates, gravel pump tin mines and tin dredge export income, annual wage bills were regressed first on same-year export income and then on the export income of the previous year, for the period 1947–72. For smallholders it is assumed that incremental export income net of duty accrues entirely to the smallholder. In fact, rubber dealers may 'cream off' incremental export income to some extent, but no data are available to make quantative estimates of this loss to smallholders.

The original form of relation calculated was a simple linear equation including a time trend. First differences were also calculated in cases where serial correlation occured (since serial correlation renders unreliable the value of the standard errors of the estimates, which means that the 'student *t*' test of significance cannot be used). Results of the regressions are shown in Table 7.5, which shows first differences where the original form was serially correlated.

In rubber, the relation between total wage payments and export income is extremely weak. Only in the first-difference unlagged version was the coefficient

TABLE 7.5 REGRESSIONS OF WAGE BILLS ON EXPORT INCOME ON RUBBER ESTATES, AND TIN MINES, PENINSULAR MALAYSIA, 1947-72

			Regression Coefficients							R^2	DW
			a		b			c			
Rubber Estates											
Unlagged First Differences	$y_t - y_{t-1}$	=	0	+	0.066^{*} (3.46)	$x_t - x_{t-1}$	−	0.169 (0.03)		0.342	2.092
Lagged First Differences	$y_t - y_{t-1}$	=	0	+	0.037 (1.66)	$x_{t-1} - x_{t-2}$	+	1.479 (0.24)		0.112	2.369
Gravel Pump Tin Mines											
Unlagged First Differences	$y_t - y_{t-1}$	=	0	+	$0.111^{*?}$ (3.58)	$x_t - x_{t-1}$	+	0.778 (0.67)		0.359	2.712
Lagged	y_t	=	$5.663^{*?}$ (2.74)	+	$0.148^{*?}$ (9.76)	x_{t-1}	+	0.155 (0.56)	(t-1)	0.938	1.372
Tin Dredges											
Unlagged First Differences	$y_t - y_{t-1}$	=	0	+	0.047^{*} (2.80)	$x_t - x_{t-1}$	+	0.123 (0.20)		0.254	2.409
Lagged	y_t	=	8.674^{*} (4.40)	+	0.049^{*} (3.82)	x_{t-1}	+	0.215^{*} (2.06)	(t-1)	0.721	1.677

Sources and Notes

(1) y is the wage bill in $million, x is export income in $million, and t is time. The t subscripts refer to time in years.

(2) Figures in brackets under values of coefficients are "Student t" statistics (not standard errors). Starred coefficients indicate statistical significance of the 5% level and absence of positive and negative serial correlation (indicated by the DW statistic). Question marks after starred items indicate that there is a possibility (but not a certainty) of serial correlation.

(3) Where the original form of the equation was subject to serial correlation, first differences were taken to try to eliminate it, and these reduced forms are therefore shown in place of the original, serially-correlated equations. Note that in the first difference version the constant c can be regarded as a time trend.

(4) See Chapters Five and Six for data sources.

statistically significantly different from zero at the 5% level of confidence (indicated by the value of the 't' statistics, which, for ease of reading the table, are given in brackets under the estimate, i.e. the bracketed items are *not* the standard errors). The equation suggests that a \$100 increase in incremental export income would generate only approximately a \$7 increase in the incremental wage bill. Moreover, the fit of the equation is very poor (R^2 only 0.342),[27] and the result should be seen against the fact that the *average* wage bill in the post-war period has been about 40% of export income. Also, no statistically significant relation between the rubber estate wage bill and the time variable could be picked up by the regression.

In gravel pump mining, the responsiveness of the wage bill to export income is much greater and in the lagged case the fit (R^2=0.938) is very good. The equation suggests that a \$100 rise in export income has generated a \$15 rise in the wage bill, which is a very high figure considering that for most of the post-war period the *average* share of wages was only \$20 in every \$100 of export income. However, there is a *possibility* of serial correlation in the gravel pump equations, but it is not certain. As in rubber, no time trend can be discerned. In dredging, the lagged version also gives the best fit, suggesting a \$5 incremental response of wage bill to \$100 of extra export income and there is a statistically significant time trend.

Taken together these results suggest that export income increases have very small proportional effects on the rubber wage bill, whereas a 100% increase of gravel pump export income leads to a 75% increase in the wage bill after a year's lag, and a 30% rise in the case of dredging (where wages on average were about 15% of output value).

Wage bills may respond to increases in the value of export output for three main reasons. First, if export earnings have increased because of a price increase with given export volume labour unions may be able to bargain for a share in the increased total revenue. Second, wage bills may rise if output expands and generates increased demand for labour at a constant wage, whether the output expansion is autonomous or in response to price increases. Third, such increases in the demand for labour may also raise wage rates. In the post-war period in rubber there has been a clearly declining trend in estate employment combined with a clearly rising trend in output, as higher yielding varieties of rubber have been introduced. In dredging, the output trend has been downwards, and associated with falls in employment and the reverse has been true of gravel pumping, which has increased its share of total tin output (see Chapters 5 and 6). In order to explain the relatively low sensitivity of rubber wage bills and the higher sensitivity of tin wage bills to export income, it is necessary to isolate the effects on wage *rates* from those resulting from changes in employment.

First therefore, figures for wage rates were regressed on export income by sector, for 1947–72. The best-fit equations (run in log-linear form in order to show elasticities) for rubber estates and gravel pumping are as follows, with stars indicating statistical significance at the 5% confidence level and with 't' statistics in brackets

Rubber

(1) $\log y = 2.698^* + 0.212^* \log x_t + 0.019^* \log t$

$\quad(7.51) \quad (3.77) \qquad\qquad (7.63)$

$(R^2 = 0.832, DW = 1.624)$

Gravel Pumping

(2a) $\log y = 2.953^{*?} + 0.304^{*?} \log x_t + 0.010 \log t$

$\quad(10.79) \quad (4.69) \qquad\qquad (1.82)$

$(R^2 = 0.867, DW = 1.318)$

(2b) $\log y = 3.687^* + 0.158^* \log x_{t-1} + 0.016^* \log (t\text{-}1)$
(17.55) (3.18) (3.48)
($R^2 = 0.869$, DW = 2.080)

In dredging, serial correlation occured in the log-linear form and first differences of the unlogged data had to be run to eliminate it

Dredging

$y_t - y_{t-1} = 5.649^* - 0.034\, x_t - x_{t-1}$

(2.85) (0.62)
($R^2 = 0.017$, DW = 1.674)

The figures show a statistically significant elasticity of wage rates with respect to export earnings of about 0.21 in rubber, and also a slight but statistically significant time trend in wage rates. In gravel pumping, the elasticity is higher (about 30%) but there is a possibility of serial correlation in the unlagged version; and lagging by one year reduces the elasticity to 16% (whereas lagging by a year in rubber leaves the elasticity unchanged), and produces a slight but statistically significant time trend. In dredging only the time trend (indicated by the value of the constant in the first difference version) is significant statistically and is upwards. Fits are good in rubber and gravel pumping, but poor in dredging.

This information may now be combined with estimates of output elasticities with respect to price, (and assuming that such induced output increases lead to increases in employment) Ariff (1970, p. 20) estimates a rubber estate output elasticity of only 0.05%, while work by David Lim (1969), pp. 41–3) suggests that gravel pumping's price elasticity of supply ranges from 0.09 to 1.43[28] using quarterly data, and 0.28 to 0.54 using annual data. The corresponding figures for dredging are -0.06 to -0.27 for quarterly data and 0.12 to 0.21 for annual data.

In rubber, therefore, the low responsiveness of wage bills (and therefore, under our assumptions, of consumption expenditure) to export income is predominantly the result of a very low output eleasticity (though presumably *supply* elasticity might be slightly higher because of the existence of stocks), which swamps the responsiveness of wage rates to prices.[29] In gravel pumping both wage rates and output respond strongly to price,[30] and wage rates may well be bid up by output expansions. In dredging, there is little responsiveness of wage rates to output value (though there is an upward time trend in wages), but wage bills expand as a result of positive output elasticity (where annual changes are considered). In general, the multiplier effects of immediate increases in export income seem slight—on rubber estates because the (large) wage bills are unresponsive, and on mines because the (responsive) wage bills are only a small proportion of output value. In the longer run, however, in rubber, wage bills increase over time, and as was shown in the previous section, the average propensity to import is low (though the marginal propensity may be higher). Also, there is evidence that the smallholder rubber elasticity of output is much higher than that of estates (approximately 0.62 according to Ariff, 1970, p. 21), so the increasing relative importance of smallholders in the rubber industry will increase export multipliers. Multiplier effects will also be increased to the extent to which workers' and smallholders' savings propensitities are low.

One might add that low export multipliers are by no means necessarily undesirable. They reduce economic instability from export earnings' fluctuations (see Chapter 2)

and if in the longer run wage bills and real wages per worker rise secularly, and if (as was shown in the previous section to have occured by the late 1960's) expenditure is directed towards local products, growth can be spread, and further employment created by the export industries without the costs of short-run instability.[31] In fact, as will be shown in Chapter 9, the upward trends in real wages have been very much stronger in tin than in rubber.

NOTES

1. Section 7.1 of this chapter is taken from Thoburn (1971, pp. 357–67). It has not been updated for publication (i.e. from 1968 to 1972) because the basic consumption data on which the analysis depends relate to 1957–8 (Statistics Dept., *HBS*, 1958) and any apparent increase in accuracy in the estimate of the share of consumption expenditure made locally, as a result of updating, would be rendered spurious because of possible further changes in consumption patterns. Since no updating has been carried out, statistics for oil palm estates and smallholdings (almost exclusively on land development schemes) have not been added, since these were not included in the original study. In fact, the estimates of local consumption expenditure made in Section 7.1 show a very high proportion of local expenditure, and for most items the criterion used to determine the existence of local expenditure (i.e. an export-sector demand : net import ratio of 1) would not be sensitive to the addition of further consumption expenditures. Section 7.2 has, however, been updated, but oil palm is not included since a sufficiently long series for oil palm wages was not calculated as part of the main commodity studies.
2. Though as Chapter 3 pointed out, the stimulus to new investment in any particular product is generally weaker than in the case of a backward or forward linkage.
3. Since there is not a wide choice of technique for many products, the introduction of new technology (discussed in Chapters 3 and 9) depends on the types of new product demanded. New products ideally should use a technology which raises domestic factor productivity without requiring increases in capital intensity.
4. Monthly incomes of \$1–\$150, \$151–\$300, \$301–\$500, \$501–\$1000; income not definite, and total all incomes.
5. There is insufficient information on the incomes of export-sector shareholders to determine consumption expenditures of dividend receivers in Malaysia. It is known that the majority of shareholders are Chinese, however. See the works cited in Chapters 5 and 6 by Yip (1968) and Mamajiwala (1963), respectively, on share-ownership in tin dredging and rubber estates.
6. In 1968 47% of the rubber estate labour force was female, 3% were young persons and 50% were males (Ministry of Labour, *HLS*, 1968).
7. Information is mainly from my own visits to estates in 1969.
8. In 1968, 77% of the rubber estate labour force was provided with free accommodation (on estates). See Ministry of Labour, *HLS*, 1968. Since Indians are only 46% of the labour force on estates (see Table 7.1) it follows that many Chinese also had free occommodation on estates (assuming that Malays would tend to come from nearby villages). Accommodation on-estate tends to increase the chance of several family members in individual households working on the estate.
9. In the *HBS* (Statistics Dept., 1958) no definition is given of 'urban'. It is assumed here that 'urban' is defined as in the 1957 *Population Census*: 'gazetted administrative areas with a population of 1000 or over' (Federation of Malaya, *Population Census*, 1957, Report No. 14).
10. In 1968 78% of rubber estate workers, and 82% and 56% of gravel pump and dredge workers, respectively, were provided with free accommodation (which is virtually always on-site). See Ministry of Labour, *HLS*, 1968.
11. In support of this classification see Fryer and Jackson (1966).
12. This involved over a thousand separate calculations as well as a similar number to convert the original consumption data from absolute figures to percentages. I am most grateful to the Departmental Assistants in the School of Social Studies at the University of East Anglia who spent several weeks doing these.
13. See Table 7.4, note 3.
14. Demands are summed because it would be difficult to use the Table 7.4 column ii measure (discussed above) for relatively small individual groups.

15. Since savings are not included in the *HBS* analysis, consumption demands will be overstated to the extent that incomes exceed expenditures. It is unlikely, however, that savings for export sector workers are more than 5% of income. See Little and Tipping (1972, p.58).
16. In fact the ratio of dependents may be less in both estate and smallholder sectors of the rubber industry where many families have several working members. This would mean that the column ii cut-off figure of 1 discussed above would show an even smaller proportion of demand met by imports.
17. The rubber and tin industries contain large groups of all three major ethnic groups, although the predominance of Indians in estate rubber would bias consumption slightly towards Indian patterns. However Indians consume very few goods not also consumed by other communities.
18. The figure is higher than 65% because excluded items include some foodstuffs. The figure for all households is 67% (see Statistics Dept., *HBS*). Unless otherwise stated, proportions of expenditure here will refer from now on to proportions of the $442.5m shown in Table 7.4.
19. These results can be compared to the average of 20–30% of income spent on food in developed countries. See Kuznets (1966, pp. 266–7).
20. In any case, many managerial personnel on rubber estates and tin dredges still are expatriates, wage payments to whom should not be considered as local earnings and much of whose expenditure may be on imported consumer goods.
21. In this context it may be noted that the highest quoted income group of Chinese (urban Chinese earning $501–1000 a month), who would provide the bulk of local management personnel, still spent almost 50% of their income on food (see Statistics Dept., *HBS*).
22. Harvie's estimate of the marginal propensities to import and to save for instance refer only to the whole economy, though he estimates marginal export tax rates and (by regression analysis) the relation between factor payments abroad and tin and rubber (and other) export earnings. Harvie does not give estimates for the goodness of fit of his regressions, nor the standard errors of the estimates. This is especially unfortunate since he has so few observations (i.e. for the years 1955–60 only).
23. Crosson (1964, p. 18) suggested that domestic *savings* depended crucially in Malaysia on export-sector profits (and tax payments). He also estimated that the marginal propensity to save with respect to export income for the period 1955–62 rose from 0.63 to 0.81 if net factor payments abroad were added to domestic savings.
24. Ariff (1969b, p. 61) in a study of the effects of export earnings' instability on the West Malaysian economy notes that government expenditures do not generally fluctuate with government revenues.
25. Under Malaysian tax laws for the period under discussion, very few export workers would pay tax, e.g. the first $3000 of annual income is tax free for a married man *Malay Mail*, 1970, p. 270).
26. MPC estimated in this fashion of course includes consumption of imports.
27. In general, if the fit for untransformed data is good, and first differences are taken solely to eliminate serial correlation we would expect R^2 to be lower in the latter case. In this case, however, R^2 in the untransformed, unlagged version was only 0.454.
28. The reason for there being a *range* of estimated supply elasticities is that Lim uses a Nerlovian adjustment model. In this model the estimate for supply elasticity increases if there is assumed to be no Nerlovian adjustment lag (the lag results from producers being able to produce less than their desired output increase). Thus the lower figures refer to an estimate with a given calculated value of the lag, and the higher estimates assume the lag to be absent. See Lim (1969, p. 36 and p. 39).
29. Ariff (1970, pp. 22–3) calculates a wage elasticity with respect to the rubber price of 0.59 for the period 1947–58, and explains it in terms of the sliding-scale wage system adopted on rubber estates following the 1951 Korean boom.
30. Lim (1969, p. 39), citing a reference by R. Krishna, suggests that the tin industry of Malaysia falls in the medium-response range of supply elasticities of primary commodities (though in fact Krishna was actually considering acreage elasticities of agricultural products, and no comparison with other minerals is given).
31. Low responsiveness of wage bills to short-run increases in export income may however shift the distribution of income away from workers (see Chapter 9).

Chapter 8
Exports and the Malaysian Engineering Industry: A Case Study of Backward Linkage[1]

In Chapter 3 it was argued that linkages are one of the most important means by which an export sector can spread growth to the rest of the economy. The linkages generated by tin, rubber and palm oil[2] exports were identified in Chapters 5 and 6, and it was decided to pick one linkage for further study. Section 8.1 discusses the choice of engineering as a case study. Section 8.2 quantifies the linkages from export industries to engineering. Section 8.3 attempts an economic analysis of the reasons for the development of engineering as a backward linkage, and relates the engineering study to the theoretical discussion of linkages in the first two sections of Chapter 3. Section 8.4 puts forward some general conclusions. The chapter is based on interviews in Malaysia with over sixty engineering firms.

8.1 ENGINEERING AS A CASE STUDY

Several industries suggest themselves as choices for a case study of export-sector linkages besides engineering, in particular electricity supply for tin mining and the production of chemical fertilizers for rubber and oil palm. Electricity supply is largely a non-traded good, owing to the limited distances over which power can be transported. Thus it fails to provide scope for study of a process of import substitution over time in response to changes in local factor supply and quality. Chemical fertilizer production owes its existence in Malaysia to tariff protection and tax incentives. A study of this industry would be tantamount to a study of government import substitution policy.[3] While this is both interesting and important, an analysis of an industry which has developed in response to market forces is more relevant to a study of linkage.

Engineering is of particular interest to less developed countries. First, as a manufacturing industry it represents the use of quite different productive techniques from that of an export sector producing primary commodities, and is a means of spreading new technology into the economy.[4] Second, it is potentially an important training ground for skilled labour, whose existence would provide external economies for the further development of manufacturing.

These remarks would apply to almost any 'modern' manufacturing industry.[5] However, engineering is sometimes assumed to be more important for further industrial development than just any manufacturing industry.[6] Certainly most developed countries, including Japan, have substantial engineering industries, which usually account for over 30% of manufacturing output (Kuznets, 1966, pp. 135–43). It does not follow from this fact that a country which acquires an engineering industry early in its development necessarily will experience faster industrial growth than one which does not. Nevertheless it is intuitively plausible that the existence of repairing and structural engineering facilities would produce externalities for other manufacturing (though it must be remembered, of course, that engineering production especially in the electrical and transport branches, also produces a substantial proportion of output for final demand use). An engineering industry would help spread what Solo has called the 'cognition of mechanism', a recognition of the value to society of mechanization and of the use of technical skills (Solo, 1966, pp. 96–7).

Finally, engineering is now a major industrial sector, accounting for over 13% of manufacturing value-added in Peninsular Malaysia (Statistics Dept., *SManI*, 1971). Yet no economic research into Malaysian engineering exists, and this study therefore fills an important gap.

8.2 ENGINEERING LINKAGES GENERATED BY MALAYSIAN EXPORT INDUSTRIES

In Chapters 5 and 6 the tin and rubber industries were each split into two sectors—tin dredging and gravel pump (or 'Chinese') mining, and rubber estates and smallholdings. This sectoral division also is associated with differences in demand for engineering products, except that rubber smallholding production on government schemes generates engineering linkages similar to those of estates. For present purposes oil palm can be considered as a single sector comprising estates and government land development schemes. Only the processing aspects of rubber and oil palm are considered, since the field operations require few engineering inputs (except for some transport equipment).[7] Also the rubber linkages set out here concern the production of Standard Malaysian Rubber (SMR) equipment, though the production of older types and smallholder equipment is discussed at various points in the next section.

The usual measure of the backward linkage effects an industry could exert is, in input–output terms, the ratio of its interindustry purchases to its total production (Hirschman, 1958, p. 107). Some of these intermediate products may be imported, so the *ex post* measure of the backward linkage actually created is the ratio of domestic interindustry purchases to total production. This measure, however, misses an important category of backward linkage investment, namely investment in the capital goods bought by the industry. These would be shown in an input–output table as deliveries to final demand. To measure this linkage, data are needed on the vector of the industry's purchases of investment goods. These will consist entirely of interindustry purchases, unless the industry itself hires primary factors to construct its capital goods.[8] What is important is the ratio of investment goods purchases locally to total investment purchases. This ratio, when prorated by the industry's capital–output coefficient, shows the extent to which backward linkage effects are exerted through capital expenditure.

Ratios of local to total capital expenditure were given for gravel pump tin mining and tin dredges and for rubber and oil palm estates. in Sections 5.3, 6.3 and 6.5, respectively. The tables in those sections also showed how the local content of investment purchases differs considerably between different items of capital expenditure, which illustrates the high degree to which engineering production can be vertically disintegrated. There is also a substantial demand for replacement parts in all

TABLE 8.1 INVESTMENT AND MAINTENANCE EXPENDITURE AND CAPITAL-OUTPUT RATIOS IN TIN, RUBBER, AND OIL PALM, PENINSULAR MALAYSIA, 1972

	Total Expenditure ($mil.)	Local Expenditure ($mil.)	Marginal Capital Net Output Ratio
Tin Dredging			
Purchase of New Fixed Assets (of which Machinery $20.5 mil.) (1970)	24	5 (20%)	3.2
Repairs and Maintenance to Machinery and Equipment (excluding vehicles) (1969)	26	5 (20%)	
Other Tin Mining			
Purchase of New Fixed Assets (of which Machinery $18.0 mil.) (1970)	37	15 (40%)	1.4
Repairs and Maintenance to Machinery and Equipment (excluding vehicles) (1969)	39	31 (80%)	
Rubber (Estates only)			
Capital Expenditure other than on Field Establishment (of which Machinery and Vehicles $8.8 mil. and excluding expenditure of $36.0 mil. on Land and Existing Buildings)	16	10 (60%)	0.3 (processing only) 2.6 (processing+field establishment)
Oil Palm			
Estimated Annual Average Expenditure (1970-75) on Mill Construction	30	13 (45%)	0.9 (processing only) 2.7 (processing+field establishment)

Sources and Notes

(1) Tin and Rubber investment figures from CMinI 1969 and 1970 and R.S.H. 1972 respectively.

(2) Oil Palm figures are a manufacturer's estimate (Interview in Malaysia, November 1970), based on an expected 30 new mills of average cost $5 mil. No official statistics are available for oil palm investment.

(3) For details of marginal capital-output ratios see Table 9.1,but note that the tin mining capital coefficients are based on 1974 capital costs in relation to 1972 output value (whereas those in Thoburn, 1973b, which are lower, were based on 1970 capital costs and 1968 output value).

(4) It is assumed in the absence of other information, that the local content of repair and maintenance expenditure in tin dredging is the same as for new investment purchases. This is likely to be an underestimate, but not necessarily a large underestimate since much of tin expenditure will consist

of imported spares. In gravel pump mining where most of the spare parts are locally produced, the local content of maintenance expenditue is assumed to be 80%.

(5) 1970 is the latest year for which tin mining investment figures are available by sector. In 1971, total purchases of new fixed assets by tin mining was \$48 mil., \$7 mil. was spent on second hand assets, and \$12 million on own construction.

four cases, especially in gravel pump mining. Table 8.1 summarizes the local content of investment expenditure and also shows the marginal capital-output coefficients for the four activities, together with the scale of investment in each in 1972 (the latest year for which statistics were available at the time of writing). The capital-output coefficients should be treated with caution in view of the differing life of the capital equipment involved, which is very short in gravel pumping and very long in rubber, oil palm and dredging. However, they do suggest that, with respect to the generation of demand for local engineering products, the low proportion of local content in dredge investment expenditure relative to the other export industries is offset by a high marginal capital-output ratio.

In an account of the economic effects of export growth the fact that a significant proportion of capital expenditure is made locally is important in itself since it can be used to refute the idea that the export industry is an enclave. To show that the industries supplying the goods to the export sector are truly examples of backward linkage, in the sense that their establishment and subsequent growth has been the result of sales to the export sector, further analysis is necessary.

A first approach is to see what proportion of engineering sales are made to the export industries. Table 8.2 gives details of engineering production in Malaysia, in relation to manufacturing and export activities. Comparison of the gross output of engineering (*major groups* 45 to 48) in Table 8.2[9] with local engineering purchases made by the export sector (from Table 8.1) shows that the latter buys about 15% of Malaysian engineering output, if the Table 8.1 figure is inflated somewhat to take account of the fact that it excludes rubber smallholdings and land development schemes. This seems a low proportion (though it was higher—25%—in 1968). However, it is not being suggested here that *all* Malaysian engineering owes its existence to export-sector backward linkage. In particular the relatively new *major groups Electrical Machinery* and *Transport Equipment*, with growth rates over the 1963-71 period of roughly double that of total manufacturing output owe much to official import substitution policy and incentives to foreign investment, though some sales (e.g. dredge electrical equipment, earth-moving machinery, tractors for estates) are made to the export sector. Sales to the export sector are concentrated in the *major groups Metal Products* and *Machinery except Electrical Machinery*, so it may be that at least 30% of output in those two groups is sold to export industries (and the figure was 40% in 1968), though a few producers selling to the export sector are classified under construction. Also, though these two groups accounted for just over 50% of value-added in engineering in 1971, they were 80% of engineering value-added in 1963 (and 60% in 1968), suggesting that the overall dependence of engineering on the export sector has been greater in the past than at present. In *Industrial Machinery and Parts*, the largest *industry* in *major group* 46, over a third of output consists of products clearly identifiable with the export sector (gravel pump parts, rubber

TABLE 8.2 PRODUCTION AND GROWTH RATES IN ENGINEERING, MANUFACTURING AND EXPORTS, PENINSULAR MALAYSIA, 1959-71

	Gross Output	Value-added ($mil at current prices)					Average Annual Growth Rates of Value-added		
	1971 ($mil.)	1971	1968	1963	1962	1959	1968-71	1963-68	1959-62
Metal Products (Major Group 45)	172	55	39	23	10	6	12.1%	11.4%	17.5%
Fabricated Structural Shapes (Industry 4510)	29	9	6	3	...	...	14.4%	11.0%	...
Machinery except Electrical (Major Group 46)	81	33	25	15	5	3	9.6%	11.3%	20.0%
Industrial Machinery and Parts (Industry 4623)	45	20	15	9	5	3	9.9%	10.8%	20.0%
Electrical Machinery (Major Group 47)	111	40	21	5	...	...	23.9%	32.9%	...
Transport Equipment (Major Group 48)	149	38	19	6	4	3	25.8%	25.7%	12.6%
All Engineering Industries (Major Groups 45-48)	513	166	104	48	19	12	17.0%	16.6%	17.9%
All Covered Industries (in Census of Manufacturing)	4164	1266	874	420	248	167	13.2%	15.7%	14.2%
Non-Residential Construction (Industry 5112)	155 (1970)	58 (1970)	33	40	...	...	32.5% (1968-70)	-1.1%	...
West Malaysia GDP at Factor Cost (Current Prices)		10529	7180 (1966)	5862	5496	4760	7.9% (1966-71)	6.9% (1963-66)	4.9%
Export Industries		Gross Outputs ($mil.)					Average Annual Growth Rates of Gross Output		
Rubber (gross exports)		1417	1301	1374	1368	1722	0.9%	-1.1%	-7.4%
Tin Dredging (production)		250	220	210	215	126	4.3%	0.9%	19.5%
Gravel Pump Tin Mining (production)		425	413	182	166	93	0.9%	17.8%	21.5%
Palm Oil and Kernels (gross exports)		362	131	76	72	57	40.3%	11.4%	8.0%
		Price Indices							
Retail Price Index (1959=100)		111	108	103	100	100	0.9%	1.0%	-0.1%

Sources and Notes

(1) Group and Industry numbers refer to the Malaysia Industrial Classification, which is based on the United Nations Standard Industrial Classification (with some modification).

(2) Value-added figures from Statistics Dept., *CManI* 1959, 1963, 1968 and *SManI* 1971; *SCI* 1963, 1968 and 1971. Retail price indices from *MSB* 1975, 1959 and 1971. GDP figure from Prime Minister's Dept., 1966 and 1973, and 1963 and 1966 figures from Statistics Dept., *NA* 1960-66. Export industry figures from *MSB* 1975.

(3) Growth rates calculated as average annual compound rates, from unrounded figures.

(4) 1962 and 1963 output statistics are not comparable, because of a major extension in Census of Manufacturing Industries coverage in 1962-3. Under the pre-1963 classification Industry 4623 was the only industry covered in Group 46. Growth rates from 1968, and output figures for 1971 will be understated for manufacturing industries because the *SManI* coverage is less than that of the *CManI*.

machinery, and so on), together with many other items (gears, engine parts) bought both by the export sector and domestic manufacturing (Thoburn, 1971, p. 417). Moreover, in a 20% sample survey of that *industry* which was conducted by the author in the two states (Perak and Selangor) where over 75% of its output is produced, it was found that 80% of employment was in firms whose main product was sold to the export sector (Thoburn, 1971, pp. 503–5). Further analysis along these lines is difficult[10] because the various groups of producers making engineering products for the four export activities are not each classified under the same *industry*, (except for firms making Chinese mining equipment, which are almost all listed under *Industrial Machinery and Parts*).

Second, to see if a relationship can be established between past growth in exports and growth in engineering it would be useful to be able to fit a regression of time series of engineering output on time series of export investment expenditures. Unfortunately no series are available for export investment for any year before 1968, except for rubber where data are available from 1961 (in Statistics Dept., *RSH*). Engineering output series from the *Census of Manufacturing* date back to 1959, but in 1963 there was a major change of *Census* coverage, so that no series of sufficient length is available to compute meaningful regressions even if fuller export investment data were available. As a second-best alternative, growth rates in engineering and in export outputs can be compared, and both are shown in Table 8.2. In 1959–62 exceptionally rapid growth in the value of tin mining output was accompanied by equally rapid growth in *major groups* 45 and 46, substantially in excess of manufacturing growth as a whole and quadruple that of GDP. Over the 1963–8 period when mining grew more slowly so did *major groups* 45 and 46, and *major group* 45 grew slightly more slowly in 1968–71, in face of stagnant tin output. Over all three periods, however, rubber exports either fell in value, or grew very little, but the lack of growth in rubber may have been counterbalanced in part by expansion in the oil palm industry, with its higher marginal capital–output ratio than rubber, and in any case Table 8.1 suggests that export-sector engineering demand is dominated by tin mining.

A third method of determining whether engineering in Malaysia is truly an export-sector linkage is to examine the history of engineering firms to see the extent to which their establishment and growth has depended on export-sector sales, and interviews were used for this purpose. The producers for each of the four export activities are distinct groups, in the sense that they each tend to specialize in equipment for a particular export activity, and they are dealt with here in turn. In dredging, the main producers are three Malaysian–Chinese firms, all large by local standards (i.e. a hundred workers or more), and the European firm United Engineers. The three local firms were all established before the Second World War as specialist dredge erectors. They have extended their activities not only into other aspects of dredge construction, but also into general industrial structural steelwork. Nevertheless dredging business is in all cases over half of the total value of their sales. United Engineers is in a class of its own and is discussed further in Section 8.3. Its dredging business is but a small part of total turnover. Two other large firms make dredging spare parts and although they depend heavily on dredging business (the ratios of dredging to total turnover were not obtained) they moved into the field at a later stage, having previously produced Chinese mining machinery. Also, the Dutch firm IHC Holland, one of the largest builders of dredges in the world, and with important shipbuilding interests was set up in Malaysia in 1972, with a shipyard in Penang (Interview, 1974).[11]

In Chinese mining machinery the position is more complicated, because there are a large number of small firms. In the sample survey of *Industrial Machinery and Parts*, previously mentioned, almost all the firms interviewed who produced Chinese mining equipment depended on it for more than half their sales, though there was a tendency for larger ones to branch out into other lines, particularly dredge spares. There was no evidence to suggest that their establishment was due to any products other than mining equipment.

Following the introduction of the Standard Malaysian Rubber scheme in the mid-1960s major changes occurred in rubber factory design, and production moved out of the hands of numerous small workshops of the type producing Chinese mining equipment into those of a small number of larger more specialist producers. Nowadays SMR machinery is made in Malaysia under a two-tier system, whereby factories are designed by firms who in most cases subcontract the actual manufacturing to others. For none of the designers (about whom more in Section 8.3) is design work an important part of turnover. Of the manufacturers, one is United Engineers for whom rubber machinery is a small part of turnover. At least three local firms manufacture under subcontract, with some 70% of turnover dependent on SMR rubber machinery. These firms were all founded over 30 years ago and previously produced older types of rubber machinery. These is also some independent manufacture by other local firms but the proportion of turnover in these cases is not known. There is still some production of older types of rubber machinery mostly by small firms but usually as a sideline to mining equipment.

It appears then that the development of firms producing dredging, gravel pump, and SMR rubber machinery is due predominantly to sales to the export sector and is thus an example of linkage investment. Whether the manufacture of oil palm machinery is also a linkage is less certain. As in rubber there is a two-tier system with design provided by a Dutch company working with United Engineers, and by specialist French and Australian firms in Malaysia who subcontract to local manufacturers. This second tier consists of at least seven local firms, for whom, with one exception, oil palm work is over half of turnover. None was established to produce oil palm machinery, however. Three were founded in the early 1950's during a boom in structural steel construction, and moved into oil palm at a later stage; three were formed before the Second World War as contractors doing rubber estate construction and factory work; and only one was established in the 1960's as the boom in oil palm mill construction started.

It is worth noting at this stage too that engineering for the export sector has developed largely without government support. The establishment of very many of the engineering firms antedates the government's import substitution policies of the 1960's and 1970's and with minor exceptions, they have not received import protection under those policies. Indeed Power's study of the structure of protection in Malaysia concluded that the local manufacture of machinery is on average subject to a negative effective rate of protection since imports of its inputs (steel for instance) are protected while, with some exceptions imports of final engineering products are not restricted (Power, in Balassa, 1971, pp. 212–7).

8.3 FACTORS IN THE GROWTH OF ENGINEERING

Although there are various differences in the way in which engineering production developed for each of the four export activities discussed in this chapter, a number of general factors can be identified which have contributed to the establishment and growth of engineering. This section looks at the importance of the high degree to which engineering can be vertically disintegrated; at its factor intensity of production, the reasons why it did not develop as an export industry in its own right and whether the linkage investment represented new capital formation or reallocation of existing investment funds; at economies of scale; and at the role of foreign and European firms in fostering the growth of local firms. Finally, it examines the time sequence of development in order to see the extent to which particular types of engineering have helped the growth of other types.

8.3.1 Vertical Disintegration and the Development of Factor Quality

In economic theory, especially (until very recently) in the theory of international trade, industries usually are assumed to be vertically integrated. Yet the technology of most industries permits vertical disintegration, and the degree of disintegration is a matter of economic decision (Corden, 1971, p. 29). As Chapter 3 suggested, a country may be able to produce efficiently at world market prices in one stage of a production process, but other stages may require quite different factor proportions, managerial techniques and labour skills from those locally available. Many branches of engineering can be vertically disintegrated to an unusually high degree. Tin dredges and oil palm mills in particular are extremely divisible products, consisting of many thousands of components requiring a variety of production processes–structural steelwork, castings in iron and in steel, motors, electrical equipment, hydraulics, and so on. This divisibility has meant that local production could be established in the particular components suited to the then-existing factor endowment and skills, and as more capital, experience and labour skills accumulated, increasingly more sophisticated items could be made in Malaysia, raising the local content of export-sector investment expenditure. Reference to Tables 5.20, 5.25, 6.22, 6.25 will show how in each of the export industries, local content still varies enormously between different items of capital expenditure. Thus in tin dredging local purchases are concentrated on fabrication, erection and some machinery; in gravel pumping there is extensive local purchase except of engines; in rubber factories much of the switch gear, electrical equipment and generators is imported; while oil palm mills import their steam and generating plant and their hydraulic equipment while buying much of their other machinery locally.

The process is most clearly seen in tin dredging. To understand it, some grasp of the technology is necessary since the operation of economic forces has been conditioned by technological possibilities.[12] The building of a dredge can be divided into five stages:- design, manufacture of machinery and parts, fabrication of the structure, site work and erection of the dredge. Designing a dredge requires the services of a highly qualified staff and has never been attempted by local (i.e. non-European) firms. It is usually performed by an overseas consulting firm, though the largest European mining company and in the past United Engineers (and, from 1971, IHC) have also done designing work. Who does the designing is significant not only because of its share (about 6%) in the total cost of the dredge but because it is the designer who organizes the project and calls for tenders. From the very first days of dredging in Malaya in the 1910's and 1920's the final stages of construction–site work and erection–have been given to local Malaysian-Chinese firms. Site work–clearing jungle, excavating the pond in which the dredge will float, preparing drainage, etc.–could well have been done by unskilled local workers under minimal expatriate supervision. It required no particular expertise and was unlikely to develop any local ability to undertake a larger share of the construction project. Dredge erecting was quite a different matter, and called for considerable skill in work with structural steel. Doubtless in the early days foreign supervision was used, and United Engineers also did erection work. Nevertheless, dredge erecting laid the experience both for managers and workers, on the basis of which the local contractors would later take over a larger share of construction. Increases in the local share occured in the 1950's and especially the 1960's, associated with moves from erection into fabrication, as experience was gained from the extensive repair work which the local contractors had undertaken since the Second World War and as the result of a single technological change—that of fabrication on-site.

Until 1965 dredge components had been fabricated abroad or at United Engineers, Singapore. In that year the first contract for on-site fabrication was awarded—to a local Chinese contractor, and perhaps significantly by the first local Chinese public dredging company to be set up in Malaysia. As one contractor explained to the author, after that date designers saw that local contractors were capable of a much greater share of the work than had previously been thought possible, and now most dredges are fabricated on-site by local contractors at considerable cost savings over the previous method.

In oil palm a similar process occured. Structural steel construction firms, though they had not gained their early experience from palm oil mill construction, found that their skills lay not only in putting up mill buildings. Many pieces of so-called 'machinery', such as threshers, could be fabricated from structural steel, and this was true also of machinery platforms and other parts of the mills. Thus it was possible for much of the mill to be made locally. The parts that are imported are usually of a more sophisticated type, such as hydraulic equipment and boilers, produced by large overseas firms. It is significant that one of the major foreign suppliers is a huge combine, in Holland, employing over 25,000 workers and making similar equipment for some twenty industries including petrochemicals, sugar refining and dairying. It suggests that production of the equipment involved is subject to considerable economies of scale which can be reaped only by a large market for similar equipment in other industries. Similarly in dredging, the components which are not made locally include some heavy steel castings, castings in manganese steel which require an unusually high degree of casting accuracy, motors, etc., for which a sufficient market does not exist locally, or in the region, for firms to consider making the substantial investment needed to produce these items. However, since 1971, the firm of Bradken Malaysia, a subsidiary of the large Australian steel foundry Bradford Kendall has been in operation (near Ipoh). Founded as a joint venture, it is able to make a variety of steel castings (including dredge buckets and bucket bands), though imported castings still take a large share of the market.[13]

The role of product divisibility is less striking in gravel pump mining equipment and rubber machinery. The engineering equipment for a gravel pump mine is fairly simple, consisting mainly of gravel pumps and parts and piping made from cast iron, wooden constructional work and engines. It is the cast-iron work which has led to local engineering. As gravel pumping developed in the early years of the century, foundries were set up to cast parts, which could be sold after simple machining. Expansion into more sophisticated items has not involved increases in the local content of gravel pump mines' investment expenditure because there is little more than can be made in Malaysia other than engines[14] and some steel piping; and so larger engineering shops have branched into spare parts for diesel engines for other industries and into dredge

TABLE 8.3 VALUE-ADDED AND FIXED ASSETS PER WORKER AND PER UNIT OF OUTPUT, SELECTED INDUSTRIES, PENINSULAR MALAYSIA, 1971

	Annual Non-Wage Value-Added per Full Time Worker ($)	Annual Wage per Full Time Worker ($)	Value of Fixed Assets per Full Time Worker ($)	Ratio of Fixed Assets to Annual Value-Added
Metal Products (Major Group 45)	3422	2315	7511	1.25
Machinery except Electrical Machinery (Major Group 46)	2429	2273	2163	0.46
Industrial Machinery & Parts (Industry 4623)	1998	2248	1650	0.39
Electrical Machinery (Major Group 47)	7813	2761	11472	1.08
Transport Equipment (Major Group 48)	4494	2670	7132	1.00
All Covered Industries	5472	2199	7808	1.02
Pioneer Industries	7976	2477	16225	1.55
All Covered non-Pioneer Industries	4586	2100	4829	0.72
Non-Residential Construction (Industry 5112) (1970)	1374	2085	...	...
Rubber Smokehouses Off Estates (Industry 1122)	3628	1434	2997	0.59
Manufacture of Chemical Fertilizers (4113)	13537	4392	45719	2.55
Rubber estates (1972)	1790	1764	...	...
Oil Palm estates (1972)	1470	1800	...	...
Tin Dredging (1972)	17370	3588	...	) 1.88
Gravel Pump Tin Mining (1972)	3920	2448	...	)

Sources and Notes

(1) All figures, except Construction and export industries, calculated from Statistics Dept., SManI 1971. Construction figures from SCI 1970, and Export figures from Statistics Dept., RSH 1972, OPCTS 1972, PR 1972 and CMinI 1971.

(2) Inclusion of part-time workers would produce slight differences in relative values between industries, but would not affect the general orders of magnitude.

(3) Division, Major Group and Industry codes are from the Malaysia Industrial Classification.

(4) Pioneer industries are industries to which special tax concessions, and often tariff protection, have been given, and they are often branches of multinational companies.

(5) Average wages for export industries include the value of labour benefits. Note that the value-added figures for tin mining are inflated to take account of the fact that the PR and CMinI report gross output net of export duty and smelting charges.

spares. Some expansion of business has come from the fact that some Chinese mines now run ore treatment plants similar to those of dredges,[15] but most of this business has gone to the dredge builders.

Early types of rubber machinery consisted of cast-iron rollers powered by imported engines, and using many small imported parts. Here however the experience gained in making these simple items led to the ability to make the more complex SMR machinery.

8.3.2 The Factor Intensity of Malaysian Engineering Production

Implied in the previous subsection was the idea that the local engineering which has developed is suited not only to local labour skills but to the country's overall factor endowment—in other words it has a high labour intensity of production.

A simple attempt to test this proposition can be made by looking at non-wage value-added (NWVA) per worker in engineering. NWVA has been widely used as a measure of capital intensity, indicating the value of flows of capital services per time period.[16] It may give misleading results if the rate of profit differs between industries (e.g. because of differing degrees of competitiveness between industries or because some industries are producing new products) or if the capital–labour ratio (which NWVA indicates) differs from the capital–output ratio *vis a vis* other industries. Total value-added per worker (i.e. NWVA + wage payments) in addition takes into account the flow of human services.

A ranking of industries by NWVA per worker, if the ranking is the same from country to country (i.e. if no factor-intensity reversal occurs), provides a country with valuable information about the products in which it is likely to have a comparative advantage. Thus a less developed country would choose industries low on the ranking. A recent study (Lim, 1970) has shown that no significant factor-intensity reversals occur between Malaysia and its major trading partners. Table 8.3 shows that for the engineering *major groups* (45 and 46) which have developed through export-sector backward linkage, NWVA per worker is substantially below the average for manufacturing and lower even than those for some of the primary product exports, while in Lim's study (1970, p. 22) these two major groups were in the lowest of a ranking of 21 manufacturing sectors by VA per worker. The ranking produced by NWVA per worker is substantially the same as that produced by fixed assets per worker (as an alternative measure of the capital–labour ratio) and fixed assets per unit of output (indicating the average capital–output ratio), also shown in Table 8.3., with the important exception of *major group* 45's relatively high fixed asset ratios. For *Industrial Machinery and Parts*, and *Non-Residential Construction*, the NWVA per worker figures are particularly low. Smokehouses and chemical fertilizer manufacture are included in the table to provide comparisons with one of the most 'traditional' and the most 'modern' activities, respectively.

8.3.3 Reasons for Development through Backward Linkage rather than Direct Export

Since it seems clear that Malaysia may have a strong comparative advantage in engineering of the type producing inputs for tin, rubber and oil palm, the obvious question arises why the industry did not develop as an export industry in its own right, as suggested by the arguments of Little and Mirrlees outlined in Chapter 3. Several of the theoretical counterarguments in Chapter 3 apply to the Malaysian case. Much of Malaysian engineering is still in the hands of small firms who would lack the expertise required to export, and for whom the risks of producing for a distant foreign market would be considerable. Of course, such factors did not prevent primary product exporting by small units, with export marketing done by European firms, but engineering products have quite different characteristics from those of primary products. Whereas primary products are homogeneous and sold on well-organized world markets, engineering products are highly diverse and specialized, and to sell them often requires close contact with individual customers. The earliest forms of Malaysian engineering, gravel pump and rubber machinery, were not in sufficient demand outside Malaysia for European firms to be willing to act as middlemen with export customers. Also such equipment was heavy and bulky relative to its value (the basic items were iron castings) so transport costs would have been high. The need for close contact with customers is illustrated by the fact that a number of foreign suppliers have now set up in Malaysia (though they usually subcontract the actual manufacture and confine themselves to design work). Indeed, even within Malaysia there is a regional specialization, and engineering firms in Perak related that they had found it impossible to enter the oil palm or SMR rubber fields since the firms only a hundred miles away in Kuala Lumpur had such close contact with the planting company head offices there.

The process described in Subsection 8.3.1 whereby larger proportions of export investment projects were accounted for over time by local engineering production is also relevant. Dredging work in particular started on essentially non-traded items such as site preparation and erection. Only after labour and management skills had developed and more capital funds accumulated did work begin on items which could in principle be exported, but even to these items (e.g. various types of dredge, and oil palm machinery) the arguments used above about limited information and the need for customer contact apply.

Nowadays, however, Malaysian engineering firms do export. Local dredge erectors for example has had contracts in Thailand and Indonesia; and the local supplier of dredge electrical equipment, Tamco, exports 25% of its output (FIDA, *MID*, 1971, 1st Quarter).

8.3.4 Reallocation or New Capital Formation?

Next, there is the question of whether engineering investment represents new capital formation or merely a reallocation of existing investment resources. Such a question is impossible to answer conclusively—one cannot know what investment would have been in the absence of engineering—but one major pointer does exist. Probably the most important alternative investment opportunity in the inter-war period, when most of the larger engineering firms were set up, was investment on the export sector itself. Yet for most of this period, from the early 1920's, investment in both tin and rubber was curtailed as the result of various government restriction schemes, so that linkage investment provided an alternative to the other favourite local uses of profits—private residential construction and the remission of profits to India and China. However, to argue in this fashion is to argue that the binding constraint on savings and investment in Malaya at the time was indeed the supply of investment opportunity and not for instance the supply of domestic savings itself, or foreign exchange, labour skills or entrepreneurship. In fact there is good reason to suppose that none of these factors constituted a constraint. During the rubber boom in the early years of the century, Malayans had been able to mobilize massive amounts of domestic savings, such that expansion of the rubber industry (at least in some boom years) did not involve a net inflow of foreign resources and the balance of payments was chronically in surplus.[17] Equally, a large supply of entrepreneurs appears to have been available not only to invest in rubber but also in tin mining and a host of trading activities associated with the export industries. Many skilled workers too had been trained in the tin industry and their skills were usable in manufacturing activities. At the same time, the profitability of domestic manufacturing of consumer goods during the depression would have been low, whereas export industry income, though much reduced, was still substantial so that backward linkage investment in products to be sold to the export sector was still profitable during a period of export restriction.

8.3.5 Economies of Scale

It has been shown that the particular branches of the engineering industry which have been set up in Malaysia are ones with a factor intensity of production suitable to the country's resource endowment. There is also evidence to suggest that much of Malaysian engineering is not subject to large economies of sale.

Ideally, in order to support this contention, data should be presented on the unit-cost functions both of engineering firms in Malaysia and, for reasons discussed below, of firms producing similar products overseas. In the absence of such data for Malaysia, two kinds of evidence are available. First, there are statistics of the size distribution of firms. The Malaysian *Census of Manufacturing* unfortunately does not show size distribution by *major groups*, only by some individual *industries*, so the size distribution statistics cannot be directly linked to the factor-intensity statistics in Table 8.3. However, in the *major groups* most dependent on export-sector sales (i.e. *groups* 45 and 46), size distributions are available for the two most important *industries* (*Industrial Machinery and Parts*, and *Fabricated Structural Shapes*) containing firms producing for the export sector. In both industries over three-quarters of the firms employed under thirty workers, and over a third employed under ten.

Second, there is the evidence from interviews and visits to engineering firms. Such information is necessarily impressionistic but the sample of firms was a large one so there is good reasons to believe the 'impressions' are valid. Input divisibility, which makes for an absence of economies of scale, is particularly a feature of firms making Chinese mining equipment and the older types of rubber machinery. A visitor to such firms is struck by the extent to which the larger ones appear to be duplications of the smaller. The larger have similar facilities for casting (though their melting furnaces are usually larger), and the machinery consists of small lathes and other metal-working equipment, essentially the same as in small firms. Such input divisibility has been crucial in the industry's growth since it fits in well with local methods of business finance through small-scale trade credit and retained earnings. Typically a firm will be established by a worker from an existing firm who decides to set up on his own. His first orders will come on subcontract from his former employer[18] and machinery will be acquired piece by piece, often second-hand from abroad.

In dredge erecting and fabrication and in oil palm mill construction there also do not appear to be great economies of scale, in the sense that structural steelwork and metal fabrication and erection do not require many large items of machinery. However, a certain minimum size of firm (say 50 workers) is needed to undertake the contracts involved, though initial capital costs (both for fixed and working capital) are minimized by an extensive use of subcontracting for both manufactured parts and skilled labour. It is not possible to determine the minimum size of firms producing SMR rubber machinery since all local firms in Malaysia in this field previously produced old-style rubber machinery, and were already large when they switched to SMR.

The fact that at least in the most important type of Malaysian export-sector engineering, Chinese mining equipment, there seem to be few economies of scale in the range of outputs produced by Malaysian firms, does not mean that for larger outputs there might not be substantial unit-cost reductions. If this is the case, then although local firms could in principle be set up on a small scale, they would not be able to compete with imports unless other factors gave them protection. Evidence on overseas engineering cost functions is not easy to use because of classificatory difficulties in matching engineering branches in Malaysia with overseas industries, but such as there is indicates that the Malaysian market is too small to support standardized basis which is necessary if economies of scale are to be achieved.[19] High transport costs relative to value on the many simple iron castings used in mining also give a degree of natural protection.

8.3.6 The Role of Foreign and European Firms[20]

Non-local firms in Malaysia have played two roles. First, one large European firm, United Engineers, has pioneered the development of engineering production in the country. Originally established as a firm of shipbuilders in Singapore in the nineteenth century, the company took up the production of rubber machinery and dredge building at an early stage (United Engineers, undated), and has been a training ground for many of the proprietors of present-day Chinese engineering firms. It has been common practice for former workers in the firm to set up in business on their own in both the two main engineering and manufacturing centres in Malaysia, Kuala Lumpur and Ipoh, where United Engineers maintains workshops.

Second, a variety of non-local firms in Malaysia have formed the first tier of a two-tier system under which, in oil palm, SMR rubber and tin dredge construction, the first tier designs the project but subcontracts the manufacture to local firms. In rubber and tin dredging, European planting and mining companies have organized manufacture of equipment by local firms (and in rubber have done a small amount of manufacturing themselves, though one large agency house with facilities to manufacture rubber machinery in Malaysia in fact imports most of its machinery from a U.K. subsidiary). In SMR and more especially in oil palm, foreign firms have moved in to Malaysia specifically to organize local production. In the case of oil palm this has included the largest world supplier of oil palm equipment which has been forced to enter Malaysia, because of effective local competition. In rubber, a foreign company, owning estates outside Malaysia has set up in Malaysia as part of a move into design work, and a multinational electrical company in Malaysia has also diversified into rubber factory design. Essentially this is an aspect of the product divisibility discussed above, but it is interesting to see how local firms have been able to compete effectively in manufacture, while foreign firms only operate in those particular parts of the production process for which their expertise is suited. The positive role played by foreign firms should not be exaggerated, though. They certainly have helped local firms in recent years to enter the oil palm and SMR rubber machinery fields but in all cases the firms concerned were already in existence when the link with foreign firms was formed.

The recent (1972) founding of a shipyard in Penang by IHC may represent a partial reversal of the trend towards subcontracting, however, since IHC apparently plan to prefabricate dredge parts to a greater extent than has been usual in the immediate past, with a corresponding reduction of work for second-tier firms (Interview, 1974).

8.3.7 The Time Sequence of Development and Interrelations between Engineering Sectors

The oldest form of non-European local engineering is the manufacture of Chinese mining machinery. Of the firms now in existence, over half of the total number with about three-quarters of total production, very probably were formed before the Second World War and several before the First World War.[21] Chinese mining machinery involves iron casting and simple machining, and rubber machinery of the old type also requires casting, with more complicated machining and assembly. Hence the development of rubber machinery manufacture can be based on techniques acquired in making Chinese mining machinery. In the past many workshops made both types, but with the SMR scheme rubber machinery has switched to specialist manufacturers, who also learnt their trade making old-style rubber machinery. Chinese machinery has also led to the making of dredge spare parts, many of which are castings, and in the case of three large local firms to casting in steel, including some work for oil palm mills. Indeed many larger firms making engineering products have become reluctant to do business with Chinese miners, because of extensive credit facilities the miners expect, and this has been an additional reason why such firms have tended to diversify out of gravel pump machinery.

In spite of these moves by firms into dredge and oil palm parts, the major dredge and mill builders have followed a different path from the foundries and machine shops making rubber and gravel pump mining equipment. As was shown earlier, they moved from structural steel erection into the fabrication of parts. What is surprising is the lack of cross-fertilization between the two fields. Only in two cases were they found to be linked. In one, the paid manager of a dredge building firm left to set up his own steel-building business, developing work in both dredge parts and oil palm mills. In another, a mill-making firm received a recent order to fabricate part of a dredge.

One general and important way in which firms have aided the establishment and growth of other firms, both within engineering and in manufacturing in general, has been in the training of skilled workers. Most firms interviewed and all the larger ones, has apprenticeship schemes under which about a third of the total workforce would be under training. The training would be financed by the workers themselves who would receive low wages initially, gradually rising to full skilled rates. Engineering workers have skills highly usuable by other industries. Moreover dredge building and oil palm mill construction have led to the establishment of the floating labour force (estimated by one contractor in 1970 to be about a thousand) whose workers move from contractor to contractor and who are able to turn their hand to most types of engineering construction under contract, including such tasks as the recent building of oil refineries.

8.4 CONCLUSIONS OF THE ENGINEERING CASE STUDY

It has been shown in this chapter that primary product exports have given rise in Malaysia to a substantial light engineering industry. The technological feasibility of a high degree of vertical disintegration in engineering production appears to have allowed those types of engineering to develop which are of a low capital intensity, suited to the country's factor endowment. As capital accumulation has progressed and more expertise developed, a process of import substitution has occured, especially in the building of tin dredges and oil palm mills, through which larger proportions of the export-sector demand for capital goods have been met locally. The absence of economies of scale made it easy for local people to establish engineering firms, especially in rubber and Chinese mining machinery. Foreign firms have been important in providing design facilities but local producers have held their own in manufacturing. Engineering production would not have developed as an export industry in its own right without backward linkage since its origins were in the production either of essentially non-traded goods or goods of highly localized demand, and exporting engineering products requires much more specialized knowledge and more customer contract than do primary product exports. Nowadays however, many of the larger engineering firms have export business in neighbouring countries. There is also at least some circumstantial evidence that engineering linkage investment was not at the expense of investment elsewhere in the economy.

Whether this import substitution process, which has proceeded largely without government protection, can continue is doubtful. What has developed is essentially a *light* engineering industry. The items which are imported are the products either of heavy engineering (e.g. many dredge castings) or technologically sophisticated items (e.g. oil palm hydraulic presses), all subject to large economies of scale and dependent on sales to a much wider range of industrial customers than can be found in Malaysia. Moreover, expansion of dredge building beyond erection and on-site fabrication faces the problem that very large firms (such as IHC) can reap economies of scale by combining their dredge work with various kinds of shipbuilding activity. Whether such economies of scale will mean that local firms will lose fabrication business remains to be seen.

It is also interesting that in oil palm and dredging, local engineering development has depended on foreign engineering firms either not having a monopoly of design technology (e.g. because consultancy firms will sell designs) or their being willing to subcontract manufacture. That subcontracting has taken place seems to be the result of local price-competitiveness. Of course this gives an opportunity for the exploitation of local firms, but no local contractor who was interviewed complained of this. In any case, there are opportunities for local firms, having learnt their trade through work for the primary export sector to branch into new lines of engineering for the domestic economy.

To what extent does this case study vindicate linkages as a tool in the analysis of less developed countries? The validity of the concept depends on how widely applicable are the limitations set out in Chapter 3, namely that linkages may involve mere reallocations of investment resources, that backward linkages could develop equally well as exports, and that some linkages may be 'bad' ones. The restriction on investment in Malaysian export industries in the inter-war period, from which it was concluded in Subsection 8.3.4 that engineering linkage investment may not have been at the expense of investment elsewhere in the economy, is clearly a special case, but there is some empirical evidence (e.g. Wolf and Sufrin, 1955, especially pp. 11–13) that many less developed countries suffer from a shortage of investment outlets. Second, there are good reasons why Malaysian engineering did not develop on its own through direct export. The initial production of goods subject to high transport costs with a high degree of 'natural' protection from imports, is a way in which 'learning by doing' (Arrow, 1962) can start as a preliminary to producing items more subject to foreign competition and it is an activity in which exporting is unlikely in the early stages. The high degree of sales expertise and customer contact important in engineering is likely to apply to many intermediate manufactured products which backward linkage may develop. Third, since Malaysian engineering production for the export sector has developed largely through market forces, there is no reason to suppose it is a 'bad' linkage, especially in view of the unpriced externalities it generates.

It has been shown therefore that major linkage effects do indeed occur, in contradiction to the Little–Mirrlees arguments set out in Chapter 3. Moreover, in view of the new savings and the particularly important unpriced externalities generated by engineering, a case could be made that the industry's establishment should have been aided by the government preferably by a subsidy paid to customers on the purchase of local engineering products. From the wider viewpoint of development strategy, the Malaysian case provides some vindication of Hirschman's unbalanced growth approach by showing how market forces may respond to new investment opportunities. It also shows that primary product exports can be important promoters of industrial growth, not the least by conditioning responsiveness to economic opportunity.

Finally, there is the question of whether engineering could have been promoted by the government in some way other than through backward linkage. The high degree of vertical disintegration in engineering enabled the industry to avoid the usual 'infant industry' difficulties with foreign competition by producing first only those items on which there was substantial natural protection. This in turn was possible only because of the existence of a local backward linkage demand. Had engineering been established to export from the beginning, it would have needed substantial subsidies and the costs involved might have exceeded the eventual benefits (Little and Mirrlees, 1968, p. 210). Thus recognition is required on the part of policy makers that some manufacturing industries producing intermediate products are likely to develop only through backward linkage. Such recognition must be combined with a realization that the fact that an industry is a linkage does not of itself make it appropriate for local production—the title linkage can never confer on an investment an 'immunity from economic analysis' (Little and Mirrlees, 1972, p. 156).

NOTES

1. This chapter is a revised version of Thoburn (1973b). The interviews on which the chapter is based were carried out in the autumn of 1970. Although some updating has been possible as the result of newer statistics, published information, and a brief visit to Malaysia in 1974, the

chapter essentially refers to the situation in 1970. It has also been necessary to shorten the study for publication, and more details about individual engineering firms and their growth are given in Thoburn (1971, Chapter 8).

2. Timber, the third and most rapidly growing export, also generates some demand for engineering goods. Timber was excluded from this case study owing to a lack of research time but some information on timber and the growth of engineering was collected as a by-product from interviews.
3. For a very full study of import-substituting industrialization policy in Malaysia see Edwards (1975).
4. See Section 9.1 for a further discussion of the role of exports in introducing new technology into less developed countries.
5. Manufacturing in Malaysia also includes many 'traditional' activities such as carpentry. The term 'modern' is difficult to define, but certainly one criterion would be the extensive use of powered machinery.
6. This is reflected in the fact that the *Mid-Term Review of the First Malaysian Plan 1966–70* (Prime Minister's Dept., 1969, pp. 73–4) singles out 'industries manufacturing capital or intermediate goods for which extensive markets already exist or are in prospect, e.g. machinery for rubber and palm oil processing and for lumber mills', as one of the four types of manufacturing activity to which special encouragement should be given. In fact, little specific encouragement has been given to these industries to date, other than to the Malayawata steelworks, and the more recent (1971 and 1972) joint ventures with the Australian Steel Foundry Bradken (making dredge supplies), and the Dutch shipbuilding firm IHC Holland, which is aiming to build dredges (and similar items) in Malaysia, Malayawata is rather outside the scope of this study, since its existence depends largely on tariff protection.
7. In 1968 the total purchases of vehicles by tin mining and by rubber estates amounted to 8% of the value of output of *major group* 46 (Transport Equipment) (Thoburn, 1971, p. 420).
8. This is not true of rubber factory construction, palm oil mills or tin dredges, where the engineering contractors themselves hire workers. On gravel pump mines some constructional work is done by mine workers, but most would be arranged by the contractor (see Table 8.1, note 5).
9. The italicized terms, *major groups* and *industries* refer to the two- and four-digit level classifications, respectively, of manufacturing activity in the *Malaysia Industrial Classification* used in the *Censuses* and *Surveys of Manufacturing*.
10. However, an attempt to determine the share of engineering output sold to the export sector by various *industries* and *major groups* is made in Thoburn (1971, pp. 415–20) which looks at the classification of engineering producers.
11. Although IHC had supplied dredges to Malaysia before 1933, it had no other business there until it built a large new dredge in 1971–3. It had, however, built dredges in recent years for Indonesia.
12. This is not to say that technology in the long run may not itself be a variable, changing according to economic and political forces. For further discussion, see Chapter 11.
13. Information from interview in 1974 and from Jeffress (1972). Bradken (as of 1974) did not have tariff protection.
14. It was reported in 1971 (FIDA, *MID*, 2nd Quarter) that the firm of Hargill Engineering was soon to start local production of diesel engines.
15. It was reported in 1973 (FIDA, *MID*, 1st Quarter) that a new plant was to be built by Hargill Engineering to make magnetic and electrostatic separators for the tin industry.
16. This is the approach used for example by Lary (1968).
17. For a discussion of this point see Drake (1972, pp. 951–3).
18. The system of subcontracting is facilitated by the close proximity of engineering workshops. Most firms in Kuala Lumpur are in the Sungei Besi/Chan Show Lin Roads complex on the South-West of the city, and in Ipoh most foundries are on the Lahat Road continuing out of town to the suburbs of Menglembu and Pusing.
19. This information is mainly from the Industrial Profiles Annex to Little and Mirrlees (1968) which suggests that in the manufacture of iron castings (which are the most important item in Chinese mining machinery) economies of scale are linked to a switch from production on a jobbing basis to standardized production on single items on a scale of some 6000 tons per year. This compares to a total use of cast iron of only 11,000 tons by the *industry Industrial*

Machinery and Parts in Malaysia for the whole range of different engineering items. This *industry* is the major producer of castings in Malaysia.

20. A 'European' firm is one founded by Europeans in Malaysia and is distinguished from a 'foreign' firm, which is one founded overseas and having a subsidiary in Malaysia. The term 'European' would also be applied to a firm which, like many of the early tin dredging and rubber companies, kept its headquarters abroad but which generated its turnover in Malaysia.
21. This contention is based on the results of a 20% sample survey of firms in *industry* 4623 conducted by the author. For further details see Thoburn (1971, pp. 503–5).

Chapter 9
Technology, Employment Creation, Income Distribution and Poverty

It is now widely accepted that economic growth in itself may not be sufficient to bring about 'development'.[1] In particular sustained increases in output per head may be accompanied by widespread and often growing unemployment; and growth may proceed in the face of highly (and possibly increasingly) unequal income distribution, leaving virtually untouched the incomes of the poorest sections of the economy. Chapter 4 has shown that Malaysia faces serious problems of absorbing into employment new entrants into the labour force, currently growing at about 3% per year, and unemployment in 1973–4 was about 7% (Treasury, *AR*, 1973–4, p. 67). In the recent study *Redistribution with Growth*, conducted by the World Bank and the Sussex Institute of Development Studies (Chenery, Ahluwalia, Bell, Duloy and Jolly, 1974, p. 8) Malaysia was listed as among the 'high-inequality' group of developing countries (i.e. where the bottom 40% of income recipients receive less than 12% of GNP), though absolute poverty in Malaysia was much less than in many other countries (11% of the population received less than U.S. $50 per year, compared to 36% for all Asian countries included in the study, and 30% for the Third World as a whole—Chenery *et al*, 1974, p. 12).

This chapter therefore tries to broaden the scope of the enquiry and considers the employment-creating effects of primary commodity exporting in Malaysia, and also its impact on income distribution. Both employment and distributional effects are closely linked with export technology. Export technology too is important in the generation of economic growth *per se*. The chapter therefore starts with an analysis of the introduction of new technology by the export industries into Malaysia, and also looks (in Section 9.2) at technological externalities generated by export growth. Section 9.3 then considers employment creation and Section 9.4 income distribution and poverty. The analysis concentrates on tin and rubber, but palm oil is also discussed, mainly in comparison with rubber.

9.1. THE DEVELOPMENT OF EXPORT INDUSTRY TECHNOLOGY AND THE SPREAD OF NEW TECHNOLOGY BY THE EXPORT INDUSTRIES

Both rubber and gravel pump tin mining and dredging involved the introduction of 'new' technology into Malaysia not only in the sense that the industries themselves were new to the country (though the earlier Chinese open cast mining was essentially a very much larger-scale version of the small-scale open cast tin mining that had been going on in the Malay Peninsula for many centuries), but also in the sense that their technology did not exist in other countries in a form immediately transferable to Malaysia (with the exception that the company which developed tin dredging operated both in Thailand and Malaya, and in fact launched its first bucket dredge in Thailand shortly before dredges were established in Malaya). Thus (with that exception) tin was not mined by dredging or gravel pumping elsewhere in the world prior to the introduction of these techniques to Malaya, nor was rubber produced elsewhere using the same methods which were to be used in Malaya. The development of the tin and rubber (and palm oil) industries has been described in earlier chapters, and only certain features of this development need be drawn out here.

TABLE 9.1 CAPITAL INTENSITIES AND RATES OF RETURN IN TIN MINING AND RUBBER AND OIL PALM ESTATES

	INTERNAL RATE OF RETURN (PRIVATE) 1974	INTERNAL RATE OF RETURN (SOCIAL) 1974	CAPITAL - NET OUTPUT RATIO 1972	ANNUAL NON-WAGE VALUE-ADDED PER WORKER ($) 1972
Gravel Pump Tin Mining	56%	>100%	1.4	3920
Tin Dredging	42%	53%	3.2	17370
Rubber Estates	26%	...	2.6	1790
Oil Palm Estates	27%	...	2.7	1470
All Manufacturing	...	...	...	5340

Sources and Notes

(1) Non-Wage Value-Added figures calculated from Statistics Department, RSH, OPCTS, and PR 1972 for rubber, oil palm, and tin and manufacturing, respectively.

(2) Capital-output ratios use 1972 product prices but (in absence of 1972 capital cost data) use 1974 capital good price for tin (interviews, 1974) and 1970 capital good prices for rubber and oil palm (Thoburn, 1971, p. 501-2). This of course will somewhat overstate the capital-intensity of mining *vis à vis* estates.

(3) Tin rates of return are from Thoburn (1976) and rubber and oil palm from Pushparaja, Chan, and Ti (1974 p. 82). In tin, price assumed is M$1000 per picul; and 140 cents/kilo and $590 a tonne for rubber and oil palm respectively. No recent social rates of return for estate cultivation are readily available, but Little and Tipping (1972) calculated that social rates of return on past rubber and oil palm investments were 4-5% points higher than private rates. Private rates of return are before tax, and also before export duty in the case of tin mining.

In tin the early development of the industry by Chinese immigrants used extremely labour-intensive methods and only the most simple equipment. Western firms attempted through the last quarter of the nineteenth century to introduce Western methods and organization, but could not compete with the simple Chinese methods. Technical developments were largely confined to the introduction of steam pumps for drainage in the open cast mines. The importance of western firms dates from the transfer of the dredging technology used in gold mining in Australia to Malayan tin. There are some preliminary indications that dredging may be a technology 'inappropriate' for the local factor endowment (about which problem more in Section 9.3). First, reference to Table 9.1 shows that its capital intensity measured in terms of non-wage value-added per worker is very high, about three times greater than that of domestic manufacturing.[2] Second, although local people have been buying shares in dredging companies on a large scale since the 1950's (see Section 5.2), no entirely locally financed and controlled company was able to enter dredging for over fifty years after its introduction in 1912, the barrier being the large initial capital sums required. Thus it has remained primarily a 'foreign' sector.

The introduction of gravel pumping is partly a result of the transfer of China-clay mining technology from England by western firms, but also the result of the quick recognition by Chinese miners of the potentialities of hydraulic mining with artificial power, once these had been demonstrated by the otherwise unsuccessful technique of suction dredging (discussed in Section 5.1). Gravel pumping is an adaption of overseas technology to local conditions by local (though immigrant) people. Its suitability to local factors endowment is demonstrated by the speed of its spread in the 1920's among the local Chinese mining community.[3] Its capital intensity is markedly lower than that of dredging (see Table 9.1) and it is subject to few economies of scale. Technical change in both tin sectors has done little to alter their basic economic characteristics, except by increasing somewhat the capital requirements for gravel pump mining, and increasing the economies of scale of dredging.

The rubber industry's technology was to an important extent developed by the government of the Federated Malay States.[4] Rubber was one of a series of crops with which various officials experimented in an attempt to promote agricultural development (see Section 4.2) and after rubber was grown successfully, experiments were devised to develop systems of tapping and processing. In many respects the early growth of the industry represented the drafting of an alien sector on to the domestic economy, as not only was much of the initial capital and management imported but also most of the labour.[5] Yet local participation in rubber growing increased rapidly after the introduction of the crop, and, as reference back to Table 4.7 shows, by 1910 'Asian' annual new plantings exceeded European new planting. Most important, not only were estates and smallholdings opened by immigrant Chinese and Indians but a large acreage of smallholdings was planted by the indigenous Malays (and also by some immigrant Malays from the then Dutch East Indies). While estates were subject to economies of scale in the sense that they used heavy processing machinery, indivisible to a certain extent, and European management which represented an overhead charge which needed to be spread over a large acreage, it was possible for smallholdings to be opened on a small scale using the peasants' own labour. In processing, a choice of technique was available and smallholders processed latex into rubber using simple coagulating pans and hand mangles to press the coagulum into sheets, in contrast to the more elaborate coagulating tanks and creping batteries used by the early estates.

It is interesting to ask to what extent the estate sector was responsible for the development of the Malay smallholding sector. Unfortunately little information is available on this or indeed on Asian participation generally in the early rubber industry (Drabble, 1973, p. 41). It is clear that expansion of smallholdings lagged behind that of estates to about 1909 after which there was a boom in Asian planting (estates *and* smallholdings) (Figart, 1925, p. 277). The development of tapping methods depended more on government action than on estates. Few Malays were employed by estates so that tapping and cultivation methods cannot have been learnt by Malays on any large scale from estate work. Little is known about the initial spread of the simple processing methods used by smallholders. It seems likely that the estate-sector's influence was limited to showing the economic potential of rubber, and helping to establish a network of dealers (mostly Chinese) who would buy unsmoked rubber at the kampong level. Estates seem to have had little influence on the direct transfer of rubber growing and processing technology to smallholdings.

Technical change in rubber has not radically altered factor proportions since the Second World War, except possibly in processing. Research centred largely in the Rubber Research Institute of Malaysia has brought about substantial rises in yield per acre but this is essentially technical progress of a Hicks-neutral type, raising factor productivities with a given capital–labour ratio.[6] In processing, the SMR scheme has meant increased initial capital requirements but processing in rubber can be undertaken separately from growing, and latex (and scrap) can be delivered to central processing factories (mostly government run) while growing remains in the hands of smallholders.

In contrast to rubber, oil palm was introduced entirely as an estate crop, until FELDA developed smallholder production with centralized processing in the 1960's. Reference to Table 9.1 shows palm oil to be a more capital-intensive crop than rubber in terms of its capital/net output ratio. In terms of its capital/labour ratio it would also be more capital intensive since fewer workers per acre are employed on oil palm estates and capital costs per acre in palm oil are higher (see Section 6.5). In terms of NWVA per worker however oil palm seems relatively less capital intensive, though this probably reflects the fact that for oil palm estates as a whole profits are lower than those of rubber because the proportion of oil palm acreage which is immature is higher. In general, capital intensity in oil palm will be somewhat lower than rubber because of the former's shorter immature period but higher in terms of processing factory investment. Indeed it is the technology of processing oil palm fruit in Malaysia which prevented smallholders from entering the industry. Fresh fruit bunches need to be brought very quickly to the factory before their quality deteriorates (due to a rise in fatty acids content) and the very high initial capital cost of mill construction would preclude anything but centralized off-estate processing for all but large estates.

The effect of a new industry such as rubber, or a new technology in an existing industry (such as the introduction of gravel pumping or dredging into a tin industry dominated by open cast methods) on factor productivity to a certain extent must be considered together with an analysis of the generation of unpriced externalities by the industry to the rest of the economy (to be considered in the next section). Thus if a new technology improves local peoples' ability to act as an industrial workforce, or if it requires and develops new labour skills which are usable elsewhere, it has both increased factor productivity and generated externalities. A 'purer' productivity effect would be to raise the return on capital or th productivity of labour given quality, though in this case too the benefits would be spread to the rest of the economy if capital and labour were drawn in from other sectors so raising the productivity of the remaining factors in these other sectors (except in the case of labour in perfectly elastic supply). Effects of the latter type are difficult to quantify because little information exists on the returns to capital and labour before the export technologies were developed. Perhaps the most which can be said is that high present returns on capital, and high wages (at least in tin mining), indicate positive effects on factor productivity; though with the two provisos, that local capitalists must be able to enter the industry, and that there may be a trade-off between labour productivity improvements per worker on the one hand and the number of workers whose productivity is improved on the other (and also that wage differentials may reflect that the bargaining power of workers in tin is probably greater than of those in rubber–see Section 7.2).

Improvements in labour quality and productivity can be presented more clearly as part of an analysis of labour skills in the next section, though it is worth noting here that they varied considerably between the export industries. Gravel pump mining represents an excellent compromise between the direct employment of a large number of workers in the wage economy (as in rubber) and the improvement of the skills and earnings of a small number of workers (as in dredging). The labour coefficients in Table 9.4 will show labour-use per unit of output in gravel pumping is nearly twice that of dredging, and about a quarter of that of rubber. Gravel pumping pays high wages relative to estates and its wages are similar to those in manufacturing. Its earnings-improvement effects are less than those of dredging but more widespread if the wages of its unskilled workers–which are higher than those of estate workers–are taken into account. Finally, even on estates wages are four times what one study has calculated to be the shadow wage of the Malaysian economy.[7] Estate wages are also in excess of average rubber smallholder earnings.[8] This substantial excess of estate wages over subsistence-sector productivity is particularly interesting. Whatever the original effects of large-scale immigration from India in reducing wages to the level of an overpopulated underdeveloped country, present estate wages are well above earnings in the subsistence sector.[9,10]

It was argued in Chapter 3 that not only could the spread of new technology be facilitated by the export industry generating unpriced externalities which increase the responsiveness of the rest of the economy to new techniques, but also that spread effects could work on the demand side, in the sense that linkage investment induced by exports could also embody new techniques. The linkage effects of tin and rubber and palm oil were set out in Chapters 5 and 6 but it is worth discussing very briefly their technology. The main linkages of rubber and oil palm growing are chemical fertilizer and other agricultural chemical production, and off-estate processing. Petroleum refining, electricity production and smelting are the main linkages to tin. All three industries have also generated substantial local engineering production (see Chapter 8). Agricultural chemicals and petroleum represent technologies transferred from abroad in recent years, mostly in 'packages' as part of foreign direct investment and as the result of official import substitution policy. Electricity production too is a technology entirely transferred from abroad, though the industry was set up by local European firms and by the government.

Off-estate processing is a 'satellite' industry (see Sections 5.4 and 6.4) and its technology does not require separate discussion from that of processing within the estate sector, except to note the speed and ease with which commercial processing factories were set up off-estate, mostly by Malaysian Chinese dealers.

Tin smelting uses techniques basically similar to that for smelting other metals (though with far fewer economies of scale than, say, aluminium), but nevertheless the industry grew up gradually in Malaysia to a certain extent developing its own technology as it went along. Engineering too, though using foreign methods, grew up through a process of gradually acquiring skills and techniques to perform increasingly sophisticated tasks (see Chapter 8).

A comparison of capital intensities and rates of return is given in Table 9.1. Using 1972 prices tin dredging is seen as substantially more capital intensive than gravel pumping, which in turn is less capital intensive in terms of the capital–output ratio than estates. The NWVA per worker criterion produces different rankings, with estates appearing to be of very low capital intensity, because of their very high labour requirements per unit of output (see Table 9.4 in the next section). However, the capital-intensity figures, particularly the capital–output ratio, should be treated with considerable caution. Comparison between different commodities is greatly affected by product prices in the particular year in question, which *in general* fluctuate far more than the price of capital goods, though the rise in mining capital–output ratios *vis-à-vis* estates since the late 1960's (Thoburn, 1973b, p. 101) is likely to have been a genuine reflection of increases in capital-good prices (especially imported steel and engines).[11] Similarly, comparisons of rates of return are sensitive to price assumption, and actual price changes since 1968 would be enough to reverse the rankings between tin on the one hand and rubber and oil palm[12] on the other (Thoburn, 1976).

9.2 UNPRICED EXTERNALITIES

The generation of unpriced externalities is one of the most important and yet one of the most intangible aspects of export growth. The development of an industry can familiarize people with the use of mechanized techniques, with keeping regular hours in factories and acting as an industrial workforce generally. Managing or acting as a supervisor in an enterprise, or as a peasant producer of cash crops, develops a familiarity with making economic transactions. But many of these externalities are difficult to quantify and analysis of them must necessarily be impressionistic, though an important exception is labour training, on which the present section concentrates.

9.2.1 Unpriced Externalities other than Labour Training

In many respects tin mining is an industrial technique. Many workers on a mine will be concerned with the operations of maintenance of machinery and equipment. A breakdown of the skill structure of the mining labour force is given in the next subsection, but it needs to be said that even unskilled workers from mines would be more suitable for subsequent industrial empoyment than would workers from, say, subsistence agriculture. Similar considerations apply to the processing operations of rubber and oil palm.

Rubber introduced many peasant producers to the idea not only of cash crop production but also of investment in a product with a long gestation period and returns over a period of years. This lengthening of time horizons can be over-stressed however. Rubber trees would be planted in ground cleared near the kampong (village) and left with minimum maintenance until maturity. Meanwhile the peasant could live on his subsistence crop (see also Chapter 1). The spread of rubber among Malays was

TABLE 9.2

WAGES AND STRUCTURE OF LABOUR FORCE ON GRAVEL PUMP TIN MINES AND TIN DREDGES, 1972

GRAVEL PUMP MINES

	% OF TOTAL WORKFORCE	AVERAGE MONTHLY EARNINGS ($)
Supervisory and Administrative		
Kepalas	2	347
Assistant Kepalas	4	223
Clerical	4	190
Skilled and Semi-Skilled		
Engine Drivers (1st class certificate)	3	247 (326)
Engine Drivers (2nd class certificate)	2	184 (205)
Engine Drivers (uncertificated)	4	117 (146)
Chargemen (with certificate)	2	250
Chargemen (uncertificated)	5	105 (103)
Excavator and Bulldozer Drivers	2	232
Unskilled Workers		
Male	)	157-199
Female	) 47	125
Male Indian	)	127
Cooks	1	110
Others	20	...
1971 Average Monthly Earnings (all workers, including salaried staff)		154
1971 Average Labour Benefits per Month		50

DREDGES

	% OF TOTAL WORKFORCE	AVERAGE MONTHLY EARNINGS ($)
Supervisory and Administrative		
Foremen	2	488
Kepalas	5	213
Clerical	4	...
Skilled and Semi-Skilled		
Workshop Skilled	8	257
Workshop Semi-Skilled	2	177
Drivers	4	184-228
Dredge Crew Skilled	10	275
Dredge Crew Semi-Skilled	5	175
Apprentices	1	155
Male Ore Washers	1	224
Unskilled Workers		
Workshop	1	140
Outside Workers	11	131
Dredge Crew	42	144
Female Ore Washers	...	159
Others	4	...
Average Monthly Earnings		274
Average Monthly Labour Benefits		25

Sources and Notes

(1) Average earnings calculated from Statistics Dept., C Min I 1971. Bracketed earnings refer to workers employed on contract. Labour benefit figures based on Thoburn (1971 p. 403).

(2) All earnings statistics from Ministry of Labour, AR 1972 and private communication with Ministry of Labour (March 1970).

facilitated by the fact that (mostly) Chinese provided a network of dealers to collect and sell the rubber, but this also lessened the degree of change required of Malay economic organizations (and widened the scope for possible exploitation of smallholders—see Aziz, 1964, and Section 9.4.).

TABLE 9.3 WAGES AND STRUCTURE OF LABOUR FORCE ON RUBBER AND OIL PALM ESTATES, 1972

	RUBBER		OIL PALM	
	% OF TOTAL LABOUR FORCE	AVERAGE MONTHLY EARNINGS ($)	% OF TOTAL LABOUR FORCE	AVERAGE MONTHLY EARNINGS ($)
Supervisory and Administrative				
Mandores/Kepalas	3	150	3	147
Clerical	1	...	1	...
Factory Workers				
Skilled	2	134	4	168
Unskilled	4	95	4	97
Field Workers				
Tappers/Harvesters	68	108	19	130
Weeders	13	68	31	68
Arsenite Sprayers	1	107	2	106
Transporters	...	...	5	114
Pruners	...	...	1	91
Other Workers	8	...	31	...
Average Earnings (all workers, including salaried staff)		122		125
Estimated Monthly Labour Benefits		25		25

Sources and Notes

(1) All individual wage rates (except factory workers) from Ministry of Labour, AR 1972 Factory worker proportions of skilled and unskilled from interviews (1970), and breakdown used to calculate unskilled workers wages (Ministry of Labour AR 1972 gives factory wages for skilled and for all factory workers only).

(2) Average earnings from Statistics Department, RSH 1972 and OPCTS 1972 and for Labour Benefits see Table 6.12.

The development of an elaborate system of trade and other credit in Chinese tin mining provided familiarity with methods of acquiring and giving credit useful for other industrial development, such as engineering production. Similarly the agency house system was enlarged and developed by the growth of European rubber planting and tin dredging.

The transport system associated with tin mining helped not only the establishment of rubber but also spread the market economy throughout the west coast.

9.2.2 Labour Skills

A comparison between the skill structures of rubber, palm oil[13] and tin mining is given in Tables 9.2 and 9.3. Skill structure is defined in two ways. First, there are the proportions of each industry's workforce in particular occupational categories. Second, the average earnings within each category provide a comparison of the quality of labour relative to labour in the same category in other industries. Similarly, average earnings in an industry can be compared to those of other industries as an indication of labour quality (though bargaining power and alternative employment opportunities for workers are also a factor in wage determination). Four skill categories are used here: supervisory and management staff (both senior and junior), clerical workers, artisans (both skilled and semi-skilled) and unskilled workers.

The relative importance of supervisory and management staff in tin, rubber and oil palm is shown in the Table 9.2 and 9.3, where it can be seen that both dredging and gravel pumping employ proportionately twice as many (7% and 6% of workforce respectively) in the junior supervisory staff category (foremen, kepalas, assistant kepalas and mandores), as do oil palm and rubber (3% of workforce). The higher quality of junior staff in mining is indicated by the fact that in gravel pumping their average earnings are 75% higher, and those in dredging over twice as high, as in rubber or oil palm. Particularly on dredges, supervisors are likely to be skilled artisans who have been promoted. No figures are shown to relate management and other senior supervisory salaries in the four industries. It is likely that estate managers in rubber and oil palm earn similar salaries, while oil palm factory managers and engineers (who are in extremely short supply) earn much more than their counterparts in rubber. Thus an oil palm mill engineer with a steam certificate and several years experience could command in 1970 a salary of over $3500 a month,[14] a salary rarely matched for work in a rubber factory. Dredges employ dredgemasters and shift engineers. The manager of the dredging site is normally a dredgemaster.

Tables 9.2 and 9.3 show that the proportion of clerical staff in rubber is rather less than in gravel pump mining and dredging, and the same as in oil palm. No obvious explanation suggests itself for the low proportion in rubber. Gravel pumping's high proportion (and to a lesser extent that of dredging) is probably accounted for by the fact that the industry is organized into relatively small-scale units of employment. No wages data are available for clerical staff other than in gravel pumping where clerks are paid at a rate comparable with skilled artisans. On estates particularly, clerks often perform supervisory functions. Thus a factory clerk would supervise the weighing in and recording of latex bought by the tappers, and might earn over $500 a month.[15] Clerks in palm oil factories are similarly well paid.[16]

It is the employment of artisans which accounts for the much higher skilled proportion of the workforce in mining than in estates. In oil palm and rubber artisans are employed almost entirely in factory (and workshop) work, accounting for 4% of the workforce in oil palm and 2% in rubber. In gravel pumping nearly 9% of the workforce are qualified artisans (and drivers) and about 30% in dredging.

In the unskilled category, the quality of the labour force also appears higher on mines than estates (or its bargaining power greater). Gravel pump mine unskilled male workers earn generally about over \$150 a month compared to about \$140 for unskilled dredge crews and dredge workshop workers. Tappers on estates earn only \$100 while oil palm harvesters earn \$130; and labour benefits on gravel pump mines are much higher (mainly because they provide free food). Few mine workers earn below \$100 (excluding labour benefits). On estates, especially oil palm, there are substantial proportions of much lower paid workers (especially weeders) who earn only about \$70.

The overall average wages in both gravel pumping are somewhat higher (when labour benefits are included), than in manufacturing industry as a whole in Peninsular Malaysia and dredging wages are 50% higher. Those in estates are substantially lower than manufacturing.[17] Thus the overall quality of the labour force in mining is comparable with manufacturing.

Wage differentials reflecting time spent in the acquisition of skills specific to individual export industries indicate increases in labour quality. Such quality increases are important in themselves since they raise productivity and *per capita* incomes within the export sector. For the sector to generate *externalities* to other industries, skills must be transferable. The skills of artisans, such as fitters, boilermakers, electricians etc., are the most obviously transferable. They are usable by almost any manufacturing industry, and elsewhere in the economy. To a certain extent, management supervisory and clerical skills are also transferable. Managers of rubber estates can switch to palm oil or other crops (though transferability would be more limited on the factory side). The executive responsibilities and general engineering knowledge of mine engineers could be transferred, although their specific mining skills could not. More junior supervisory positions are often given to older men, especially in Chinese mines, who have had long experience in the industry. As such, their experience may be difficult to transfer. The same difficulty applies to clerical staff (on mines and estates) to the extent to which, as is often the case, they exercise some supervisory functions. Tapping skills are of little use outside the rubber industry, although the existence of a labour force already used to estate work is valuable to new estate crops such as oil palm. Of course, familiarity with the rubber industry lends itself to workers setting up as smallholders, but in fact this process is restricted by institutional constraints. Indians, who are the bulk of the estate labour force, would find difficulties in acquiring new land for rubber.

Most skilled occupations in the export industries discussed are performed by local people. Expatriates are confined entirely to the administrative and managerial staff. No detailed figures are available for European employment, but the total proportion in 1972 of 'other races' (i.e. non-Malay, non-Indian, non-Chinese) was 0.4% in rubber, 0.3% in oil palm and 0.5% in tin (Ministry of Labour, *AR*, 1972). This category includes all Europeans, as well as other non-Malaysian Asians such as Japanese. If it is assumed that senior administrative and supervisory staff are about 1½% of the workforce in rubber, and 2½% in oil palm,[18] then it can be seen that much of management is Malaysian. The tin figure (1 to 2%) conceals the fact that since virtually no Europeans (except for a few companies such as Gopeng) are employed in gravel pump mines the 272 'others' employed in tin will be mostly on dredges. Allowing say 20 Europeans for work in non-dredging, non-gravel pump tin mines such as Pahang Consolidated, this gives a proportion of 2.6% of the dredging workforce, indicating that much of the management may still be European.

Europeans have not been employed in artisan, junior supervisory or clerical capacities since long before the Second World War. Writing in 1916 on tin dredging in Malaya, H. D. Griffiths noted that local skilled labour for workshops was easily obtainable, and that European staff was confined to managers, dredge masters and winchmen. Even at that time European winchmen were being replaced by Chinese (Griffiths, 1917, pp. 19 and 26). Gravel pump mines, predominantly Chinese, never employed Europeans except in the small minority of European-owned mines. Even early accounts of the rubber industry such as D. M. Figart's (1925) do not speak of Europeans employed as conductors, mandores, etc.

9.3 EMPLOYMENT CREATION

Chapter 4 has discussed in general the problems faced by the Malaysian government in devising policies to absorb the rapidly growing labour force and to reduce existing unemployment; and it has considered the role of the primary export sector in those policies. This section tries therefore to look in more detail at the employment-creating effects of the various primary exports, bearing in mind that for rubber and oil palm there exist abundant land resources for further expansion (if demand conditions are favourable) whereas for tin the expansion prospects (excepting off-shore dredging and the long-discussed but so far little-realized potential of ore reserves to be found in Malay Reservations) are poor and more attention needs to be given with tin therefore to the possibilities of altering the relative shares of the two main techniques in total production.

In order to assess employment creation through export expansion essentially the same mechanisms can be used as those outlined in Chapter 3 to assess trade and growth. This is hardly surprising since employment is created by short-run changes in output and long-run changes in capacity. Thus once the structure of growth effects through forward and backward linkages and the multiplier effects (or 'final demand linkages') of export growth are known, employment creation in principle can quickly be determined with the aid of incremental labour/output and labour/investment coefficients. This is not to say, however, that maximizing output growth necessarily maximizes employment growth. Techniques for example which have high capital–labour ratios sometimes have higher output–capital ratios than techniques with lower capital–labour ratios (i.e. the high K/L techniques may 'dominate' the lower K/L techniques—see Stewart, 1972; Thoburn, 1976). In general though, over long periods of time, employment/output conflicts are likely to be less severe than is often supposed, since higher future output presents an opportunity of generating more future employment (Stewart and Streeten, 1971, pp. 162–3). Nevertheless output growth may generate insufficient opportunities to employ new entrants to the labour force (or to reduce existing unemployment), and changes in output mix or in techniques (or both) could often reduce the problem (since unemployment is typically due to a shortage of complementary factors rather than a deficiency of Keynesian aggregate demand). This is not to say that increasing employment creation would necessarily reduce growth. Indeed, and perhaps ironically, the influential International Labour Office missions to Colombia, Ceylon and Kenya (and Iran) recommended employment-creating policies which actually required for their implementation rates of economic growth *faster* than those of those countries' recent experience (Thorbecke, 1973, p. 422).

The effects of tin, rubber and palm oil on employment creation historically (say prior to the Second World War) are problematical and not particularly interesting since the country suffered from a labour shortage. For rubber estates the labour force was largely imported from India with minimal effects on local employment (though a few Malays and local Chinese were also employed). In tin mining, employment effects were negative since the changes in techniques at the start of the twentieth century (and this is true of gravel pumping as well as dredging) employed fewer workers per unit of output (or investment) than the earlier open cast techniques used during the massive influx of Chinese in the late nineteenth century. On rubber smallholdings, self-employment opportunities were generated for some Chinese and Indians, but Malays tended to grow rubber instead of (or often in addition to) rice. Oil palm, prior to the Second World War, was exclusively an estate crop, and of minor importance (at least in comparison to rubber).

In the post-war period, employment on rubber estates has declined, and output increases have been the result mainly of increasing output per acre from high-yielding varieties of rubber. Rubber estate acreage has declined somewhat as the estate sector of relatively constant total size, has diversified into oil palm. In tin, taking the early 1950's as the base period (i.e. excluding 1946–9, to allow for post-war reconstruction) output declined relatively in the late 1950's, but by the late 1960's, was substantially higher. In contrast, by the late 1960's employment was at about the 1950 level. The potential lagging of employment has, however, been substantially cushioned by switches of output from dredging to the more labour-intensive gravel pumping, but even gravel pumping has substantially reduced its labour requirements per unit of output as it has increasingly mechanized (Thoburn, 1976).

With regard to present and possible future employment creation by the export industries, a first impression can be gleaned from Table 9.4, which shows labour use per unit of output and per unit of initial investment by sector. Between the two tin mining sectors differences in labour requirements in relation to investment are more marked than in relation to output. This is mainly because much of the equipment in gravel pump mines has a relatively short life, which reduces initial capital requirements (though substantially more replacement investment, relative to initial investment, and relatively more maintenance expenditure is needed throughout the life of the ore deposit than is the case in dredging). It is also possible that *incremental* labour requirements in gravel pumping may be overstated relatively to dredging in that output expansion might well occur in 'best-practice' mines which could have lower labour use.[19] Reference back to Table 9.1 shows that both techniques are viable from the private investor's viewpoint of current (1976) tin prices of $1000 a picul[20], and the difference in private rates of return (calculated from data from individual interviews) between the techniques at $1000 a picul are possibly small enough to be due to sampling error (though there are not enough observations to test this statistically). It was shown in Subsection 5.1.2 that the two techniques are competing ones over much of the mining area of Malaysia, in the sense that most dredging deposits could, from a technical point of view, be worked by gravel pumps. The labour/investment ratio suggests therefore there is a real conflict between output growth and employment, in the sense that while a given initial capital sum will generate a similar private rate of return in both techniques, gravel pumping investment will generate four times more jobs; and thus if new investment is in dredging then potential jobs will be sacrificed for no gain in output. If the supply of mining land, rather than the supply of capital is regarded as the binding constraint, a similar picture

TABLE 9.4 EMPLOYMENT CREATION AND SKILLED LABOUR COEFFICIENTS ON GRAVEL PUMP MINES, TIN DREDGES, AND RUBBER AND OIL PALM ESTATES, 1972

	VALUE OF OUTPUT ($ MIL)	WORKFORCE	PROPORTION OF WORKFORCE SKILLED	SKILLED WORKERS PER $ MILLION OF OUTPUT	SKILLED WORKERS PER $ MILLION OF INVESTMENT	TOTAL WORKERS PER $ MILLION OF OUTPUT	TOTAL WORKERS PER $ MILLION OF INVESTMENT
Gravel Pump Tin Mines	442.7	30,450	0.29	19.9	12.2 (1974)	68.8	41.9 (1974)
Tin Dredges	248.3	9,710	0.43	16.8	4.2 (1974)	39.1	9.6 (1974)
Rubber Estates	704.6	196,314	0.06	16.7	4.7 (1970)	278.6	78.4 (1970)
Oil Palm Estates	255.7	47,470	0.08	14.8	2.7 (1970)	185.6	34.3 (1970)
All Manufacturing Industry (1971)	4164.1	165,027	...	...	...	39.6	...

Sources and Notes

(1) Output and Workforces from Chapters 5 and 6, for tin and rubber (and oil palm) respectively. Manufacturing figures from Statistics Department S Man I 1971. Investment coefficients for rubber and oil palm from Thoburn (1971, p. 340), and from interviews 1974 for tin.

(2) Skilled worker coefficients from Table 9.2 and 9.3, treating tappers, harvesters etc. as unskilled, but clerical workers as skilled, and adding 1% point to skilled figure to take account of management staff.

(3) Since indirect labour requirements for mining are higher than oil palm and rubber, the former's total labour coefficients would be higher in relation to the latter's than they appear in the table.

emerges with gravel pumps mines employing roughly twice the number of workers per acre[21] as dredging. At low tin prices, as I have shown elsewhere (Thoburn, 1976) a conflict emerges since dredging then generates a higher private (and social)[22] rate of return, whereas at high tin prices gravel pumping becomes more profitable privately and socially.[23] It could be argued, however, that at low tin prices the fact that dredging's social profitability is higher than gravel pumping's renders the output/employment conflict irrelevant. This would be a reflection of the weights used in the social profitability appraisal being such as to value the gains in output growth higher than the losses from a lower rate of job creation.

Within the estate sectors, rubber generates twice the number of jobs per unit of investment as palm oil, and uses substantially more labour per unit of output. A similar picture emerges if labour use is estimated on an acreage basis. Thus in 1972 only 0.08 workers were employed on oil palm estates per planted acre, compared to 0.13 on rubber estates, though the difference is somewhat overstated since the proportion of immature acreage, with lower labour requirements, was higher in oil palm (31% compared to 14%—see Statistics Dept., *RSH* and *OPCTS*, 1972).

Statistics for rubber smallholdings and rubber and oil palm land development schemes are not given in Table 9.4. Aggregate statistics for labour use on rubber smallholdings would be misleading, since, because of the very small acreage size of holding and the consequent need for outside employment for many smallholding families, the incremental employment from new land development for smallholders, would differ considerably from average labour use. In general smallholdings use labour more intensively than estates. Basically this is because they have no cash wage costs and therefore attempt to maximize output per planted acre (Bauer, 1948b, p. 363; Sen, 1975, pp. 63–64). With a higher planting density of trees per acre (say 180, instead of the 120 or less usually found on estates) and a more intensive tapping system (say daily, instead of alternate days) a single smallholder could manage about 3½ acres (see also note 8), compared to 7.7 workers on rubber estates per acre in 1972 (Statistics Dept., *RSH*, 1972). Even taking into account the understating of smallholder labour requirements as a result of off-estate processing of smallholder rubber, does not greatly alter the orders of magnitude. On FELDA rubber schemes the modal size of holding was until recently 8 acres (now 10 acres) for a *family* (i.e. usually with more than two workers). On FELDA oil palm schemes the modal size is 10 acres (though in 1973 it was announced that the holding size on new FELDA schemes would be increased to twelve acres for rubber and fourteen acres for palm oil—see Prime Minister's Dept., *MTR*, 1973, p. 8). Capital costs on schemes tend to be somewhat higher than on private estates, partly reflecting the location of schemes in virgin areas to which labour must be transported but also the use of less efficient technical and managerial resources (Lim and Chong, 1973, pp. 18–19), so that the higher labour/land ratios are partly counterbalanced by higher capital/land ratios. On smallholder and scheme rubber and oil palm there is also considerable scope for factor substitution, in the sense that the existing sizes of holdings are smaller than could be operated in principle by the settler families (i.e. assuming for example that teenage children work on the holding) and thus are a compromise between income and employment generation. For this reason Lim Sow Ching (1972) has argued that larger (ten-acre) holding is necessary to provide adequate income from rubber (but see also Section 9.4 where some criticisms of these large holdings are discussed).

It is not possible from existing data fully to take into account on a sectoral basis the indirect effects of export expansion on employment. With respect to backward and forward linkages, the latest input–output table (Statistics Dept., *IAA*, 1965) treats estate, smallholder and land development scheme rubber as a single sector. Tin mining too is treated as a single sector and oil palm is not distinguished from agriculture in general. A study by C. B. Edwards (1975, pp. A3/4) based on the 1965 input–output table estimates *total* (i.e. direct and indirect) labour requirements for rubber growing as 642 workers per $ million of final demand, compared to 629 for all agriculture (excluding rubber) and 89 for mining. This gives useful orders of magnitude as far as direct employment and total backward linkage is concerned. Forward linkages for both tin and rubber have already been shown to be small. As between sectors in rubber, little more can be determined except that estates generate more backward linkages than smallholdings (because their use of fertilizers, etc. is greater). Between the tin mining sectors, gravel pumping generates almost double the backward linkage (as a share of gross output) of dredging, but gravel pump linkages are concentrated on petroleum refining which is very much less labour intensive (8 workers per $ mil. of final demand) than is electricity (125 workers per $ mil. of final demand), which is dredging's main produced input purchase.

Final demand linkages have been calculated in the present study (in Chapter 7) in aggregative terms which do not permit sectoral comparisons (though the probable total size of multiplier effects is discussed on a sectoral basis). Some general observations can, however, be made. First, for the tin and rubber industries combined (and almost certainly for oil palm too since its workers' income levels and ethnic composition are very similar to that of rubber), a very high proportion of consumption expenditure is made locally in the first instance (i.e. for the first round of multiplier effects after the initial receipt of export income). Moreover, these purchases are mostly of simple foodstuffs and other consumer goods where there is a good *a priori* reason for expective employment intensity to be high (Singer, 1975b, p.11; Lydall, 1975a and 1975b). However, Chapter 7 also showed that the total size of multiplier effects (i.e. irrespective of the proportion spent locally) is likely to be small for any given increase in export income. This is because on tin mines wages are only a small proportion of output value, and on rubber estates because there is little sensitivity of wage payments to export income. Thus the multiplier effects of export expansion are likely to be much greater, both in terms of value and of employment creation, if in the rubber industry (and probably in oil palm too) export expansion is concentrated on smallholdings (and to a lesser extent also on land development schemes). In contrast, export expansion centred on estates and (to a lesser extent on mines) will mainly generate, at least in the short run, increases in profits (where marginal propensities to consume will almost certainly be lower and propensities to imports will be higher), though there will also be increases in taxation (which eventually will have multiplier effects of its own through government expenditure); and on mines (as will be shown in the next section) real wages (and therefore potential final demand linkage) have risen substantially over time.

9.4 INCOME DISTRIBUTION AND POVERTY

It was noted in the introduction to this chapter that the distribution of income in Malaysia (the distribution by income-size groups that is, rather than the distribution between broad categories of factors of production) was highly unequal compared to many other developing countries. Moreover, there is some evidence (though it is still rather tentative) that over the last decade inequality has increased.[24] Although it was also noted that Malaysia's highly unequal income was not associated with absolute poverty to the same extent as in many other countries (only just over a third of her bottom 40% had annual incomes below U.S. $50 per year), nevertheless the impact of the export industries on Malaysia's poor (defined here along 'Redistribution with Growth' lines simply as the bottom 40% or 50%) is worthy of consideration as a distinct issue.

9.4.1 Income Distribution

The impact in historical terms of the introduction of tin and rubber (and later palm oil though its effects would be similar to rubber and confined initially to the estate sector) into the economy is highly problematic. Clearly, if personal incomes on the rubber estates differed from those in the rest of the economy, income distribution would change, but far more interesting is the effect of the introduction of Indian estate labour on incomes elsewhere in the economy. Historically the rubber estates could be depicted as introducing the low wage levels associated with more heavily populated Asian countries (in this case India) to a country where labour was scarce. In fact it is unlikely that Indian immigrant labour would greatly have affected the wage rates of local Malays, because the Malay population was at the time not short of land and wage labour on estates (and even more so on mines where conditions were more arduous) would have been unattractive even at much higher wages to peasant farmers with adequate income. It is possible, however, that the introduction of Indian labour at a time when the mines were beginning to switch to less labour-intensive techniques lessened the possibilities of mining workers (who had also emigrated from a relatively low wage area—Southern China) from being reabsorbed into rubber. Thus over the period 1910–19, as figures from Chapters 5 and 6 show, rubber estate employment in the Federated Malay States rose from nearly 130,000 to nearly 240,000, while mining employment *fell* by a similar amount from its 1913 peak (225,000) to 113,000 by 1919. Thus in mining there would have been downward pressure on the wage rates of unskilled workers, which *could* have been relieved by offtake into other sectors and *was* also relieved by the return of workers to China.

At the present time, rubber estate employment offers wages substantially in excess of those for many households in the subsistence sector and in smallholder rubber (see note 8 for instance, on rubber), and indeed an increasing number of Malays have taken estate employment (33% of the 1972 rubber labour force were Malays, compared to only 2% in 1938). The share of Chinese in the rubber estate labour force also rose from 17% to 26% over the same period, while that of Indians fell from 80% to 40% (see Table 6.6). Whether rubber estates (and also oil palm estates, where average earnings are similar) have had a depressing effect on wages elsewhere is not certain. Probably they have not, since Tamils from the estates are a non-competing group for other employment to a much greater extent than are Chinese. Thus over 30% of the Indian workforce still works on rubber (and oil palm) estates compared to only 3% of Chinese on tin mines. Average earnings on mines are very much higher, being $154 per month in gravel pumping and $274 in dredging, compared to only $122 on rubber estates (see Tables 9.2 and 9.3). Gravel pump wages are very similar to average wages in manufacturing ($183 per month in 1971). Dredging wages are certainly higher, but the differential *vis-à-vis* other sectors is minute compared to those found for example in the oil industry in, say, Venezuala or Iran, which (as Chapter 10 describes) have biased the pattern of domestic demand in favour of luxury consumer goods, and have influenced wages in other sectors, thereby adversely affecting the rate of growth of employment.

With regard to the effects of estates and mines on distribution with respect to other sources of factor income, conclusions must be still more uncertain and opinions even more impressionistic. Not only is it impossible adequately to hypothesize the 'without-tin', 'without-rubber' and 'without-palm oil' situations, but data on the distribution of local capitalists' profits from the export industries is lacking. Although factorial distribution of income can be obtained for gravel pumping (almost entirely a local sector) and for the local sector of the rubber estate industry, no information is available on the size distribution of the profits *between* capitalists. Thus many gravel pump mines are owned by partnerships of unknown size, and, conversely, for example many individual urban dwellers own unknown areas of rubber land. Earlier in this chapter it was suggested that very high rates of profit could be earned in tin mining, and it seems likely that these high returns will have concentrated much of the financial returns from tin mining in the hands of a relatively small number of local Chinese capitalists, thus worsening distribution, though making available funds for reinvestment elsewhere in the economy. Local rentiers will have derived income too from share ownership in tin dredging companies.

Before considering smallholder rubber and the effects more generally of export growth on poverty, the distribution of income on a comparative basis between export sectors is worth discussion. It was shown earlier in the chapter that tin mining has demanded a much greater improvement in the average quality of its labour force (in terms of generating demand for skilled workers) than has rubber or palm oil. What is also noticeable is that there are large differentials not only in average earnings between the sectors (which reflect different skill mixes) but also with respect to unskilled wages. On rubber estates, the factorial distribution of income seems to have worsened since the end of the Second World War, compared to mines.[25] Since there are many workers and few capitalists, this would be associated with a relative worsening of the size distribution of income within the rubber industry compared to mining. Two pieces of information are available to support this contention. First, indices of real wages were calculated for rubber estates and the two main mining sectors (using the retail price index as a deflator). Wage data are available from the appendices to Chapters 5 and 6 and need not be repeated here, and we simply compare therefore five-year averages of real wages in each sector for the period 1947–51 (i.e. including the Korean boom) with those for 1968–72. In tin dredging the ratio of the latter average real wages to the former is 2.14, in gravel pumping 1.60, and on rubber estates only 1.31. Obviously the relatively poor performance of rubber wages might reflect a lower rate of labour productivity growth (including a possibly lower rate of growth of labour skills). To test this proposition average wages were regressed in log-linear form (so as to show elasticities) on the value of output per worker for the 1947–72 period, and the following were the best-fit equations for rubber estates and gravel pump mining, where the figures in brackets under the coefficient estimates are Student 't' statistics (not standard errors), and where y_t is the wage rate in year t and x_t is the value of output per worker in year t, and t is time in years:

Rubber Estates

$$\log y_t = 2.505^* + 0.205^* \log x_t + 0.016^* \log t$$
$$(5.45) \quad (3.36) \qquad (5.32)$$
$$(R^2 = 0.819, DW = 1.498)$$

Gravel Pump Mines

$$\log y_t = 1.934 + 0.386^* \log x_t + 0.012^* \log t$$
$$(1.66) \quad (5.13) \qquad (2.39)$$
$$(R^2 = 0.878, DW = 1.8065)$$

In the case of dredging positive serial correlation occured in the log-linear form, so first differences (of unlogged data) were taken to eliminate this—

Dredging

$$y_t - y_{t-1} = 6.359^* - 0.001\, x_t - x_{t-1}$$
$$(3.14) \quad (1.31)$$
$$(R^2 = 0.069, DW = 1.5864)$$

The starred coefficients are those which are significant (by the Student 't' test) at the 5% confidence level. In rubber and gravel pumping there is a very slight time trend, and a substantial difference in the elasticities of wage rates with respect to value of output per worker. In rubber, a given increase in total labour productivity is associated with a 20% rise in wages; and with a 39% rise in gravel pumping. Lagging the equations by a year does not increase the rubber elasticity (it stays at approximately 20%) though the gravel pump elasticity falls to 15%, indicating that rubber estate wage increases *partially* catch up with gravel pumping's after the longer lag. In dredging, no statistically significant relation could be identified between wage rates and labour productivity, but there was a statistically significant positive time trend (indicated by the value of the constant in first differences). The fit of the dredging equation was very poor, but it is worth pointing out that the fit of the untransformed (and unlogged) equation (not shown) was much better ($R^2 = 0.958$, though there was serial correlation), and first differences were a transformation imposed on the data merely to eliminate serial correlation.

The relative failure of wage rates to keep pace with labour productivity in rubber, and the unskilled wage differential *vis-à-vis* mining, suggests that the bargaining power of workers on rubber estates may be weaker. Certainly estate workers are highly unionized, but the alternative employment opportunities for Indian workers (who still are the largest single ethnic group on estates) are limited. Traditionally few Indians work in mines, and language difficulties (reinforced by a history of vernacular education, which meant that until the recent introduction of Malay-medium primary education for everyone, Tamil workers tended to be able to speak only Tamil) make jobs hard to find where industry is run by Chinese, or where (in the case of foreign companies) preferences may be given to Malays or where a knowledge of English might be required. In contrast, Chinese unskilled workers often move between estates and Chinese mines according to prevailing wages, and the demand for labour,[26] and are highly mobile into other sectors of the economy, where Chinese business firms are widespread. It is worth adding, in passing, that mobility *within* the Chinese community has probably been aided by vernacular education, since Malaysian Chinese primary education in Mandarin has been a force breaking down barriers between different dialect groups (Cantonese, Hokkien, Hakka, etc.).

9.4.2 Poverty

In some developing countries (Jamaica is perhaps an example) the 'poor' can be identified predominantly with the unemployed. Therefore measures to create employment will also improve income distribution and, given the frequent difficulty of using fiscal measures for redistributive purposes (Chenery, Ahluwalia, Bell, Duloy and Jolly, 1974, p. xii), they may well be the most important means of doing so.[27] In other countries, of which Malaysia is one, the poorest section of the community is self-employed farmers.[28] In Malaysia, of the poorest 49% of the population 52% are self-employed, for instance, compared to 39% in the community as a whole (Chenery *et al.*, 1974, p. 23) though of course the 'self-employed' also include petty traders in urban areas. Moreover, although the inequitable distribution of income in Malaysia is by no means entirely a 'racial' problem since there are substantial inequalities *within* as well as between ethnic groups,[29] nevertheless the poorest people in Malaysia are undoubtedly rural Malays. The average size of Malay smallholding for example (and Malays own most of the padi smallholdings, and about half of the rubber smallholding acreage) is only 3.3 acres compared to a national average of 6.6 acres. Forty-two percent of Malay smallholdings are below three acres (Prime Minister's Dept., *MTR*, 1973, p. 11) which, as will be shown below, is a size insufficient to generate adequate income in either padi or rubber. Indeed, according to the 1960 *Census of Agriculture*, 10% of the total number of smallholdings were less than one acre (and 28% less than two acres) and virtually all of these very small farms were in areas of long-standing Malay settlement (Rudner, 1971, p. 85).

Although Malays in recent years have increased their participation in the mining and estate labour forces, historically the main effect of primary commodity exports on the Malay peasant community has been through opportunities to grow rubber as a smallholder crop. Specialization on the traditional peasant crop, rice (though a minority of peasants specialize on coconut growing, and in coastal regions on fishing) varies considerably between regions in Peninsular Malaysia. In the North Western states of Kedah and Perlis, and in Penang and Province Wellesley, where there are large-scale irrigation works and where double-cropping of padi characterizes the economy, the degree of specialization on rice is high. In the central states of Malaysia, such as Selangor, Malacca or Negri Sembilan, where yields per acre are somewhat lower,[30] rubber growing frequently is pursued along with the growing of padi (and fruit, and livestock and poultry rearing). Probably about a third of rubber smallholders, for example, grow some padi.[31] Rubber in such circumstances provides regular cash income (either for owner-tappers, or sharetappers, and sometimes for paid estate work outside the village), while rice is grown mainly for subsistence (Swift, 1965, pp. 26–77). In spite of restrictions placed on Malay cultivation of rubber during the early years of the industry's expansion (see e.g. Drabble, 1973, p. 101), Malay peasants found rubber growing more profitable than increasing padi output to meet the potential demand for rice by Chinese and Indian workers (Bauer, 1948b, pp. 60–65).

Rural Malay proverty today in rubber and padi growing (and presumably in coconut growing too, though it has not been investigated in this book) springs from a combination of the small size of holding,[32] low productivity per acre (in relation to potential productivity) and the possible exploitation of peasants by dealers (mostly Chinese) and by landlords. Although rice has not been considered explicitly so far (except briefly in Chapter 4) it is the most obvious practical alternative to rubber for most peasants. In padi, fragmentation of holdings under the Islamic law of inheritance has gradually decreased average size (Lim Chong Yah, 1967, pp. 170–71). Yields vary considerably between areas in Malaysia (depending on soil, rainfall and irrigation facilities). By world standards Malaysian rice yields per acre are low and her costs high,[33] and in a recent study Y. Huang (1972, p. 95) was pessimistic about the income-generating possibilities of even double-cropped rice on adequately sized holdings[34] with the possible exception of double cropping in such highly favourable areas as the Muda scheme in Kedah and Perlis. In rubber in contrast, adequately sized holdings even at conservative future price estimates, yield much higher incomes.[35]

In Malaysia, with its large reserves of unused land, the main device for increasing average holding size has been a variety of schemes for new land development (which have been described in Chapter 6, and also discussed in Chapter 4, and of which FELDA has been the most successful), which have resettled families onto new and larger holdings (with special preference given in FELDA to young married Malays who are actually landless). Replanting of smallholdings with high-yielding rubber has also been discussed in Chapter 6, but it is worth stressing again here how difficult this is on the typical Malay holdings of 2–4 acres. Thus success in the replanting programme depended on better financial arrangements for replanting, which were made especially following the first general election in 1955 and the election campaign of 1959 (Rudner, 1970, pp; 325–6), as the ruling Alliance party courted support among Malay peasants.

Ungku Aziz (1964) has argued that the root cause of rural poverty (in both rubber and padi) is a exploitation of peasants by dealers and landlords.[36] Such exploitation not only deprives peasants of existing income, but may discourage them from introducing new methods, making investment on the holding, etc. With regard to landlordism, in padi insecurity of tenure is a serious problem. In the 1950's for instance, in a study of the important rice-ground state of Kelantan (where yields however are low) over 40% of tenanted padi land was found to change hands annually (Lim Chong Yah, 1967, p. 169). In rubber, absentee landlordism significantly increased during the 1950's as a result of estate subdivision (as foreign interests sold out during the Emergency).[37] since subdivided land frequently was bought by urban dwellers. Landlordism, especially in rubber, should not necessarily be equated with exploitation, however. As Swift has shown in his study of Negri Sembilan (1965, p. 57) the categories of owner-operator, sharetapper and smallholder owner are not clear income classes. In particular many village landlords may be older people who can no longer tap rubber themselves. With regard to dealers, Aziz suggests that the system of Chinese dealers, which was so useful in easing the Malay village economy into rubber, has fossilized the rural economy, since dealers may take excessive margins, buy produce from indebted producers at low prices, sell on truck, etc. Widespread evidence is lacking on this contention, though Aziz's own assertions spring from wide experience in rural areas, particularly as part of his studies of the effects of estate subdivision. Swift (1965, pp. 62–3) says that Chinese dealers in his area of study formed a price ring, though they sometimes competed on a non-price basis, and took a margin of about 10 cents per kati on the RSS 1 price in Singapore (very roughly a 10% reduction, in Swift's period—the late 1950's—though equal to about 20% at late 1960's prices.). Writing about an earlier period (the 1930's) Bauer (1948b, p. 59) noted that dealer margins were relatively low. Studies in the mid-1960's of dealers' margins over most of Peninsular Malaysia at the first-trade level found margins of 8–11 cents per 1b for unsmoked sheet (Lim Sow Ching, 1968a, p. 4). Lim Sow Ching also found, in the important rubber-growing state of Selangor, that only 32% of customers (and only 25% of Malay customers) were indebted to dealers, and that there was indeed no evidence to show that indebtedness was an important factor in causing smallholders' adherence to one dealer (p. 7). Lim did, however, conclude that for unsmoked sheet (which accounts for about 70% of smallholders' sales) marketing margins were 'excessive' (in relation to processing costs). Official measures to improve smallholder marketing arrangements (and to upgrade their produce) have included the encouragement of small, group-processing centres, and the establishment of central processing factories which buy smallholder latex and unsmoked sheet for processing into SMR grades (see also Chapter 6).

With regard to possible connections between primary commodity exporting and the deterioration in income distribution in Malaysia over the last decade some general observations can be made. Reference has already been made to the employment creation (and therefore redistributive) effects of the switch in tin mining from dredging to gravel pumping. On estates, on the other hand, a slightly declining trend in acreage has been accompanied by a switch from rubber to oil palm, which reduces labour requirements per acre. No information has been presented on timber, but its substantial expansion will have had obvious employment-creating effects. Apart from timber (where capitalists will have made high speculative profits as well as creating employment), the main effect on distribution will have been through new state and federal land development. Snodgrass in a recent paper (1974, pp. 282–5) has suggested that, though distribution in Malaysia has become more unequal, the fiscal system (and particularly public expenditure) has worked against this trend (at least in so far as inequality is associated with inequality between ethnic groups—since public expenditures have mainly benefitted Malays). As Chapter 4 has shown, land development has been an important part of the public expenditure programme[38] though taxation (mainly the export duty) on rubber smallholders is regressive (Snodgrass, 1974, p. 284).[39] Nevertheless, as the riots in November 1974 in Baling (and later in Kuala Lumpur), over low rubber incomes in a period of inflation, showed,[40] much rural discontent persists, and much progress in eliminating rural poverty remains to be made. In any case land development has only affected directly a small proportion (under 5%) of the rural population.

NOTES

1. The acceptance of the importance of the distributional and employment-creating aspects of development owes much to the International Labour Office missions to Colombia, Ceylon and Kenya in the early 1970's. For a convenient discussion and critique of these missions (and also of the later ILO mission to Iran) see Thorbecke (1973). The *Redistribution with Growth* study referred to in the text found that although income inequality tends to increase in the very early stages of economic growth (say up to U.S. $200 per head per year), after that point there can be found a great variety of experiences. Taiwan, Korea and Tanzania for instance are among countries where growth has been accompanied by trends towards more equal income distribution, whereas in other cases it has worsened (Chenery, Ahluwalia, Bell, Duloy and Jolly, 1974, p. xv). For further discussion of *Redistribution with Growth*, see Jolly (1975) and Leys (1975a).
2. To the extent that the effective rate of tariff protection on tin mining is negative (because its output is subject to export taxes and some of its inputs are subject to import duties) and since

domestic manufacturing has a positive ERP the NWVA figure of manufacturing will be overstated relative to that of dredging (but note NWVA in table is *gross* of export duty).

3. It is interesting to speculate why gravel pump mining was not also taken up by Malays. One reason is that few Malays were employed on Chinese mines (due in part to language and cultural difficulties) and so had no opportunity to learn the necessary techniques. Again, the same language and cultural barriers might have prevented them from acquiring small-scale credit and finance, also at that time mainly a Chinese preserve.
4. Drabble (1973, pp. 42–7, 86–91, 118–22, 150–4, 199–204) provides a very detailed account of both private-sector and government research. As Section 6.5 shows, government research was also important in establishing the palm oil industry in Malaysia, though it had already been grown as an estate crop in Indonesia for ten years prior to its introduction to Malaysia.
5. This imported labour is the basis of the present Malaysian–Indian community. The contrast with Chinese tin mining is that European rubber (and tin dredging) companies were owned outside the country whereas the Chinese were immigrants who raised capital from within the Malay peninsula. Reinvested profits, however, were important in the growth of European rubber companies.
6. However the reductions in labour use and supervisory staff per acre during the inter-war depressions referred to in Subsection 6.2.1 greatly reduced the labour–capital ratio. Since then as Table 6.11 shows, the use of workers per acre has changed little in the forty years to 1972, though research resulting in the reduction of the immature period of rubber would have reduced the capital–output ratio somewhat.
7. Little and Tipping (1972, pp. 69–70). Their shadow wage ($25 a month) is the estimated marginal product of labour in Malaysia, measured as the output of the landless or near landless peasant. It should be remembered however that a shadow wage used, say, in a planning model is not necessarily equal to the social marginal product of labour. See Hornby (1968, p. 101).
8. On the average 1966 rubber holding in West Malaysia of 6.4 acres, 1.5 workers would be employed, giving a labour intensity of 4.2 acres per worker compared to 7.3 on estates. With high-yielding material and f.o.b. prices of 50 cents/lb this gives a net monthly return per worker of $110, slightly below the average estate wage. With low-yielding material this would fall to $55, less than half the estate wage. A rise in the rubber price (53 cents/lb in 1968) would of course raise these returns. According to the Statistics Dept., *RSH*, 1968 at least 720,000 acres (27% of smallholding 1968 acreage) were planted with old (low-yielding) rubber. Smallholding incomes from Barlow and Chan (1968, pp. 22–3). Barlow and Chan's figures can be compared to those of Fisk's Rasa study, where average income per family member is $13 or $31 per worker assuming Barlow and Chan's worker–dependents ratio of 1:1:3. The average potential household land holding in Rasa was 8 acres which is the basis for the above figures. In fact, 42% of households owned no land. (see Fisk, 1961, p. 19). However, in the Ulu Selangor study by Fryer and Jackson, average Chinese rubber smallholdings were 6.8 acres yielding average monthly income of $181 with a price of 63 cents/lb, compared to Barlow and Chan's $164 with high-yielding material (see Fryer and Jackson, 1966, p. 209). In comparison, the average monthly income on FELDA scheme, assuming a rubber price of 50 cents/lb, would be $149 a month for a ten-acre holding ($112 for an eight-acre holding) for the first fifteen years of tapping, after deducting loan repayments of $172 a month ($144 for an eight-acre holding) (FELDA, 1970, pp. 27–8).
9. Some useful generalizations on the effects of immigration into countries such as Malaysia are to be found in Myint (1967, pp. 53–68).
10. Of course, earnings in the subsistence sector are likely to be equal to *average* rather than *marginal* product, but the very large excess of estate wages over marginal product suggests an excess over average subsistence earnings too.
11. In fact over the period 1968–72 tin prices rose and rubber prices fell, which would tend to raise the K/O of rubber relative to tin, but this was outweighed by a very substantial increase in mining capital costs. The considerable rise in the gravel pump mine capital/output ratio since the late 1960's shown in a previous publication (Thoburn, 1973b, p. 101) where a value of 0.5 is given is partly the result of increased capital costs but also of an allowance for initial site work and excavation not included in the 1968 estimate, but included in dredging.
12. Oil palm rates of return are rather more sensitive to price changes than are those of rubber, presumably because of oil palm's shorter gestation period (Pushparajah, Chan and Ti, 1974, p. 82).

13. For conciseness, the terms 'rubber' and 'palm oil' will refer in this section to the estate sectors only, unless otherwise stated.
14. Interview with an oil palm mill manager in Johore, September 1970. This salary would be for a local person. An expatriate might get more.
15. One factory visited in December 1969 paid its clerk $630 a month.
16. An oil palm mill visited in September 1969 paid its clark $550 a month.
17. In 1972, average wages per full worker in manufacturing were $179 per month (Statistics Dept., *PR*, 1972).
18. Estimates devised by subtracting the supervisory and administrative staff in Tables 9.2 and 9.3 (who are all fairly junior) from the total 'Administrative, Managerial and Supervisory' figures given in Ministry of Labour, *AR*, 1972.
19. The gravel pump mines from whose investment costs the coefficient in Table 9.4 is taken are mostly the traditional small mines of 20–30,000 cubic yards/month capacity. There also exist larger-capacity mines which use more mechanical power (earth-moving equipment etc) and have lower labour coefficients. See Thoburn (1976).
20. After tax and export duty payments are deducted from the cash flow the internal rates of return for gravel pumping and dredging reduce to 13% and 21% respectively (Thoburn, 1976). The reversal of rankings compared to the pre-tax and duty situation is due to the fact that the substantial export duty is levied on gross output value not on profits, and so bears more heavily on the profits of the technique with higher operating costs (gravel pumping).
21. This is based on the Table 9.4 labour/output coefficients, on the assumption that output per acre from a deposit of given richness would be the same for both techniques. In practice dredging recovery rates would be slightly higher. To assume that land is the binding constraint on dredging investment, and that capital is not 'rationed' to the individual investor, would favour the use of a Net Present Value rather than an Internal Rate of Return investment criterion. In fact, rankings by NPV at realistic discount rates (5% to 15%) are broadly similar in tin mining to those by IRR, though in theory this need not be the case (see Hirschleifer, 1958).
22. The fact that reworking the profitability analysis in terms of social net benefits results generally in a greater proportionate increase in gravel pumping's social profitability is primarily a reflection of gravel pumping's higher labour use, and strengthens the argument that there is an employment–output conflict.
23. This reversal in rankings as the tin price changes is the result of differences in time profiles between the two techniques including (but not exclusively the result of) a much longer gestation lag in dredging than in gravel pumping (Thoburn, 1976).
24. According to the Treasury, *AR* (1973–4, p. 84), the top 20% of households received approximately half of national income in 1957, and the bottom 60% received 30% of income. By 1970, the top 20% had increased their share, to 56%, and the share of the bottom 60% of households had fallen to 25% of total income. For a fuller discussion of income distribution in Malaysia, see Snodgrass (1974 and 1975). Snodgrass contends however that the degree of inequality in Malaysia is *not* particularly high for a country at its stage of development (1974, p. 272).
25. This argument is based on the regression of wage bills on export income in Chapter 7, where only a very weak relation could be found in rubber compared to stronger relations in tin. This may seem surprising statement nevertheless, since the share of wages in export income on rubber estates seems to have stayed roughly constant (at around 40%). This implies in turn that wage bills do catch up, but with longer lags. However, in the time while wages are catching up, and with a secularly increasing total output value, income is redistributed away from workers. This is clear from the current payments data in Chapter 6 (Tables 6.12 and 6.17) where the wage share falls sharply in years of very high prices (e.g. 1951, 1955), but does not rise greatly when price is low.
26. This statement is based on interviews with a large number of Chinese mining firms in Malaysia in 1969, 1970 and 1974, who regarded themselves as being in close competition for labour with nearby rubber estates.
27. D. R. Snodgrass (1974) argues that Malaysia is a country in which the fiscal system can, and *has* since Independence, redistributed incomes, though more by expenditure than taxation, and more towards poor Malays than to poor people of other ethnic groups (pp. 269–91).
28. This point is clearly brought out in *Redistribution with Growth* (Chenery *et al.*, 1974, p. 22) and it has long been argued with respect to Malaysia by Ungku Aziz (1964).

29. According to Snodgrass (1975), in 1970 mean household incomes were $177, $399 and $310 per month for Malay, Chinese and Indian households, respectively. However the degree of inequality within each ethnic group was rather similar, with the top 20% of income receivers earning 52.5%, 52.6% and 54.2% of total income, respectively; and 12.7½, 13.9% and 14.3% in the case of the bottom 40% of those households. Over the period Snodgrass considers, inequality has risen within each group, though somewhat more for Malays and less for Chinese (see especially pp. 262–64).
30. Note however that although the most important rice states, Kedah and Perlis (producing 50% of 1972–3 output) have high yields, high yields are also found in some states (such as Selangor) whose output is small, whereas Kelantan (which produces 12% of Peninsular Malaysian rice output) has low yields (356 gantangs per acre for the main-season crop, compared to 552 for Kedah) (figures from Statistics Dept., *MSB*, Sept 1974).
31. This statistic is based on figures from a study by Selvadurai, published 1972 (and cited by Edwards, 1975, pp. 261–3) in which it is estimated that half of Malaysian smallholders grow some padi, and a quarter specialize on padi (i.e. it accounts for over three-quarters of their acreage). Since (with the minor exceptions of coconuts, tapioca, etc.) padi and rubber are almost the only crops grown by smallholders (excluding those on federal and state schemes) this implies that of the three-quarters (maximum) of smallholders specializing on rubber, one-third grow some padi.
32. Smallness of holdings may be overstated slightly if peasants own both rubber and padi plots, which are counted separately (see also 31).
33. Thus in 1970 yields in Malaysia were 14.5 cwt per acre (Statistics Dept., *MBS*, Sept 74) compared to 15.4 cwt in China, 30.5 cwt in the U.S.A., and 32.6 cwt in Japan (*National Grindlays Review*, 1974, p. 7). Also, Malaysian costs for a given yield were higher than those of some of her immediate neighbours. The rice exporting countries, Burma and Thailand, though their yields per acre were only 9.2 cwt and 9.5 cwt per acre, respectively, could produce rice at between a half and a third of the Malaysian cost per cwt (Lim, 1973, p. 245).
34. Huang appears to regard four acres as an adequate holding for double-cropped padi. This figure is rather larger than that implied by J. T. Purcal's (1975) study of rice in villages in Province Wellesley where twenty-five households (of which two were landless, and provided paid labour) in a double-cropping area cultivated a total of 55.7 relongs (= 39.5 acres, i.e. on average 1.6 acres per household) in the main season, and 50.2 relongs for the off-season crop. Sizes of individual holdings ranged from 1–2 to 6–8 relongs. In the peak (harvesting) months of July unemployment in terms of number of hours worked relative to labour time available was only 2% for males (27 of them) and 12% for females (23 of them). During July however, one-third of male labour time was spent on non-padi work (mostly off-farm) and the corresponding figure for women was 23% (though their non-padi work was mostly on-farm). For the whole year, unemployment was 33% of available male and 57% of available female labour-time, and on-and off-farm padi work comprised 48% of total employment for men and 8% for women (work on rubber was 1% for women and 17% for men).

    Huang unfortunately does not discuss the possibilities for adapting 'miracle rice' strains to Malaysia, or the likely effect of such adaptation on yields (or on the padi economy's economic and social structure, since high-yielding varieties tend to require more purchased inputs and thus benefit owners of larger holdings). (For a discussion of 'miracle rice' and other aspects of the 'Green Revolution' see Myint, 1972, pp. 42–57.)
35. Lim Sow Ching's (1972) study of the economic viability of future rubber smallholdings in Malaysia estimated a minimum size of ten acres for a household to provide an income of $250 per month, which is his estimated income for a household whose members were employed as rubber estate workers. Since rubber-tappers wages are about $100 a month (see Chapter 6), this implies household size of 2.5 full-time workers. Indeed 2.5 workers (say parents and one teenage child) would be needed to work a ten-acre holding (say 180 trees per acre, tapped two out of three days), and R. Wikkramatileke (1972, p. 113) has raised serious doubts as to whether settler families can manage a ten-acre rubber plot, since wives often work off-farm and children attend school. Lim's income estimate (after deduction of FELDA loan repayments) is $260 per month at a price of 40 cents per lb, with high-yielding trees on a FELDA ten-acre holding (p. 29). After the fifteenth year of tapping, when loans have been repaid, income rises by over $40 per month (p. 28). Of course, these figures concentrate on household income in a land-abundant situation. When the supply of new land in Malaysia becomes exhausted, the fact the padi involves a much higher man–land ratio would become

more important than at present. It is also worth noting that in 1973 it was announced that the size of FELDA plots was to rise from ten acres to twelve, and from ten to fourteen for oil palm (Prime Minister's Dept., *MTR*, 1973, p. 8).

36. For a discussion of some other factors in rural Malay poverty, mainly social and psychological, see Parkinson (1967).
37. Between 1957 and 1960, 230,000 acres of rubber estate (equivalent to 16% of the present (1973) rubber estate acreage was sold and subdivided. Only 8% of these subdivided holdings were worked by their owners, and the rest were let mainly by small businessmen (Rudner, 1970, p. 327).
38. Land development schemes accounted for 12.6% of the public development expenditure allocation under the First Malaysia Plan (and rubber replanting a further 3.7%) (Prime Minister's Dept., *MTR*, 1973, p. 98).
39. On the other hand, the government's Guaranteed Minimum Price for padi has been designed as a means of increasing the income of (the mainly Malay) padi farmers, though there is much potential conflict between this policy and that of providing cheap wage-goods for Malaysian workers. For a highly critical review of rice price-support policy see David Lim (1973, pp. 234–45).
40. An account of these riots is given in the *Far Eastern Economic Review*, 10 January 1975.

Part III
Primary Commodity Exports as a Source of Development

Chapter 10
Other Empirical Studies of Commodity Exporting and Economic Development

Following the Malaysia case study of Part II, this chapter reviews evidence from work on other countries. Sections 10.1 and 10.2 present, respectively, case studies of some of the more important mineral and agricultural exports; and the greater length of the mineral section is a reflection of the larger number of major studies of mineral exporting. In general Sections 10.1 and 10.2 cover only modern studies made from the trade and development perspective.[1]

As far as possible, the empirical evidence is organized around the methodological framework developed in Chapter 3, namely

1. Proportion of current export income paid locally (or 'retained value').
2. Proportion of capital expenditure made locally.
3. Possibilities of direct entry by local producers if the export industry is foreign-owned.
4. Generation of forward and backward linkages.
5. Creation of a local market through final demand linkage.
6. Introduction of new technology and creation of unpriced externalities.
7. Employment creation and influence on income distribution.

10.1 MINERAL EXPORTS

The minerals chosen for this section are copper, petroleum and bauxite. Petroleum and copper are by value the two most important mineral products from less developed countries entering into world trade (see Chapter 1), and exhibit interesting comparisons with tin in terms of technology, ownership patterns and vertical integration. Bauxite is chosen for its dominant role in certain economies as well for the contrast it provides in economic structure and marketing arrangements.

10.1.1 Copper

Unlike tin, where production is located almost entirely in the Third World and output almost exclusively exported, at least half of world copper output is produced by rich countries—U.S.A. with 21% of world output, the U.S.S.R. (15%), Canada

(11%) and Australia (3%).[2] The U.S.S.R. however is virtually self-sufficient, and the domestic consumption of the U.S.A. usually exceeds its domestic production. Of the three largest producers only Canada is an important exporter (exporting 70% of its output). Underdeveloped countries therefore are more important in world trade, and the main producers are Chile (10% of world output), Zambia (9%) and Zaire (6%). Peru and the Philippines produce similar amounts to Australia and the output of Chile is only slightly higher than the U.S. import surplus. A full length study has been made of Chile from 1925 to 1959 by Reynolds (in Mamalakis and Reynolds, 1965), and updated by Mamalakis (in Mikesell, 1971) to 1967. Baldwin (1966) has written a book on copper in Zambia (to 1960), and there is a shorter, more recent study of Zambia by Fry and Harvey, and of Zaire by Mikesell (in Pearson and Cownie, 1974), though the Zaire study is not included here for reasons of space.

Until the 1960's most copper production in less developed countries was in the hands of foreign companies. In Chile a thriving domestic sector in the early 19th century declined after the 1880's, when Chile was the world's largest supplier, with the depletion of high-grade ores. American firms entered Chile from the mid-1900's with a technology developed in the United States suitable for Chile's large reserves of low-grade (porphyry) ores, and by 1918 96% of production was in the hands of three mines owned by two large American copper companies (Anaconda and Kennecott), comprising the so-called *Gran Mineria* (or *GM*). A fourth company the Cerro Corporation, a subsidiary of an American firm important in Peru, entered later. In Zambia intensive exploration in the 1920's led to the formation of four foreign copper companies, with capital raised mainly from the U.K., the United States and South Africa (Prain, 1975, p. 28). This followed the establishment of the copper mining industry in the Belgian Congo (Zaire) on Belgian and British initiative, and in fact the copper industry of the Congo had provided rail transport which the Rhodesian mines were able to utilize. However, although foreign firms predominated in all three major producers there was little vertical integration between them and copper fabricators and manufacturers, except in the case of U.S. firms operating overseas (principally in Chile). In this respect copper resembles tin and is in sharp contrast to bauxite or petroleum.

Since the early 1960's there has been a substantial increase in public ownership. Prain (1975) notes that over the period 1960–70 the proportion of output in non-Communist countries from mines in which the State had an interest rose from 2½% to 43%, of which 25 percentage points were accounted for by wholly government-owned mines and another 12% by mines in which governments had a majority interest. In Chile the Frei government initiated a state participation programme with agreements to acquire 25% holdings in the Cerro Corporation, a 25% share in a new Anaconda Mine and a 51% share in Kennecott. Further nationalization measures were taken around 1969. These were speeded up under the Allende regime, and have not been reversed following Allende's overthrow (Prain, 1975, p. 225). In Zambia in 1969 foreign mines were asked to sell a 51% interest to the government, and in Zaire nationalization eventually followed independence in 1960.

Chile

In the two studies of Chile attention is concentrated on the share of export incomes initially retained locally ('retained value' or *RV*). In Chile's case it is payments to the government which have been the main determinant of retained value. Since 1925, when a special tax on copper was first introduced, the importance of retained value has grown substantially. The following figures represent the average share of tax in retained value over periods to 1959:

1925–31 17%
1932–37 19%
1938–49 35%
1950–55 53%
1956–59 52%

Indeed the average figures understate the importance of tax in certain years. In 1953, tax represented about 60% of retained value, and increases in taxation have been the main force driving up the share of RV in export earnings. Taxation of copper dates from the decline of the Chilean nitrates industry, a traditional source of tax revenue, after competition from synthetic nitrate production overseas following the First World War, and by the early 1960's copper taxes paid by the GM generated 20% of government revenue. Tax policy in Chile has been discussed at length by Reynolds, Mamalakis and also by Mikesell (1971), and at least until the New Deal legislation of 1955 it has been severely criticized. First, assuming that the maximization of the long-run tax share in export value is a desirable policy objective, significant conflicts have arisen between short-term and long-term maximization. From the 1930's to the 1950's, and brought about by substantial rises in taxation, the retained-value share of production (excluding local purchases on capital account) rose from 35% (1930–39 average) to 55% (1940–54), reaching the extraordinary peak of 94% in 1953, and averaging 82% for the 1950–55 period alone. Accompanying this rising RV share however was a relative decline in copper output from a 21% world market share in 1948 to 14% in 1953, as the American copper companies were (apparently) forced close to bankruptcy and ran down their Chilean operations to some extent, preferring to open marginal mines in the United States rather than expand operations in Chile (Mikesell, 1971, p. 370).

The second criticism of tax policy is that it was not part of a consistent strategy to increase RV from copper, even in the short run. Not only were there certain inconsistencies among different taxes, but in particular in 1932 following the inter-war depression, a multiple exchange rate system was in force which worked to raise implicit tax revenue while discouraging the growth of other elements in RV. Thus the companies of the GM had to meet a large portion of their production costs (their 'legal costs of production', estimated by Reynolds as 63% of total costs in 1951) in local currency purchased at a greatly overvalued rate. In 1952 Mamalakis estimates that the company's exchange rate was overvalued threefold, and in 1951 Reynolds calculates that the exchange rate effect raised total tax take from U.S. $53.8 million (explicit tax plus import duty) to U.S. $89 million. This artificial increase in legal production costs of course stimulated the GM to economize both on local labour and on local capital goods and intermediate products, since capital goods and intermediate products could be imported directly by using dollar revenue from exports.

Tax provisions were changed considerably in the 1955 New Deal legislation with the generally lower rates, simplified structure and incentives to increase production by means of a surtax which was progressively reduced with output expansion; and the abolition of the multiple exchange rates. The most important influence on development however is the government's use of tax revenue. Although some copper revenue has been channelled to development projects especially through CORFO (the national development corporation founded in 1938) and although copper earnings have helped guarantee export credits, writers on Chilean affairs are in general agreement that very much has been spent on current expenditure. Mamalakis for example quotes the telling instance that over the 1960–64 period 60–80% of the government's copper surplus went to finance the operating deficit of the state railway. Moreover, very little control was exercised through the Central Bank towards encouraging the import of capital goods with copper export earnings.

The importance of retained value from copper in the Chilean economy can be seen in relation to other economic quantities. In 1956–8 gross retained value (i.e. including local investment expenditure, which adds about 8% to RV 1955–64) averaged U.S. $170 million, while government expenditure was U.S. $453 million and total gross investment in Chile was U.S. $273 million. Whilst tax was the largest single component in the post-war years when retained value has risen sharply, there is evidence of increasing local purchases of investment goods and intermediate products. From 1956–64 the local consumption of intermediate products rose from 31% to 56%, partly as a result of a buy-local government policy, and Mamalakis (Mikesell, 1971, p. 413) quotes figures for Anaconda's El Salvador mine which suggests that over 60% of capital expenditure was locally made. Local products supplied to the GM particularly included construction items and fabricated steel shapes made by the local steel mills. From 1950–60 intermediate products, according to Chilean national accounts, averaged 15.9% of production value and wages and social security payments another 13%. Real-wage costs per worker apparently rose substantially over the period covered by the studies (1925 to the 1960's), but falls in employment kept the wage bill roughly constant and the overvaluation of the company's exchange rate from 1932–1955 prevented much of the real-wage rise accruing to the workers themselves. Consumption expenditure by workers was probably local however following import restrictions imposed in the 1930's, and 90% of the wage and salaries bill accrues to local workers.

The RV measure catches tax payments, and backward and potential final demand linkages. Forward linkages from copper seem to have been slight. Some 8% of copper output is retained in Chile for fabrication (into wire, rods, etc.), though because of the substantial weight loss in smelting, most copper from GM, located in the remote north of the country, is milled and smelted at the mine prior to export. Some smaller mines nearer the coast export concentrates (and Japan in particular has been keen to import concentrates to keep her own smelting capacity occupied). Some mines also sell concentrates to government smelters. Also, the RV figure overstates gains, in that Chilean copper has been valued for two periods (during the Second World War and briefly during Korea) at a price set by the United States government below world price.

Employment creation has been minimal. The GM produces 10% of GDP with ½% of the Chilean labour force. The multiple exchange rate policy (1932–55) mentioned above has operated in favour of a high capital–labour ratio, though technical progress appears to have been both capital and labour saving (K/O in 1960 was only 1.5); and Reynolds lists employment coefficients for the GM of only approximately 20 workers per pound of copper mined, compared to 155 for five large mines in Zambia, a difference too great to be explainable in terms of different grades of ore worked. However, declines in GM employment have been matched by an expansion in the small to medium mining sector, which though it produces still only a small percentage of the total output employs approximately as many workers (about 17,000) as the GM.[3]

Zambia

The major study of the Zambian copper industry by Baldwin (1966) is concerned more with the spread effects of copper expansion rather than with RV as such, though information is given from which RV can be estimated. Spread effects are analysed along very similar lines to those suggested in Chapter 3 (which indeed derives much from Baldwin's own work—Baldwin, 1963). The brief Fry and Harvey account (in Pearson and Cownie, 1974) is useful for updating and for a fuller discussion of tax policy. In comparison with Chilean copper RV over the period which Baldwin covers (which antedates Independence and the major changes in taxes and ownership which occured thereafter) is low. In 1956–7 Baldwin's figures suggest a retained value somewhat over 50% (or just under 40% if European workers' wages are excluded), with tax payments the largest item (23.5%) followed by European and African wages (11.5% and 4.6% respectively) and domestically produced intermediate products equal to a little over 10% of the gross output value. By 1967 Fry and Harvey estimate RV at 70%. Of the components of RV, the size and use of tax revenue can best be left until the discussion of post-Independence tax policy below, and linkages are considered first therefore. Some important backward linkages have been generated. According to Baldwin over half of the output of railway services is purchased by the copper industry. Foundries and metal products, and electrical power supplies are also industries heavily dependent on copper sales, while saw mills, petroleum products, cement, road transport and several other sectors depended in the 1960's for more than 10% of their sales on copper (Pearson and Cownie, 1974, pp. 209–12). Overall, domestic purchases of intermediate products accounts for 19.9% of gross output in 1967 and imported ones 7.7%. Forward linkages are confined to a new copper fabrication plant, though Fry and Harvey seem sceptical of its prospects. Copper ornaments are also made in Zambia, but of imported copper! Local content of capital good expenditure in copper is given by Fry and Harvey as 70% (p. 200). Baldwin estimates that about 40% of capital expenditure could be for labour costs, some of which will be locally supplied and purchases from the construction industry also would be made locally. Equipment, however, would normally be imported.

Final demand linkages and the development of a domestic market have been rather less conducive to further growth than have backward linkages. In 1967 wages and salaries accounted for 18.6% of gross output which by standards of mining is not particularly low. However, Baldwin's earlier figures for 1956–7 show that of the then total of 16.1% for wages and salaries only 4.6% was for Africans and 11.5% was for Europeans (and this in spite of a European: African workers ratio of about 1:8). Neither Fry and Harvey nor Baldwin present figures on the local content of workers' expenditure but one may presume that the European workers consume a high proportion of imported goods. One important effect of final demand purchases however has been the stimulus to domestic agriculture, both European and African. Baldwin records that in 1937 the mines consumed 80% of the beef produced in Northern Rhodesia and that there has been a great increase in maize output especially by African farmers. Development has been stimulated too by the fact that the railways serving the mining community run through particularly good agricultural land which eases considerably the problem of marketing.

Before discussing tax policy, nationalization and the government's use of its share of the copper surplus, it is worth trying to see copper's development effect in Zambia in perspective. Unlike Chile with a population of eight million, where copper, though important, generates only 10% of national income, Zambia is a country with a much smaller population (2 million) and depends almost totally on copper. Copper generates 95% of visible export earnings, two-thirds of government revenue and about half of GDP (though this figure, of course, varies considerably with fluctuations in the copper price). Some favourable backward linkages have been generated and electric power supply, railways and metal foundries have obvious potential for further growth. Yet Baldwin, though feeling Zambia's development potential is considerably better than most African countries', comes to pessimistic conclusions about copper's past growth effects. Probably the most important reason concerns employment. Though copper in Zambia is more labour-intensive than in Chile or the U.S.A., its impact on total employment is small. African employment in the late 1960's was under 50,000 and European about 6000, compared to a total Zambian work force of perhaps 1,000,000. Labour coefficients in railways and construction were somewhat higher but those in electricity lower, and the indirect employment creation through backward and forward linkages was therefore slight. The employment coefficient in maize growing is high (1.3 workers per U.S. $1000 of output, compared to 0.146 in metal mining, 0.945 in electricity and 0.603 on railways) but only less than 20% of gross output (i.e. the wages and salaries bill) was available for domestic multiplier effects (though there would be further multiplier effects through factors employed in linked industries). The high wages of Europeans and of Africans relative to Africans employed in other sectors gives rise to demonstration effects on consumption elsewhere in the economy. Baldwin also refers to a more severe labour surplus on the copper belt than existed in the 1930's depression. Indeed, one of the most striking effects of copper in Baldwin's view has been to increase the dualistic nature of the economy and worsen income differentials. Thus while transport and communications are generally good along the twenty-mile wide strip along the railway line, beyond this point roads are poor and marketing difficult. European workers on average enjoyed in Baldwin's period wages over sixteen times as high as Africans, and African workers in turn well over double the money wages elsewhere in the economy. Indeed the monopoly power of European trade unions in copper and in railways was an important factor retarding African advancement, at least until Independence. However, since the 1930's the quality of the African labour force has increased greatly and turnover rates have been much reduced. Baldwin (1966, p. 93) records how these improvements have led to greater use of African labour and have slowed down the introduction of labour-saving equipment. Skills learned by Africans and savings accumulated by them have given them the opportunity of leaving copper mining to set up in business on their own (though this applied with even greater force to European workers).

In an industry where gross profits account for nearly 60% of the value of gross output, tax policy is of obvious importance in the disposition of gains from exports. Since Independence in 1964 several changes have occurred. Royalty payments, 80% of which were previously paid to the British South Africa Company, at a rate equal to about 13% of output value, have been entirely to the Zambian government (and before 1950 *all* royalties went to the British South Africa Company). Also, since 1966, the marginal tax rate has been increased (from 52% to 74%). Since 1969, the Zambian government has had a 51% interest in copper, but Fry and Harvey show that this nationalization may actually reduce the local share, because as much as two-thirds of government revenue from copper is being used to make compensation payments and because the government relaxed an earlier (1968) regulation which forced mines to keep half of their post-tax profits in the country (though in fact this regulation had simply led to a build-up of liquid balances). Figures for 1967, cited by Fry and Harvey, show that the tax share was 21.2% of gross output, and the operating surplus 29.4%. Independence, and the end of the Federation of Rhodesia and Nyasaland has however stopped the partial diversion of Zambian revue to Southern Rhodesia, and has also given the government freedom of action to check the unrestricted flow of manufactured imports from Southern Rhodesia and South Africa, which helped prevent the establishment of domestic manufacturing.

10.1.2 Petroleum

The oil industry is the most extreme case of mineral extraction carried out by vertically integrated multinational firms. Before the formation of OPEC in 1960 (see also Chapter 2) the seven largest oil companies (the so-called 'seven sisters') controlled 84% of crude oil production, 74% of refining capacity and 70% of marketing, as well as exerting considerable influence on smaller companies through marketing and supply contracts (Dasgupta, 1974, pp. 46–67). Since then there has been some growth of state participation in producing countries and, especially since 1973, there has been direct intervention in the formation of prices, which in the early years were fixed almost entirely on the basis of intra-firm transfer pricing. The largest producers in OPEC are Saudi Arabia (24% of 1973 OPEC production), Iran (19%), Venezuala (12%), Kuwait (11%) and Libya and Nigeria (7%) each (figures from Ellis, 1974). OPEC countries in 1972 produced 53% of world output and the bulk of non-OPEC production came from North America (22%) and the Communist bloc (16%). The U.S.A. however is a net importer of oil though Canada has a small export surplus. Studies of oil export and growth in Saudi Arabia, Iran and Venezuela are given in Mikesell's (1971) collection of papers on foreign investment in mineral and petroleum production, and a convenient short study of Nigeria by Meyer and Pearson is given in Pearson and Cownie (1974). Very much common ground exists in the findings of these studies and therefore the treatment of each country given here concentrates on the particular points best illustrated by that country's experience. All these studies antedate the massive oil price increases of 1973–4, however, and thus the figures for the share of oil in GDP etc. will be understated.

Saudi Arabia

The dominance of oil in Saudi Arabia is clear from the fact that oil revenues in the 1960's constituted 80–90% of total government revenue and government revenue in turn generated about two thirds of GDP. Oil, however, only employed 2.3% of the salaried work force. Expenditure on Saudi-Arabian labour by Aramco, the major oil consortium consisting of four multinational companies, was equal to only 2% of the value of oil exports (Aramco constitutes 80% of local oil disbursements so the share of Aramco wages and salaries in total exports will not greatly understate the total share of wages and salaries) and other local payments 5%. In such a situation payments to the government (and also forward linkages, discussed below) are the major channel by which growth can be transmitted.

The Aramco concession dates back to 1933 though the major expansion in Saudi production did not occur until after the Second World War. Shifts from royalty payments to royalties plus taxes on profits had been accompanied by rises in the government's share of oil earnings until by the late 1960's RV was approximately 60% of export earnings of which all but about 6 percentage points would be payments to government (Mikesell, 1971, p. 232). The Saudi government has also let minor concessions out to small foreign companies and in 1962 launched a state oil enterprise, Petromin. Probably the most important area of bargaining has been over so-called *posted prices*, which are used for tax reference purposes since most oil is marketed at internal transfer prices which are fixed mainly to suit the companies' accounting convenience. Bargaining under the auspices of OPEC in which Saudi Arabia took a leading part was particularly successful in the early 1960's in keeping posted prices constant at a time of excess supply.

Some forward linkage investment has occurred largely on the initiative of Petromin including fertilizer production and a sulphur extraction plant. Oil revenues have also been channelled into the establishment of a steel mill and some 17% of government expenditure is used on development projects including an extensive road-building programme.

Iran

Iran is the oldest oil producer in the Middle East, with production dating from 1908. Oil generates some 80% of Iranian export earnings but its share of national income is substantially less than Saudi Arabia's, being 19% of GDP in the late 1960's. The input structure is somewhat similar to Saudi Arabia with oil only employing 1% of the total labour force though the wage share in total output is somewhat higher. RV was about three-quarters of export earnings in 1966 and of this RV 70% consisted of tax revenue from foreign companies, 19% wages and salaries, and 1% purchases of Iranian goods and services. About 84% of retained value was derived from a consortium of foreign companies, about 12% from the National Iranian Oil Company and the rest was from other foreign companies (Mikesell 1971, pp. 244–5). The most interesting aspect of the Iranian experience is the use of oil revenue by the government. Oil revenue has been used to meet over three-quarters of the outlays under a series of development plans. Oil revenue obtained by the NIOC has been channelled into the establishment of an extensive oil marketing network overseas. Oil and gas exports to the U.S.S.R. have resulted in financial and technical aid in the establishment of a steelworks, grain silos and other projects, and in 1965 the National Petroleum Company was set up as a subsidiary of NIOC to establish a petrochemical industry. Yet the bulk of Iran's 28 million population remains untouched by the oil industry and problems of employment creation and low rural incomes are intensified by an exceptionally rapid rate of population growth. In the opinion of Bartsch, the author of the case study (in Mikesell, 1971), unless capital-investment projects are more slanted towards agriculture Iran will continue to be a dual economy and substantial rises in oil revenue will not greatly change its structure (Mikesell, 1971, p. 263).

Venezuela

The conclusions of W. G. Harris (in Mikesell, 1971) about the impact of petroleum on Venezuelan development are pessimistic. In Venezuela petroleum exports account for 90% of visible exports and 25% of GDP, and petroleum expansion has resulted in an overall rate of growth in the economy of over 5% over the period 1950–57 though thereafter growth has slowed down as investment in petroleum slackened during a period of conflict between the host government and the foreign investors.

Following the establishment of tax reference prices after a government claim for back taxes from the foreign petroleum companies (and in Venezuela three foreign companies produce about 75% of the petroleum output) RV reached approximately 70% of export income by the mid-1960's. The composition of RV is similar to that of other petroleum exporters though because Venezuela is a relatively high-cost producer the share of wages and intermediate products is somewhat larger. In 1964 wages and salary payments constituted 16% of RV, domestic purchases of goods and non-traded services 9% (though this represents about 60% of total petroleum industry inter-industry purchases) and revenue to the government 75%.

One of Harris's main criticisms of Venezuelan development concerns the extremely uneven income distribution which petroleum produced and the consequences of this distribution for further development. Only 2% of the workforce is in petroleum, but the demonstration effect of high petroleum wages (combined with the general shortage of labour skills) has spread to other sectors such as transport, construction and electric power. This income distribution has produced demand patterns biased in favour of luxury consumer goods, either locally assembled or imported at low rates of duty. A major forward linkage of petroleum has been automobile assembly and tyre manufacturing, and domestic refining capacity and a petrochemical industry have also been established. But industrial exports constitute only ½% of total exports and only 7% of non-petroleum exports, and domestic capital-goods production is far below the level of other Latin-American countries. Industrial expansion thus has been of a high-cost, import-substituting variety and has failed to reduce the prevailing high levels of unemployment.

Nigeria

Nigeria is a relatively new petroleum producer, the first commerical strike being in 1956. The input structure is again similar to that of other producers. In 1971 wages and salaries and other local purchases comprised only 11% of gross output value, while direct payments to government were 60%; and the government owned substantial equity shares in many of the foreign companies. The residual share accruing to foreign investors was 14% in 1971. Backward linkage investment has taken place, mainly for local services rather than goods, but these have frequently been established by foreign firms in Nigeria. Various forward linkages have been proposed but aside from refining capacity few have yet come to fruition.

Thus petroleum's impact on development mainly springs from the use of government revenue (75% of which was produced by petroleum exports), and in contrast to many other producers the high priority of the Nigerian government policy has been to use oil revenue to finance agricultural development (Pearson and Cownie, 1974, p. 174). Nevertheless the authors of that case study feel future development is by no means assured, though it might seem that prospects are somewhat more favourable than in Venezuela.

10.1.3 Bauxite

The largest producer of bauxite is a developed country, Australia (with 24% of 1973 world output–British Government, 1975, p. 81). The second largest producer is Jamaica (18% of world output) which produces over twice as much bauxite as any other producing country. Like petroleum, bauxite mining is a highly vertically integrated activity and most sales are transactions between or within multinational companies. Nine major companies produce 90% of world aluminium output and four North American companies 60%. Two trade and growth studies have been made of Jamaica (Huggins, 1965; Meier, 1974), and there is also a 'dependency' study of Jamaica by Girvan discussed in the next chapter.

Jamaica

Following the first shipment of bauxite in 1952, Jamaican bauxite exports grew rapidly and Jamaica become the world's largest producer until overtaken by Australia in 1972. All bauxite in Jamaica is mined by six North American companies but there is no domestic smelting. The payment structure of the industry allows for considerably more direct integration of the industry into the economy than does say petroleum. Domestic wages and salaries payments constituted 18% of 1972 output value and total local expenditures were 28%. Government revenue amounted to 13% of output value. There are great variations in local content between items however. Within the total wages and salaries bill only 1% was for foreign expenditure but over 70% of materials and services are imported and the main local supplies are in fact services. Of total 1972 capital expenditure 50% was local though the bulk of this was for constructional items and only 8% of machinery and equipment was locally supplied. Overall retained value (59% in 1972) has risen somewhat since the late 1960's when Huggins calculates total local expenditure as 52% of bauxite output value. RV in this industry however is a somewhat misleading measure since the main gains from bauxite lie in further processing. Thus bauxite mining itself accounts for only 10% of total aluminium costs, alumina 25% and smelting over 60%, but because of large economies of scale no smelting takes place in Jamaica. Sixty percent of bauxite is refined into alumina prior to export however.

The relatively smaller role of payments to government compared to petroleum or copper is illustrated by the fact that though bauxite and alumina generate two-thirds of export earnings they produce only 10% of government revenue. However its impact on total employment is small, its 15% contribution to GDP being matched by employment of only 0.8% of the labour force, and this in an economy where unemployment is *officially* estimated at 25%, and higher in major cities. Thus although local construction and services have been stimulated and there will have been some significant local market generation (though the import content of worker expenditure is not known), the direct benefits of the industry are spread very unevenly. Further processing, which is more labour intensive per unit of output, would improve employment creation, but smelting is restricted not only by economies of scale but by the U.S. tariff on aluminium imports (but since 1971 alumina imports have been free of duty).

10.2 AGRICULTURAL EXPORTS

The range of empirical studies of the development effects of major agricultural exports is smaller than for minerals, and individual studies are usually much shorter. Accordingly studies are presented here of only three of the eight most important agricultural exports (see Chapter 1)—tea, cocoa and cotton.

10.2.1 Tea in Sri Lanka

A study of the tea industry in Sri Lanka (then Ceylon), the second largest world producer (India is the largest), has been made by Youngil Lim (1968a and b) explicitly along the lines of Baldwin's (1963) theoretical analysis, covering the period to 1960.[4]

Sri Lanka is exceptionally dependent on agricultural exports, with tea generating over 60% of current export earnings, and tea, rubber and coconuts together generating 90% (Bond, 1974, p. 4). Because of substantial economies of scale up to 500 acres in growing, and further economies in processing (Lim, 1968b, p. 250) smallholder tea growing is of minimal importance compared to estate production and in turn foreign ownership in the industry accounted for about 60% of acreage in the 1950's. At present (prior to nationalization announced in December 1975) tea companies with British connections controlled about a third of the tea exports from Ceylon (Bond, 1974, p. 11), and a predominance of tea manufacturing companies amongst these parallels the vertical integration in many mining export activities.

In the foreign sector of the tea industry Lim's studies suggest that RV is high, and of course higher still in the domestic sector since profits are not remitted abroad. The bulk of RV consists of payments to labour, accounting for 60–70% of total production costs and 50% of output value in 1960, and nearly 46% on average over the period 1920–60. Lim does not produce figures from which an exact RV can be calculated but he notes that many ancilliary services, including the manufacturing and servicing of tea processing machinery, are locally produced. The tea industry has also been largely responsible for a comprehensive road and rail system (necessary for collecting tea over a wide area), which serves both plantations and the rest of the economy. Figures however are not presented for the share of local intermediate input purchases in total output, and tax policy is not discussed, though it is indicated the total surplus for distribution between government and foreign investors is 20–30% of output value (29.8% for the 1920–60 period as a whole).

Lim concludes that tea is by no means an enclave, and that its effects on growth should not be disregarded. Aside however from its backward linkages and contribution to net foreign exchange revenue, tea has had little other favourable effect on the growth of the economy. Although the large wage bill with its high proportion of expenditure on clothing and foodstuffs generates considerable potential domestic market demand, in fact foods and cotton goods are important imports, and about 40% of a working-class family budget was spent on imports in 1950 (Lim, 1968b, p. 253);

so the local market potential to a large extent has not been realized. Also tea has done little to improve labour skills and such skills as it uses tend to be specific to the industry. Thus in 1952 under 3% of the tea (and rubber) labour force was in skilled jobs such as machine minding, managerial occupations and clerical work.

Up to 1959 Lim's study shows a substantial increase (about 80%) in real wages over pre-war years, though almost all of this occurred in the early 1950's with gradual improvements (about 10%) thereafter. Lim also concludes that there was no significant worsening of the commodity terms of trade of Ceylon over the period 1900–61. Yet a recent *War on Want* investigation (Bond, 1974) found widespread starvation and disease among workers on tea estates in Sri Lanka. On the assumption (which cannot be proved without further research) that this represents a worsening in tea workers' living standards *since* Lim wrote on the industry, three factors seem to be involved. First, a deterioration in the terms of trade for tea since the late 1950's, the tea price having been static in face of rising import costs and new production elsewhere such as East Africa (which has reduced tea-growing profits to virtually zero). Second, a virtual halt in foreign investment in tea, especially in the early 1970's in face of uncertainty about government intentions towards the industry and third, Sri Lanka's growing foreign exchange shortage, which has resulted in reductions of basic food rations. Moreover the bargaining position of workers in tea is extremely weak. Eighty percent are Tamils and 75% of these are stateless, which means they not only fail to qualify for ration books for food but are effectively barred from employment elsewhere in the economy (Bond, 1974).

10.2.2 Cocoa in Ghana

Ghana is the world's largest producer of cocoa, accounting for 29% of world production in 1973, almost double that of the next largest producer, Nigeria (British Government, 1975, p. 47). Although a long historical study of the establishment of the industry in the then Gold Coast has been written by Szereszewski (1965), the main up to date material is a short study by Sara Gordon (in Pearson and Cownie, 1974).

Cocoa is grown in South America on plantations, but in Africa it is a small farmer's crop, and was established in Ghana by migrants with profits derived from earlier growing of oil palm; though Szereszewski has argued that much of the industry's growth was financed by capitalization of surplus labour time. By 1911 Ghana was the world's largest supplier although the infrastructure in the form of railways and roads to service the industry was not constructed until the next two decades.

Gordon's general conclusion is that cocoa exporting has not diversified the economy and has therefore failed to promote sustained economic growth. This is argued mainly on the basis of linkages. Forward linkages in the form of processing into butter and paste have probably resulted in net foreign exchange losses, though they have generated some employment and labour training. Backward linkages, apart from transport, have been few—the production of cocoa bags and of chemicals. Transport however has been an important linkage, with road building having been undertaken firstly by farmers and later by the government.

In 1960 about a fifth of the total Ghanian labour force of 2.6 million was engaged in cocoa growing or marketing. With such widespread participation in the industry and an RV figure of over 90% final demand linkages are of great potential importance, but in fact Gordon suggests that the growing market for mass-produced goods in the 1950's and early 1960's was supplied mainly by imports.

From just after the Second World War to the mid-1960's Gordon estimates that about a third of Ghanian cocoa income accrued to the government in the form of marketing board surpluses, export duty and other duties. Some of this revenue was ploughed back into the industry to combat disease and also into various forms of social overhead capital. Gordon feels, however, that taxation may well have been at the expense of private capital formation. Evidence from sample surveys in the 1950's suggests that cocoa farmers have extremely high propensities to save (between a quarter and a third of their total income), and their savings have been used particularly to finance investment in the road haulage industry and for education (even if Ghanaian education apparently is of a highly academic kind not strongly conducive to training for industrial development).

During the late 1960's cocoa prices were low in comparison to earlier periods, new planting was minimal, and disease increased. Nevertheless, Gordon concludes that a rehabilitated cocoa industry could still make a substantial contribution to development in Ghana if cocoa linkages were strengthened and the manufacturing sector extended.

10.2.3 Cotton in Uganda

In 1973 34% of world cotton exports were produced by developing countries (IBRD, 1973). Of the latter, only Egypt (with 15% of world exports) had a world export share of over 5%, and the rest was therefore produced by a variety of smaller producers of which Uganda is one with 1.7% of 1973 world exports. Unfortunately no study of present-day Egypt, the largest supplier, has been made along the lines of the other studies in the chapter.[5]

Jamal's study (in Pearson and Cownie, 1974) looks both at the pre-war situation in Uganda, where cotton was the largest export earner, and at the present day when cotton has been surpassed by coffee.

Cotton in Uganda is a peasant crop, grown mostly on holdings of under 5 acres where it occupies only a small proportion, perhaps a quarter to a third, of the farm's acreage. In the earlier years of this century after the distribution of seeds by the colonial government, cotton spread rapidly through Uganda in advance both of road construction and ginning capacity. Ginning capacity did not catch up until 1918 and road building until the 1920's.

Although intermediate products account for only 16% of output value linkages in Jamal's opinion have been of considerable importance, in that two-thirds of intermediate products are locally made, and important forward linkages have been generated in oil milling and textile manufacture based on local lint. Moreover final demand linkages by growers are 90% local, and overall it is estimated that the share of linked industries in monetary GDP is as large as that of cotton itself (6% for each).

Two factors modify the conclusion that cotton has been favourable to development in Uganda. First, Uganda by international standards is still an extremely poor country (U.S. $110 per head of population in 1969), and growers' incomes are particularly low in comparison to those of other Ugandans. Second, historically the gains from cotton have been quite unevenly distributed. Skilled jobs in ginneries, trading, etc. have gone to Ugandan Asians and in 1937 Jamal estimated that whereas £2.9 million was spread among 800,000 growers, £600,000 accrued in profits to only 143 ginnery owners. Taxation moreover was relatively regressive, imposed more heavily on Africans than on Europeans or Asians.

NOTES

1. This is not to deny that more general empirical studies of export economies, or purely historical work, would not also be helpful in understanding trade and development, but their inclusion would increase the scope of this chapter beyond manageable proportions. Where such studies are useful on specific points they are brought into the discussion in Chapter 11. There have been no other trade and growth studes published, unfortunately, on tin and rubber (except for a brief discussion of rubber in Ceylon (Sri Lanka) in Lim, 1968b). For a cross-sectional study of trade and growth covering many countries, see Emery (1967).
2. These figures are from British Government (1975).
3. Unfortunately the empirical studies have very little to say about this small-scale sector.
4. Lim (1968b) also considers the effects of growth of rubber and coconut exports in Sri Lanka.
5. There is a study of cotton exports in Egypt before the First World War in Lewis (1970).

Chapter 11
An Overview of the Evidence

In the Malaysian study and in the studies reviewed in Chapter 10, development through export expansion has been seen in terms of the direct income earning opportunities in the export industry, and of spread effects from the export base in the form of forward and backward linkages and the development of a local market for consumer goods (final demand linkage). Both direct participation in the export industry and the various spread effects may generate increased capital formation at a given income level if the economy is short of investment opportunities, and increased export income provides a surplus for potential reinvestment elsewhere.[1] Exports may also introduce new technology into the economy, raising returns to existing factors, and provide unpriced externalities in the form of labour and management training and the learning of entrepreneurial skills. Where the export sector is domestically owned and controlled, the direct growth effects depend on the distribution of income between workers, capitalists and the government, but where the industry is initiated by foreign direct investment the degree of possible local participation is crucial. Local participation is important too in terms of whether potential linkages effects are translated into local production. Spread effects often are seen as more important than direct effects. This is partly because of the way the multiplier magnifies spread effects through final demand if local capacity can develop; and partly because spread effects may give an opportunity for diversification into growth ultimately independent of the export activity. The latter aspect is particularly important where the export is an exhaustible natural resource. Diversification also gives an outlet through which export factors can be withdrawn if their productivity increases in the face of price-inelastic foreign demand, and so avoids passing on productivity gains to consumers in the form of lower prices (though this also would be achieved by diversifying into other exports).

As was argued in Chapter 3, these effects depend to an important extent on the technological nature of the export-good's production function and on those of linked industries, which determine the commodity's input–output relations in a given situation. The basic proposition, which derives originally from the North American staple theorists, but whose wide influence has been largely the result of work by Robert Baldwin (1956 and 1963), is of course that production functions, and thus growth effects, differ significantly between commodities. Whether this apparently technologically determinist view can be accepted, or whether technology is itself more a reflection of (for example) the economic and political power structure, is taken up in Section 11.2 and also in Section 11.3 on 'dependency'. First, however, Section 11.1 asks how far the industries studied conform to Baldwin's famous (1956 and 1963) stereotypes of minerals, planatation and family farm (or in most of these cases, peasant) exports.

11.1 MINERAL VS. PLANTATION VS. PEASANT EXPORTS

In Baldwin's formulation neither minerals nor plantation crops could be expected to generate much growth, either directly or through spread effects. In minerals considerable economies of scale and a high elasticity of substitution of capital for labour in the export good itself, in the production of its capital goods and in its intermediate products and processing, would tend to reserve mineral production for foreign investors and to mean that backward and forward linkages and capital-good production would be in the hands of overseas suppliers or foreign-owned firms located in the host economy. Apart from taxation by the government, local participation would be limited to wage labour. Employment creation would however be small, though workers would be highly paid. Their high pay would reflect their acquisition of skills over time and might allow them to accumulate savings both of which would be important favourable effects on growth since their skills would be transferable to other industries and their savings help them to set up as entrepreneurs. Because of the limited linkage generation however, and the small size of the local market for wage goods (many of which, anyway, might be something of a luxury character since workers were highly paid—and the goods might therefore be imported), little demand for local production would be generated. In general, the export industry would be poorly integrated with the rest of the economy, except for tax payments to the host government.

Plantation crops on the other hand, would be more closely integrated into the host economy by virtue of their high ratios of labour to capital investment (though in practice plantations have often imported their labour forces—witness the Tamils in Sri Lanka and Malaysia—who have subsequently been isolated socially and economically from other ethnic groups). This large labour force would be poorly paid and unskilled, however and would generate little savings of its own whereby its members could set up in business outside the export sector or help facilitate the establishment of new industry. Final demand linkage might be considerable, but for a limited range of goods. These goods, though, might be highly labour-intensive and create further employment.[2] Economies of scale in production and processing and the need for specialized management would limit local entry, though linked industries and capital goods might be less capital- and high-technology intensive than in the case of minerals; but plantations would do little to condition local factor supplies to be able to meet these demands. Family farm crops, however, would have a high degree of local participation since little management expertise would be required, and the absence of economies of scale *combined* with a high elasticity of substitution of capital for labour would mean that capital per worker could be raised gradually over time, increasing labour productivity. The family farm formulation however, is discussed by Baldwin (1956) in relation to an 'empty' region such as parts of North America before settlement, and is especially concerned with factor inflow—which in this case would be of relatively skilled people with capital of their own. Whether it fits peasant crops such as cocoa is an interesting question, taken up below.

Before looking at the differences between these three types of export production in the available case studies, one important similarity is striking; namely that retained value is almost uniformly high. Retained value (RV), or the proportion of export income paid locally, is in effect a summary measure of an export development contribution, although it does of course miss forward linkages and it may be made artificially high if output is sold at transfer prices below world market price (and for some goods such as bauxite world free market prices scarcely can be said to exist since so much of exports are intra-company transactions). A high RV in a foreign-owned sector contradicts the most obvious of the enclave assertions of the Singer–Myrdal–Prebisch hypothesis that export income leaks abroad immediately. Thus in the studies of foreign investment in minerals and petroleum by Mikesell and his associates (1971), in nine commodity and country studies RV typically was at least 65–70%. In Pearson and Cownie's wide-ranging investigation, covering eleven case studies in Africa, the unweighted mean RV was 76%, and though this average included some wholly locally owned activities, the major foreign investments in Nigerian oil, and Zambian and Zaire copper all had RV's over 70%. These figures accord with the results of foreign investment in rubber and tin in Malaysia, in Part II, while the domestic rubber and tin sectors have even higher RV's. Some exceptions were found, however. In bauxite in Jamaica, RV was little over 50%, and tax revenue seemed low in comparison to other minerals. In Pearson and Cownie's study, timber in Ghana and large-scale diamond mining in Sierra Leone RV's were slightly under 50%, mainly because of high foreign factor costs and remitted profits (Pearson and Cownie, 1974, pp. 263–5). It is interesting, in spite of this evidence, that it is still sometimes asserted that RV in export industries is low.[3]

The high-employment, high wage bill characterization of plantation exports *vis-à-vis* minerals generally is borne out by the evidence, but between minerals especially there is considerable variation. Petroleum extraction is the extreme case. In Saudi Arabia, Saudi labour accounts for only 2% of output value, and in Nigeria local labour gets only 1%, though in Iran it is 14% (but the Iranian figure may include expatriate salaries too). In Venezuela (a relatively high-cost producer) it is 11%. What is more striking is the lack of integration of the oil industry with its host economies. In Venezuela, oil generates 25% of GDP but employs less than 2% of the labour force, in Iran 19% and 1%, and in Saudi Arabia 40% and 2% respectively. Similarly in bauxite, 15% of Jamaican GDP comes from bauxite and alumina exports, but the industry employs less than 1% of the labour force, though in Jamaica 18% of output value is paid as wages and salaries. Copper, especially in Africa, is somewhat more labour intensive than petroleum, with wages and salaries in Zambia accounting for nearly 19% of output value, though at least until the late 1950's (and possibly later) European workers earned about two-thirds of this sum. In contrast to petroleum too, tin dredging in Malaysia pays about 12–15% of its output value to its workforce, and the European salaries share is very small; and the locally owned sector, gravel pumping, pays over 20% of its output value in wages and salaries. The lack of employment creation in many minerals is a severe disadvantage—in Zambia Baldwin (1966) suggested that the Copper belt labour surplus was more severe than in the 1930's depression, and in Jamaica there is *officially* estimated to be 25% unemployment, which capital-intensive bauxite production does almost nothing to alleviate. In view of these relatively small wage bills, potential final demand linkage is small, and is frequently biased towards luxury consumer goods which cannot be locally produced except with high effective rates of protection. The further effects of this highly uneven pattern of income distribution in many mineral-export economies is taken up later in the section on dependency.

Local backward and forward linkage investment depends both on the extent to which the export good uses intermediate products and requires further processing, but also on the appropriateness of the linkages to the host economy. Similar arguments apply to capital goods. Before any substantial range of developing-country case studies had been built up, Canadian and American staple theorists (mostly economic historians) had made familiar the possibilities that certain export goods might have almost no favourable spread effects on development, or that their potentialities might be lost to other countries (or regions).[4] Harold Innis' seminal study of the fur trade in Canada (Innis, 1930) depicted a commodity which required minimal material inputs (simple goods for trading with the Indians, wooden canoes and trapping tools) and only circulating capital; and fur did nothing to encourage settlement and urbanization (the latter being an important factor in domestic market creation), and was exported unprocessed. Wheat, in contrast, encouraged urbanization, extensive transport investment, and a move towards the use of fixed capital. Douglas North (1966) shows how potential linkages from cotton plantations in the ante-bellum U.S. South were lost to other regions. Food for the South was grown in the American West, services and further processing and textile manufacture were located in the North East, little urbanization developed outside of the ports, and transport was mainly by sea. Family farm crops in the West and North West in contrast were more easily processed on the spot and the more even distribution of income which was associated with them made for a broader based domestic market.

In general the potential for backward linkage investment has been greater in minerals. Except for petroleum in Saudi Arabia, an exceptionally low-cost producer, intermediate product purchases are usually in the range of 15–25% of output value, and in bauxite and in gravel pump tin mining in Malaysia well over 30%. Plantation exports seem to generate fewer potential linkages, normally under 15% of output value. The proportion of intermediate products supplied locally varies considerably both between commodities and between countries producing similar commodities. In copper, local firms in Zambia produce over 70% of the industry's intermediate products, and about 55% in Chile. In petroleum locally based firms supply just over a third of petroleum's intermediate products (and many of these firms are foreign owned), whereas the figure is 60% for Venezuela. In Jamaican bauxite, local firms produced only 10% of the industry's purchases of goods and services, and in fact local supply is mainly of services alone. In rubber in Malaysia, the estate sector buys about half of its materials locally, and in Sri Lanka a large proportion of intermediate products (exact figures are not given) are local. In Malaysian tin mining in the foreign sector about 60% of materials purchased are local, and 50% in the local mining sector. In capital expenditure too local content is substantially higher for mineral exports than might have been expected. In Zambian copper it is 70%, on a recently opened mine in Chile 62% and in Jamaican bauxite 50%. In this case, the Malaysian mining figures of 25–30% local content for dredging and just over 40% for gravel pumping are relatively low, but Chapter 8 has shown that they have generated a wider range of local engineering production than many other minerals. Exact figures are not available for tea estates to provide a comparison with rubber, but since much of the expenditure is on labour and Sri Lanka tea equipment is locally made, the proportion is likely to be high, as in Malaysian rubber (about 60% for factory equipment, and almost entirely local field establishment). Similarly, in Malaysian oil palm most field establishment costs are local, and about 40% of factory costs are locally spent.

The degree of processing required varies enormously between agricultural and mineral exports and between different types of minerals, even if one considers forward linkage only up to the fully processed raw material stage, and there is further variation, obviously, where end use is concerned. An extreme case is aluminium. Bauxite mining accounts for only 10% of final aluminium costs. Refining the bauxite into alumina accounts for another 25%, but two-thirds of the cost is smelting. Most less developed bauxite-producing countries export the bulk of their output as alumina, though there are still substantial bauxite exports. Production of alumina is in fact somewhat more labour-intensive per unit of output than bauxite mining, so the securing of alumina capacity is valuable where mining itself creates so little employment. Smelting is subject to enormous economies of scale and needs considerable amounts of hydroelectric power, with the result that it is located in consuming countries. Tin ore on the other extreme is easily concentrated at the mine, and smelting costs the equivalent of 2–3% of the value of the refined tin. Malaysia, the largest producer, smelts her entire output (and some of her neighbours' output too). Similarly the processing of rubber, tin and oil palm constitutes a relatively small proportion of total production costs and is normally located in the producing country.

A particularly important aspect of linkage generation is whether the linkages themselves give rise to further spread effects. In mining industries, a high proportion of intermediate purchases are for power and transport services. Electric power provides obvious external economies for further development of industry. Transport services also have this potential, and serve to widen domestic markets. Tin in Malaysia and rubber in Sri Lanka have given rise to road and rail transport facilities which provide an almost ready-made system for other economic activities to use. Petroleum on the other hand is transported in pipelines which do not serve other uses. In general much of an export industry's development potential depends also on its geographical location. Tin in Malaysia is mined near what are now major centres of population and economic activity, and the large cities (Kuala Lumpur, Ipoh, Taiping) were originally mining towns. Tin in Indonesia on the other hand is mined on three relatively remote islands, and Chilean copper mostly comes from a region far from the main centres of population and urban development. Another important linkage is engineering production. The engineering chapter (Chapter 8) of the Malaysia case study traced in detail how tin, rubber and oil palm had given rise to the domestic production of capital goods and spare parts, and both mechanical and structural engineering capacity are easily turned to other uses. Tea in Sri Lanka similarly has given rise to engineering facilities, and fabricated steel parts are made in Zambia and Chile for the copper industry. The high proportions of capital expenditure made locally in a number of the studies frequently only reflect the use of local construction facilities but in the Malaysian engineering study it was shown how engineering construction can give rise to machinery manufacture.

In spite of what seems to be a more favourable picture in terms of backward linkage than might have been expected from the Baldwin characterization, very large proportions of mineral export income would accrue as profits to foreign firms in the absence of action by the host government. Petroleum of course is the extreme case, where the industry's favourable effects on development depend almost entirely on how much tax revenue the government can raise (or how much equity participation it can secure, or whether the industry could be run successfully as a nationalized concern). With regard to the size of the tax take there are two policy problems. First, short-run maximization of the government's share in some cases may have been at the expense of its long-run maximization, where heavy taxation has induced foreign investors (or indeed domestic investors) to run down their operations, for example in Chile and Venezuala. To some extent this problem can be solved by agreements among producing countries to treat foreign companies in similar fashion so that multinational companies have no incentive to switch their source of supply, though of course it is possible that in some cases the absolute level of taxation has been so high that, especially at times of low prices, export firms have not earned an adequate rate of return in comparison to other investment opportunities. Tea in Sri Lanka in recent years may be a case in point, but tax policy is only one of that industry's problems (which are discussed further below). Second, maximization of the government share may reduce other items of retained value, as in Chile for many years where the government forced foreign companies to finance much of their domestic expenditures in local currency bought at an overvalued rate, which encouraged the minimization of such local expenditure. Also where some investors are local and have high propensities to save and reinvest, taxation may reduce private capital formation, as was argued in the case study of Ghana (Pearson and Cownie, 1974).

The uses to which governments have put tax revenue especially from mineral exports, where it is largest, are discussed further below in the section on dependency. For the moment one may note that far less success has been found here than might perhaps have been expected. Whilst some governments, such as Iran, have used revenue for development projects (in Iran's case particularly to develop a petrochemical industry), others such as Venezuala and Chile have used revenue mainly for current expenditure.

So far this section has concentrated on mineral and plantation exports. Peasant exports such as cocoa, cotton and smallholder rubber are also of great importance to particular countries. The family farm crop of Baldwin's (1956) presentation was depicted as a powerful force for development. Abstracting from the fact that much of the family farm crop's favourable effects spring from its inducing an inflow of skilled immigrants with capital, and recognizing that family farm crops in less developed countries were not normally developed by large-scale immigration, it is in by creating a large and varied domestic market that such crops would spread growth. Market creation would be the result of high average (i.e. modal) farm income levels, reflecting an even distribution of income, and opportunities for increasing the capital/labour ratio gradually over time, without economies of scale or the need for skilled management precluding entry. In fact an identification of the most common peasant crops with North American family farm crops such as wheat is tenuous, and many peasant crops in fact are plantation products developed by smallholders, sometimes coexisting with large-scale plantations. This of course in itself represents a significant modification to the 'plantation' characterization. Rubber certainly can be grown on smallholdings without specialist management, and Bauer's (1948b) classic study of the inter-war rubber industry in Malaya and the then Dutch East Indies showed that smallholders frequently were economically more efficient than estates (though this would be less likely today since replanting with high-yielding varieties has been carried much further on estates than smallholdings). It is interesting too that cotton, Douglass North's archetypal plantation crop, is grown by peasants on one or two acres in Uganda. The technological reasons why peasants have been able to enter plantation crop production, and why there has been little parallel entry in mining, are taken up further in the next section.

An important feature of peasant entry into export agriculture is, as noted by Myint (1958), that little change in technique has been required. Labour time has been capitalized to produce the 'capital goods' required, and 'waiting' for final output (five to seven years for a rubber tree, for instance) has been financed by subsistence crop production. Skills are easily learnt and there has been little substitution of more capital for labour. Retained value for peasant exports is usually extremely high, often over 90%, since few material inputs are used (and since profits are retained locally), and the corollary is that few backward linkages are generated. With regard to forward linkages, similar arguments apply as to plantation crops grown by estates, but usually only the simplest processing is in the hands of the peasants themselves. Thus in rubber in Malaysia and Indonesia peasants process their rubber into unsmoked sheet using simple coagulating pans, acid and mangles, and sell the product to dealers who have it smoked prior to export, or to government processing centres making new-process crumb and other rubbers. In Uganda, until the formation of state corporations and ultimately the expulsion of most Asians by General Amin, cotton ginning and trading was in the hands of immigrant Indians. Some further processing of peasant crops is also found, such as the Malaysian rubber products industry, the production of cocoa butter in Ghana and cotton textiles in Uganda. Whether these forward linkages are uniformly 'good' ones (i.e. whether they generate a positive social net present value at appropriate social discount rates in the countries concerned, or indeed a positive social rate of return at all) is by no means certain, and there has been some evidence presented to the contrary in the foregoing studies.

For any given level and distribution of income, final demand linkage depends on the responsiveness of the domestic economy to investment opportunities in consumption good production. In Uganda, cotton incomes apparently have generated substantial production of food and textiles for local consumption, in Sir Lanka demand from rubber smallholders (and tea workers) has been met more by imports, competition from Indian textiles for instance being particularly severe. In Ghana increases in cocoa incomes have been accompanied by a high marginal propensity to import.

Income levels and income distribution for workers or peasants are, however, by no means equal in different types of export production. In Uganda, very large shares of cotton income accrued to dealers and ginners, in Zambia European workers comprising less than 10% of the copper mining labour force earned in total nearly three times as much as Africans. The influence of highly skewed income distribution in further development is taken up in the dependency section, but the present argument can be concluded by an observation which is obvious perhaps, but often overlooked or played down. This is the distinction between the *mechanisms* through which exports can generate further growth and the level of the flows of income which are channelled through those mechanisms. It is ironic that in two of the studies where many of the mechanisms seem particularly favourable to further growth, tea in Sri

Lanka and cotton in Uganda, (though in Sri Lanka many of the final demand linkage opportunities have been missed) that actual income levels of workers on tea estates are near starvation level and in Uganda, a country not greatly richer than India per head of population, the cotton farmers enjoy some of the lowest incomes in the country. Such low incomes of course are not only lowering the welfare of the direct participants but reduce spread effects. Moreover it cannot be assumed that income *increases* will be channelled in the same way as existing incomes—there is considerable evidence that marginal propensities to import among consumers are higher than average propensities.

Neoclassical economic theory in its naivest form leads one to believe that income levels for individuals are dependent on labour 'quality' (skills, education, etc.), and in simple international trade models flows of commodities between countries will equalize prices of factors of production of given quality. Factor price equalization is dependent of course on the strictest of assumptions. Trade does *not* equalize returns in practice and bargaining is extremely important. Bargaining between countries as part of the New International Economic Order was discussed in Chapter 2, but bargaining *within* developed countries is also of the greatest importance. In Sri Lanka, tea profitability has been low, taxation high, and there has been little replanting. Yet even if the position of the industry improved, the tea workers—Tamils who are mostly stateless and debarred from other activities—would have little bargaining power to secure a share of export income increments. Whether the newly announced (December 1975) nationalization of the tea industry improves their position remains to be seen. Similarly peasant growers' income is frequently creamed off by dealers, who, with higher income levels may well have higher propensities to import.

11.2 TECHNOLOGY AND OWNERSHIP

Many of the different effects of export expansion on growth between the various commodities have depended on differences in input–output coefficients. While the Baldwin-staple approach used in most of the studies does not assume coefficients are fixed, it does suggest (e.g. Baldwin, 1963) that there are significant differences in elasticities of factor substitution as between commodities, and also differences in economies of scale. These technological differences not only condition the effects of export expansion, but also the type of ownership pattern likely to be established. In a less developed country, especially in colonial times and with no organized capital market, capital-intensive sophisticated technology and high economies of scale operations may preclude local capitalist entry and reserve an activity for foreign investors. Similarly the technological characteristics of potentially linked industries may greatly influence whether they are set up in the export economy.

It would be absurd to contend however, that technology is a purely independent variable. It is obviously influenced by economic forces (for example), and the concentration of technical progress in rich countries (with high labour costs) whose applied research is directed towards finding efficient labour-saving processes, for example, has resulted in many activities where high capital/labour processes 'dominate' less capital-intensive ones (i.e. the former use less of *both* factors per unit of output). Equally, it is hardly surprising that exporters have engaged in technological research to improve their competitive position—witness the enormous increases in rubber yields due to high-yielding varieties of tree. Political efforts may be made too as in Douglass North's study of the Pacific North West in the 19th Century United States, for example to induce the government to improve transport technology.

More interesting is where major changes in the available range of techniques have been made by foreign firms wishing to gain entry or strengthen their positions in a less developed country. A good example comes from Malaysia, where European tin mining firms unsuccessfully competed against immigrant Chinese for over thirty years until they developed a relatively efficient and capital-intensive technology (tin dredging), and from then on received considerable help (especially in land allocation) from the colonial government to establish themselves. Equally interesting in this case is that the Chinese miners were not forced out of business as their original technique of open cast, dry mining was rendered obsolete by European competition and decreasing ore richness. In contrast to local Chilean copper miners in the nineteenth century for example, they developed a new technique of their own (gravel pumping) by copying and *adapting* selected pieces of European technology to suit their needs. Their resilience in the face of European competition can hardly be explained solely in terms of economic and technological possibilities. Of great importance also was the highly socially integrated nature of the Chinese business community, with its members' wide access to credit from other local Chinese firms and suppliers for new ventures, its control of the labour supply to European firms through secret societies; and also the fact that local Chinese also owned one of the large tin smelters and had their own network of ore dealers.

Nevertheless the evidence suggests that plantation crops resist attempts to raise their capital/labour ratios more successfully than do minerals. As a result foreign estates frequently have imported labour when they were unable to induce local people to take up wage employment in sufficient numbers at the wages offered.

In spite of their relatively low capital/labour ratios, plantations have been depicted as having high initial capital requirements, largely because of economies of scale, and this, it is argued, would prevent smallholder entry. Whilst there are some crops where economies of scale do prevail in growing (e.g. tea, where Lim, 1968a found economies of scale to 500 acres), economies of scale are more usually found in processing. In this case much depends on whether processing, or at least some processing, can be split from the growing operation. In oil palm in Malaysia, for instance, where the oil is to be sold on the world market and must have a low free fatty acid (FFA) content, the fruit has to be processed within a few days at most after harvesting (otherwise the FFA content builds up) and the processing is a highly capital-intensive, large-scale operation. Peasant producers would have difficulty in transporting their fruit to processing plants within the time available, since storage of unprocessed fruit is virtually impossible. Also, such peasants would be in an extremely weak bargaining position regarding processing charges. As a result, in Malaysia until the spread of government FELDA and state land development schemes, oil palm was entirely an estate crop. Rubber, in contrast, as noted in the previous section, can be processed into unsmoked sheet to prevent immediate deterioration (in this case natural coagulation into scrap, which has much lower value), and then sold to dealers. In fact, oil palm is unusual among plantation crops in its processing requirements, and smallholder entry into plantation crops is quite common.

11.3 GOVERNMENT POLICY, 'DEPENDENCY' AND INTERSECTORAL RELATIONS

The Singer–Myrdal–Prebisch hypothesis, of the 1950's set out in Chapter 3, described a variety of ways in which export expansion might fail to promote development. Multiplier–accelerator effects of expansion might be lost to foreign factors and firms through income leakages, declining terms of trade might transfer gains from domestic producers to foreign consumers, and the spread effects of expansion might be outweighed by backwash effects (such as the drawing off of much-needed capital, entrepreneurship and skilled labour from other sectors). Chapter 2 has discussed the terms of trade argument, and the high retained value figures for almost all export commodities discussed here nullify the high-leakage argument. To Myrdal's 'backwash' effects the so-called 'dependency' theorists of Latin America and the Carribean have added a number of insights, sometimes as part of a Marxist view of 'imperialism'.

The Latin American dependency theorists have been interested primarily in the effects of the new dependency of import-substituting industrialization as a reaction to primary production, whereas Carribean writers such as Beckford and Girvan have been concerned more directly with plantation and mineral economies, though, for reasons to be discussed below, these are in many cases essentially only differences in emphasis.

Both Beckford and Girvan are concerned with foreign-owned enterprises, and especially with export by local subsidiaries of multinational companies. The main arguments about plantations' adverse effects on development are, first, that plantations compete too successfully for land resources, and so inhibit food production which supposedly has a higher income elasticity of demand than plantation crops—with the result that a faster growth of plantation output is required to finance a given growth in food demand. For plantation crops grown by domestic producers, planned expansion of plantation output rather than a switch to food crops would involve forecasting errors about future demand (though switches would be inhibited by specificity of existing skills and equipment). For foreign producers who were part of a multinational organization, a fall in the relative price of their raw material might represent gain rather than loss for the organization as a whole. The racial pluralism associated with plantations, Beckford's second argument, clearly has been associated with lack of social economic mobility. The Sri Lankan Tamils are one of the worst examples, but the mobility of Tamil workers in Malaysia beyond the estates (and railways) has also been limited, with the result that the workers' bargaining position has been poor and their wages low. Third, the concentration of research on export crops is most marked between say, foreign estate crops such as rubber and oil palm on the one hand, and mainly peasant crops such as coconuts on the other (Hicks and McNicholl, 1971, pp. 205–7), though the major Asian food crop, rice, has also experienced great yield increases as a result of research. However, yield improvements in most crops are associated with the use of higher productivity varieties of trees, etc., which require more complementary inputs, particularly fertilizer, if their higher yields are to be achieved, which further strengthens the position of larger producers (domestic and foreign) *vis-à-vis* smaller ones and worsens the distribution of income.

Beckford's description of the loss of linkages from sugar to branches of the multinational sugar corporations is paralleled in the mineral dependency studies. Girvan argues that, though technological conditions (especially economies of scale) account for the growth of vertically integrated firms, first in developed economies and then spreading as multinationals into the Third World, ownership conditions rather than domestic resource endowment in the host economy account for the loss of linkages. Multinationals may prefer to locate processing plants (though particularly those subject to very large economies of scale such as aluminium smelting) in the metropolitan country so they can switch their source of supply as they wish. Multinationals may prefer to buy equipment from metropolitan suppliers to standardize their operations in several countries. Also, ownership of transport facilities (especially shipping) by multinationals may induce them to have their subsidiary import metropolitan equipment so as to use otherwise empty capacity.[5]

The evidence of loss of linkages, however, is by no means conclusive. Substantial local shares of backward linkage investment and of capital-good production have been found in many of the empirical studies reviewed in this chapter, even in such cases as Jamaican bauxite (one of the industries studied by Girvan, 1970) where retained value is low. To dismiss local capital-good construction in some case studies as construction, while equipment and marketing is imported, is to miss the important lesson of the Malaysian engineering case study that much 'machinery' or 'equipment' can be made by firms in engineering 'construction', and construction may well form a basis for further development.

One interesting aspect of dependency work is the light it sheds on intersectoral relations in primary production. An important (but rarely remarked) inconsistency in the Singer–Myrdal–Prebisch hypothesis is that it can scarcely be argued seriously that gains from primary production are lost by the exporting country through deteriorating terms of trade at the same time as arguing that considerable potential gains are lost to foreign investors through leakages of income etc. Unless the foreign firms are subsidiaries of metropolitan firms consuming the primary product, they could hardly be 'gaining' anything if income gains are transferred to consumers (though, as shown in Chapter 2, various definitions of the terms of trade allow for ambiguity). This is especially important if there coexist a foreign and a domestic sector producing the same export commodity, as is commonly the case with rubber for instance. If potential gains *are* being lost to foreign investors (i.e. if any terms of trade deterioration is not sufficient to transfer all gains to foreign consumers), then an obvious remedy is the development of a local sector, either private or run by the state (unless foreigners have a monopoly of technology which prevents both private and state entry, in which case taxation, equity participation or nationalization—with appropriate use of foreign consultants—are the alternative.)

The dependency theorists have shown mechanisms whereby the local primary sector may be exploited by the foreign sector. A.G. Frank's (1966) well-known imperialist *chain-of-exploitation* may take the form of local smallholders selling crops to foreign firms for processing at discounts on world market prices far greater than costs of processing, trading and transport. Cotton in colonial Uganda (Pearson and Cownie, 1974, p. 142) is an example, but there is evidence, for example, that rubber dealers' margins in Malaysia are greater than would need to be charged by state processing centres (see for example Lim Sow Ching, 1968a, p. 8). Similarly foreign firms may control the distribution of imported (and sometimes domestically produced) inputs and charge high margins, as could be the case with agricultural inputs sold by the agency houses in Malaysia who also own a large share of the estate rubber and oil palm acreage. State enterprises of course are much less susceptible to this particular form of exploitation (though losses may occur through corruption).[6]

Finally, Girvan in particular has argued that what he calls the external diseconomies of mineral export production (Girvan, 1970, pp. 520–6) have greatly restricted scope for independent government policy and have generated 'growth without development', a situation where growth of average income per head proceeds in the face of widespread poverty, and unemployment, and eventually halts as resource restraints become binding. Perhaps the most important diseconomy, noted in the earlier studies of oil extraction in most countries, and in Jamaican bauxite, and copper, is the highly skewed income distribution which results in a biased demand pattern towards luxuries, which are either imported or locally assembled by foreign firms and with a high import content. Similarly, the high capital/labour ratios in mineral export production, which result in the demand bias, have a demonstration effect on wages in other sectors, again reducing employment and further biasing demand. Accelerated urbanization and urban unemployment along Harris–Todaro lines, (see e.g. Harris, 1970) again influence demand as well as retarding agricultural development. The result is continued dependence on imports and a need therefore to maintain primary commodity production for foreign exchange if domestic manufacturing cannot compete at world market prices.

These possibilities are illustrated in the study of exports and growth in the Philippines by Hicks and McNicholl (1971), which, though it does not regard itself as a 'dependency' study, strengthens the dependency theorists' case. Following their open dual economy theory of growth (set out in our Chapter 3) they argue that rapid Philippine growth has been dependent on extraction of exhaustible minerals and increasing the margin of cultivation of agricultural land to produce export commodities, both of which are essentially 'vent-for-surplus' mechanisms. The continued dependence of the Philippines on primary production of a vent-for-surplus type is the result of the need to import capital goods for manufacturing development, in the absence of a domestic capital-goods industry and the uncompetitiveness of tariff-protected import-substituting industry, which precludes transformation of manufacturing consumption goods into capital goods by direct export. This is a similar perspective to the starting point of the Latin American dependency theory, and brings the argument full circle from colonialized primary production to new industrialized dependency. In the Hicks–McNicholl system, ultimate stagnation can be postponed by improvements in agricultural productivity (either in export agriculture itself, or in subsistence agriculture to release land for other crops), and can be averted by developing manufacturing export capacity and a domestic capital-goods industry, or both.

Whether manufacturing *per se*, even if developed for export, offers really more favourable growth prospects than primary product export expansion is not certain. In recent years, along with a process of metropolitan firms subcontracting the manufacture of labour-intensive stages of industrial production to developing countries (see Sharpson, 1975), there has developed the practice of multinational firms establishing subsidiaries in the Third World to manufacture labour-intensive products or components. Myint (1954–5) has long since argued that had foreign firms in the past established a 'cheap labour' policy in manufacturing in colonial territories instead of plantation exports, the effects on development would have been far (or even) less favourable. While such labour-intensive export manufacturing, like estate agriculture, avoids creating the unemployment which follows capital-intensive import substitution, nevertheless it confines the workforce to largely unskilled tasks, and fails to generate further growth if linkages are appropriated by the multinational. Hoffman and Tan (1973) argue that in Malaysia, for instance, export promotion of labour-intensive manufactures would create new comparative advantage. Whether such export expansion is preferable to expanded primary production both through yield increases and new land expansion, unless the factors complementary to labour come entirely from overseas (and there is evidence that multinationals increasingly have tapped local funds, especially through joint ventures, to establish and expand subsidiaries—Barratt Brown, 1974, pp. 268–9) is questionable, especially with regard to agricultural commodities where there is more likely to be a choice between dependent industrial development or state-run primary production. Indeed Professor H.W. Singer, one of the most influential of the writers in the early post-war period who advocated industrialization as an escape from dependent primary export production, has recently (and convincingly) argued that the really important issues are not primary production *versus* manufacturing, but the *control* of production and technology (and access to information in general) (Singer, 1975a). The present study has shown, I hope, how different technologies and forms of control have influenced development through primary production, and similar considerations can apply to manufactures.

NOTES

1. Balogh (1959) has argued, however, that in Malaya and other parts of the British Empire, the banking system in colonial times (and to a lesser extent subsequently) tended to hold its assets in Britain and thus syphon off from domestic use some locally generated investment funds. Yet Drake's (1969) research on the new-issue boom in shares in Malaya and Singapore in 1961–4 suggests there was a plentiful local supply of funds for new issues.
2. This was true of final demand linkage industries in the Malaysia case study (see Chapter 7).
3. This is asserted by Girvan (1970) in an otherwise extremely useful article. Of course, other exports not covered by the main trade-and-development studies discussed in this chapter may have low RV's—banana exports from the Caribbean are one possibility—but the evidence that RV's generally are high is becoming increasingly strong.
4. In general, when it is found that a particular export in a developing country leads to few linkages, it is usually the case that there are *potential* linkages but that they are lost to overseas suppliers.
5. This is an interesting revival of the stress on transportation found in the staple theories of Harold Innis—see his essays on transportation and excess capacity as factors in Canadian economic development in Innis (1956), and the discussion in Thoburn (1971, pp. 37–43)
6. For example state officials may be bribed to buy foreign equipment rather than local equipment (though local firms also may engage in bribery!).

Appendices and References

(*Note: for ease of printing, the symbol – used in the Appendices indicates that a statistic is 'not available'*, not *that it is zero or negligible.*)

APPENDIX 5.1 TIN MINING WAGES AND LABOUR BENEFITS

(a) Wages 1964–72

From 1964 onwards the wage bills and labour benefits for each sector are given annually in the *Census of Mining Industries* (Statistics Dept., *CMinI*, 1964–71 and *PR*, 1972). Prior to 1964 the wages bill had to be calculated by using estimates of average wages, given below in (b). The following figures show how these estimates compare to those of the *Census of Mining Industry*, for the first five years of the *Census* sectoral wage bills.

	DREDGING		GRAVEL PUMP MINING	'OTHER TIN MINING'
	CALCULATED WAGE BILL	*CENSUS* WAGE BILL	CALCULATED WAGE BILL	*CENSUS* WAGE BILL
1964	13.1	11.9	16.6	22.2
1965	13.7	11.3	17.9	20.9
1966	12.3	13.3	19.5	23.3
1967	14.8	15.0	20.2	23.7
1968	15.0	15.1	20.3	23.4

(*Note*–All Wage Bills include benefits except for free accommodation, which is not valued in the *Census* and has therefore been excluded from the Calculated Wage Bills. Calculated Wage Bills do not include an estimate of free medical expenses; however, in *Census* figures these were only 0.2% for Dredging and 0.1 overall.)

(b) Wages 1946–68

	DREDGING			GRAVEL PUMP MINING		
	(i) AVERAGE MONTHLY WAGE ($)	(ii) EMPLOYMENT	(iii) ANNUAL WAGE BILL INCL. MANAGEMENT & PROFESSIONAL SALARIES ($MIL.) (i x ii x 12 x 1.3)	(iv) AVERAGE MONTHLY WAGE ($)	(v) EMPLOYMENT	(vi) ANNUAL WAGE BILL INCL. MANAGEMENT & PROFESSIONAL SALARIES ($MIL.) (iv x v x 12 x 1.2)
1946	*80.6	8,184	10.2	*41.0	7,882	4.6
47	80.6	12,493	15.7	41.0	19,418	11.4
48	56.3	15,235	13.8	70.9	23,611	24.1
49	68.5	15,776	16.8	68.8	23,584	23.4
1950	*81.6	15,732	20.0	98.1	15,732	22.2
51	*94.7	15,486	22.9	*96.2	23,707	32.8
52	*107.8	14,882	25.0	*94.3	23,179	31.5
53	120.7	13,488	25.4	92.5	17,172	22.9
54	124.5	14,077	27.3	96.3	21,915	26.8
55	126.1	14,442	28.4	*97.5	19,163	26.9
56	128.2	14,322	28.6	98.7	26,240	41.6
57	140.4	15,170	33.2	114.3	19,940	32.8
58	*136.8	9,555	20.4	*102.2	19,292	23.4
59	133.1	8,593	17.8	90.2	10,703	13.9
1960	142.4	11,334	25.2	104.4	12,771	19.2
61	148.2	11,438	26.4	110.0	15,471	24.5
62	*159.5	10,933	27.2	*114.0	16,567	27.2
63	170.8	11,156	29.7	*118.0	17,984	30.5
64	182.2	12,340	35.1	122.1	22,646	39.8

65	182.0	11,126	40.3	134.0	29,294	56.5
66	*188.0	10,785	31.6	*141.2	32,608	66.3
67	194.0	11,738	35.5	148.4	32,290	69.1
68	198.0	10,720	33.1	142.6	35,514	66.7

Sources and Notes

(1) Calculation of average monthly wage is discussed below. Asterisked items are estimates for years for which no wage data are available.

(2) Employment figures are the largest of Ministry of Labour, Mines Dept. and Statistics Dept., *CMinI* sources. Ministry of Labour figures are from the Ministry's *AR*'s to 1965 and the *HLS*, 1967; Mines Dept. figures are from *BSMI*'s.

(3) The conversion factor of 1.3 used in column iii is derived from a cost sheet supplied by a dredging company in Malaysia in 1970. On that sheet 'supervision' costs were equivalent to an additional 30% of the wages bill. The figure of 1.2 for gravel pump mines is arbitrarily assumed at a lower value than for dredges. These coefficients compare well with the results of dividing *CMinI* wage bills (which include management and professional salaries) by wage bills derived from average wages from Ministry of Labour sources (which do not).

Calculation of the Average Wage

The main source of data are the *AR*'s of the Ministry of Labour. These give detailed breakdowns of wages for different occupational groups within each industry, and proportions of the workforce in each group. For certain years the *AR*'s are missing, probably not published. In such cases an average of the preceding and following years' wages is taken. If the gap is for more than a single year, the difference is spread between the preceding and following year evenly over the intervening period. The 1946 wage is assumed the same as that for 1947. The 1967 and 1968 figures are from Ministry of Labour, *HLS*, 1967 and 1968. The 1950 wage is from Siew in Silcock (1961, pp. 428–9). Wages do not include free food and accommodation (see part c of this Appendix). For a general discussion of mining wages and employment see Lee (1966).

(c) **Labour Benefits in Tin Mining, 1946–68**

	DREDGING		GRAVEL PUMP MINING		
	(i) MONTHLY VALUE OF FREE ACCOMMODATION ($)	(ii) ANNUAL TOTAL VALUE OF FREE ACCOMMODATION ($000)	(iii) ANNUAL TOTAL VALUE OF FREE ACCOMMODATION ($000)	(iv) MONTHLY VALUE OF FREE FOOD PER WORKER ($)	(v) ANNUAL TOTAL VALUE OF FREE FOOD ($000)
1946	8.45	830	236	18	1362
47	8.45	1267	582	18	3355
48	8.45	1545	708	25.6	5794
49	8.6	1628	736	30.2	6837
1950	8.8	1661	491	35.0	5286
51	9.0	1672	768	39.5	8990
52	9.1	1625	751	44.0	9791
53	9.3	1505	577	48.6	8008
54	9.5	1605	649	43.8	8127
55	9.6	1664	666	39.0	5109
56	9.8	1684	913	37.0	8971
57	10.0	1820	718	37.0	6197
58	11.1	1273	368	37.0	3301
59	12.1	1248	424	37.0	3802
1960	13.2	1795	613	37.0	4550
61	14.2	1949	798	37.0	4595
62	15.3	2007	914	34.8	5535
63	16.4	2195	1057	32.6	5628
64	17.4	2577	1413	30.5	6631
65	18.3	3188	1933	30.7	8690

66	19.1	2472	2230	37.2	11646
67	20.0	2817	2325	40.2	12617
68	20.0	2573	2557	40.2	13704

Sources and Notes

(1) Annual Values = Monthly Values x 12 x Labour Force x % of Workers receiving benefits.

(2) Monthly Values of Free Accommodation in Dredging–figures available for 1948, 1957, 1964, 1967. Intervening years figures are estimated as an average of the preceding and following years, spread evenly over all intervening years. The years 1946 and 1947 are assumed to be the same as 1948; 1948 and 1957 are from Ministry of Labour, *AR*; 1964 is from Rubber Research Institute of Malaya, *Guide to Estate Management*, 1968, p. 30. Housing facilities on rubber estates and tin dredges to some extent are similar. 1967 is from *Fourth Biennial Report 1965–7, National Mining Workers Union of Malaya.* This report cites $23 a month as the housing allowance to be paid under the 1967 Agreement between the NMWUM and the Malayan Mining Employers Association. This figure is reduced to $20 for purposes of calculations since other figures reflect the value of accommodation in terms of its actual cost, rather than its opportunity cost in the open market. Normally all dredge workers have free accommodation. 1968 is assumed to be the same as 1967.

(3) Monthly Values of Free Accommodation in Gravel Pump Mining–taken as 0.3 of the Dredge figure. Accommodation on Chinese gravel pump mines is of a very rudimentary form–usually wooden kongsi houses roofed with atap. It seems logical therefore that the monthly value should be lower. The figure of 0.3 was arrived at as follows (figures from personal enquiries in Perak, November 1969).

Cost of kongsi house	$15000
Number of men housed	30
House lasts 5 to 10 years	
Monthly cost per worker if house cost is depreciated over 10 years:	$4
over 5 years:	$8
Cost of dredge housing:	$20

Therefore cost is approximately a third of dredge housing cost.

(4) Monthly Value of Free Food–figures from *AR*, Ministry of Labour, for 1947, 1953, 1956, 1957, 1960. Calculated from *CMinI*, 1964–7; and from Siew Nim Chee (in Silcock, 1961) for 1950. Other years are estimated in same fashion as for accommodation. Eighty percent of workers are assumed to receive free food unless another figure is available (57% in 1955, 77% in 1956, 70% in 1957, 81% in 1964 and 1967).

(d) Tin Mining Wages 1913–30

	(i) MONTHLY WAGE OF UNSKILLED WORKERS ($)	(ii) TOTAL ANNUAL DREDGING WAGE BILL (ALL WORKERS) ($000)	(iii) TOTAL ANNUAL NON-DREDGING WAGE BILL (ALL WORKERS) ($000)
1913	10.0	41	30,930
14	10.0	91	23,552
15	10.0	274	21,953
16	9.0	311	19.707
17	10.0	388	16,321
18	10.75	496	20,568
19	10.75	529	15,976
1920	12.5	640	10,003
21	8.75	883	9.493
22	10.0	934	10,350
23	11.25	1,135	13,771
24	11.25	1,333	15,106
25	11.25	1,538	15,079
26	18.75	3,057	24,809
27	12.5	2,502	18,756
28	12.5	3,198	15,894
29	12.5	3,784	14,605
1930	10.0	2,213	9,056

Sources and Notes

(1) To 1930, no wage data are available for tin mines. Column i is rubber tappers' daily wage x 25 (number of working days a month), from Labour Department, *AR*'s, 1913–30. No wages data are available for before 1913. For the 1930's, when mining wage data are available, tappers' wages do compare *roughly* with those of unskilled mining labour. For the 1931–9 period, unskilled mining wages were 92% of tappers' wages on average with a standard deviation of 37.3% of the mean. Mining wages were higher in three of the nine years, lower in five, and the same in one.

(2) To obtain the dredge wage bill, column i is multiplied by 12 x 1.5, the 1.5 being a conversion factor to take account of skilled workers wages and managerial salaries, 1.5 is obtained as follows: for 1946–67 the average ratio of skilled to unskilled workers wages in dredging is 1.25, and as described in part (b) a conversion factor of 1.3 is then applied to take account of management salaries. No comparable figures are available for before 1946. Therefore 1.5 can be taken as a *minimum* ratio of average to unskilled dredge wages. (Of course, this ratio is much smaller than the ratio of average skilled to average unskilled wages, because in the overall average skilled wages carry only a small weight.)

(3) Column iii is derived as follows: the total *tin* mining labour force is taken as 96% of the total mining labour. The 96% figure is the approximate ratio of tin to total mining employment in the years for which tin employment figures are first available. Tin dredge labour force is deducted from the resulting figure, which is then multiplied by column i x 12 x 1.17. The conversion factor of 1.17 comprises 1.06 as ratio of skilled to average wages in gravel pump mines (from 1931–9 data) multiplied by a management salaries correction factor, taken arbitrarily as half the post-war figure of (1.2).

(e) Wages and Labour Benefits, 1928–39

	DREDGING		GRAVEL PUMP MINING			
	(i) AVERAGE MONTHLY UNSKILLED EARNINGS ($)	(ii) ANNUAL WAGE BILL ($000)	(iii) AVERAGE MONTHLY UNSKILLED EARNINGS ($)	(iv) ANNUAL WAGE BILL ($000)	(v) MONTHLY VALUE OF FREE FOOD ($)	(vi) TOTAL ANNUAL VALUE OF FREE FOOD ($000)
1928	12.5	3198	12.5	10,450	Included	Included in
29	12.5	3784	12.5	10,379	in Monthly	Annual Wage
1930	10.0	2213	10.0	5,767	Wages	Bill
31	7.5	1244	4.5	1,616	3	922
32	7.5	944	4.5	1,045	3	596
33	11.85	1473	8.75	2,165	4.1	867
34	14.65	2356	9.25	3,734	5.4	1864
35	14.65	2779	9.25	4,034	5.4	2013
36	14.65	4089	9.25	5,479	5.4	2734
37	24.0	6979	18.6	12,372	5.4	3070
38	12.9	3003	7.5	2,446	5.4	1506
39	19.15	3666	13.75	7,058	5.4	2369

Sources and Notes

(1) Average monthly earnings of unskilled workers in dredges assumed to be equal to gravel pump mine wages plus free food. Unskilled average daily wage rates are from *AR*'s, Perak, 1931–9, monthly rates calculated on basis of 25-day working month. The 1928–30 wages, and value of free food except for 1931, 1932 and 1939, are from section (d) of this Appendix. The same skilled labour and management salaries correction factors have been used as in sect.(d) to correct the unskilled wage before multiplying by the employment figures (x 12) (not shown) to derive an annual bill. The 1931 and 1932 food cost is estimated as follows: an adult male consumes approximately 8 gantangs (gallons, equal to about 8 lb each) of rice a month, which at a rice price of 25 c a gantang is $2. This, plus 50% for other food makes $3. The 1939 food costs are assumed the same as for 1938.

(2) Figures are taken from 1928 because this is the first year for which output statistics are broken down by mining method.

Tin Mining Wage Bill, 1931–9

	(i) TOTAL ANNUAL NON-DREDGING WAGE BILL ($000)	(ii) TOTAL ANNUAL WAGE BILL FOR ALL TIN MINING ($000)
1931	4,432	5,676
32	3,372	4,316
33	5,651	7,124
34	8,083	10,439
35	9,093	11,872
36	11,281	15,320
37	21,018	27,997
38	6,370	9,373
39	12,666	18,332

Sources and Notes

(1) Column i calculated by multiplying Gravel Pump Wage Bill (Column iv of first table of part e of this Appendix) by total non-dredge employment in tin divided by gravel pump employment (not shown).

(2) Column ii is column i + column ii of first table of part (e) of this Appendix.

APPENDIX 5.2 **SMELTING AND TRANSPORT CHARGES**

(a) 1946–67

(All Tin Mining)

	(i) TOTAL SMELTING CHARGES ($000)	(ii) RAILWAY RECEIPTS FROM TRANSPORT OF TIN ORE ($000)	(iii) RECEIPTS FOR TRANSPORT OF TIN ORE BY NON-RAIL TRANSPORT ($000)
1946	768	195	–
47	2462	419	38
48	4083	719	38
49	5029	884	38
1950	5263	920	64
51	5229	1031	57
52	5199	1176	32
53	5138	1136	48
54	5551	1188	78
55	5579	1200	62
56	5606	1269	217
57	5402	1232	181
58	5269	618	283
59	5126	777	245
1960	7100	1277	99
61	7653	1252	110
62	8005	1237	224
63	8189	1211	302
64	8197	1225	175
65	8697	1320	196
66	9410	1379	189
67	9852	1388	282

Sources and Notes

(1) Smelting Charges—derived by multiplying smelting charges per ton of ore by total tin output converted to an ore equivalent. Charges per ton were $103 for 1958–67, and a minimum of $68.6 for 1946–57 (from private communication from Straits Trading Company, April 1970). Conversion factors of metallic tin into ore: 1.32 for 1946–55, 1.326 for 1956, 1.328 for 1957, 1.326 for 1959–66 (from Statistics Dept., *MSB*, July 1969). Assay deductions have not been included in the table. Smelting charges levied by Eastern Smelting Company were not obtained, but in a competitive (oligopolistic) situation they could differ little from those of the STC. Yip Yat Hoong, 'The marketing of tin ore in Kampar', (1959), quotes smelting charges for 74% ore of $5.20 a pickul ($84 a ton) in Kampar, Perak, with 1% assay deduction, for 1956. Unfortunately he gives no other years. Since the charges tend to stay constant for long periods and to rise in single discontinuous jumps, the usual practice of spreading changes evenly over time has not been adopted for the 1946–58 period, and the $68.6 figure has been used in preference to Yip's.

(2) Railway receipts from tin—derived from *AR*'s of Railway Administration Dept., 1946–67. Non-rail transport charges per ton are assumed to be the same as for rail transport. Non-rail transport tonnage is derived by subtracting tin ore tonnage carried by railways from tin ore production figure.

(3) For the purpose of Chapter 5, total smelting and transport charges can be allocated between types of tin mining in the same proportion as the proportion of total output produced by each type. There is no *a priori* reason to believe that smelting or transport charges per ton differ appreciably, if at all, between mining methods.

(Note—in Chapter 5 for present day, i.e. 1972–3 smelting charges, information from Company reports has been used.)

(b) Smelting and Transport Charges 1913–39

	(i) RAILWAY RECEIPTS FROM TRANSPORT OF TIN ORE ($000)	(ii) NON-RAILWAY RECEIPTS FOR TRANSPORT OF TIN ORE ($000)	(iii) RAIL CHARGES ON COAL, COKE AND FIREWOOD ($ PER TON)	(iv) RAIL RECEIPTS FOR TRANSPORT OF FUEL TO MINES ($000)	(v) LOCAL CHARGES ($ PER TON)	(vi) TOTAL SMELTING CHARGES ($000)
1913	—	—	*1.2	*411	43.68	3043
14	—	—	*1.2	*577	50.57	3447
15	—	—	*1.2	*652	38.64	2511
16	220	2	1.2	869	35.28	1931
17	*202	3	1.2	856	74.42	3914
18	195	4	1.2	978	78.62	3885
19	199	5	1.2	1073	58.63	2806
1920	193	1	1.3	1141	65.13	2971
21	237	14	1.7	1407	61.82	2713
22	223	10	1.7	1378	62.83	2838
23	231	18	1.6	1515	74.59	3655
24	355	13	1.9	2156	49.22	2746
25	387	25	1.9	2999	47.04	2591
26	329	17	1.9	2275	33.77	1811
27	365	12	1.9	2370	35.45	2194
28	422	9	2.0	2037	29.90	2143
29	449	9	2.1	2084	23.02	1688
1930	409	9	2.2	1669	39.65	3002
31	332	2	2.1	1057	34.10	2735
32	180	—	2.0	591	23.52	703
33	227	3	1.9	413	12.77	654
34	157	—	2.1	660	—	—

35	264	—	2.1	797	—	—
36	439	—	2.4	—	—	—
37	585	—	2.7	2089	—	—
38	339	—	2.3	1101	—	—
39	413	—	2.2	—	—	—

Sources and Notes

(1) Columns i and iii from Railway Dept., *AR*'s 1913–39.

(2) Column ii derived from multiplying the rail charges per ton (assumed equal to the charges for road and other transport) by the difference between total exports and tons carried by rail.

(3) Column iv calculated by multiplying total tonnage of coal, firewood and diesel carried by column ii (except that for diesel which requires more elaborate transport facilities, the charge per ton is doubled). The tonnage figures are in Appendix 5.3. This is an important item since local coal prices are quoted ex-pithead and imported coal and diesel are prices c.i.f. at the port of entry.

(4) Local charges from Mines Dept., *AR's*, 1913–33. They represent charges levied by the smelter for smelting handling, and transport (normally paid for by smelter). Column vi derived by multiplying total exports of ore by column v and subtracting transport charges (i + ii).

APPENDIX 5.3 TIN MINING CONSUMPTION OF FUEL

(a) 1946–72

From 1964 detailed figures for fuel consumption by sector are available from the *Census of Mining Industries* (Statistics Dept., 1964–71, and *PR*, 1972).

For the period 1946–63 no statistics on mining diesel consumption are available, but electricity consumption by mining sector is given in *AR*'s of the Central Electricity Board (later named the National Electricity Board, and later the Lembaga Lektrik Negara). Unit value figures were obtained from the Mines Dept., *BSMI*'s, and the calculation of the value of electricity consumption is therefore straightforward. For the pre-war period, construction of the various time series for fuel consumption is more complicated, and the figures and their derivation is given below.

(b) 1910–39

Coal

	(i) TOTAL MINING CONSUMPTION COAL (TONS)	(ii) CONSUMP-TION OF LOCAL COAL (TONS)	(iii) LOCAL COAL PRICE PER TON EX-PITHEAD ($)	(iv) ANNUAL VALUE OF LOCAL COAL CONSUMPTION ($000)	(v) FOREIGN COAL CONSUMP-TION (TONS)	(vi) FOREIGN COAL UNIT VALUE ($)	(vii) ANNUAL VALUE OF FOREIGN COAL CONSUMPTION ($000)
1910	–	–	–	–	–	–	–
11	44,607	–	–	–	–	–	–
12	53,365	–	–	–	–	–	–
13	35,795	–	–	–	–	–	–
14	37,434	–	–	–	–	–	–
15	40,528	*10,000	4.94	49	30,528	15.9	487
16	72,952	*35,000	4.73	167	37,952	21.9	833
17	62,044	*45,000	5.37	242	17,044	64.7	1,103
18	62,290	66,500	6.93	461	–	79.8	–
19	88,839	87,060	6.75	588	1,779	64.5	115
1920	102,270	115,041	8.63	993	–	43.4	–
21	105,724	92,728	8.91	826	12,996	25.3	329
22	103,916	72,678	7.87	572	31,238	22.3	698
23	146,545	100,846	7.42	748	45,699	18.3	836
24	167,378	145,969	7.23	1,055	21,409	13.3	285
25	194,995	174,011	7.26	1,263	20,984	21.6	453
26	204,419	210,732	7.28	1,524	–	11.8	–
27	287,508	241,139	6.74	1,625	46,369	10.9	503
28	305,099	285,065	6.29	1,793	20,034	10.5	211
29	303,827	297,486	5.90	1,755	6,341	13.5	85

1930	236,110	213,288	5.77	1,231	22,822	10.3	234
31	158,285	156,942	5.77	906	1,343	8.9	12
32	76,268	73,359	5.61	412	2,909	8.2	24
33	41,277	47,566	5.53	263	—	7.8	—
34	81,101	82,505	4.81	397	—	7.7	—
35	128,599	103,681	4.88	506	24,918	7.6	189
36	—	170,708	4.98	850	—	7.2	—
37	399,117	187,313	6.37	1,206	149,804	8.8	1,326
38	165,733	133,453	6.75	901	32,280	10.1	327
39	—	124,819	5.51	688	—	10.2	—

Sources and Notes

(1) Columns i and ii from Mines Dept., *AR*'s 1911–39; column iii from Mines Dept., *BSMI*, to 31 December 1955; column v = i – ii; column vi derived by dividing value of coal imports by their tonnage from British Malaya, *Imports and Exports* (annual), 1930–39, and *AR*'s of Trade and Customs Dept., 1915–29

(2) Local coal consumption estimated for 1915–17 on basis of the proportion of mining consumption to local coal production (1/3). Production figures not shown here.

Diesel Oil and Wood Fuel, 1913–39

	(i) TOTAL CONSUMPTION OF DIESEL OIL BY MINES (TONS)	(ii) DIESEL UNIT VALUE ($)	(iii) TOTAL VALUE OF DIESEL CONSUMPTION ($000)	(iv) TOTAL CONSUMPTION OF WOOD FUEL BY MINES (TONS)	(v) WOOD FUEL UNIT VALUE ($)	(vi) TOTAL VALUE OF WOOD FUEL CONSUMPTION ($000)
1913	1,481	—	—	303,500	3.0	910
14	1,640	—	—	439,800	3.0	1,320
15	3,727	—	—	495,628	3.0	1,486
16	3,107	—	—	645,280	2.8	1,806
17	2,538	—	—	646,285	3.2	2,068
18	3,488	—	—	741,357	4.2	3,114
19	3,397	—	—	798,363	4.0	3,194
1920	2,702	—	—	769,990	5.2	4,004
21	2,577	—	—	713,183	5.4	3,872
22	2,640	—	—	701,137	4.8	3,366
23	4,576	—	—	791,015	4.4	3,480
24	8,070	—	—	951,042	4.4	4,184
25	20,860	58.0	1,210	1,380,012	4.4	6,072
26	32,325	49.1	1,587	928,456	4.4	4,084
27	53,875	47.7	2,570	852,148	4.0	3,408
28	66,100	49.5	3,272	581,775	3.8	2,210
29	73,356	50.3	3,690	541,849	3.6	1,950
1930	69,396	46.3	3,224	556,752	3.4	1,212
31	47,781	38.3	1,830	249,473	3.4	848
32	27.741	39.2	1,087	163,655	3.4	556
33	22,024	37.3	821	131,561	3.4	448
34	31,121	36.1	1,123	173,314	2.8	486

35	39,219	34.8	1,365	172,166	3.0	316
36	—	35.7	—	*195,710	3.0	*587
37	107,659	38.2	4,113	219,255	3.8	834
38	76,425	37	2,828	160,068	4.0	640
39	—	—	—	*160,068	3.4	*544

Sources and Notes

(1) Diesel consumption from Mines Dept., *AR*'s, 1913–39. Diesel Unit Values from British Malaya, *Imports and Exports*, 1930–39 and 1925–9 from Trade and Customs Dept., *AR*, 1929. No attempt made to estimate consumption for 1936 and 1939, because of great variability in other years.

(2) Total firewood consumption from Mines Dept., *AR*'s, 1913–39. This series is especially suspect and the Mines Department suggests they are only very rough estimates. The price of firewood (excluding transport charges to mine) is also only a very rough estimate. It is calculated as 0.6 of the local price of coal on the basis that the FMS Railways Dept. (*AR*, 1935) calculates that one ton of jungle wood is equal in calorific value to ⅔ of a ton local coal. Estimate for 1936 is an average of preceding and following year, and 1939 is assumed same as 1938.

(c) Electricity, 1928–39

	(i)	(ii)	(iii)	(iv)	(v)	(vi)	(vii)	(viii)	(ix)	(x)	(xi)	(xii)
	SALES BY PERAK RIVER HYDRO-ELECTRIC COMPANY (000 UNITS)			SALES BY SELANGOR GOVERNMENT (000 UNITS)								
	TO DREDGES	TO 'OPEN CAST' MINES	ALL MINING SALES	TO DREDGES	TO 'OPEN CAST' MINES	ALL MINING SALES	TOTAL ALL MINING PURCHASES	TOTAL ALL MINING CONSUMPTION (000 UNITS)	PRICE OF ELECTRICITY PER UNIT ($)	TOTAL VALUE OF DREDGE PURCHASES ($000)	TOTAL VALUE OF 'OPEN CAST' MINING PURCHASES ($000)	TOTAL VALUE OF ALL MINING PURCHASES ($000)
1928	–	–	27,520	–	–	7,620	35,140	106,478	.0275	–	–	966
29	–	–	31,698	–	–	12,825	44,523	165,445	.0275	–	–	1,224
1930	–	–	53,231	–	–	12,248	65,479	–	.0265	–	–	1,719
31	–	–	–	–	–	–	–	–	.0265	–	–	–
32	–	–	–	–	–	–	–	–	.0265	–	–	–
33	–	–	–	–	–	–	–	–	.0265	–	–	–
34	–	–	–	–	–	–	–	–	*.0265	–	–	–
35	–	–	–	–	–	–	–	194,653	*.0265	–	–	–
36	66,301	131,052	197,353	–	–	61,800	259,153	344,050	*.0265	–	–	–
37	74,935	166,514	241,449	15,595	41,364	56,959	298,408	467,171	*.0265	2,376	5,457	7,833
38	–	–	148,511	11,957	25,560	37,517	186,028	266,773	*.0265	–	–	4,883
39	–	–	108,920	–	–	*40,000	*150,000	–	*.0265	–	–	*3,937

Sources and Notes

(1) Column ix from FMS, *Manual of Statistics*, 1928–33. The 1934–6 *Manuals* were not available, and the 1937–9 issues did not give electricity rates. The 1934–9 rates are assumed not to have altered—this gives a *minimum* value of electricity purchases.

(2) All 1928–30 figures except column viii are from Mines Dept., *AR*'s, FMS, 1928–30.

(3) Columns i to iii from Perak, *AR*'s, 1936–9. Columns iv to vi from Electricity Dept., *AR*'s, 1936–8. The 1939 figure in column vi is estimated on the basis of a large increase mentioned in the 1939 *AR* of the Electricity Department.

(4) Column viii from FMS, *AR*'s Chief Secretary, 1936–8. *Consumption* of electricity differs from *Purchases* mainly by the extent of self-generated electricity. It can be seen how the proportion of Purchases rose over time.

(5) Perak and Selangor are the main tin mining areas. There was little or no generation of electricity for mines by the government in Perak, or by private firms in Selangor.

APPENDIX 5.4 OWNERSHIP OF SHARES IN TIN DREDGING COMPANIES

The survey covered the following companies:

Malaysian–incorporated Companies
Austral Amalgamated Tin Bhd.
Berjuntai Tin Dredging Bhd.
Johan Tin Dredging Bhd.
Kampong Kamunting Tin Dredging Bhd.
Kampong Lanjut Tin Dredging Bhd.
Kuala Kampar Tin Fields Bhd.
Larut Tin Fields Bhd.
Lower Perak Tin Dredging Bhd.
Petaling Tin Bhd.
Rantau Tin Dredging Sdn. Bhd.
Selangor Dredging Bhd.
Sungei Way Dredging Bhd.

1. **1970 Value of Issued Capital**–$204.4 million
2. **Average Malaysian Share Ownership** 56.3%
3. **1970 Value of Issued Capital of Malaysian Companies (2) not Covered**–$4.2 million

U.K.–incorporated Companies
Kamunting Tin Dredging Ltd.
Southern Kinta Consolidated Ltd.
Ampat Tin Dredging Ltd.
Malayan Tin Dredging Ltd.
Southern Malayan Tin Dredging Ltd.
Renong Tin Dredging Co. Ltd.
Ayer Hitam Tin Dredging Ltd.
Tronoh Mines Ltd.

1. **1970 Value of Issued Capital**–£32.4 million
2. **Average Malaysian Share Ownership** 20.0%
3. **1970 Value of Issued Capital of U.K. Companies (7) not Covered**–£3.7 million

The names of companies were obtained from Yip (1968, pp. 81–2). Of the 18 Malaysian-incorporated companies in Yip, 4 have been omitted as operating in Thailand (Aokam, Katu, Pungau, Tongkah Harbour). Of the 17 Overseas-incorporated companies, one is omitted as operating principally in Thailand (Siamese Tin Syndicate) and another as Australian (Sungei Bidor) for which the necessary data are not available. Thus there are 14 Malaysian and 15 U.K.-incorporated companies covered. Par values of issued capital were obtained from Stock Exchange of Malaysia and Singapore (1970), except for Rantau (from Yip, 1968, p. 81).

Information on Malaysian shareholdings is from Yip (1968, p. 83) for Malaysian companies; and for the U.K. firms information was obtained from a postal survey in March–April 1970 to which 8 out of 15 companies responded. The 8 U.K. companies, however, constituted 89–90% of the total issued capital of all 15 companies, and the Malaysian companies nearly 98% of all Malaysian dredging issued capital. To calculate the shareholdings shown in Chapter 5, it was assumed that companies not covered had on average the same local shareholdings as the covered U.K. and Malaysian companies, respectively. Share prices for U.K. and Malaysian companies were obtained from the *Financial Times* and the *Straits Times*, respectively. Malaysian share ownership probably includes Singaporean shareholders in some cases, but no further details could be obtained. Shareholdings by local nominee companies also complicate the picture somewhat.

APPENDIX 6.1 CALCULATION OF ESTATE OUTPUT UNIT VALUES

Estate output unit values used in tables in the text for the period 1946–72 are equal to net export unit values (derived from foreign trade statistics) plus one cent per pound. This is arrived at as follows, using statistics for a convenient recent year (1968).

	1968 PRICE	WEIGHT (PROPORTIONS OF TOTAL OUTPUT)	
Smallholders			
RSS 1 and 2	52.57	0.26	
3	51.30	0.45	
RSS 4 and Lower Grades	47.15	0.29	
	Unit Value of Smallholder Output		50.42
Estates			
Latex Concentrate	60.0	0.13	
RSS 1	53.12	0.72	
Lower Grades	47.15	0.15	
	Unit Value of Estate Output		53.11

	1968 OUTPUT (MIL.TONS)	UNIT VALUE
Smallholders	563	50.42
Estates	472	53.11
Total, and Overall Unit Value	1,035	51.64

Thus, estate unit value less overall unit value = 1.47 cents. Since the estimates of the proportion of RSS 1 in estate output are based on best rather than average practice, the excess of estate over overall unit value is taken to be one cent per pound. Note that over the post-1946 period there is a close correspondence between export unit values and RSS 1 price. Average export unit values 1947–68 are 0.997 of the average RSS 1 price.

For the period to 1939 output unit values for estates have been assumed to be the same as overall net export unit values. In the pre-war period latex concentrates' manufacture was less important than post-war, and it is the manufacture of latex concentrates, with its high premium over the RSS 1 price, which primarily accounts for the post-war differential in estates over overall export unit values.

Sources and Notes

(1) Proportions of smallholder output from Fryer and Jackson (1966, p. 225); Estate figures assume most latex concentrate is produced by estates (latex concentrate was 14.3% of West Malaysian 1968 rubber exports by weight, and a higher proportion by value–Statistics Dept., *RSH*, 1968), and that 15% of output is of lower grades. According to RRIM (1968, p. 14) 90% of an RSS estate crop can be processed into RSS 1, SMR rubber is excluded as being unimportant for the post-war period as a whole.

(2) Prices and output figures from Statistics Dept., *RSH*, 1968 except for latex concentrate, the premium for which is estimated from an interview in Malaysia with a latex concentrate manufacturer, December 1969. The absolute price differentials between grades change little with the level of rubber prices, except for the latex concentrate premium which tends to move independently of the RSS price.

APPENDIX 6.2
SHAREHOLDINGS IN U.K.-INCORPORATED RUBBER PLANTING COMPANIES

Local shareholdings in rubber companies incorporated in Malaysia are given in the 1967 *Survey of Limited Companies* published by the Malaysian Department of Statistics. In order to find the proportion of Malaysian shareholdings in U.K.-incorporated companies, questionnaires were sent, in March and April 1971, to all Secretaries of rubber planting companies operating in Malaysia whose shares were quoted on the London Stock Exchange. The list of Secretaries was taken from the 1969 edition of Zorn and Leigh-Hunt, *Manual of Rubber Planting Companies*. Replies were received from 20 of the 27 Secretaries, in several cases after follow-up letters had been sent assuring the companies that their information would be kept confidential.

Of the replies received three indicated that the company (or companies) concerned had sold their interests and had become investment companies, two were in liquidation, and two were unable to provide the information requested. The 13 positive replies covered 31 companies (since generally Secretaries act for several companies), and indicated very low Malaysian shareholdings. Only 7 companies had more than 6% of their shares owned by Malaysians. These had from 8% to 61% of their shareholding in Malaysian hands.

In order to arrive at an average shareholding, individual companies' shareholdings were weighted by the *current* value of their issued capital. Current share values were used in preference to par value because the former give a clearer indication of recent and expected profitability. Current share prices were obtained from the *Financial Times* (of London). For 13 of the companies no current share price was available, presumably because no trading in the particular share had occurred recently. In these cases share prices were taken from the 1969 Zorn and Leigh-Hunt. It was found that the 1971 share price of companies quoted in the *Financial Times* was in almost all cases very near to the 1968 higher share price (a highest and a lowest price were quoted) in Zorn and Leigh-Hunt. Thus the 1968 high share price was used in the calculation. For two very small companies (each with annual output below a million pounds of rubber) no share prices were given in Zorn and Leigh-Hunt, so these companies' issued capital was weighted by the par value of their shares. The calculation is of exactly the same form as that used for tin dredging companies, discussed in Appendix 5.4. No calculations are shown here for rubber companies, because several companies gave information on the strict condition that their individual shareholdings should not be shown. Since it would be possible to recognize companies from their issued capital and share prices even if names are not given, no worksheet can be shown which would effectively disguise companies' identities.

The results of the survey were as follows. The 31 companies had a mean Malaysian shareholding of 6.68%, with standard deviation of 0.1590. Confidence intervals, using Student t distribution, at the 5% level of significance indicated a possible range of Malaysian shareholdings from 1.22% to 12.14%. Since the sample represented a large proportion (exactly half) of all U.K.-registered rubber companies, a finite population correction factor (FPCF) was applied, reducing the confidence limits to a range of 2.78% to 10.57%.

It is also possible to argue that the size of the sample relative to the population of rubber companies should be seen in terms other than the number of companies. The 31 companies in the sample had a total issued share capital currently valued at

£96.8m, in relation to the current value of issued capital of all Zorn and Leigh-Hunt Malaysian rubber companies (i.e. all rubber companies operating in Malaysia with shares quoted on London Stock Exchange) of £123.4m. Also, the output of the sample companies in 1968 was $200.8m compared to $307.4m for all Zorn and Leigh-Hunt companies. This information cannot properly be used in a FPCF, but it is a further indication of the large size of the sample relative to the total population of companies.

Of course, such confidence intervals must be treated in any case with extreme caution, since the 'randomness' of the sample depends on the pattern of self-selection of the respondents. However, the confidence intervals may be better quoted than not, unless the pattern of non-response shows some particular bias, (e.g. companies might fail to respond if they thought there were political disadvantages to having low local shareholdings. Since most respondents indicated low local shareholdings the sample would not be biased by the exclusion of others with similar characteristics.)

Several other points of caution need to be made. First, part of the Malaysian holdings may be in the hands of nominee companies which themselves have small local shareholdings. Two large companies mentioned this problem. One suggested that most of its Malaysian-held shares were owned by institutional nominees and therefore the true Malaysian holdings (i.e. holdings in the hands of private Malaysian residents or companies which themselves had a predominant Malaysian shareholding) were small. Another suggested that most of its (large) Malaysian holding was in the hands of private individuals. Second, local shareholding include holdings of resident expatriates. Third, in some cases 'Malaysian' holdings quoted refer to residents of both Malaysia and Singapore. These are all factors which would tend to overstate local shareholding. Since average local shareholdings are found to have been low anyway, the fact that this low proportion may be overstated is less important than if the proportion were high. On the other hand, the local holding may be understated to the extent that Malaysians purchase shares on the London Stock Exchange and thus are not included on companies' Malaysian share registers.

(a) Wages 1946–68, Peninsular Malaysia

	(i) AVERAGE MONTHLY WAGE ($)	(ii) EMPLOYMENT	(iii) ANNUAL WAGE BILL INCLUDING MANAGEMENT & PROFESSIONAL SALARIES (i x ii x 12 x 1.2) ($000)
1946	–	332,300	–
47	61.12	289,200	254,533
48	52.58	287,000	217,303
49	44.24	257,800	175,700
1950	*60.60	281,600	–
51	*85.80	282,800	349,405
52	*74.10	280,000	298,771
53	62.77	281,390	254,345
54	64.35	267,981	248,322
55	70.50	278,200	282,429
56	75.88	280,200	306,167
57	78.77	276,740	313,903
58	*78.00	281,900	316,635
59	78.74	282,510	320,326
1960	92.24	285,300	378,951
61	80.48	285,560	330,939
62	83,39	286,220	343,683
63	79.02	286,320	325,820
64	88.35	275,410	350,388
65	85.88	270,160	332,933
66	91.95	249,500	330,370
67	92.89	231,900	310,171
68	97.68	206,680	290,714

Sources and Notes

(1) Wages to 1961 are calculated from *AR*'s of Ministry of Labour/Labour Department to 1961. The 1962 and 1963 wages are calculated from column (iii) wage bill from Statistics Dept., *RSH*, 1962 and 1963. The 1962 and 1963 *RSH* wage bills are given for December only, and have been prorated with the average total wage bill ÷ December wage bill from *RSH*'s, 1964–8 in order to arrive at an annual total.

(2) Employment figures are also from *AR*'s of Ministry of Labour/Labour Department. Employment in years for which *AR*'s not available is from Thomas and Fong (1968, p. 36).

(3) The conversion factor of 1.2 in column (iii) takes account of the fact that management salaries are not included in the average wage computations. In the 1964 RRIM *Survey of Estates* (Chan, Ng and Barlow, 1969), (Labour Costs + Management Costs) ÷ (Labour Costs) = 1.19, say 1.2. This conversion factor gives wage bills which agree closely with those of the *RSH* (see below part b).

(4) Estimates (asterisked) for years for which data are missing are calculated as follows: 1958–in view of the slight fall in rubber prices between 1957 and 1958 and the fact that 1959 and 1957 wages are almost identical, 1958 wages are assumed to be a figure ($78) rounded down from the 1957 wage rate. 1951 and 1952–estimated from details of union wage agreement in rubber industry for 1951 and 1952 for rubber price range of $1.50–$2 per lb for 1951 and

80–90 for 1952. Checkroll tappers' wage for 1951 is $3.30, equivalent to $85.80 at 26 days a month and $74.10 for 1952. For most years tapper's wage is very close to overall average wage. Data from Gul (1968, p. 25). 1950 wage estimate based on a wage index from Ma (1959).

(5) 1947 calculated using 1948 weights, as no weights are given for 1947.

(6) Wages for 1967 are calculated from Statistics Dept., *HLS*, 1967 and 1968. No Ministry of Labour figures are available for 1962, 1963 and 1966, hence the use of *RSH* data. Where *RSH* data are used to calculate average wage (*RSH* gives only the total wage bill), the wage bill is first divided by 1.2 (see note 3).

(b) Reconciliation of Wage Statistics from Rubber Statistics Handbook and Ministry of Labour Sources

In the text the wage statistics in part (a), which are calculated from Ministry of Labour sources, are used only up to 1963, after which wage bills are available from the *Rubber Statistics Handbook* of the Statistics Dept. To compare the two series, wage bills for a further five years (1964–8) are given in part (a), which can be compared to *RSH* figures as follows, and it can be seen that the two series are very close.

Wages as Percentage of Annual Value of Output

	RSH WAGE BILL	M OF L WAGE BILL
1964	47.0	46.8
1965	42.7	43.0
1966	42.3	–
1967	46.0	45.8
1968	41.4	42.2

(c) Wages, 1910–1939, Federated Malay States

	(i) ESTIMATED TOTAL WORKFORCE	(ii) AVERAGE MONTHLY WAGE ($)	(iii) ANNUAL WAGE BILL INCLUDING MANAGEMENT SALARIES ($000) ((i) x (ii) x 12 x 1.3)	(iv) LABOUR BENEFITS ($000)
1910	115,601	6.0	10,820	–
11	149,081	10.3	24,040	3,991
12	169,997	11.6	30,849	4,787
13	179,477	10.0	27,915	4,362
14	–	9.0	–	–
15	160,552	8.9	22,273	3,508
16	178,472	12.3	34,177	4,520
17	201,331	12.8	40,056	4,891
18	181,676	13.9	39,528	4,827
19	213,415	10.1	33,809	4,534
1920	194,929	12.4	37,679	5,642
21	141,489	12.3	27,190	4,466
22	151,537	10.9	25,879	4,229

(c) Wages, 1910-1939, Federated Malay States (continued)

23	141,121	11.0	24,163	3,833
24	143,581	10.3	23,036	3,825
25	165,550	13.7	35,329	4,773
26	221,097	16.2	55,933	6,289
27	202,021	15.5	48,734	6,275
28	200,294	15.6	48,876	5,974
29	231,091	17.4	62,598	7,611
1930	151,340	9.7	22,792	4,104
31	126,668	8.9	17,603	2,925
32	111,844	6.1	10,608	1,713
33	123,924	8.3	16,000	2,260
34	161,408	8.9	22,307	3,219
35	145,899	9.0	20,505	3,369
36	153,455	9.5	22,805	3,702
37	199,199	11.5	35,747	5,863
38	170,932	10.1	26,818	4,567
39	174,084	11.3	30,728	5,224

Sources and Notes

(1) Column i from FMS Agriculture Dept., *AR*'s for 1911–13 and 1915; 1916–30 from FMS, *AR*'s Resident-General/Chief Secretary; 1931–2 from FMS, *AR*'s Department of Labour; 1933–9 from Statistics Dept., *RSH*, 1933–9. To 1932 the original figures include workers on estates growing crops other than rubber (usually 10% of total). Figures in column (i) have been adjusted to include only rubber estate workers, since, up to 1932, workforce statistics included workers on coconut estates, etc. Adjustment is by multiplying workforce by the proportion of rubber in total acreage (i.e. assuming rubber labour requirements are similar to those of other crops). Acreage figures are from Agriculture Dept., *AR*'s, and FMS, *AR*'s to 1932.

(2) Column (ii) calculated from daily wages, assuming 24 working days per month (in contrast to 26 for post-war years). Daily wages from same sources as labour force statistics to 1932, except for 1910 and 1914 wages which are from Figart (1925, p. 179). 1932–9 wages data are supplemented by information and fragmentary wage data from Bauer (1948b) and Parmer (1960).

(3) Conversion factor in column (iii) is arbitrarily assumed 1.3. It is thereby assumed that management salaries are higher in relation to estate workers than is the case in the years after the Second World War (when the conversion factor is known to be 1.2—see part (a).

(4) Labour benefits are assumed to be equal to 30% of the non-Chinese workers' wage bill. Chinese workers earned higher daily wages and did not receive non-monetary benefits. See Bauer (1948b, p. 219) who estimates that labour benefits add another third to the total wage bill.

References

Abdul Rahman, Tungku (1969), *May 13, Before and After,* Utusan Melayu Press, KL.

Agriculture Dept. (of FMS, MU, FM)—references cited in full in text using abbreviations shown on pp. xv-xvi.

Ahluwalia, M., Bell, C. Chenery, H. and Duloy, J. (1975) 'Redistribution with growth—a comment', *IDS Bulletin*, August.

Allen, G. C. and Donnithorne, A. G. (1954), *Western Enterprise in Indonesia and Malaya. A Study in Economic Development*, Allen and Unwin, London.

Allen, R. G. D. (1967), *Macroeconomic Theory. A Mathematical Treatment*, Macmillan, London.

Anjaria, S. J. (1975) 'The MTN and tariff reduction' *Finance and Development*, IMF and World Bank, December.

Ariff, K. A. M. (1969a) 'On the export instability of West Malaysia', *Kajian Ekonomi Malaysia*, June.

Ariff, K. A. M. (1969b) 'The impact of export instability on the domestic economy of West Malaysia', *Kajian Ekonomi Malaysia*, December.

Ariff, K. A. M. (1970) 'The effect of price instability on employment, wages and profits in the national rubber industry of West Malaysia', *Kajian Ekonomi Malaysia,* June.

Arrow, K. J. (1962) 'The economic significance of learning by doing', *R. econ. Stud.*

Aziz, U. A. (1964) 'Poverty and rural development in Malaysia', *Kajian Ekonomi Malaysia*, June.

Balassa, B. (1971), *The Structure of Protection in Developing Countries*, John Hopkins Press, Baltimore.

Baldwin, R. E. (1956) 'Patterns of development in newly settled regions', *Manchester Sch. econ. soc. Stud.*, May.

Baldwin, R. E. (1963) 'Export technology and development from a subsistence level', *Econ. J.*, March.

Baldwin, R. E. (and thirteen other authors) (1965), *Trade, Growth, and the Balance of Payments. Essays in Honor of Gottfried Haberler*, North Holland, Amsterdam.

Baldwin, R. E. (1966), *Economic Development and Export Growth: A Study of Northern Rhodesia 1920–60*, California University Press, Berkeley.

Balogh, T. (1959) 'A note on the monetary controversy in Malaya', *Malayan econ. R.*, October.

Baran, P. (1952) 'On the political economy of backwardness', *Manchester Sch. econ. soc. Stud.*, January.
Barker, C. and Page, B. (1974) 'OPEC as a model for other mineral exporters', *IDS Bulletin*, October.
Barlow, C. (1967) 'The marketing of smallholders' rubber', RRIM, KL.
Barlow, C. and Lim Sow Ching (1965), *A Report on the Malay Group Processing Centres*, RRIM, Economic Report No. 1, KL.
Barlow, C. and Lim Sow Ching (1967) 'The effect of density of planting on the growth, yield, and economic exploitation of *Hevea brasiliensis*', *Journal of the RRIM*, 1.
Barlow, C. and Ng Choong Sooi (1966) 'Budgeting on the merits of a shorter immature period', *Planters' Bulletin*, November.
Barlow, C. and Chan Chee Kheong (1968), 'Towards an optimum size of rubber holding', Natural Rubber Conference, KL, Preprint.
Barratt Brown, M. (1974), *The Economics of Imperialism*, Penguin, London.
Bateman, L. C. (1965) 'Natural rubber in modern dress', Address delivered to the Rubber Division of the American Chemical Society, Miami Beach, Florida, May 1965, reprinted by RRIM, KL.
Bauer, P. T. (1947) 'Malayan rubber policies', *Economica*, May.
Bauer, P. T. (1948a), *Report on a Visit to the Rubber Growing Smallholdings of Malaya, July–September 1946*, Colonial Office, London.
Bauer, P. T. (1948b), *The Rubber Industry. A Study in Competition and Monopoly*, Longman, Green & Co., London.
Bauer, P. T. (1959) 'International economic development', *Econ. J.*, March.
Bauer, P. T. (1971), *Dissent on Development: Studies and Debates on Development Economics*, Weidenfeld and Nicholson, London.
Beckford, G. L. (1972), *Persistent Poverty. Underdevelopment in Plantation Economies of the Third World*, Oxford University Press, New York.
Bevan, J. W. L. and Goering, T. J. (1968) 'The oil palm in Malaysia: an estimate of product prices and returns to investment', in Turner (1968).
Bhagwati, J. N. (1958) 'Immiserizing growth: a geometrical note', *R. econ. Stud.*, June.
Bhagwati, J. N. (1969) 'Optimal policies and immiserizing growth', *Amer. econ. R.*, December.
Blake, D. J. (1973) 'Unemployment: the West Malaysian example', *United Malayan Banking Corporation Economic Review*, 1, reprinted in Lim (1975), to which page numbers refer.
Bond, E. (1974), *The State of Tea. A War on Want Investigation into Sri Lanka's Tea Industry and the Plight of the Estate Workers*, War on Want, London.
Briscoe, L. (1975) 'The growth and structure of international trade since the Second World War', *British Journal of International Studies*, October.
British Government (1975), *World Economic Interdependence and Trade in Commodities*, Her Majesty's Stationery Office, London (Cmnd. 6061).
British Malaya–references cited in full in text, including reports of individual Malay states.
Brown, C. P. (1975), *Primary Commodity Control*, Oxford University Press, KL.
Bruno, M. (1972) 'Domestic resource costs and effective protection: clarification and synthesis', *J. polit. Econ.*, January/February.

Bruton, H. J. (1969) 'The two gap approach to aid and development: comment', *Amer. econ. R.*, June.

Cairncross, A. K. (1961) 'International trade and economic development', *Economica*, August.

Cairncross, F. and McRae, H. (1974), *Capital City: London as a Financial Centre*, Eyre Methuen, London, revised edn.

Caves, R. E. (1960), *Trade and Economic Structure: Models and Methods*, Harvard University Press, Cambridge, Mass.

Chai Hon Chan (1964), *The Development of British Malaya, 1896–1909*, Oxford University Press, KL.

Challis, J. (1968 and 1969), *Annotated Bibliography of Economic and Social Material on West Malaysia*, Part I, *Government Publications*, Part II, *Non-Government Publications*, Economic Research Centre, University of Singapore.

Chambers, E. F. and Gordon, D. F. (1966) 'Primary products and economic growth—an empirical measurement', *J. polit. Econ.*, August.

Chambers, E. F. and Gordon, D. F. (1967) 'Primary products and economic growth: a rejoinder', *J. polit. Econ.*, December.

Chan Chee Kheong, Ng Choong Sooi and Barlow, C. (1969), *Results of the 1964 Sample Survey of Estates in West Malaysia*, RRIM, KL.

Chang Wai Pong, Pillai N. M. and Chin Peng Sung (1969) 'Developments in polybag collection', RRIM Planters' Conference, KL, Preprint.

Chenery, H. B. (1959) 'The two-gap approach to aid and development: a reply to Bruton', *Amer. econ. R.*, June.

Chenery, H. B. and Watanabe, T. (1958) 'International comparisons of the structure of production', *Econometrica*, October.

Chenery, H. B. and Bruno, M. (1962) 'Development alternatives in an open economy. The case of Israel',, *Econ. J.*, March.

Chenery, H. B. and Strout, A. M. (1966) 'Foreign assistance and economic development', *Amer. econ. R.*, September.

Chenery, H. B., Ahluwalia, M. S., Bell, C. L. G., Duloy, J. H. and Jolly, R. (1974), *Redistribution with Growth*, Oxford University Press, London, for the World Bank.

Chenery, H. B. and Syrquin, R. (1975), *Patterns of Development 1950–70*, Oxford University Press, London, for the World Bank.

Colonial Office (1900), *Confidential Correspondence on Native States in the Malay Peninsula 1860–1894*, London.

Coppock, J. D. (1962), *International Economic Instability. The Experience after World War II*, McGraw-Hill, New York.

Corden, W. M. (1971), *The Theory of Protection*, Oxford University Press, London.

Crosson, P. R. (1964) 'Exports and economic growth: Malaya, a case study', Working Paper for National Planning Association, Washington, D.C., mimeographed.

Cutajar, M. Z. and Franks, A. (1967), *The Less Developed Countries in World Trade. A Reference Handbook*, ODI, London.

Dales, J. H., McManus, A. and Watkins, M. H. (1967) 'Primary products and economic growth: a comment', *Canadian J. Econ. & polit. Sci.*, December.

Dasgupta, B. (1974) 'Large international firms in the oil industry', *IDS Bulletin*, October.

Dellar, L. V. (1963), *The World of Tin*, Oxford University Press, KL.

Doyle, P. (1879), *Tin Mining In Larut*, E. and F. N. Spon, London.

Drabble, J. H. (1967) 'The plantation rubber industry in Malaya up to 1922', *Journal of the Malaysian Branch, Royal Asiatic Society*, 1.
Drabble, J. H. (1973), *Rubber in Malaya, 1876–1922. The Genesis of the Industry*, Oxford University Press, KL.
Drabble, J. H. and Drake, P. J. (1974) 'More on the financing of Malayan rubber 1905–23', *Econ. Hist. R.*, 1.
Drake, P. J. (1969) 'The new issue boom in Malaya and Singapore 1961–64', *Econ. Develop. cult. Change*, 1, reprinted in Lim 1975, to which page numbers refer.
Drake, P. J. (1972) 'Natural resources *vs.* foreign borrowing in economic development', *Econ. J.*, September.
Dunning, J. H. (1964) 'Capital movements in the 20th century', *Lloyds Bank Review*, April.
ECAFE (1962), *Electric Power in Asia and the Far East 1956–60*, Bangkok.
ECAFE (1972), *Report of the Asian Industrial Development Council Consultative Mission on the Oil Palm Industry*, Bangkok.
Eckhaus, R. S. (1955) 'The factor proportions problem in underdeveloped areas', *Amer. econ. R.*, September.
Edwards, C. B. (1975) 'Protection, profits, and policy: an analysis of industrialization in Malaysia', *Ph.D. thesis* (in two volumes), University of East Anglia, Norwich.
Edwards, C. T. (1970), *Public Finance in Malaya and Singapore*, Australian National University Press, Canberra.
Electricity Dept. (of FMS, MU, FM, Malaysia)—references cited in full in text using abbreviations set out on pp. xv–xvi.
Ellis, F. (1974) 'Diary of events in the oil market 1971–74'; and 'Statistical background', *IDS Bulletin*, October.
Emery, R. F. (1967) 'The relation of exports and economic growth', *Kyklos*, 2.
Emmanuel, A. (1972), *Unequal Exchange: A Study of the Imperialism of Trade*, New Left Books, London.
Evans, D. (1975) 'Unequal exchange and economic policies: some implications of the neoRicardian critique of the theory of comparative advantage', *IDS Bulletin*, March.
Federated Malay States—reference to FMS documents such as *Annual Report* of Secretary General are cited in full in the text, using abbreviations shown on pp. xv–xvi, except:
FMS (1938), *Methods and Conditions of Employment of Chinese Labour in the Federated Malay States.*
FMS Railways (1935), *Fifty Years of Railways in Malaya, 1885–1935.*
Federation of Malaya (1952) *Progress Report on the Development Plan of the Federation of Malaya 1950–52*, KL.
Federation of Malaya (1954) *Report of the Mission of Enquiry into the Rubber Industry of Malaya* (the '*Mudie Report*').
Federation of Malaya (1955) *Taxation and Replanting in the Rubber Industry. Statement of the Federal Government on the Report of the Mudie Mission and on Certain Proposals made by the Rubber Producers Council*, KL.
Federation of Malaya (1961) *Second Five Year Plan 1961–65*, KL.
Federation of Malaya (1963a) *Interim Review of Development in Malaya under the Second Five-Year Plan*, KL.
Federation of Malaya (1963b) *Report of the Subdivision of Estates Committee*, KL.
Fei, J. C. H. and Ranis, G. (1964), *Development of the Labor Surplus Economy*, Irwin, Homewood, Illinois.

Fei, J. C. H. and Ranis, G. (1971) 'Development and employment in open dualistic economy', *Malayan econ. R.*, October.

FELDA (undated), *The Role of Land Settlement in the Economic Development of West Malaysia.*

FELDA (1966), *Land Settlement in Malaysia under the FLDA.*

FELDA (1967), *Jengka Triangle Report.*

FELDA (1970), *A Review of the FLDA, its Policies and Operations.*

FELDA *Annual Reports* are cited in full in text.

Fermor, Sir L. L. (1939), *Report upon the Mining Industry of Malaya,* Government Printer, KL.

Figart, D. M. (1925), *The Plantation Rubber Industry in the Middle East,* U.S. Government Printing Office, Washington DC.

Findlay, R. (1973), *International Trade and Development Theory.* Columbia University Press, New York.

Firth, R. and Yamey, B. S. (Eds.) (1964), *Capital, Saving and Credit in Peasant Societies. Studies from Asia, Oceania, the Caribbean and Middle America,* Allen and Unwin, London.

Fisk, E. K. (1961) 'Productivity and income from rubber in an established Malay reservation', *Malayan econ. R.*, April.

Flanders, M. J. (1964) 'Prebisch on protectionism: an evaluation', *Econ. J.*, June.

Fox, W. (1974), *Tin. The Working of a Commodity Agreement,* Mining Journal Books, London.

Frank, A. G. (1966) 'The development of underdevelopment', *Monthly Review,* September, reprinted in Rhodes (1970), to which page numbers refer.

Fryer, D. W. and Jackson, J. C. (1966) 'Peasant producers or urban planters? The Chinese rubber smallholders of Ulu Selangor', *Pacific Viewpoint,* September.

Gamba, C. (1962), *The National Union of Plantation Workers,* Donald Moore, Singapore.

GATT (1974), *International Trade 1973–74,* Geneva.

Giersch, H. (Ed.) (1974), *The International Division of Labour. Problems and Perspectives,* Mohr, Tubingen.

Girvan, N. (1970) 'Multinational corporations and dependent underdevelopment in mineral export economies, *Soc. econ. Stud.*, 4.

Graham, D. J. and Morris, J. E. (1968) 'New processes and the SMR scheme', *Planters' Bulletin,* November.

Green, R. H. and Singer, H. W. (1975) 'Towards a rational and equitable new international economic order: a case for negotiated structural changes', *World Development,* June.

Greenwood, J. M. F. (1964) 'Rubber smallholdings in the Federation of Malaya', *Journal of Tropical Geography,* August.

Griffiths, H. D. (1917), *Bucket-Dredging for Tin in the Federated Malay States,* reprinted in book form by the publishers of *The Mining Magazine*, London.

Grindlays Bank Review (1975) 'What help for commodities', November.

Grist, D. H. (1930) 'The Malayan oil palm industry in 1929', *Malayan Agricultural Journal,* July.

Grubel, H. G. (1967) 'Intra-industry specialization and the pattern of trade', *Canad. J. Econ. & polit. Sci.*, August.

Gul, A. M. F. (1968), 'Wages and prices with reference to the rubber industry in West Malaysia', BA Graduation Exercise, University of Malaya, KL.

Harris, J. H. (1959) 'Innovations in gravel pump treatment plant, *Mining Journal,* January–February.

Harris, J. R. (1970) 'Migration, unemployment, and development: a two-sector analysis', *Amer. econ. R.*

Harris, S. and Hagelberg, G. B. (1975) 'Effects of the Lomé convention on the world's cane-sugar producers, *ODI Review,* 2.

Harvie, C. H. (1964) 'Export multipliers and the stability of the Federation of Malaya's economy, *Malayan econ. R.*, April.

Helleiner, G. K. (1972), *International Trade and Economic Development,* Penguin Books, London.

Helleiner, G. K. (1973) 'Manufactured exports from less developed countries and multinational firms, *Econ. J.*, March.

Helm, A. R. (1969) 'Some aspects of postwar agricultural policy in West Malaysia', *M.Sc* (Econ.) *thesis,* University of Hull.

Hicks, G. L. and McNicholl, G. (1971), *Trade and Growth in the Phillipines. An Open Dual Economy,* Cornell University Press, Ithaca and London.

Hicks, J. R. (1959), *Essays in World Economics,* Oxford University Press, London.

Hilgerdt, F. (1945), *Industrialization and Foreign Trade,* League of Nations, Geneva.

Hirschleifer, J. (1958) 'On the theory of the optimal investment decision', *J. polit. Econ.*

Hirschman, A. O. (1958), *The Strategy of Economic Development,* Yale University Press, New Haven.

Hodgkinson, E. (1975) 'The international development situation: reacting to recession', *ODI Review,* 2.

Hoffmann, L. and Tan Siew Ee (1973) 'Employment creation through export growth: a case study of West Malaysia's manufacturing industries', Kiel conference 'Verein for Socialpolitik' paper, reprinted in Lim (1975), to which page numbers refer.

Hornby, J. M. (1968) 'Investment and trade policy in a dual economy', *Econ. J.*, March.

Huang, Y. (1972) 'Some reflections on padi double-cropping in West Malaysia', *Malayan econ. R.*, April, reprinted in Lim (1975), to which page numbers refer.

Huggins, H.D. (1965), *Aluminium in Changing Communities,* Deutsch, London.

Hughes, J. R. T. (1959) 'Foreign trade and balanced growth: the historical framework', *Amer. econ. R. Papers and Proceedings,* May.

IBRD (1955), *The Economic Development of Malaya. Report of a Mission,* John Hopkins Press, Baltimore.

IBRD (1963), *Report on the Economic Aspects of Malaysia,* KL.

IBRD (1973), *Commodity Trade and Price Trends,* report prepared by the Commodities and Export Projections Division, Washington, DC.

IMF (1975), *IMF Survey*—Tokyo Round Issue, 10 March, Washington, DC.

Innis, H. A. (1930), *The Fur Trade in Canada. An Introduction to Canadian Economic History,* page numbers refer to revised edn. prepared by S. D. Clark and W. T. Easterbrook, University of Toronto Press, 1962.

Innis, H. A. (1956), *Essays in Canadian Economic History* (Ed. M. Q. Innis), University of Toronto Press.

Jackson, J. C. (1968), *Planters and Speculators. Chinese and European Agricultural Enterprise in Malaya, 1786–1921,* University of Malaya Press, KL.

Jackson, R. N. (1961), *Immigrant Labour and the Development of Malaya, 1786–1920,* Government Printer, KL.

Jeffress, R. (1972) 'Establishing and operating a foundry in Malaysia', *South East Asian Steel Industry Quarterly*, October.

Johns, B. L. (1973) 'Import substitution and export potential—the case of manufacturing industry in West Malaysia', *Austral. econ. Pap.*, December.

Johnson, H. G. (1967), *Economic Policies towards Less Developed Countries*, Allen and Unwin, London.

Johnson, H. G. (Ed.) (1971), *Trade Strategy for Rich and Poor Nations*, Allen & Unwin, London.

Jolly, R. (1975) 'Redistribution with growth—a reply', *IDS Bulletin*, August.

Jones, W. R. (1925), *Tinfields of the World*, Mining Publications, London.

Kenen, P. B. and Voivodas, C. S. (1972) 'Export instability and economic growth', *Kyklos*.

Khoo Swee Joo (1964) 'The Malayan oil palm industry', *Kajian Ekonomi Malaysia*, June.

Kidron, M. (1973) 'Imperialism. Highest stage but one' and 'International capitalism', *International Socialism* (originally published in 1962 and 1965, respectively).

Kilby, P. (1972) 'Farm and factory: a comparison of the skill requirements for the transfer of technology', *J. Develop. Stud.*, October.

Kravis, I. B. (1970) 'Trade as a handmaiden of growth: similarities between the nineteenth and twentieth centuries', *Econ. J.*, December.

Kuznets, S. (1966), *Modern Economic Growth. Rate, Structure and Spread*, Yale University Press, New Haven.

Labour Dept. (FMS, MU, FM)—references to publications are cited in full in text using the abbreviations set out on pp. xv–xvi.

Lall, S. (1973) 'Transfer pricing by multinational manufacturing firms', *Oxford Bulletin of Economics and Statistics*, August.

Lary, H. B. (1968), *Imports of Manufactures from Less Developed Countries*, Columbia University Press, New York.

Lee, J. K. (1971) 'Exports and the propensity to save in less developed countries', *Econ. J.*, June.

Lee Thong Cheong (1966) 'A study of employment and wage structure in European dredges and Chinese tin mining in Malaya', BA Graduation Exercise, 1965–66, University of Malaya, KL.

Lenin, V. I. (1917), *Imperialism. The Highest Stage of Capitalism. A Popular Outline*, reprinted in *The Essentials of Lenin in Two Volumes*, Lawrence and Wishart, London, 1947, to which page numbers refer.

Levin, J. V. (1960), *The Export Economies. Their Pattern of Development in Historical Perspective* Harvard University Press, Cambridge, Mass.

Lewis, W. A. (1952) 'World production, prices and trade, 1870–1960, *Manchester Sch. econ. soc. Stud.*, May.

Lewis, W. A. (1954) 'Economic development with unlimited supplies of labour', *Manchester Sch. econ. soc. Stud.*, May.

Lewis, W. A. (1958) 'Unlimited labour: further notes', *Manchester Sch. econ. soc. Stud.*, January.

Lewis, W. A. (1969), *Aspects of Tropical Trade 1883–1965*, Almqvist and Wiksell, Stockholm (the 1969 Wicksell lectures).

Lewis, W. A. (1970), *Tropical Development 1880–1913. Studies in Economic Progress*, Allen & Unwin, London.

Leys, C. (1975a) 'The politics of redistribution with growth', *IDS Bulletin*, August.

Leys, C. (1975b), *Underdevelopment in Kenya. The Political Economy of Neocolonialism 1964–71*, Heinemann, London.

Li, D. J. (1955), *British Malaya. An Economic Analysis*, The American Press, New York.

Lim Chong Yah (1967), *Economic Development of Modern Malaya*, Oxford University Press, KL.

Lim, D. (1969) 'The supply response of tin miners in Malaysia', *Kajian Ekonomi Malaysia*, December.

Lim, D. (1970) 'Export-orientated industrialization: a case study of Malaysia', *Kajian Ekonomi Malaysia*, December.

Lim, D. (1973), *Economic Growth and Development in West Malaysia 1947–70*, Oxford University Press, KL.

Lim, D. (1974) 'Export instability and economic development: the example of West Malaysia', *Oxford econ. Pap.*

Lim, D. (1975), *Readings on Malaysian Economic Development*, Oxford University Press, KL.

Lim Sow Ching (1968a) 'Analysis of smallholders' rubber marketing in West Malaysia, Natural Rubber Conference, KL, 1968, preprint.

Lim Sow Ching (1968b), *A Study of the Marketing of Smallholders' Rubber at the First Trade Level in Selangor*, RRIM, *Economic Report*, No. 4, KL.

Lim Sow Ching (1972) 'Economic viability of future smallholdings', in Rajarao and Foo (1972).

Lim Sow Ching and Chong, K. M. (1973) 'Merits of estate participation and incentive wage system in public sector land development', in Rajarao and Foo (1973).

Lim Sow Ching and Chong, K. M. (1974) 'Replanting cess and replanting on estates', in Sim (1974).

Lim Sow Ching, Ho, Y. C. and Yoon, P. K. (1973) 'Economics of maximizing early yields and shorter immaturity', in Rajarao and Foo (1973).

Lim Sow Ching and Ghazali Noor (1974) 'Use of public funds on unsatisfactory land schemes', in Sim (1974).

Lim, Y. (1968a) 'Impact of the tea economy on the growth of the Ceylonese economy', *Soc. econ. Stud.*, December.

Lim, Y. (1968b) 'Trade and growth: the case of Ceylon', *Econ. Develop. cult. Change*, 2.

Linder, S. B. (1961), *An Essay on Trade and Transformation*, Almqvist and Wiksell, Stockholm.

Linder, S. B. (1967), *Trade and Trade Policy for Development*, Pall Mall Press, London.

Little, I. M. D. (1975) 'Economic relations with the third world—old myths and new prospects', *Scott. J. polit. Econ.*, November.

Little, I. M. D. and Mirrlees, J. (1968), *Manual of Industrial Project Analysis in Developing Countries* (in two volumes), Organization for Economic Cooperation and Development, Paris.

Little, I. M. D. and Mirrlees, J. (1972) 'A reply to some criticisms of the OECD manual', *B. Oxford Univ. Inst. Econ. Statist.*, **1**.

Little, I. M. D. and Mirrlees, J. (1974), *Project Appraisal and Planning for Developing Countries*, Heinemann, London.

Little, I. M. D., Scitovsky, T. and Scott, M. F. (1970), *Industry and Trade in Some Developing Countries. A Comparative Study*, Oxford University Press, London.

Little, I. M. D. and Tipping, D. G. (1972), *A Social Cost Benefit Analysis of the Kulai Oil Palm Estate*, OECD, Paris.

Lo Sum Yee (1972), *The Development Performance of West Malaysia 1955–67*, Heinemann, KL.

Lydall, H. F. (1975a), *Trade and Employment. A Study of the Effects of Trade Expansion on Employment in Developing and Developed Countries*, International Labour Office, Geneva.

Lydall, H. F. (1975b) 'Employment effects of trade expansion', *International Labour Review*.

Ma, R. (1959) 'Company profits and prices in the rubber industry in Malaya 1947–58', *Malayan econ. R.*, October.

MacBean, A. I. (1966), *Export Instability and Economic Development*, Allen and Unwin, London.

MacDougall, G. D. A. (1960) 'The benefits and costs of foreign investment from abroad. A theoretical approach', *Econ. Rec.*

McHale, T. R. (1965) 'Rubber smallholding in Malaya. Their changing role and prospects', *Malayan econ. R.*, October.

McHale, T. R. (1967), *Rubber and the Malaysian Economy*, MPH Publications, Singapore.

Maizels, A. (1968a), *Exports and Economic Growth of Developing Countries. A Theoretical and Empirical Study of the Relationship between Exports and Economic Growth, with Illustrative Projections for 1975 for the Main Overseas Sterling Countries*, Cambridge University Press, London.

Maizels, A. (1968b) review of MacBean (1966), *Amer. econ. R.*, June.

Malaya/Malaysia—reference to documents published under this heading are cited in full in the text, using abbreviations set out as pp. xv–xvi.

Malay Mail, The (1969 and 1970), *Malaysia Yearbook, 1968–69, and 1970*, Straits Times Press, KL.

Mamajiwala, P. K. (1963) 'Ownership and control of public limited rubber companies incorporated in the Federation of Malaya, 1948–58, *MA thesis*, University of Malaya, KL.

Mamalakis, M. and Reynolds, C. W. (1965), *Essays on the Chilean Economy*, Irwin, Homewood, Illinois.

Manning, C. (1971) 'The timber boom with special reference to Kalimantan', *Bulletin of Indonesian Economic Studies*, November.

Marco, L. E. di (1972), *International Economics and Development* (Essays in honour of R. Prebisch), Academic Press, New York.

Meerhaeghe, M. A. G. van (1966), *International Economic Institutions*, Longmans Green, London.

Meier, G. M. (1953) 'The problem of limited economic development', *Econ. int. (Genova)*, 4.

Meier, G. M. (1958) 'International trade and international inequality', *Oxford econ. Pap.*, October.

Meier, G. M. (1968), *The International Economics of Development*, Harper, New York.

Meier, G. M. (1973), *Problems of Trade Policy*, Oxford University Press, New York.

Meier, G. M. (1974), *Problems of Cooperation for Development*, Oxford University Press, New York.

Melvin, J. R. (1969) 'Demand conditions and immiserizing growth', *Amer. econ. R.*,

September.
Mikesell, R. F. (Ed.) (1971), *Foreign Investment in the Petroleum and Mineral Industries. Case Studies in Investor–Host Country Relations,* John Hopkins Press, Baltimore.
Mill, J. S. (1848), *Principles of Political Economy with some of their Applications to Social Philosophy,* New impression, Longmans Green, London, 1900, to which page numbers refer.
Mincing Lane Tea and Rubber Share Brokers Association Ltd. (1925), *Rubber Producing Companies 1924. Official Guide for Investors in Rubber Shares,* privately published, London.
Mines Dept. (FMS, MU, FM)—references cited in full in text using abbreviations set out on pp. xv–xvi.
Ministry of Agriculture (1960), *Census of Agriculture,* KL.
Ministry of Agriculture (1966), *The Oil Palm in Malaya,* KL.
Ministry of Labour (FM, Malaysia)—references to publications are cited in full in the text using the abbreviations set out on pp. xv–xvi.
Ministry of Lands and Mines (Malaysia)—references cited in full in text using abbreviations set out on pp. xv–xvi.
Morris, J. E. (1964) 'Sole crepe', *Planters' Bulletin,* September.
Munro, G. R. (1973a and 1973b) 'The Malaysian balance of payments to 1980', Parts I and II, *Kajian Ekonomi Malaysia,* June and December, reprinted in Lim (1975), to which page numbers refer.
Myint, H. (1954) 'An interpretation of economic backwardness', *Oxford econ. Pap.,* June.
Myint, H. (1954–5) 'The gain from international trade and the backward countries', *R. econ. Stud.*
Myint, H. (1958) 'The "classical" theory of international trade and the underdeveloped countries', *Econ. J.,* June.
Myint, H. (1965) 'Economic theory and the underdeveloped countries', *J. polit. Econ.,* October.
Myint, H. (1967), *The Economics of the Developing Countries,* Hutchinson, London, 3rd edn.
Myint, H. (1972), *Southeast Asia's Economy. Development Policies in the 1970's,* Penguin, London.
Myrdal, G. (1956a), *An International Economy,* Routledge, London.
Myrdal, G. (1956b), *Development and Underdevelopment. A Note on the Mechanism of National and International Inequality,* National Bank of Egypt, Cairo.
Myrdal, G. (1957), *Economic Theory and Underdeveloped Regions,* Duckworth, London.
Myrdal, G. (1968), *Asian Drama, An Enquiry into the Poverty of Nations,* Penguin Books, London.
Nair, S. and Lee, A. K. (1972) 'Speciality natural rubbers in relation to the SMR scheme', in Rajarao and Foo (1972).
National and Grindlays Review (1974) 'The riddle of rice', February.
National Operations Council (Malaysia) (1969), *The May 13 Tragedy, A Report,* KL.
Ness, G. D. (1967), *Bureaucracy and Rural Development in Malaysia. A Study of Complex Organisations in Stimulating Economic Growth in New States,* University of California Press, Berkeley.

Ng Choong Sooi (1967) 'Some aspects of estate replanting and new planting costs, *Planters' Bulletin,* October.
Ng Choong Sooi (1969) 'Economic aspects of replanting on rubber estates', *M.Sc*(Agric.) *thesis,* University of Malaya, KL.
Ng Choong Sooi (1972) 'Profitability of investments in replanting and new planting on estates', in Rajarao and Foo (1972).
Ng Choong Sooi, Barlow, C. and Chan Chee Kheong (1968) 'Factors affecting the profitability of rubber production on West Malaysian estates', Natural Rubber Conference, KL, 1968, preprint.
Ng Eng Kok, Ng Choong Sooi and Lee Chew Kang (1968) 'Economic analysis of tapping experiments', Natural Rubber Conference, KL, 1968, preprint.
Noor bin Wahab, Mohd. and Arun, K. C. (1968) 'Smallholdings in West Malaysia', Natural Rubber Conference, KL, 1968, preprint.
North, D. C. (1955) 'Location theory and regional economic growth', *J. polit. Econ.,* June.
North, D. C. (1959) 'Agriculture in regional economic growth', *Journal of Farm Economics,* December.
North, D. C. (1966), *The Economic Growth of the United States, 1790–1869,* Norton, New York.
Nurkse, R. (1953), *Problems of Capital Formation in Underdeveloped Countries,* Oxford University Press, London.
Nurkse, R. (1962), *Patterns of Trade and Development,* Basil Blackwell Ltd., Oxford (the 1959 Wicksell lectures).
Ooi Jin Bee (1955), 'Mining Landscapes of Kinta', *Malayan Journal of Tropical Geography,* reprinted in Silcock (1961), to which page numbers refer.
Osborne, F. D. (1920) 'Hydraulic mining in the Federated Malay States', *Mining World,* March.
Oxaal, I., Barnett, T. and Booth, D. (Eds.) (1975), *Beyond the Sociology of Development. Economy and Society in Latin America and Africa,* Routledge and Kegan Paul, London.
Pahang Consolidated (1967), *Sixty Years of Tin Mining. A History of the Pahang Consolidated Company, 1906–1966,* London.
Parkinson, B. K. (1967) 'Non-economic factors in the economic retardation of the rural Malays', *Mod. Asian. Stud.,* January, reprinted in Lim (1975), to which page numbers refer.
Parmer, J. N. (1960), *Colonial Labor Policy and Administration. A History of Labor in the Rubber Plantation Industry in Malaya, 1910–1941,* J. J. Augustin, New York.
Pearce, D. W. (1975), *The Economics of Natural Resource Depletion,* Macmillan, London.
Pearson, S. R. and Cownie, J. (1974), *Commodity Exports and African Economic Development,* Heath, Lexington.
Prain, R. (1975), *Copper. The Anatomy of an Industry,* Mining Journal Books, London.
Prebisch, R. (1962) 'The economic development of Latin America and its principal problems', *UN Economic Bulletin for Latin America,* February.
Prebisch, R. (1963), *Towards a Dynamic Development Policy for Latin America,* UN, New York.
Prebisch, R. (1964), *Towards a New Trade Policy for Development,* UNCTAD, New

York.
Prime Minister's Dept. (Malaysia) (1966), *First Malaysia Plan, 1966–70*, KL.
Prime Minister's Dept. (1969), *Mid-Term Review of the First Malaysia Plan, 1966–70*, KL.
Prime Minister's Dept. (1971), *Second Malaysia Plan 1971–75*, KL.
Prime Minister's Dept. (1973), *Mid-Term Review of the Second Malaysia Plan*, KL.
Purcal, J. T. (1975) 'Employment pattern in the rice growing areas of West Malaysia', in Lim (1975).
Purcell, V. (1948), *The Chinese in Malaya*, Oxford University Press, London.
Pushparaja, E, Mohd. Johar bin Mohd. Rashid, Subramaniam, S, Ti, T. C. and Yoon, P. K. (1973) 'Towards modernization of smallholders', in Sim (1974).
Pushparaja, E., Chan, H. Y. and Ti, T. C. (1974) 'Organization of land use for rubber and oil palm', in Sim (1974).
Putucheary, J. J. (1960), *Ownership and Control in the Malayan Economy*, Eastern Universities Press, Singapore.
Railways Dept./Railways Administration (FMS, MU, FM)—Annual Reports cited in full in text.
Rajarao, J. C. and Foo Kah Yoon (Eds.) (1972), *Proceedings of the RRIM Planters' Conference 1972*, KL.
Rajarao, J. C. and Foo Kah Yoon (Eds.) (1973), *Proceedings of the RRIM Planters' Conference 1973*, KL.
Rao, V. K. R. V. (1952) 'Investment, income and the multiplier', *Indian econ. R.*
Reddaway, W. B. (1968), *Effects of UK Direct Investment Overseas: Final Report*, Cambridge Univerity Press, London.
Rhodes, R. I. (Ed.) (1970), *Imperialism and Underdevelopment. A Reader*, Monthly Review Press, New York.
Ricardo, D. (1817), *The Principles of Political Economy and Taxation*, Modern Library edition, J. M. Dent, London.
Robertson, D. H. (1938) 'The future of international trade', *Econ. J.*, March.
Robinson, J. (1971), *Economic Heresies. Some Old Fashioned Questions in Economic Theory*, Macmillan, London.
Rowe, J. W. F. (1965), *Primary Commodities in International Trade*, Cambridge University Press, London.
RRIM (1967), *The Estate Management Handbook*, Economic Report No 3, KL.
RRIM (1968), *Guide to Estate Management*, Economic Report No 5, KL.
Rudner, M. (1970) 'The state and peasant innovation in rural development: the case of Malaysian rubber', *Asian Afr. Stud.*, reprinted in Lim (1975), to which page numbers refer.
Rudner, M. (1971) 'The Malayan quandary: rural development policy under the first and second five-year plans', *Contributions to Asian Studies*, reprinted in Lim (1975), to which page numbers refer.
Sandhu, K. S. (1969), *Indians in Malaya: Immigration and Settlement 1786–1959*, Cambridge University Press, London.
Schweinberger, A. G. (1975) 'The Heckscher–Ohlin model and traded intermediate products', *R. econ. Stud.*, April.
Scitovsky, T. (1964), *Papers on Welfare and Growth*, Allen and Unwin, London.
Selvadurai, S. (1972), *Padi Farming in West Malaysia*, Ministry of Agriculture and Fisheries, KL.

Selvaratnam, V. (1974) 'Decolonization, the ruling elite and ethnic relations in Peninsular Malaysia', *IDS Discussion Paper* No. 44, Sussex.

Selwyn, P. (1975) 'Trade expansion, employment and country selectivity', *IDS Bulletin*, March.

Sen, A. K. (1966) 'Peasants and dualism with or without surplus labor', *J. polit. Econ.*, October.

Sen, A. K. (1975), *Employment, Technology, and Development*, Clarendon Press, Oxford.

Sethu, S., Soh York Beng and Hoo Hok Kim (1972) 'Present trends in new rubber processing methods', in Rajarao and Foo (1972).

Sharpson, M. (1975) 'International sub-contracting', *Oxford econ. Pap.*, March.

Short, A. (1975), *The Communist Insurrection in Malaya, 1948–1960*, Muller, London.

Silcock, T. H. (Ed.) (1961), *Readings in Malayan Economics*, Eastern Universities Press, Singapore.

Silcock, T. H. and Fisk, E. K. (Eds.) (1963), *The Political Economy of Independent Malaya. A Case Study in Development*, University of California Press, Berkeley.

Sim Lee Ling (Ed.) (1974), *Proceedings of the RRIM Planters' Conference 1974*, KL.

Singer, H. W. (1950) 'The distribution of gains between investing and borrowing countries', *Amer. econ. R., Papers and Proceedings*, May.

Singer, H. W. (1970) 'Dualism revisited: a new approach to the problems of the dual society in developing countries', *J. Develop. Stud.*, October.

Singer, H. W. (1975a) 'The distribution of gains from trade and investment—revisited', *J. Develop. Stud.*, July.

Singer, H. W. (1975b) 'Trade expansion, employment, and income distribution', *IDS Bulletin*, March.

Singer, H. W. *et al.* (1973) 'Trade liberalization, employment and income distribution. A first approach', *IDS Discussion paper*, No 31, Sussex (with eight other authors).

Smith, A. (1776), *An Enquiry into the Nature and Causes of the Wealth of Nations*, Methuen, London, 1930 edn., Vol 1, Ed. E. Cannon.

Snodgrass, D. R. (1974) 'The fiscal system as an income redistributor in West Malaysia', *Publ. Finance*, **1**, reprinted in Lim (1975), to which page numbers refer.

Snodgrass, D. R. (1975) 'Trends and patterns in Malaysian income distribution, 1957–70', in Lim (1975).

Solo, R. (1966) 'The capacity to assimilate an advanced technology', *Amer. econ. R.*, **1**.

Spooner, R. J. (1969) 'Elements of importance in feasibility studies for oil palm development enterprises in Malaysia', in Turner (1969).

Sraffa, P. (1960), *Production of Commodities by Means of Commodities. Prelude to a Critique of Economic Theory*, Cambridge University Press, London.

Stahl, K. M. (1951), *The Metropolitan Organization of British Colonial Trade. Four Regional Studies*, Faber and Faber, London.

Statistics Dept. (MU, FM, Malaysia)—publications of the Statistics Department are cited in full in the text, using the abbreviations set out on pp. xv-xvi.

Stewart, F. (1972) 'Choice of technique in developing countries', *J. Develop. Stud.*, October.

Stewart, F. and Streeten, P. P. (1971), 'Conflicts between output and employment objectives in developing countries', *Oxford econ. Pap.*, **2**.

Stewart, F. and Streeten, P. P. (1972) 'Little–Mirrlees methods and project appraisal', *B. Oxford Univ. Inst. Econ. Statist*, February.

Stigler, G. J. (1951) 'The division of labor is limited by the extent of the market', *J. polit. Econ.*, June.

Stillson, R. T. (1971) 'The financing of Malayan rubber, 1905–23', *Econ. Hist. R.*

Stillson, R. T. (1974) 'The financing of Malayan rubber, 1905–23: reply', *Econ. Hist. R.*, 1.

Stock Exchange of Malaysia and Singapore (1970 and 1973), *Company Reports. Handbook of Malaysian and Singapore Companies on the Official List*, privately published, Singapore.

Straits Settlements—publications of the SS are cited in full in the text, using the abbreviations set out on pp. xv–xvi.

Straits Times, The (1970), *The Straits Times Directory 1970*, Straits Times Press.

Straits Times, The (1973–6), Monthly Survey of Singapore and Malaysia, Singapore.

Streeten, P. P. (1961) *Economic Integration*, A. W. Sythoff, Leyden.

Streeten, P. P. (1971) 'Technology gaps between rich and poor countries', *Kajian Ekonomi Malaysia*, June.

Sumitro Djojohadikusumo (1968), *Trade and Aid in South-East Asia*, Vol. I, *Malaysia and Singapore*, F. W. Cheshire Publishing, Melbourne.

Swerling, B. C. (1961) 'Some interrelationships between agricultural trade and economic development', *Kyklos*.

Swettenham, Sir F. A. (1907), *British Malaya. An Account of the Origin and Progress of British Influence in Malaya*, Allen and Unwin, London.

Swift, M. G. (1965), *Malay Peasant Society in Jelebu*, The Athlone Press, London.

Syed Hussain Wafa (1972 and 1973) 'Land development stategies in Malaysia: an empirical study' (in two parts), *Kajian Ekonomi Malaysia,* December issues.

Szereszewski, R. (1965), *Structural Changes in the Economy of Ghana, 1891–1911*, Weidenfeld and Nicholson, London.

Taib, H. A. (1968), *The Application of Strategy to Tactics: FLDA, a Case Study*, FELDA, KL.

Tan, A. H. H. (1967) 'The incidence of export taxes on small producers', *Malayan econ. R.*

Tan Theong Hean (1966) 'A study of the sources and nature of credit in Chinese tin mining in Malaya', BA Graduation Exercise, University of Malaya, KL, 1965–66.

Theberge, J. D. (Ed.) (1968), *Economics of Trade and Development*, Wiley, New York.

Thoburn, J. T. (1970) 'Ownership of shares in UK-incorporated public rubber planting and tin dredging companies in Malaysia', *Kajian Ekonomi Malaysia*, December.

Thoburn, J. T. (1971) 'Export expansion and economic development in West Malaysia', unpublished report to Overseas Development Administration, Foreign and Commonwealth Office, London.

Thoburn, J. T. (1973a) 'Exports and economic growth in West Malaysia', *Oxford econ. Pap.*, March, reprinted in Lim (1975).

Thoburn, J. T. (1973b) 'Exports and the Malaysian engineering industry. A case study of backward linkage', *Oxford Bulletin of Economics and Statistics*, May, reprinted in Lim (1975).

Thoburn, J. T. (1976), 'Commodity prices and appropriate technology: some lessons from tin mining', *J. Develop. Stud.*, forthcoming.

Thomas, P. O. and Allen, P. W. (1973) 'Some aspects of competition between natural and synthetic rubber', in Rajarao and Foo (1973).

Thomas, P. O. and Fong Chu Chai (1968), *Rubber Industry Statistics*, RRIM, KL.

Thorbecke, E. (1973) 'The employment problem: a critical evaluation of four ILO comprehensive country reports', *International Labour Review*, June.

Treasury, The (1974–5), (annual) *Economic Report*, KL.

Tregonning, K. C. (undated), *Straits Tin. A Brief History of the First Seventy-five Years of the Straits Trading Company, 1887–1962*, Straits Times Press, Singapore.

Turner, P. D. (Ed.) (1968), *Oil Palm Developments in Malaysia,* Proceedings of the First Malaysian Oil Palm Conference, sponsored by the Incorporated Society of Planters and the Agricultural Institute of Malaysia, and held in Kuala Lumpur, November, 1967.

Turner, P. D. (Ed.) (1969), *Progress in Oil Palm*, Proceedings of the Second Malaysian Oil Palm Conference, sponsored by the Incorporated Society of Planters, held in Kuala Lumpur, November 1968.

UN (1968), *Mining Developments in Asia and the Far East*, New York.

UNCTAD (1972), *Handbook of International Trade and Development Statistics*, New York.

UNCTAD (1974), *Report of the Trade and Development Board 1973–4*, New York.

UNESCO (1972), *International Bibliography of Economics*, prepared for International Committee for Social Science Information and Documentation, Tavistock Publications, London.

United Engineers Group (undated), *Progress: United Engineers*, KL (probably published *c*1968).

Vernon, R. (1966) 'International investment and international trade in the product cycle', *Quart. J. Econ*.

Viner, J. (1953), *International Trade and Economic Development*, Lectures delivered at the National University of Brazil, Oxford University Press, London.

Voon Phin Keong (1967) 'Chinese rubber smallholdings industry in Selangor', *MA Thesis*, University of Malaya, KL.

Wang Gungwu (Ed.) (1964), *Malaysia: A Survey*, Pall Mall Press, London.

Warnford-Lock, G. C. (1907), *Mining in Malaya for Gold and Tin*, Crowther and Goodman, London.

Watkins, M. H. (1963) 'A staple theory of economic growth', *Canadian J. Econ. & polit. Sci.*, May.

Wells, S. J. (1965), *Trade and International Inequality*, Fabian Society, London.

Wheelwright, E. L. (1965), *Industrialization in Malaysia*, Melbourne University Press, Melbourne.

Wikkramatileke, R. (1972) 'Federal Land Development Authority in West Malaysia 1957–71', *Pacific Viewpoint,* May, reprinted in Lim (1975) to which page numbers refer.

Wilson, T., Sinha, R. P. and Castree, J. R. (1969) 'The income terms of trade of developed and developing countries', *Econ. J.*, December.

Winstedt, Sir R. O. (1968), *A History of Malaya*, Marican & Sons, KL, 3rd edn. revised.

Wolf, C. and Sufrin, S. C. (1955), *Capital Formation and Foreign Investment in Underdeveloped Areas*, Syracuse University Press, Syracuse.

Wong Lin Ken, (1965), *The Malayan Tin Industry to 1914, with special reference to the States of Perak, Selangor, Negri Sembilan and Pahang*, Arizona University Press, Tucson.

Wood, R. (1975) 'Justice, power and commerce in the new international economic order', *ODI Review*, 2.

Yates, P. L. (1959), *Forty Years of Foreign Trade*, Allen and Unwin, London.

Yip Yat Hoong (1959) 'The marketing of tin ore in Kampar', *Malayan econ. R.*, October.

Yip Yat Hoong, (1964) 'Post war international tin control with special reference to Malaysia', *Kajian Ekonomi Malaysia*, December.

Yip Yat Hoong (1966) 'Tin export earnings and the early economic growth of Malaya', *Kajian Ekonomi Malaysia*, December.

Yip Yat Hoong (1968) 'Recent changes in the ownership and control of locally incorporated tin dredging companies in Malaya', *Malayan econ. R.*, April.

Yip Yat Hoong (1969), *The Development of the Tin Mining Industry of Malaya*, University of Malaya Press, KL.

Young, A. (1928), 'Increasing returns and economic progress', *Econ. J.*, December.

Zorn and Leigh-Hunt, Messrs. (stockbrokers) (1938, 1953, 1959, 1965 and, 1967a, 1969a), *Manual of Rubber Planting Companies*, published for private circulation, London, annually since 1908.

Zorn and Leigh-Hunt, Messrs. (1967b, 1969b, 1970b), *Manual of Tin Mining Companies*, published for private circulation, London, annually since 1967.

Zorn and Leigh-Hunt, Messrs. (1974), *Manual of Rubber and Tin Producing Companies*, privately published, London (replacing the two publications cited above).

Author Index

Subject Index